STUDIES IN SCRIPTURE
IN EARLY JUDAISM AND CHRISTIANITY

Editor
Craig A. Evans

21

Published under

LIBRARY OF SECOND TEMPLE STUDIES
94

Formerly Journal for the Study of the Pseudepigrapha Supplement Series

Editor
Lester L. Grabbe

Editorial Board
Randall D. Chesnutt, Philip R. Davies, Jan Willem van Henten,
Judith M. Lieu, Steven Mason, James R. Mueller,
Loren T. Stuckenbruck, James C. VanderKam

Founding Editor
James H. Charlesworth

SCRIBES AND THEIR REMAINS

Edited by

Craig A. Evans
and
Jeremiah J. Johnston

LONDON • NEW YORK • OXFORD • NEW DELHI • SYDNEY

T&T CLARK
Bloomsbury Publishing Plc
50 Bedford Square, London, WC1B 3DP, UK
1385 Broadway, New York, NY 10018, USA

BLOOMSBURY, T&T CLARK and the T&T Clark logo
are trademarks of Bloomsbury Publishing Plc

First published in Great Britain in 2020
Paperback edition first published 2021

Copyright © Craig A. Evans, Jeremiah J. Johnston and contributors, 2020

Craig A. Evans and Jeremiah J. Johnston have asserted their right under the Copyright, Designs and Patents Act, 1988, to be identified as the Editors of this work.

All rights reserved. No part of this publication may be reproduced or transmitted in any form or by any means, electronic or mechanical, including photocopying, recording, or any information storage or retrieval system, without prior permission in writing from the publishers.

Bloomsbury Publishing Plc does not have any control over, or responsibility for, any third-party websites referred to or in this book. All internet addresses given in this book were correct at the time of going to press. The author and publisher regret any inconvenience caused if addresses have changed or sites have ceased to exist, but can accept no responsibility for any such changes.

A catalogue record for this book is available from the British Library.

A catalog record for this book is available from the Library of Congress.

ISBN: HB: 978-0-5676-8804-0
PB: 978-0-5677-0040-7
ePDF: 978-0-5676-8805-7
eBook: 978-0-5676-9345-7

Series: Library of Second Temple Studies, 2515-866X, volume 94

Typeset by Forthcoming Publications (www.forthpub.com)

To find out more about our authors and books visit
www.bloomsbury.com and sign up for our newsletters.

CONTENTS

Preface vii
Abbreviations ix

INTRODUCING SCRIBES AND THEIR REMAINS
    Craig A. Evans and Jeremiah J. Johnston xi

1   TEXT AS ARTIFACT: AN INTRODUCTION
     Stanley E. Porter 1

Part I
SCRIBES, LETTERS, AND LITERACY

2   LONGEVITY OF LATE ANTIQUE AUTOGRAPHS AND FIRST COPIES:
    A POSTSCRIPTUM
     Craig A. Evans 17

3   GREEK WRIT PLAIN:
    VILLAGE SCRIBES, Q, AND THE PALAEOGRAPHY
    OF THE EARLIEST CHRISTIAN PAPYRI
     Gregg Schwendner 88

4   MY LORD AND PROTECTOR:
    PAPYRI AND *SKEPĒ* PATRONAGE IN SIRACH AND *3 MACCABEES*
     Christopher J. Cornthwaite 120

5   HILARION'S LETTER TO HIS WIFE, CHILD EXPOSURE,
    AND EARLY CHRISTIANITY
     Jeremiah J. Johnston 146

6   FETISHIZING THE WORD:
    LITERACY, ORALITY, AND THE DEAD SEA SCROLLS
     Ian C. Werrett 163

Part II
WRITING, READING, AND ABBREVIATING CHRISTIAN SCRIPTURE

7 SIGNED WITH AN "X":
Σταυρός AND THE STAUROGRAM AMONG THE *NOMINA SACRA*
Benjamin R. Overcash   187

8 NEW LIGHT FROM THE PAPYRI:
THE SACRED BACKGROUND OF βίβλος IN MATTHEW 1:1
Michael P. Theophilos   205

9 THE EARLY PAPYRI, "GOSPEL-PARALLEL" VARIANTS,
AND THE TEXT OF THE NEW TESTAMENT IN THE SECOND CENTURY
Roy D. Kotansky   224

10 TERMS OF KINSHIP FROM USAGE IN EVERYDAY LANGUAGE
TO OFFICIAL CHRISTIAN LIFE
Eleonora Angela Conti   281

11 EARLY CHRISTIAN ROLLS
Marco Stroppa   290

Index of References   300
Index of Authors   315

Preface

Studies in Scripture in Early Judaism and Christianity (SSEJC) was founded almost thirty years ago by Craig A. Evans and James A. Sanders. More than twenty volumes have been published to date. Many of them have focused on the function of Israel's sacred Scripture in early Christian writings, whether in those writings eventually recognized as canonical or in those not so recognized. Most of these volumes have appeared in the "blue series," that is, the Library of New Testament Studies (LNTS), though a few have appeared in the "red series," that is, the Library of Second Temple Studies (LSTS).

The present volume has been included in the red series and should be viewed as a companion to *Jewish and Christian Scripture as Artifact and Canon* (LSTS 70), a collection of studies published a few years ago that has been well received by papyrologists, biblical scholars, and scholars interested in ancient book culture. The present volume, *Scribes and Their Remains*, brings together several studies that address aspects of book culture in late antiquity, both in the world at large and in the context of the Christian Church. Scribal practices, literacy, personal letters, and the longevity of literary texts, including autographs, are some of the topics that are investigated.

The editors of the present SSEJC volume are grateful to its contributors, especially to Eleonora Angela Conti and Marco Stroppa whose first language is not English. Our volume has been enriched by the insights of these Italian papyrologists. The editors are also grateful to Professor Stanley Porter for taking the time to write an Introduction to the volume and to bring into play his considerable experience working with papyri and ancient codices. We also thank Professor Peter Arzt-Grabner who at the outset of this project recruited some of the contributors and along the way provided advice and guidance. We are deeply grateful to him.

Craig A. Evans
Jeremiah J. Johnston

Abbreviations

AB	Anchor Bible
ACW	Ancient Christian Writers
AGJU	Arbeiten zur Geschichte des antiken Judentums und des Urchristentums
AJP	*American Journal of Philology*
AKG	Arbeiten zur Kirchengeschichte
AnBib	Analecta biblica
AnPap	*Analecta Papyrologica*
APF	*Archiv für Papyrusforschung*
AYB	Anchor Yale Bible
BARev	*Biblical Archaeology Review*
BASOR	*Bulletin of the American Schools of Oriental Research*
BASP	*The Bulletin of the American Society of Papyrologists*
BBR	*Bulletin of Biblical Research*
BETL	Bibliotheca ephemeridum theologicarum lovaniensium
Bib	*Biblica*
BibInt	Biblical Interpretation series
BICS	Bulletin / University of London. Institute of Classical Studies
BJS	Brown Judaic Studies
BZAW	Beihefte zur ZAW
CBQ	*Catholic Biblical Quarterly*
CLGP	Commentaria et Lexica Graeca in Papyris reperta
CP	*Classical Philology*
CPF	Corpus dei Papiri Filosofici
CSEL	Corpus scriptorum ecclesiasticorum latinorum
DACL	F. Cabrol and H. Leclerque, *Dictionnaire d'archéologie Chrétienne et de liturgie*, vol. 1. Paris: Letouzey et Ané, 1924
DELG	P. Chantraine, *Dictionnaire Étymologique de la Langue Grecque*, vol. 1. Paris: Éditions Klincksieck, 1968
DJD	Discoveries in the Judaean Desert
DSD	*Dead Sea Discoveries*
ETL	*Ephemerides Theologicae Lovanienses*
GRBS	*Greek, Roman, and Byzantine Studies*
HTB	Histoire du texte biblique
HTR	*Harvard Theological Review*
ICC	International Critical Commentary
JBL	*Journal of Biblical Literature*
JCS	*Journal of Cuneiform Studies*
JETS	*Journal of the Evangelical Theological Society*

JJP	*Journal of Juristic Papyrology*
JNES	*Journal of Near Eastern Studies*
JRS	*Journal of Roman Studies*
JSJ	*Journal for the Study of Judaism*
JSJSup	*Journal for the Study of Judaism*, Supplement Series
JSNT	*Journal for the Study of the New Testament*
JSNTSup	*Journal for the Study of the New Testament*, Supplement Series
LCL	Loeb Classical Library
LNTS	Library of New Testament Studies
MH	*Museum Helveticum*
MPER	Mitteilungen aus der Papyrussammlung der Österreichischen Nationalbibliothek in Wien
NovT	*Novum Testamentum*
NovTSup	*Novum Testamentum*, Supplements
NTS	*New Testament Studies*
NTTSD	New Testament Tools, Studies, and Documents
OTL	Old Testament Library
OSAE	Oxford Studies in the Ancient Economy
RAC	*Reallexikon für Antike und Christentum*
RE	A. Pauly and G. Wissowa, *Realencyclopädie der classischen Altertumswissenschaft: neue Bearbeitung*. Stuttgart: A. Druckenmüller Verlag, 1893–1978
REG	*Revue des Études Grecques*
RevQ	*Revue de Qumran*
SCJ	Studies in Christianity and Judaism
SCL	Studies in Classical Literature
SCS	Septuagint and Cognate Studies
SHR	Studies in the History of Religions
SNT	Studien zum Neuen Testament
SPap	*Studia Papyrologica*
StAA	Studia antiqua australiensia
STDJ	Studies on the Texts of the Desert of Judah
TENTS	Texts and Editions for New Testament Study
TSAJ	Texte und Studien zum antiken Judentum
TU	Texte und Untersuchungen
WBC	Word Biblical Commentary
WUNT	Wissenschaftliche Untersuchungen zum Neuen Testament
VC	*Vigiliae christianae*
VTSup	*Vetus Testamentum*, Supplements
ZNW	*Zeitschrift für die neutestamentliche Wissenschaft*
ZPE	*Zeitschrift für Papyrologie und Epigraphik*

Editions of papyri, parchments, ostraca, and tablets are abbreviated according to J. F. Oates, et al., *Checklist of Editions of Greek, Latin, Demotic and Coptic Papyri, Ostraca and Tablets*, 5th ed., BASPSup 9 (Oakville: Oxbow, 2001), online version: J. D. Sosin, et al. (eds.), *Checklist of Editions of Greek, Latin, Demotic, and Coptic Papyri, Ostraca, and Tablets*: papyri.info/docs/checklist.

Introducing Scribes and Their Remains

Craig A. Evans and Jeremiah J. Johnston

Scribes and Their Remains begins with an introductory essay by veteran Greek grammarian, exegete, papyrologist, and textual critic Professor Stanley Porter. His essay addresses the principal theme of our book: the text as artifact. On the face of it, says Porter, a text seems like a relatively stable notion, but nothing could be further from the truth. Once one begins to think about text and how to define it, the difficulties seem to multiply. #In fact, he argues, there are numerous intellectual and academic traditions for which the text is central and that have consequently come to view text in particular ways. These include the fields of text-criticism, philology, literature, linguistics, phenomenology, philosophy, and of course biblical studies. Most of these disciplines view the text as a bounded entity. This changed, Porter believes, as a result of the poststructural revolution. The result is the emergence of what has been called the semiological text, that is, the text as a socially and culturally embedded and unstable semiological system, with shifting relations to society, culture, the author, the reader, and even language itself. In his stimulating essay Porter explores the implications of the semiological text in light of the essays that follow.

Five studies appear under the sub-heading, "Scribes, Letters, and Literacy." In the first, lengthy study Craig Evans develops further a paper he published in 2015, in which he argued that the archaeological, artifactual, and historical evidence suggests that New Testament autographs and first copies may well have remained in circulation for one century or more, having the effect of stabilizing the text. Evans critically evaluates the testimony of second- and third-century Christian leaders and writers, such as Tertullian and Bishop Peter of Alexandria, as well as the testimony of non-Christian writers, such as Aulus Gellius, Strabo, Pliny the Elder, and Galen, who claim to know of or even possess in some cases autographs and copies that are two hundred years old or older. Evans also considers the archaeological evidence relating to how long books in libraries remained in use before being cast out (as at Oxyrhynchus) or destroyed (as at Herculaneum). The evidence again suggests that literary works remained in use for 200 and in some cases 300 years. The implications this longevity may have for New Testament criticism calls for exploration.

Gregg Schwendner explores the important question of late antique literacy levels and the composition of the hypothetical dominical source known as Q. Who compiled, composed, and copied the source material (Q) of the Synoptic Gospels? Schwendner notes that John Kloppenborg's theory that village scribes living in northern Galilee could have done so has been supported by recent work by Giovanni Bazzana, who draws on comparative evidence from Ptolemaic and Roman Egypt. Schwendner's paper offers a papyrological perspective on the question raised by their work, in three parts. Beginning with what we know about the educational levels in villages in Egypt, especially in the Fayum, and the role played by sub-literary texts, he concludes with a palaeographical question: Why were so many early Christian texts written in a plain, non-cursive documentary script, rather than in book scripts? Schwendner also very helpfully provides a palaeographical appendix examining the similarities between the plain documentary style of writing and how early Christian papyri were written.

Christopher Cornthwaite observes that studies of benefaction and patronage and their influence on Judaeans and Christ groups have become common, yet we still have much to learn about regional variations in practices of protection, how these relationships were formed and evolved, and how they influenced texts. This chapter explores the *skepē* (protection) practices in the papyri from Ptolemaic and early Roman Egypt. These were protections offered by agreements of trust (*pisteis*), which were constructed between two people using moral language. Within these relationships credit and debt could be established, and workers' productivity could be protected. Cornthwaite's study shows that this social context is witnessed in the Greek translation of the LXX and uses the additions in Sirach and 3 Maccabees as examples of direct incorporation of *skepē* traditions into new texts.

Jeremiah Johnston treats in detail the oft-mentioned letter of Hilarion to his wife Alis (P.Oxy. 744). This disturbing turn-of-the-era letter, which advises Alis to cast out her newborn should it be a female, is frequently mentioned in critical literature but has not been studied in detail. Johnston interprets the text line by line, then sets the letter in its social and historical context, especially with reference to exposure and infanticide in late antiquity. He looks at the reasons for exposure and infanticide, including economics, superstition, the health of the child, suspect parentage, gender, and deformities. Johnston also reviews the advantages and disadvantages to those who rescue or take in unwanted infants and children. He then contrasts Jewish and Christian practices with Pagan practices, observing how the compassionate practices of the former sometimes gave opportunity to criticism and sinister charges on the part of the latter.

The final article in the first major section of the book is by Ian Werrett, who challenges the notion held by some that the scribes and interpreters of Qumran held a "relaxed" view of the text of Scripture. Werrett wonders if some of these hypotheses have been driven by a post-canonical mindset that fetishizes the Hebrew Bible and/or awards pride of place to those manuscripts that are the most intact. He observes that because the vast majority of individuals would have heard the stories of the "Bible" as opposed to reading, writing, or editing them, it stands to reason that the physical form of the written texts, be they "biblical" or some other genre, would have been influenced by the sensibilities and practices of the culture in which they were created. Werrett tries to show how the scribes of the Second Temple period, and their writings, were affected by low literacy rates and the prevailing trends of the oral tradition. He hopes to challenge the notion that the Qumran community had a "relaxed" attitude towards textual pluriformity and move us closer to understanding the literary perspectives of those who lived in the waning days of the pre-canonical era.

Five studies fall under the second sub-heading of our book, "Writing, Reading, and Abbreviating Christian Scripture." The first paper is by Benjamin Overcash who investigates the *stauros*, or cross, as a *nomen sacrum*. The contracted form of the Greek word for "cross," σταυρός, is not usually considered to be among the so-called "primary" group of *nomina sacra*, which includes the four most widely attested examples of this practice—God, Lord, Jesus, and Christ. But a close analysis of the occurrences of the noun σταυρός in New Testament manuscripts conventionally dated up to the third/fourth century reveals a surprising consistency in its treatment as a *nomen sacrum* when compared to these primary four. Hence the question must be asked: How did the word for "cross" come to be included with such remarkable consistency in a practice almost exclusively reserved for names and titles? In addressing this question, Overcash first examines the data that prompt it, before offering a solution that positions this phenomenon within the tradition of the *tav* of Ezek. 9:4-6, which ancient Christians associated with the divine name that was applied to baptismal initiands in the form of the sign of the cross. Overcash then explores how the staurogram embedded in the *nomina sacra* for "cross" and "crucify" might create a potent visual metonym that points intersemiotically to this baptismal ritual, thus necessitating and validating the treatment of these words as *nomina sacra*.

Michael Theopholis observes that recently published documentary papyri significantly enhance our understanding of the sacred background of βίβλος (Matt. 1:1). In light of some notable Greek parallels attested in the Septuagint (Gen. 2:4; 5:1; Exod. 32:32-33, et al.) commentators have characteristically viewed the word as reminiscent of Hellenistic Jewish use. This view, says Theopholis, overlooks considerable Greco-Roman papyrological material which sheds much light on the use of the word in the wider Mediterranean world. Of special interest are the sacred dimensions of the word, which are analyzed in his paper and applied to the biblical material.

Roy Kotansky considers the significance of the numerous Greek New Testament papyri that have been published since the appearance of NA[27] in 1993. To what degree, he asks, has this new body of evidence contributed to our understanding of the text of the Gospels in the second century? Kotansky concludes that the text of the early papyri still points to a particular period, c. 200 and earlier, as one of considerable scribal diversity in terms of textual variants and text-families. Textual variants embedded in Gospel parallels found in harmonized or assimilated passages, observes Kotansky, sometimes offer variants that differ noticeably from versions of the majority manuscript readings of the parallel Gospels from which they derive. This may indicate textual diversity before the period c. 200 CE.

Eleonora Angela Conti investigates the papyrological evidence concerning two kinship terms, that is, the child's words *amma* and *appa*, and their evolution from private use, typically inside the family, to a more extensive and consequently more official use, inside the Christian world and monastic life. This evolution, which is clear from the private letters on papyri, begins in the second century, when we record the first evidence of the noun *amma* on papyri. The nouns *amma* and *appa*, also attested in the pre-Christian era, testify to the transition of these everyday Graeco-Roman nouns to Christian language and their subsequent change of meaning.

Marco Stroppa finds that among the papyrological studies of recent years, many have concentrated on the transition between the two book formats, roll and codex, and the adoption of the latter by Christian communities. The scholarly studies have properly focused on the evidence of the oldest Christian codices. However, a less investigated area of study concerns the existence of rolls that are definitely Christian: such pieces cover a wide timespan, ranging from the second to the eighth centuries. The collection and the investigation of about twenty fragments from the second and the third/fourth centuries will provide us, says Stroppa, with insight with respect to the technical and material features of these books and allow us to view them within the historical and social context of early Christianity. In his paper he compares diverse elements of early Christian rolls, including their content, the kind of roll (in particular the use of recto and verso), the dating, and the writing. Stroppa also analyzes in detail some papyri which have special features compared to the general framework of the other documents.

1

Text as Artifact:
An Introduction

Stanley E. Porter

The notion of *text* has been around for a considerable amount of time, at least as far back as the ancient Greeks and probably even earlier.[1] As a result, texts are frequently referred to in both common and intellectual parlance, and appear to be the essential elements of many, if not most, academic disciplines so as to invite little to no comment. In some ways, this volume is a work that seems to assume a common understanding of the notion of text, such that most of the articles will assume our familiarity with not only such a concept but such an entity. On the face of it, a text seems like a relatively stable notion, but nothing could be further from the truth. Once one begins to think about text and how to define it, the difficulties seem to multiply. This has not always been the case but has become a recent issue of greater significance.[2] For example, the philosopher Jorge J. E. Gracia offers the following sentences to illustrate the problem of definition of text:

1. The text we shall discuss today is a novel.
2. Give me the text that is in front of you.
3. Do not throw away the text.
4. That text is ungrammatical.
5. The text we have been discussing is logically incoherent.[3]

---

1. See Anne H. Stevens, *Literary Theory and Criticism: An Introduction* (Peterborough, ON: Broadview, 2015), who labels Plato the first literary theorist.
2. The last thirty to forty years have seen a significant increase in literature discussing the notion of text. I do not make an attempt to refer to all of that literature, but select several significant works that touch on important matters that help to situate this volume within a larger discussion. A helpful collection of essays on the notion of text is found in Mario J. Valdés and Owen Miller (eds.), *Identity of the Literary Text* (Toronto: University of Toronto Press, 1985).
3. Jorge J. E. Gracia, *A Theory of Textuality: The Logic and Epistemology* (Albany: State University of New York Press, 1995), xx.

As he points out, the word *text* is being used in a number of different ways within just these five sentences—many more of which sentences could be suggested to further illustrate the problem (e.g. Our class is going to study Matthew's Gospel as an oral text). To illustrate some of the differing conceptions, the first definition probably conforms to the definition that most people have in mind when they use the word *text*. This text is written and has literary pretentions attached to it, quite possibly in distinction from other types of written literary texts, such as poems, plays, and the like. The literary understanding of text has been a widespread definition of text and perhaps the place where most discussion of texts occurs and hence has come to dominate the notion of text. The problem with such a definition is that it masks more than it hides, as it seems to assume a static object that can be examined and interpreted, and perhaps even manipulated, without reference to any other factors, whether individual or communal. The second and third sentences, according to Gracia, convey the notion that text is a physical object, one with distinct physical boundaries and characteristics, and that it can be treated as any other physical object can be treated—passed around between people and even thrown away if it is judged no longer useful. This characterization of text is probably most closely associated with a very narrow definition of text as artifact—although as we shall see below, such a narrow definition does not do justice to the notions either of text or of artifact. The fourth sentence characterizes text as a linguistic entity. In other words, without reference to whether it is written or otherwise and whether it is part or whole, this usage conveys the idea that text is linguistically analyzable in relationship to something else, presumably something that is thought or said to be grammatical. This definition of text as linguistic item also reflects a relatively common use of the word text, even if not as frequent as the one of text as literary entity. However, the characterization of text according to its grammaticality opens up some perspectives on the definition, because the text is seen as an instance of a language system, which is outside of or larger than (the ways of characterizing it may vary) the instance itself, according to which it can be evaluated. The fifth and final definition of text implies that text is a philosophical notion, or at least one that conforms or not to a viewpoint that one might have of various ideas or concepts, that they can be coherent or not, according to some kind of external (here logical) standard. Like the fourth sentence, this definition also opens up the possibilities, even if only slightly, regarding the notion of text. However, rather than appealing to a linguistic system that might produce such a sentence, this sentence appeals to a philosophical or even ontological framework of understanding.[4]

4. Ibid.

As I stated above, a few moments of thinking will reveal that there are many other ways of thinking about the notion of text. In fact, even though the Greeks may have been some of the earliest to think about text, consideration of what constitutes text has continued to the present, and in fact is in many ways a very current topic. It may at first glance seem unusual to introduce a volume such as this with an introduction of this sort, but I think that noting something about the wider notion of text helps us better to understand how each of the contributions here is a contribution not just to a particular issue related to texts but to a wider notion of what constitutes a text. This volume—or should I say, text—for which I am writing this introduction falls within the general area of biblical studies, but this is only one of many disciplines for which texts have played an important role. There are numerous intellectual and academic traditions for which the text is central and that have consequently come to view text in particular ways. These include the fields of text-criticism, philology, literature, linguistics, phenomenology, and philosophy, among no doubt others in what has come to be identified with the modernist tradition.[5] There are a number of areas of overlap among how these various traditions reflect upon text, but each also makes a distinct contribution by treating text in slightly different ways.

Texts in textual criticism place high emphasis upon an actual, physical text, as textual criticism consists in comparing not just texts, but specific wordings of texts for their similarities and differences.[6] Texts are not just bounded entities but they are recognizably finite and even flawed, and as a result suitable for comparison at the most minute levels for their convergences and divergences. Textual criticism, although it implies a perhaps unachievable text (the original or *Urtext*), operates on a horizontal level of seeking an elusive original text, but the comparison is between one text and another (even if the notion of original text is idealized in many ways). At most, a given text is a representation, even if flawed, of the original text. This text-critical perspective played a huge role in the notion of textual studies in the nineteenth and into the early twentieth century especially in the study of ancient texts, including the Bible.

---

5. Many of my comments have been greatly aided by the analysis of recent developments in thought about text in John Mowitt, *Text: The Genealogy of an Antidisciplinary Object* (Durham, NC: Duke University Press, 1992), including many if not most of the categories I use in my taxonomies below, supplemented by the perspective of Gracia, *Theory of Textuality*.

6. Cf. Mowitt, *Text*, 223–4. New Testament scholars will be very familiar with this notion of text, especially in terms of lower criticism, where the "text" is foundational for higher criticism.

The philological text has similarities with the text-critical one, because traditional philology is concerned with establishing texts for study and appreciation.[7] The difference is that a philological text, while still an actual, physical text, is an even more narrowly defined text than a text-critical one, even if philology may make use of textual criticism. The text of philology is an instance of the preserved and best representatives of the literature of those who produced such texts, studied for artistic or literary merit, appreciation of language, use of language, and often generic exemplification. In a limited way, there is appeal to the culture that produced the text, but the notion of culture is not specifically defined but represented by the text. Much traditional biblical study has placed the philological text at the center of its discussion. The nineteenth- and early twentieth-century commentary tradition represents the philological text under close scrutiny.

The literary text is related to the philological text.[8] The literary text is in some respects the descendant of the philological text in its actual, physical representation of various literary works through the ages, not just confined to the world of philology (often associated with study of the ancients). The literary text has traditionally been seen as the direct product of the biography of the author, and having features that characterize literature, such as structure, form, and content. In more recent times, the literary text has focused upon the text itself without primary concern for author or audience. The literary text is not externally referential but self-referential, being equated with the thing in itself without regard for authorial intention or audience response. The literary text is often equated with the North American New Criticism literary movement, in which the image of the "well-wrought urn" is seen as metaphorically capturing the nature of text.[9] The literary text has had a more recent influence upon biblical studies, especially with the advent of literary studies and now narrative criticism of the Bible. The shift from a philological to a literary text in biblical studies is noteworthy and noticeable, even if not always understandable when many language-related issues remain unresolved.

7. Cf. ibid., 2–6 and 223–4. Classical studies as a discipline has traditionally been based upon this notion of text and the study of its texts described as classical philology.

8. Cf. ibid., 4, who might place rhetorical and stylistic texts in this category as well. As we will see in what follows, literary studies is an encompassing discipline in which text figures prominently in all periods.

9. One of the major works of New Criticism was Cleanth Brooks, *The Well Wrought Urn: Studies in the Structure of Poetry* (San Diego: Harcourt Brace Jovanovich, 1974), originally published in 1947.

The linguistic text is related to both the philological and literary text in its association with language, but with the distinguishing characteristic that a linguistic text is an instance of another entity, a linguistic code (apart from those non-code theories of language).[10] Whereas for the text-critical, philological, and literary text the text itself takes priority, for the linguistic text not the text but the linguistic code is the focus of attention. The text itself is merely an instance, an example, that points to the linguistic code that produced the text. There exist a variety of ways that one may relate the code to the text, such as generatively, structurally, functionally, or stratificationally, among others, with the most important of these in discussion of text being the structural conception of text. The linguistic text has made some inroads into examination of the biblical text, but remains an alternative approach to the philological and especially literary text.

The phenomenological text is both a philosophical and literary characterization of text.[11] The philosophical connections to phenomenology are a concern for the thing itself, with emphasis upon the relationship of the one who experiences the phenomenon of the text. The literary connections are to various literary movements, such as Russian formalism (itself related to phenomenology), Prague structuralism, and the Anglo-focused New Criticism, and result in text as phenomenon to be experienced and reacted to by textual participants. The focus is upon the phenomenon of the text with the participant called to respond to the text as seen diachronically in the history of its reception or synchronically in the response of the reader who is forced by the text to respond by completing it or filling in its spaces. The phenomenological text, because of its relationship to the literary text, has had influence upon biblical studies, especially as this is seen in narrative criticism, which continues to be practiced even within the scope of other types of criticism.

The ontological text is the most philosophical view of text, and it is associated with a range of views of the text as being a representation in some form of being, that is with either epistemological or metaphysical properties or characteristics.[12] This being may be conceived of in various ways, depending upon the particular philosophical view propounded. In

---

10. Cf. Mowitt, *Text*, esp. 8 but throughout 2–10. In linguistics, the notion of text has been metaphorical from the inception of the discipline, with priority given to oral over written language. See below for the relation of text to discourse.

11. Cf. ibid., 224.

12. See Gracia, *Theory of Textuality*, esp. xxii–xxiv, but who is concerned to defend the epistemological and metaphysical features of text (his emphasis is upon epistemology), even if text has other features as well that he is concerned to define.

any case, text is seen as representative of a philosophical notion, whether it is a representational or ideational reality that is reflected in text. Related to this is the notion that text is to be coherent or logical in its structure, with its representation being faithful to whatever the philosophical notion might be. The ontological text has had a surprising resilience and continued presence in biblical studies by way of its forming the presupposition of varying types of biblical theology. Biblical theology often insinuates a philosophical viewpoint regarding the nature of text.

There are no doubt other ways that text has been conceived, but the above convey at least some major characterizations made through the centuries and illustrate how it has been used within various disciplines. This includes biblical studies where texts have mostly been seen as literary, though sometimes as linguistic. Such a notion of text focuses upon text as entity, with bounded and finite parameters, usually physical representation, mostly with emphasis upon the text as opposed to any other reality, and there is an overriding sense of text being a static, fixed, and stable (and at least correctable) item. This is the notion of text that has come to be associated with text as artifact, and it has proved to be useful for a number of different academic and intellectual disciplines. These are primarily within literary and related studies (such as biblical studies), where it has probably had its greatest continuing life and influence, but also within a range of other disciplines.

That is, such was the case up to around the 1970s, when the notion of text underwent a major and radical reconceptualization on the basis of how language was reconceptualized.[13] John Mowitt summarizes some of these changes in language-perception, including the deinstrumentalization of language so that language is no longer seen as an instrument for the expression of authorial intent but part of the "cultural formation where human beings are subjected to language's codes and modes of operation."[14] Any idea of language being transcendental is eliminated and emphasis

---

13. One of the most important singular events in this transformation occurred at a conference on structuralism in October 1966 at Johns Hopkins University, where the seeds of poststructuralism first germinated. The papers from the conference are published in Richard Macksey and Eugenio Donato (eds.), *The Structuralist Controversy: The Languages of Criticism and the Sciences of Man* (Baltimore: Johns Hopkins University Press, 1972), including Jacques Derrida's "Structure, Sign, and Play in the Discourse of the Human Sciences" (247–65), in which he "deconstructs" Lévi-Strauss, one of the leaders in structuralism. See also the critical discussion that followed his talk. Other papers from the conference (e.g. by Roland Barthes) are also important in this historical development.

14. Mowitt, *Text*, 7.

placed on its being actualized.[15] The result for both text and language was to make it impossible to view text in the same way since. This reconceptualization was part of a general intellectual foment that transpired within many if not most intellectual disciplines, especially those that had structuralist underpinnings, in which many of the foundational assumptions and orientations of such disciplines—such as the notion of stable texts, something that was deeply engrained in most of these disciplines mentioned above up to this point—underwent a radical revaluation.[16] The basic transformation that occurred involved at least the following differences: between the traditional notion of text as product and the notion of text as process and the emphasis upon its productivity,[17] between text and textuality as the process by which various texts and other phenomena are interwoven into a tapestry whose result is intertextuality, between meaning as simplex and univocal to its being (to use the language of Bakhtin) dialogical and heteroglossic,[18] and between stability in interpretation and fluidity and even infiniteness or unboundedness.[19] The result is the emergence of what has been called the semiological text, that is, the text as a socially and culturally embedded and unstable semiological system, with shifting relations to society, culture, the author, the reader, and even language itself.[20] The lines were drawn in a number of different ways among various conceptual fields. These include opposition between modernists who believed in stable and fixed texts, even if they were subject to interpretation, and postmodernists who were unconvinced of such stability; structuralists who posited almost ontological categories of fundamental oppositions as a type of metaphysical framework for human existence, and poststructuralists who believed in the instability of the sign and there being nothing other than fluid notions of language

15. Ibid.
16. For a brief summary of structuralism, see Stanley E. Porter and Jason C. Robinson, *Hermeneutics: An Introduction to Interpretive Theory* (Grand Rapids: Eerdmans, 2011), 154–67. The importance of this movement and its impact upon a wide variety of critical disciplines cannot be overestimated.
17. Mowitt, *Text*, 6; cf. Julian Wolfreys (ed.), *The Continuum Encyclopedia of Modern Criticism and Theory* (New York: Continuum, 2002), 870 (in the glossary).
18. Although Mikhail Bakhtin preceded this reconceptualization, his writings were important in the poststructural revolution, especially as they were reinterpreted by Julia Kristeva (see below). On Bakhtin and dialogism, see Michael Holquist, *Dialogism: Bakhtin and his World* (London: Routledge, 1990).
19. Mowitt, *Text*, 15.
20. Cf. ibid., esp. 6–7, 10, but whose entire volume is dedicated to exploring the "semiological text." The language of semiology pervades poststructuralism.

and meaning; ontologists who believed in reality other than the text and pragmatists or de-ontic thinkers who were more concerned with the notion of the creativity of language than its meaning; those who placed emphasis upon the individual, especially the individual as interpreter, and those who were concerned with rethinking the nature of the subject in light of communities of practice and belief and behavior;[21] and those who placed emphasis upon cognitive processing and its possibilities and those who emphasized knowledge as a social and communal construct to be negotiated.

The four leading proponents in this major shift in the notion of text were Jacques Derrida, Julia Kristeva, Roland Barthes, and Michel Foucault.[22] The contribution of these four major thinkers of the second half of the twentieth century cannot be underestimated. I can only summarize here what others have expatiated upon at far greater (and necessary) length and with much greater depth. Derrida, besides his dissolving the bonds between author and text, was enamored with the play of language and the instability of signification;[23] Kristeva was concerned with moving from language as a stable code to the text as process,[24] the notion of text

---

21. See Paul Smith, *Discerning the Subject* (Minneapolis: University of Minnesota Press, 1988).

22. See Mowitt, *Text*, who devotes a chapter each to Derrida (83–103), Kristeva (104–16), and Barthes (117–38). He does not devote a chapter to Foucault, but does discuss him at some length (e.g. 30–7, but also elsewhere). Mowitt notes the significance of the French journal *Tel Quel* in this intellectual movement (Kristeva was an editor and Derrida and Barthes had varying levels of involvement). For *Tel Quel*, see Patrick ffrench [sic] and Roland-François Lack, *The Tel Quel Reader* (London: Routledge, 1998), with essays by all but Derrida of those mentioned above. See James Williams, *Understanding Poststructuralism* (Stocksfield, UK: Acumen, 2005), among many volumes dedicated to this diverse movement.

23. For important sources of Derrida's perspective, see Jacques Derrida, "Semiology and Grammatology: Interview with Julia Kristeva," in his *Positions*, trans. Alan Bass (Chicago: University of Chicago Press, 1981), 15–36, which refers or alludes to his major notions; *Writing and Difference*, trans. Alan Bass (Chicago: University of Chicago Press, 1978), which also contains his "Structure, Sign, and Play in the Discourse of the Human Sciences" (see above); and *Of Grammatology*, trans. Gayatri Chakravorty Spivak (Baltimore: Johns Hopkins University Press, 1976).

24. For important sources of Kristeva's perspective, see Julia Kristeva, Σημειωτική: *Recherches pour une sémanalyse* (Paris: Éditions du Seuil, 1969), esp. the essays on "Le texte et sa science" and "La productivité dite texte"; *Revolution in Poetic Language*, trans. Margaret Waller (New York: Columbia University Press, 1984). Two useful collections of Kristeva's works are Toril Moi (ed.), *The Kristeva Reader* (New York: Columbia University Press, 1986), with pp. 75–88 for a translation of the

becoming a productive force, that is, textuality,[25] and with it the interplay of texts in intertextuality;[26] Barthes brought the notion of the text as structural artifact under attack and turned to other notions to provide justification, such as pleasure;[27] and Foucault was virtually preoccupied with social and cultural anti-conventionalism regarding structures of knowledge, power, and society.[28] The poststructuralist movement (or whatever one wishes to call what transpired in the rejection of convention in its various forms from the 1970s onwards) led not only to social and cultural transformation (some may well have thought of it as revolution) but to a radical reconceptualization of text. Text became a fluid, malleable, composite, variably interpretable, impossible to circumscribe and limit, and even deconstructive and deconstructing notion. All of the fields that I mentioned above—and many others as well that had been influenced by structuralism—were themselves forced either to outright reject or to radically rethink the notion of text. Textual criticism changed its focus from an original text to social-historical episodes of textuality (sometimes called new or material philology, and in New Testament studies narrative textual criticism), that is, a more fluid process of textual creation and reception, involving intertextuality and variant production.[29] Philological

first essay mentioned above; and Kelly Oliver (ed.), *The Portable Kristeva*, rev. edn (New York: Columbia University Press, 2002).

25. Plays on and extensions of the word "text" into such things as "textuality," "texture," "intertextuality," and the like have served to figuratively extend the notion of what a text is, does, and contains to a variety of fields.

26. The literature on intertextuality is immense and growing, especially the sanitized kind that refers to direct lines of influence (such as the Old Testament on the New Testament) in New Testament studies. For an introduction to the issues, see Graham Allen, *Intertextuality*, 2nd edn (London: Routledge, 2011).

27. For important sources of Barthes's perspective, see Roland Barthes, *Essais critiques* (Paris: Éditions de Seuil, 1964), with essays "Ecrivains et écrivants" and "L'activité structuraliste"; *Image—Music—Text*, trans. Stephen Heath (New York: Hill & Wang, 1977), containing the essays "The Death of the Author" and "The Grain of the Voice"; *The Pleasure of the Text*, trans. Richard Miller (New York: Hill & Wang, 1975); and *The Rustle of Language*, trans. Richard Howard (New York: Hill & Wang, 1986).

28. For important sources of Foucault's perspective, see Michel Foucault, *Language, Counter-Memory, Practice: Selected Essays and Interviews*, ed. Donald F. Bouchard, trans. Donald F. Bouchard and Sherry Simon (Ithaca, NY: Cornell University Press, 1977), with "What Is an Author?"; and Paul Rabinow (ed.), *The Foucault Reader* (New York: Pantheon, 1984).

29. See Matthew J. Driscoll, "The Words on the Page: Thoughts on Philology, Old and New," in *Creating the Medieval Saga: Versions, Variability and Editorial*

and literary texts moved the center of interest from the text to the reader, by means of reception history, with increasing interest in reader-oriented strategies and destructive tendencies of texts and readers.[30] With the recognition of socially and culturally embedded readers came the notion of cultural studies as the appropriate response to the understanding of texts, and along with it the development of what might appear as fragmented interests in such things as colonial and postcolonial studies, New Historicism, feminist and gender studies, and various other ideological criticisms—all reflecting in various ways the resulting intertextuality of the text as process.[31] Linguistic texts soon came to be discussed in relationship to discourse. If text is the instantiation, discourse is the socially and culturally embedded environment in which such a text functions or is used.[32]

The history of the development of the notion of text was not complete, however, with the poststructural revolt. This proved to be but one important stage in the development of notions of text, one that one could never

---

Interpretations of Old Norse Saga Literature, ed. Judy Quinn and Emily Lethbridge (Odense: University Press of Southern Denmark, 2010), 87–104; and Stanley E. Porter, *How We Got the New Testament: Text, Transmission, Translation* (Grand Rapids: Baker, 2013), 27–36.

30. See Robert C. Holub, *Reception Theory: A Critical Introduction* (London: Routledge, 1984); two helpful collections of essays in reader-response, Jane Tompkins (ed.), *Reader-Response Criticism: From Formalism to Post-Structuralism* (Baltimore: Johns Hopkins University Press, 1980); and Susan R. Suleiman and Inge Crosman (eds.), *The Reader in the Text: Essays on Audience and Interpretation* (Princeton: Princeton University Press, 1980); and, among a number of works on deconstruction, Harold Bloom, et al., *Deconstruction and Criticism* (New York: Continuum, 1979).

31. For an overview of such literary criticism, see Raman Selden, et al., *A Reader's Guide to Contemporary Literary Theory*, 4th edn (London: Prentice Hall/Harvester Wheatsheaf, 1997); Lois Tyson, *Critical Theory Today: A User-Friendly Guide*, 2nd edn (London: Routledge, 2006); and Mads Rosendahl Thomsen, et al. (eds.), *Literature: An Introduction to Theory and Analysis* (London: Bloomsbury, 2017). See also Vincent B. Leitch, *Cultural Criticism, Literary Theory, Poststructuralism* (New York: Columbia University Press, 1992), who chronicles some of the reactions to these developments.

32. See Sara Mills, *Discourse* (London: Routledge, 1997), 8–27, for varying definitions of discourse (although Mills emphasizes the role of Foucault in the development of the notion of discourse). Discourse analysis has become a dominant approach to texts, especially in linguistics. The above two paragraphs draw upon Stanley E. Porter, "The Domains of Textual Criticism and the Future of Textual Scholarship," in *The Future of New Testament Textual Scholarship*, ed. Garrick V. Allen, WUNT 417 (Tübingen: Mohr Siebeck, 2019), 131–53 (133–36).

forget and never rid oneself of. If one might characterize the longstanding notion of text as static and as product, and the reactionary notion of text as process and as productive, then the result of this dialectic (if one dares to use such a framework) is a moderating view of text that rejects the extremes of both yet appreciates what has been learned from the residual advances. In a work that to a large extent reflects this moderating view, Gracia approaches the subject as a discussion of a "theory of textuality." I note that he assumes that textuality now demands further definition, but he also recognizes that in order to do so he must begin with a notion of text. However, his notion of text necessarily takes into account the poststructural notion of textuality. As a result, Gracia offers the following definition of texts: they are "semantically significant artifacts in relation to which authors, audiences, and contexts play interesting and idiosyncratic roles."[33] This definition then forms the basis for the rest of his volume. Each of the parts of the definition merits detailed consideration. The major factors that I note are the following: the importance of meaning as indicated by their being "semantically significant" even if there is not a specific theory of meaning that is agreed upon, the status as "artifact," and their having "interesting" even if "idiosyncratic" relationships, which covers a host of non-predictable or not necessarily stable relationships, with "authors" as their producers (Gracia clearly does not go so far as to see the author as having vanished), "audiences" as their users, and "contexts" as their necessary environment of function and use (Gracia's emphasis is upon the cultural function of texts in conjunction with the above factors, as determinative of meaning, even if meaning is not finally singularly determinative). This definition, even if it would not be completely satisfactory to those of either the old or new schools of thought on texts (it introduces too much imprecision and fluidity for the former and too much certainty and fixedness for the latter), attempts to capture the reality and definable existence of the text while also recognizing that texts are not simply static products, but without introducing a number of undefinable fluid boundaries that make interpretation and analysis more problematic than they already were when texts were treated as static entities. There are many other important concepts that Gracia discusses in his definition of textuality that would be worth recounting in another context, some of them still highly debatable.

For this volume, one of the major definitional elements of text is the concept of "artifact."[34] Gracia spends a significant amount of time debating

---

33. Gracia, *Theory of Textuality*, xv.
34. Ibid., 44–52.

various definitions of "artifact," in an effort to make clear that whereas every text is an artifact, and therefore has the properties of an artifact, contrary to some every artifact is not a text and thereby subject to the same interpretation. The major components in his definition of an artifact include it being either "the product of intentional activity and design" or its having "undergone some change and/or its context [having] undergone some change," in which case this change is "the product of intentional activity and design" within a specified and appreciated context.[35] Thus texts are also products of this intentional behavior that involves activity and what he identifies as design. However, texts may also be entities that have experienced some kind of change to themselves or the environment in which they are found has experienced this change, with the emphasis here upon the importance of context and how the artifact, in this case the text, functions within this context. This definition of artifact, which is narrow enough to exclude a number of entities that rightly should be excluded but provides greater scope for what might well constitute a text, reinforces the notion that texts are artifacts (and artifacts are not necessarily texts, to be "read" or understood in the same way, even if they are metaphorically described as reflecting "sign" systems) but artifacts in such a way that they reflect intentions on the part of their creators or reflect the fact that they are contextually situated in such a way that their cultural function helps to determine their meaning and understanding. Meaning is therefore potentially not strictly or narrowly circumscribed even if it is not limitless.[36] Authors may intend texts, but they do not determine all of the meaning, because authors themselves demonstrate conventional behavior within varied contexts that give rise to the cultural function of their text. Texts therefore do not necessarily have singular or "strict and narrow" meanings but may have a "wide range of meaning as determined by the cultural function they have."[37] Cultural function is a way of capturing both the environment and the performance of a text in which the author's intended text is limited in its scope of meaning by the way that it functions according to conventional rules.

35. Ibid., 48. He recognizes that there are still some weaknesses with this definition, and he discusses things that are not simply artifacts or non-artifacts but possible quasi-artifacts.
36. Ibid., 125.
37. Ibid., 126–7. Gracia appeals to Wittgenstein's notion of language games (see Ludwig Wittgenstein, *Philosophical Investigations*, trans. G. E. M. Anscombe [Oxford: Blackwell, 1974], passim). See ibid., 125 and 127, for a different sense of the notion of game than is used by Derrida in his sense of play.

Gracia has certainly not said the last word regarding text or textuality. However, he has performed a major task in bringing to bear many of the factors involved in the understanding of texts. His approach finds a way between the structural and poststructural divide over the nature of text. Even if such poststructural considerations are often seen to be exaggerated in their claims, confused in their suppositions, and even illogical in their execution, the movement itself—if it is to be characterized as a movement, rather than as a number of people thinking out loud in the light of their times—has raised important questions regarding language, understanding, meaning, and even being. These questions needed to be raised in light of the possibility, if not the inevitability, of the traditional view of text becoming arid or insular in its claims. The inevitable appreciation of the response of the reader and the denigration of the role of the author was in many ways no more than a movement along a continuum whose projection had begun appreciably earlier. Nevertheless, once the ontological foundations had been called into question, the inevitable deconstruction was sure to follow. It is out of this that we have come to appreciate the complexity of understanding and the various and competing roles that a variety of factors play in interpretation. Texts are fundamental artifacts, and their understanding and interpretation may be ascertainable, but doing so may be difficult.

This complex of concepts focused around the notions of text and artifact, including such things as intention, specific though not narrow meaning, context, and cultural function, are appropriate points of connection with the contents of this volume—all of the essays of which are attempts to interpret texts in the light of their being reconfigured as complex artifacts. An example from textual criticism in New Testament studies will illustrate the difference between the earlier and the later view of text. Traditional textual criticism with its narrowly conceived view of text was responsible for creating the contemporary text-critical apparatus. New Testament scholars are familiar with their editions of the Greek New Testament—whether these are fuller editions or hand-texts—that are concerned not with manuscripts but with the listing of textual variants, usually at the bottom of the page. Text is concerned with the written material on the page in a narrowly conceived sense—the individual wordings of the text. The later view of text goes beyond the notion of text as wording and is concerned with such things as para-textual and meta-textual data, intertextual relations, and even cultural conditions that resulted in textual production. These elements, some of which are only accessible through reconstruction of the textual environment, become as important elements of what it means to study a text as are the individual wordings.

This later view of text is in that expanded sense reflected well in this volume. The first part of the volume is headed "Scribes, Letters, and Literacy," and it focuses upon some of the appropriate contexts in which texts are created and the conventions associated with them. This volume attempts to broaden the scope of much traditional biblical scholarship that has not taken such contexts or conventions into account in discussing texts. This is fairly typical of those who hold to the traditional and pre-revolutionary definition of text. For these texts, the world of their creation is beyond the scope of examination, with focus being given to the product, not the text as process. In this part we are introduced to some of the contextual factors that helped to create the environment for the creation of texts, such as those who wrote them and how they were able to do so and how they related to other texts that came from contexts that were in some ways compatible. In light of the post-revolutionary characterization of text, these studies are part of how we now must define a text as artifact. The text is no longer seen in isolation but as a more complex entity that functions within a set of cultural expectations and conventions.

The second half of the volume is focused upon "Writing, Reading, and Abbreviating Christian Scripture." This second part is more focused upon the sign system used within the text and how that sign system may reflect more than the simple use of letters. Sign systems and their understanding extend beyond simple wordings to encompass all of the symbols that may be used. Pre-revolutionary characterizations of text focused heavily upon the language of the text, whether the philological or the linguistic text was in view. Their domain of dominance was the language system itself. Analyses of alternative wordings or the functions of other symbol-systems, even within other semiotic-systems, extend beyond treatment of a text as simple meanings encoded in wordings to appreciation of meanings encoded in wordings that can only be understood as performing cultural functions. Determining these cultural functions is not necessarily easy, especially when one is examining ancient texts for which the very notions of authorship, audience, context, culture, and function, as well as even the language code itself, are debatable. Nevertheless, satisfactory interpretation of such meanings can only take place within the parameters of understanding their complex relationships.

Part I

SCRIBES, LETTERS, AND LITERACY

2

Longevity of Late Antique Autographs and First Copies: A Postscriptum*

Craig A. Evans

In a paper published a few years ago I reviewed a variety of evidences that suggest that New Testament autographs and early copies probably remained in circulation for a century or longer before being lost, destroyed, or retired.[1] The writings of the New Testament were not unique in this regard; apparently most literature in Jewish and Greco-Roman antiquity enjoyed longevity of one or two centuries or more. The evidence appears to be substantial. If my conclusion is valid, then I should think this would have relevance for textual criticism and could help explain why the text of the New Testament was as stable as it was in the first centuries of the Christian movement.

It was to be expected that some objections and criticisms would be raised, which so far as I can tell have been thus far limited to the internet. The objections that have been raised argue that the evidence for longevity is seen primarily in Egypt and the region of the Dead Sea, where the arid climate permits manuscripts to survive a long time. It has been claimed that the Greco-Roman practices of collecting, preserving, and handing down whole libraries over the course of generations do not apply to the autographs and early copies of the New Testament writings. Consequently, there really is no evidence that New Testament autographs and early copies survived for a century or more.

---

* I wish to thank a great many colleagues, many of whom with expertise in papyrology, textual criticism, archaeology, classics, and book culture of late antiquity, for reading all or parts of the present paper, as well as the related earlier study that appeared in 2015. I deeply appreciate the helpful suggestions and encouragement. Some of the suggestions will have to be developed in future studies, but a number of them are reflected in the pages below. Many thanks, Colleagues!

1. C. A. Evans, "How Long Were Late Antique Books in Use? Possible Implications for New Testament Textual Criticism," *BBR* 25 (2015): 23–37.

I welcome the questions that have been raised. I think more needs to be said about the role played by climate. I also think more evidence can be presented that shows that manuscripts, including autographs, could well have survived two or more centuries and could have done so in non-arid climates.

As we shall see, most books were expensive, were coveted, were sometimes stolen or confiscated, and in fact were passed on either through inheritance or purchase by people eager to expand their libraries. Early Christians evidently shared the values of classical book culture, which in many respects was pretty much the same in the Jewish world from which Christianity emerged. Papyrus, from which most books were made, is a durable medium. Paper, whether papyrus or parchment, is, says Pliny the Elder, "the material on which the immortality of human beings [*immortalitas hominum*] depends" (Pliny, *Naturalis historia* 13.70). Even in our digital age, Pliny's comment still contains a lot of truth.

In the present essay I will try to assemble most of what I regard to be the relevant evidence. This evidence clearly shows that manuscripts could and often did survive centuries when properly cared for. In light of this evidence, which includes the high value Christians placed on the antiquity of their sacred writings, I will argue that autographs and first copies of the writings of the New Testament, accepted as authoritative by their first readers and, in the passage of time, increasingly revered, in fact were extant for a long time. The evidence that supports this conclusion is largely testimonial, though there is important archaeological and artifactual supporting evidence that will also be considered.

In the present essay I will review late antique claims regarding the longevity of books under six headings: (1) Late Antique Christian Claims of Longevity, (2) Late Antique Non-Christian Claims of Longevity, (3) Late Antique Claims Regarding the Value and Cost of Books, (4) Late Antique Claims Regarding Loss of Books, and (5) Book Burning. Under the final heading, (6) Climate and Archaeology, I will discuss the role played by climate (and what is relevant and irrelevant in this respect) and what light archaeology has shed on the question of the longevity of late antique books.

Late Antique Christian Claims of Longevity

Several writers in late antiquity, both Christians and non-Christians, refer to very old writings, in some cases autographs, still in circulation. Taken at face value, their testimony suggests that bookrolls of literature, including autographs, remained in relatively good condition for centuries.

All of the testimony cited here is in reference to old writings extant in non-arid regions. I begin with Christian testimony.

The earliest relevant testimony seems to be a comment made by Irenaeus (c. 130–c. 200) with respect to the number of the Antichrist as given in Rev. 13:18. He affirms that "this number (i.e., 666) is found in all the excellent and ancient copies [σπουδαίοις καὶ ἀρχαίοις ἀντιγράφοις]" (*Adversus haereses* 5.30.1; cf. Eusebius, *Historia ecclesiastica* 5.8.5). What would count as an "ancient" (ἀρχαῖος) copy of Scripture for Irenaeus? Writing *c.* 180 an ancient copy of Scripture from his perspective likely would reach back to the beginning of the second century. Given that Irenaeus is here speaking of the Apocalypse, it could hardly be earlier. The reference to "excellent" (σπουδαῖος) is interesting too, suggesting that Irenaeus and others knew the difference between well-executed manuscripts and those poorly or carelessly written.

The most important and most direct testimony comes from Tertullian (c. 160–c. 225), a north African Church Father who was raised in a non-Christian home in Carthage. Writing c. 190 CE Tertullian states in his *Prescription against Heretics* that the autographs of seven of Paul's letters were still extant and could be viewed:

> ¹ Come now, you who would indulge a better curiosity, if you would apply it to the business of your salvation, run over the apostolic churches, in which the very thrones of the apostles are still pre-eminent in their places, in which their own authentic writings [*ipsae authenticae litterae eorum*] are read, uttering the voice and representing the face of each of them severally. ² Achaia is very near you, (in which) you find Corinth. Since you are not far from Macedonia, you have Philippi; (and there too) you have the Thessalonians. Since you are able to cross to Asia, you get Ephesus. Since, moreover, you are close to Italy, you have Rome, from which there comes even into our own hands the very authority (of apostles themselves).² (*De praescriptione haereticorum* 36.1-2)

By "apostolic churches" (*ecclesias apostolicas*) Tertullian means the churches founded by apostles. Paul, of course, did not found the church at Rome but he did visit it (or at least Tertullian assumes Paul did). The crucial question here is the meaning of *ipsae authenticae litterae eorum* (36.1), which, as we see in the English translation above, Peter Holmes in the old *ANF* series has rendered "their own authentic writings." But

---

2. Translation based on P. Holmes, "On the Prescription against Heretics," in *The Ante-Nicene Fathers*, ed. A. Roberts and J. Donaldson, 10 vols. (Edinburgh: T. & T. Clark, 1898), 3:260.

Holmes isn't quite sure how to render the Latin. In fact, he really hasn't rendered it at all. The word "authentic" is more transliteration than translation. Holmes admits his uncertainty in a footnote: "Authenticae. This much disputed phrase may refer to the *autographs* or the Greek *originals* (rather than the Latin translations), or full *unmutilated* copies as opposed to the garbled ones of the heretics. The second sense is probably the correct one."[3]

To be sure, the second sense (i.e., Greek originals rather than Latin translations) is a legitimate lexical option. But the first sense, *autographs*, is the more probable. Indeed, the *Oxford Latin Dictionary* defines *authenticus* as "An original document, autograph."[4] That Tertullian means autographs, that is, Paul's original letters—not copies—is supported by the nature of his argument. After all, *copies* of Paul's letters were available in many places. By the end of the second century most Greek-speaking leaders in the Church would have copies of them. There would be no need to travel to Greece, Macedonia, Asia Minor, and Italy to see reliable copies of Paul's letters in Greek. But one would have to do just that if one wanted to see the autographs themselves, the *authenticae litterae*.[5]

The lexical data clarify and support this interpretation. The Latin adjective *authenticus* derives from the Greek αὐθεντικός. The cognate verb αὐθεντεῖν means "to have full power over" something (LSJ), while the nominal form αὐθέντης means "one who does something with his own hand" (LSJ). The abstract noun αὐθεντία means "authority deriving

---

3. Ibid., 260 n. 12 (his emphasis).

4. See also E. A. Andrews, *A Copious and Critical Latin–English Lexicon Founded on the Larger Latin-German Lexicon of Dr. William Freund* (New York: Harper & Brothers, 1866), 182: *authenticus* is what "comes from the author...the original writing." One will want to consult K. E. Georges (ed.), *Ausführliches lateinisch-deutsches Handwörterbuch*, 2 vols. (Darmstadt: Wissenschaftliche Buchgesellschaft, 1998 [repr. of 8th edn, 1913/1918, rev. H. Georges]), 749: *die Urschrift, das Original*, etc., in both classical and ecclesiastical texts.

5. I was pleasantly surprised to discover precisely this argument in John Chapman, *Eusebius: Or the True Christian's Defense against a Late Book entitul'd the Moral Philosopher* (Cambridge and London: W. Thurlbourn, 1739), 337–9. Mr Chapman, late Fellow of King's College, Cambridge, rightly points out that in Tertullian's time Greek copies of Paul's letters were to be found in many places throughout the Roman Empire. Therefore, it would be (to quote Chapman without modernizing his English prose) "needless to send his Reader to Ephesus, Corinth, Philippi, etc. above all others for that purpose. But in order to consult the Original Manuscripts of the Apostles, this was proper advice, and therefore he undoubtedly meant those Manuscripts, by his *Literae* [sic] *Authenticae*, authentic being here oppos'd to Copy." Examination of the papyri, to which neither Chapman nor Holmes had access, will bear this out.

from oneself." Accordingly, the adjective αὐθεντικός means that the thing qualified possesses the authority of him who made it or composed it (hence we speak of an *author* of a work). In reference to a written composition, this means the writing comes from the author himself; and what comes from the author is an autograph.

The relevant Greek and Latin vocabulary in the documentary papyri is straightforward enough, but its correlation with English equivalents can at times be confusing. This is because everyday English words like "authentic," "original," "autograph," and "copy" lack precision and often overlap. It will be helpful to look at several examples in the papyri. The principal Greek vocabulary includes αὐθεντικός ("original," "authentic," "genuine"), ἰδιόχειρον / ἰδιόγραφος ("in one's own hand"), αὐτόγραφος / ὑπογραφή ("signature" or "autograph"), and ἀντίγραφον / ἀντίτυπος ("copy"). A review of a few examples where *authenticus* / αὐθεντικός occurs should make it clear that Tertullian in *De praescriptione haereticorum* 36.1-2 is speaking of Pauline autographs and not, for example, Greek copies or unabridged copies.

A receipt for rent (50 CE) concludes: "I, Gaius Cutius son of Marcus, have the original [τὴν αὐθεντικήν] of the aforesaid in my possession and will produce it if required" (P.Oxy. 38.2836, 17-19). At the conclusion of a letter regarding military recruits (103 CE): "I, Avidius Arrianaus, chief clerk of the cohort III Ituraeorum, certify that the original letter [*scripsi authenticam epistulam*] is in the files of the cohort" (P.Oxy. 7.1022, 27-31).[6] In context the "original" (receipt or letter) in these papyri is clearly intended by the adjectives αὐθεντικός and *authenticus*, respectively.

A registration of a deed (193 CE) concludes: "This contract, written by me, Papontos, in my own hand [ἰδιόγραφος μου] without erasure or insertion, is valid as though publicly registered…the authentic bond [τὸ αὐθεντικὸν χειρόγραφον] should be registered… I request you to take this authentic bond [τὸ αὐθεντικὸν χειρόγραφον] bearing my attestation that it is the autograph [ἰδιόγραφον] of Papontos…" (P.Oxy. 4.719, 26-34). In this case the authentic status of the document is confirmed by the autograph of the man filing the deed. Most autographs, of course, were written by the hand of a professional scribe, not by the author himself. The author signed his name and perhaps added a few words.[7] The word ἰδιόγραφος implies

6. For text, translation, and discussion, see also *Rom.Mil.Rec.* 87); with additional comments by P. Cugusi in *C.Epist.Lat.* 2, pp. 125–31. See also P.Ital. 1.1.10: [*ac*] *cepto facis ut authenticas ipsas* etc. For text and notes, see also P. Cugusi in *C.Epist. Lat.* 1, pp. 257–58 (no. 240).

7. This is seen several times in Paul's letters. He concludes his letter to the Galatians by saying, "See with what large letters I write to you in my own hand

that the author held the pen and that the autograph (αὐτόγραφος) is in fact in the author's own handwriting.⁸

To qualify as an autograph the document need not be in the author's hand; it need only be a document that the author has dictated and then signed (or someone else signed for him, in case the author does not know how to write). This probably applies in the case of P.Oxy. 2.260, which identifies itself in the first line as a "copy" (ἀντίγραφον), as do many documents of this nature.⁹ One Antiphanes of the city of Oxyrhynchus swears that he will appear in court on the appointed day (in 59 CE). The document concludes, "I, Theon, son of Onnophris, assistant, have checked this authentic bond [αὐθεντικῆι χιρογραφίᾳ]" (lines 19-21). Although the document in this case is itself a copy, Theon affirms that what he has copied is "authentic," which presupposes an autographic archetype, which has been reproduced exactly. In contrast with P.Oxy. 4.719 above, the text of P.Oxy. 2.260 was not penned by the author himself.

Near the end of a marriage application (201 CE) we read: "I request of you, on receiving it from me with my attestation, that the signatures [ὑπογραφάς] appended to it are autographs [ἰδιογράφους]...to register it together with this application, the original [τὸ αὐθεντικόν] at the Library of Hadrian and a copy [τὸ ἴσον] of it at the Library of the Nanaeum" (P.Oxy 12.1473, 38-41). What is rendered "copy" is literally "the same" (τὸ ἴσον), implying that the copy truly mirrors the original.¹⁰

In P.Hamb. 1.18.col. ii 6 we hear of "original epistles [αὐθεντικῶν ἐπιστολῶν] and assembled small bookrolls [βιβλιδίων]" (222 CE). These "original" or "authentic" epistles are in reference to autographs.

[Ἴδετε πηλίκοις ὑμῖν γράμμασιν ἔγραψα τῇ ἐμῇ χειρί]" (Gal. 6:11). Near the end of his brief letter to Philemon, written on behalf of the slave Onesimus, Paul assures the recipient: "I Paul write in my own hand [ἐγὼ Παῦλος ἔγραψα τῇ ἐμῇ χειρί]; I will repay" (Phlmn 19).

8. As we see here: "And the autograph signatures [αὐτόγραφοι] of many other bishops who agreed with them are contained in the same letter" (Eusebius, *Historia ecclesiastica* 5.19.4).

9. We find several examples of "copies" of letters and testaments in the apocryphal and pseudepigraphal literature, e.g., "A copy of the letter [ἀντίγραφον ἐπιστολῆς] which Sisinnes the governor of Syria and Phoenicia, and Sathrabuzanes, and their associates the local rulers in Syria and Phoenicia, wrote and sent to Darius" (1 Esd. 6:7); "The copy of the testament [ἀντίγραφον διαθήκης] of Reuben, the commands that he gave his sons before he died..." (*T. Reub.* 1:1); so all the *Testaments of the Patriarchs*. There are many examples in 1 Maccabees as well. See also *Aristeas* 21, 28, 34.

10. We have a helpful example of this terminology in P.Lond. 3.985 (p. 228; fourth century CE): "It seemed the same [τὸ ἴσον] and I have the original receipt

Near the end of an application concerning the sale of land (267 CE) we find the same closing formula: "...with his attestation that the signature [ὑπογραφήν] after the date is the autograph [ἰδιόγραφον] of Aurelius Agathinus also called Origenes, you will register the original [τὴν αὐθεντικήν] with this application in the Library of Hadrian, and a copy [τὸ ἴσον] of it with the application in the Library of Nanaeum" (P.Oxy. 12.1475, 43-45).[11] We again observe that "copy" is τὸ ἴσον. The copy is made of the "original" (τὴν αὐθεντικήν).[12]

A letter of the prefect of Alexandria (374 CE) concludes: "I, Aurelius Serapion, supervisor, have received together with my associates the original receipt [αὐθεντικὴν ἀποχήν] of which you presented this copy [ἀντιτύπου], as stated" (P.Turner 45, 23-25).[13] And in the minutes of a legal hearing (325 CE) we read: "...the inscribed heirs will see to it that they provide copies [τὰ ἀντίγραφα] of the will when they obtain the original [τὸ αὐθεντικόν]...we beg to obtain the original [τὸ αὐθεντικόν], subject to our providing copies [τὰ ἀντίγραφα], for the security of the heirs" (P.Oxy. 54.3758, 154-155, 207-209).

The legal document just quoted reflects Roman practice. For our purposes the important point is the distinction between the original or authentic document on the one hand and the copy on the other. This distinction is clearly expressed in Justinian's sixth-century Digest of

[αὐθεντικὴν ἀποχήν]" (line 18). The "original receipt" (αὐθεντικὴν ἀποχήν) is an autograph. The writer was able to say that what was before him was "the same" (τὸ ἴσον), because he was in possession of the original receipt (and not a copy, which might be inaccurate in places). So also in O.Wilck. 1010: "We acknowledge that we have the original receipt for the straw [αὐθεντικὴν ἀποχὴν ἀχύρου]." Another way of referring to a copy is found in another legal text (BGU I.326.col. ii 23), dating to the second century CE, where "a scribe declares the ἀντίγραφον before him to be σύμφωνον τῇ αὐθεντικῇ διαθήκῃ" (MM 91), that is, "in agreement with the authentic will." The scribe has declared that the copy before him is in fact an exact copy of the original, a copy that "agrees" (σύμφωνον) with the original.

11. It should be noted that knowingly putting one's signature on a false or fraudulent document was a serious offense (Suetonius, *Augustus* 33.2: *et cum de falso testamento ageretur omnesque signatores lege Cornelia tenerentur*, "and in the case of a forged will, in which all the signers were liable to punishment by the Cornelian Law...").

12. Similar formula and language are found in P.Oxy. 12.1562 (279–282 CE).

13. In legal documents, as we have seen, and sometimes in letters, scribes often identify themselves by name. One thinks of Paul's scribe Tertius, who inserts his greeting in the final chapter of the apostle's letter to the Romans: "I, Tertius, who write this letter [ἐγὼ Τέρτιος ὁ γράψας τὴν ἐπιστολήν] greet you in the Lord" (Rom. 16:22).

Roman law: *Nam et Labeo scribit, Vendita hereditate tabulas testamenti descriptas deponi oportere: heredem enim exemplum debere dare, tabulas vero authenticas ipsum retinere, aut in aede deponere* (*Digesta* 10.2.4.3), "Indeed, Labeo also writes that, when an inheritance has been sold, it is fitting that the tablets of the testament that are described be set aside: for one ought to surrender a copy [*exemplum*], but indeed, ought himself to hold the authentic tablets [*tabulas authenticas*] in reserve, or else to set them aside in a temple."[14] The *tabulas authenticas* refer to the original writings, in contrast to the subsequent *exemplum* or copy.[15]

On an inscription from Lydia, dating to about 250 CE, we read: "I deposited a copy [ἀντίγραφον] of the epistles [τῶν ἐπιστολῶν]…the original epistle [αὐθεντικὴν ἐπιστολήν] that was written…"[16] What is interesting in the latter example, which is damaged and in places indecipherable, is that in the legal context of this inscription the plural ἐπιστολαί should probably be understood as "commands." A municipal official has deposited a copy of the commands and then references the original letter, or command, that underlies them. Here αὐθεντικός takes on a nuance of great authority. The command, or epistle, comes from the hand not simply of an author but of an authority.

Additional examples could be supplied, but the above should be sufficient to show that *authenticus* routinely refers to original documents, as opposed to copies. And by "original documents" we also mean the autographs.

In *De praescriptione haereticorum* 36.1-2 Tertullian makes reference to seven autographs of Paul's letters, still extant in five cities and available for inspection.[17] If Tertullian knows what he is talking about, that is, that at

---

14. Labeo (c. 50 BCE–c. 11 CE) was a noted Roman jurist.

15. For another example of this distinction between original and copy, see *Digesta* 22.4.2: *quicumque a fisco convenitur, non ex…exemplo alicuius scripturae, sed ex authentico conveniendus est*, "Whatever is agreed upon from the treasury, must not be agreed upon from a copy of some writing [*exemplo alicuius scripturae*], but from the original [*authentico*]."

16. G. H. R. Horsley (ed.), *New Documents Illustrating Early Christianity*, vol. 2 (North Ryde: Macquarie University, 1982), 76.

17. Tertullian alludes to the apostolic autographs in his polemic against Marcion: "…if that is from the beginning which has the apostles for its authors, then it will certainly be quite as evident, that that comes down from the apostles, which has been kept as a sacred deposit in the churches of the apostles" (*Adversus Marcionem* 4.5.1). The "sacred deposit" (*sacrosanctum*) in the apostolic churches very probably alludes to the Pauline autographs mentioned by Tertullian in *De praescriptione haereticorum* 36.1-2. In his polemic with Marcion Tertullian goes on to mention the

least some of the autographs of Paul's letters were extant in his day, then these original writings would be about 130 to 140 years old. Holmes's reluctance to render *authenticae* as "autographic" in his *ANF* translation may have been due to his belief at the time he worked (c. 1870s) that papyrus was a fragile medium, a false belief that perdured in scholarly circles for almost another century.

In a Paschal homily, of which only fragments are extant, Peter, Bishop of Alexandria (d. 311 CE), refers in passing to the autograph of the Gospel of John:

> Now it was the preparation, about the third hour [cf. John 19:14], as the accurate books [τὰ ἀκριβῆ βιβλία] have it, and the autograph [ἰδιόχειρον] itself of the evangelist John, which up to this day has by the grace of God been preserved [πεφύλακται] in the most holy church of Ephesus, and is there adored [προσκυνεῖται] by the faithful.[18] (frag. 5.2)

At the time Bishop Peter wrote (c. 306 CE) and on the assumption that the Gospel of John was composed in the 90s, the autograph of the Gospel of John would have been just over two hundred years old. This would make the autograph at least 50 years older than the autographs of Paul's letters mentioned by Tertullian. Is this possible? Review of non-Christian testimony will suggest that it is. In any event, even if Peter was mistaken and the copy of John venerated by the Christians of Ephesus was not the autograph itself, the copy in their possession likely would have been very old. After all, a newish copy would hardly be mistaken for a two-hundred-year-old autograph. Even if what the church at Ephesus possessed was not the actual autograph of the Gospel of John, they at least possessed a very old manuscript.[19]

Corinthians, Galatians, Philippians, Thessalonians, Ephesians, Romans, all having received instruction from Paul. The reference to the Galatians seems to add an eighth Pauline autograph to the list.

18. Translation based on J. B. H. Hawkins, "Fragments from the Writings of Peter," in Roberts and Donaldson (eds.), *The Ante-Nicene Fathers*, 6:283. For the Greek text, see Andrea Gallandi, *Bibliotheca veterum patrum antiquorumque scriptorum ecclesiasticorum*, 14 vols. (Venice: Albritiana, 1765–81), 4:113. Volume 4 appeared in 1768. I thank Stephen Carlson for locating and making this passage available to me.

19. Tertullian may lend some support to Peter's testimony. Writing a century earlier, Tertullian says, "The same authority of the apostolic churches will afford evidence to the other Gospels also, which we possess equally through their means, and according to their usage—I mean the Gospels of John and Matthew" (*Adversus*

We should note too that Bishop Peter speaks of "the accurate books" (τὰ ἀκριβῆ βιβλία), evidently with reference to the reading "about the third hour" (ὥρα ὡσεὶ τρίτη). However, our earliest manuscripts read ὥρα ἦν ὡς ἕκτη ("it was about the sixth hour"); these include 𝔓⁶⁶ ℵ A B N W and others. A few manuscripts, including ℵ︎ᶜ L Δ Ψ, perhaps under the influence of Mark 15:25, read ὥρα τρίτη ("third hour"), the reading Bishop Peter chose. Not too many textual critics today will approve of the bishop's choice of reading, but it is telling that at the end of the third century the man was aware of variant readings and of the fact that some copies of Scripture were better than others.

The testimony seems clear enough: Both Tertullian and Peter assert that the autographs of seven (perhaps eight) of Paul's letters and of the Gospel of John remained extant anywhere from 130 to 200 years. There is also indirect testimony that implies the same. I am thinking here of polemic leveled against those accused of altering the text of New Testament Scripture or of introducing new writings altogether. To counter the newer writings or newer forms of text, Christian apologists appealed to the great antiquity of the writings that would in time be recognized as canonical. This strategy comes to expression several times.

Late second-century Theophilus, in his apology addressed to one Autolycus, remarks that "the writings which belong to us godly people are more ancient [τὰ καθ' ἡμᾶς τοὺς θεοσεβεῖς ἀρχαιότερα γράμματα τυγχάνει], yes, and are shown to be more truthful, than all writers and poets" (*Ad Autolycum* 2.30). Later in his letter Theophilus comments that "writers are fond of composing a multitude of books [πληθὺν βίβλων συγγράφειν]… on this account I also will not grudge the labor of compendiously setting forth to you, God helping me, the antiquity of our books [τὴν ἀρχαιότητα τῶν παρ' ἡμῖν γραμμάτων]…" (3.1).

Later still, Theophilus makes the point that "the Hebrews, who also are our ancestors, and from whom we have those sacred books which are older than all authors [τὰς ἱερὰς βίβλους ἔχομεν ἀρχαιοτέρας οὔσας ἁπάντων συγγραφέων], as already said, are proved to be more ancient [προγενέστεροι] than the cities which were at that time renowned among the Egyptians" (3.20). And finally, Theophilus appeals to Josephus, who "tells us in his writings that the sacred books take precedence of them in antiquity [προάγουσιν αὐτοὺς ἀρχαιότητι αἱ ἱεραὶ βίβλοι]" (3.23).

Marcionem 4.5.3). In context (see 4.5.1) Tertullian seems to be suggesting that certain churches have in their possession very old, pre-Marcionite copies of John and Matthew, even as some churches possess Pauline autographs.

The importance that Theophilus attaches to the antiquity of the sacred writings is hard to miss. What sets both the Hebrew books above the works of pagans and the Christian books above the works of heretics is their antiquity. Theophilus argues that antiquity is important because ancient books, he believes, reach back to the eyewitnesses.

Tertullian mounts similar arguments in his polemic with Marcion. He sees the futility in simply quarreling over whose version of the text is superior. What settles the matter is the antiquity of the sources:

> I say that my Gospel is the true one; Marcion, that his is. I affirm that Marcion's Gospel is adulterated; Marcion, that mine is. Now what is to settle the point for us, except it be that principle of time [*temporis ratio*], which rules that the authority lies with that which shall be found to be more ancient [*antiquius*]; and assumes as an elemental truth, that corruption belongs to the side which shall be convicted of comparative lateness in its origin [*posterius revincetur*]... we have proved our position to be the older one, and Marcion's the later...a century later than the publication of all the many and great facts and records [*opera atque documenta*] of the Christian religion....[20] (*Adversus Marcionem* 4.4.1-2)

The dispute is settled, says Tertullian, by the "principle of time" (*temporis ratio*). Authority lies with the more ancient, while corruption is found in what is late. Marcion's version of the text of Luke (which is Tertullian's main concern here) is a "century later than the publication of all the many and great facts and records of the Christian religion." By "records" (*documenta*) Tertullian means the early New Testament manuscripts, such as the autographs, that is, the *authenticae litterae*, that he discusses in *De praescriptione haereticorum* 36.1-2.

Tertullian argues in such a way here in *Against Marcion*, as well as in his *De praescriptione haereticorum*, as though older texts, even autographs in some cases, were still available for confirmation, which was not the case for Marcion's version of Luke. Accordingly, Tertullian can declare that "the Gospel of Luke which we are defending with all our might has stood its ground from its very first publication [*ab initio editionis suae*]" (*Adversus Marcionem* 4.5.2).[21] At the end of the chapter Tertullian avers that "a late date is a mark of forgers [*posteritati falsariorum praescribentem*], and that authority of churches which lends

---

20. Translation based on P. Holmes, "The Five Books against Marcion," in Roberts and Donaldson (eds.), *The Ante-Nicene Fathers*, 3:348–9.
21. Ibid., 350.

support to the tradition of the apostles (is decisive); because truth must necessarily precede the forgery, and proceed straight from those by whom it has been handed on" (4.5.7).[22]

The thinking of Serapion (d. 211), bishop of Antioch, seems similar in his decision to forbid the reading of the *Gospel of Peter* in his churches. Writing at the end of the second century, the bishop explains: "For we, brethren, receive both Peter and the other apostles as Christ; but we reject intelligently the writings falsely ascribed to them, knowing that such were not handed down to us [τὰ δὲ ὀνόματι αὐτῶν ψευδεπίγραφα ὡς ἔμπειροι παραιτούμεθα, γινώσκοντες ὅτι τὰ τοιαῦτα οὐ παρελάβομεν]" (*apud* Eusebius, *Historia ecclesiastica* 6.12.3). When Serapion says that suspect writings "were not handed down to us," he means they were not handed down *by the apostles*, that is, by *the ancients*. The *Gospel of Peter* was not "handed down" from ancient sources or ancient authorities. Rather, it is of recent origin and is therefore suspect and should not be read in the churches.

Interest in old manuscripts is also seen in Origen (c. 185–c. 253), who was born in Alexandria and lived much of his life in Caesarea Maritima in Palestine. Commenting on Origen's scholarship, Eusebius (c. 260–c. 340) relates that Origen

> got into his own possession the original writings in the actual Hebrew characters, which were extant among the Jews [τάς τε παρὰ τοῖς Ἰουδαίοις ἐμφερομένας πρωτοτύπους αὐτοῖς Ἑβραίων στοιχείοις γραφάς]. Thus, too, he traced the editions of the other translations of the sacred writings besides the Seventy; and besides the beaten track of translations, that of Aquila and Symmachus and Theodotion, he discovered certain others, which were used in turn, after lying hidden for a long time [ἔκ τινων μυχῶν τὸν πάλαι λανθανούσας χρόνον], he traced and brought to light, I know not from what recesses…and in the case of one of these he has indicated again that it was found at Jericho in a jar [ἐπὶ μιᾶς αὖθις σεσημείωται, ὡς ἐν Ἱεριχοῖ εὑρημένης ἐν πίθῳ] in the time of Antoninus the son of Severus [i.e., Caracalla, who ruled from 198–217]. (*Historia ecclesiastica* 6.16.1-3)[23]

This remarkable account took on new significance when hundreds of scrolls were discovered in caves in the vicinity of Wadi Qumran, on the northwest shore of the Dead Sea, only a few miles from Jericho. That some of the scrolls migrated from Qumran before their discovery

---

22. Ibid., 351.
23. Translation based on J. E. L. Oulton, *Eusebius Ecclesiastical History II*, LCL 265 (London: Heinemann; Cambridge, MA: Harvard University Press, 1932), 51, 53.

in the 1940s and 1950s is attested by the appearance of the *Damascus Covenant* among the genizah remains of the Ben Ezra synagogue in Cairo (at first dubbed *Fragments of a Zadokite Work*) and a Psalm attributed to David that may have been part of the Qumran library (now tentatively identified as Psalm 156).²⁴ Note too that the prepositional phrase ἔκ τινων μυχῶν literally means "out of some caves"! Some may dismiss the story as little more than a legend, but the correlation with the discovery of eleven, now twelve,²⁵ caves linked to the Qumran community has, in my view, shifted the burden of proof onto the shoulders of the skeptics. The story about Origen's acquisition of ancient Hebrew manuscripts from the vicinity of Jericho has received significant support, if not confirmation.²⁶

The point here is that Origen was interested in and greatly valued ancient manuscripts. The same thinking comes into play in a tract against one Artemon (early third century). Arguing in a manner reminiscent of Tertullian a generation earlier, Gaius (or Caius) of Rome (early third century) states:

> They [followers of Artemon] have not feared to corrupt divine scriptures... For this cause they did not fear to lay hands on the divine scriptures, saying that they had corrected [διωρθωκέναι] them. That I am not speaking falsely of them in this matter, whoever wishes may learn. For if any one will collect their respective copies, and compare them one with another [τὰ ἀντίγραφα ἐξετάζειν πρὸς ἄλληλα], he will find that they differ greatly... For you can compare those prepared by them at an earlier date with those which they corrupted later, and you will find them widely different... For they cannot deny the commission of the crime, since the copies have been

---

24. See J. H. Charlesworth, *Has Psalm 156 Been Found?* (Eugene, OR: Cascade Books, 2018).

25. Some may not know that a twelfth Qumran cave was identified in early 2017.

26. Recall too the letter (c. 800) of Timotheus I, the Nestorian patriarch, in which he refers to manuscripts found in a cave near Jericho: "We have learnt from certain Jews who are worthy of credence, who have recently been converted to Christianity, that ten years ago some books were discovered in the vicinity of Jericho, in a cave-dwelling in the mountain. They say that the dog of an Arab who was hunting game went into a cleft after an animal and did not come out; his owner then went in after him and found a chamber inside the mountain containing many books. The huntsman went to Jerusalem and reported this to some Jews. A lot of people set off and arrived there; they found books of the Old Testament, and, apart from that, other books in Hebrew script" (Letter 47, to Mar Sergius). This 1200-year-old account eerily adumbrates the discovery of the Dead Sea Scrolls in the twentieth century. It may well explain how the *Damascus Covenant* found its way to Egypt.

written by their own hands [καὶ τῇ αὐτῶν χειρὶ ᾖ γεγραμμένα]. For they did not receive such Scriptures from their instructors, nor can they produce any copies from which they were transcribed [καὶ δεῖξαι ἀντίγραφα, ὅθεν αὐτὰ μετεγράψαντο]. (frag. 3, *apud* Eusebius, *Historia ecclesiastica* 5.28.13-18)[27]

Gaius faults the followers of Artemon for altering the text of Scripture. The crime cannot be denied because comparison of their respective copies readily reveals their differences. Gaius also makes the point that the followers of Artemon cannot "produce any copies from which" their altered texts "were transcribed." Gaius's charge is fatal: The followers of Artemon cannot produce old texts; they therefore cannot establish the authenticity of their distinctive readings. The implication is that the teachers of the apostolic church *can* produce old copies of Scriptures, whereas Artemon and his followers cannot.[28]

We observe a similar perspective in Eusebius, though he was neither philologist nor textual critic. With respect to the Jewish people Eusebius remarks: "That the Hebrew nation is not new, but is universally honored on account of its antiquity [ἀρχαιότητι], is known to all. The books and writings of this people contain accounts of ancient men [παλαιοὺς ἄνδρας], rare indeed and few in number" (*Historia ecclesiastica* 1.4.5).

Near the end of his history Eusebius claims that Constantine's victory fulfilled prophecy "which had been anciently inscribed in sacred books [τὰ πάλαι...ἐν ἱεραῖς βίβλοις ἐστηλιτευμένα]" (9.9.4). In a lengthy panegyric on the restoration of the Church and the building of many churches, addressed to Paulinus bishop of the Tyrians, and after citing a string of passages from Isaiah, we hear: "These things Isaiah prophesied; these things had been anciently recorded concerning us in sacred books [ταῦτα πρόπαλαι περὶ ἡμῶν ἐν ἱεραῖς βίβλοις καταβέβλητο]" (10.4.53).

27. Translation based on K. Lake, *Eusebius Ecclesiastical History I*, LCL 153 (London: Heinemann; Cambridge, MA: Harvard University Press, 1926), 521, 523, 525.

28. Ironically, the altered texts produced by followers of Artemon, "in their own hand," are autographs of a sort. But they are third-century autographs, not first-century autographs. I might add here that among the papyri recovered from Herculaneum (which will be surveyed below) we have a text by Demetrius of Laconia (c. 100 BCE), a contemporary of Zeno of Sidon and teacher of Philodemus, in which he distinguishes "between reliable editions of Epicurus and corrupt and interpolated copies." The text is P.Herculanensis 1012 and the quotation comes from M. Gigante, *Philodemus in Italy: The Books from Herculaneum*, trans. D. Obbink (Ann Arbor: University of Michigan Press, 1995), 20. For a critical treatment of this papyrus, see E. Puglia, *Demetrio Lacone, Aporie testuali ed esegetiche in Epicuro (PHer. 1012). Edizione, traduzione e commentio*, La Scuola 8 (Naples: Bibliopolis, 1988).

It is the *antiquity* of the prophecies and the scriptures that contain them that seems to impress Eusebius, but more importantly they are intended to impress the Roman powers, including Emperor Constantine himself. The antiquity of these prophecies and the ancient books in which they are found serves an important apologetic purpose, akin to what we have already observed: older is better.

The same thinking lies behind a comment in the well-known Thirty-Ninth Festal Letter by Athanasius of Alexandria (c. 296–373). In it he asserts that apocryphal books are "a fabrication of the heretics, who write them down when it pleases them and generously assign to them an early date of composition in order that they may be able to draw upon them as supposedly ancient writings [παλαιά]..."[29] Athanasius is quite correct; pseudepigraphal writings not only claim spurious authorship, they also claim great antiquity. This is because antiquity brings with it authority and respect.

We probably have the same idea at work in the much-disputed Muratorian Fragment. Although this Latin fragment has been traditionally dated to the late second century, recent scholarship has made, in my opinion, a convincing case for a late fourth-century date.[30] The relevant portion reads as follows:

> But Hermas wrote the Shepherd very recently, in our times [*vero nuperrime temporibus nostris*], in the city of Rome, while Bishop Pius, his brother, was occupying the (episcopal) chair of the church of the city of Rome. Therefore it ought indeed to be read; but it cannot be read publicly to the people in church...for it is after (their) time [*in finem temporum potest*].[31] (lines 73–80)

---

29. Translation from W. Schneemelcher, "General Introduction," in *New Testament Apocrypha*. Vol. 1, *Gospels and Related Writings*, ed. W. Schneemelcher, rev. edn (Cambridge: James Clarke; Louisville: Westminster John Knox Press, 1991), 50.

30. For a review of the relevant issues, see L. M. McDonald, *The Formation of the Biblical Canon*. Vol. 2, *The New Testament: Its Authority and Canonicity* (London and New York: Bloomsbury T&T Clark, 2017), 274–304; C. Rothschild, "The Muratorian Fragment as a Roman Fake," *NovT* 60 (2018): 55–82. Rothschild's case for a fourth-century date is compelling. McDonald also supports the later date. But see E. J. Schnabel, "The Muratorian Fragment: The State of Research," *JETS* 57 (2014): 231–64.

31. The English translation, which reflects the "corrected" version of the Latin, is adapted from McDonald, *The Formation of the Biblical Canon*, 278. The original and restored Latin of the Muratorian Fragment can be found in D. J. Theron, *Evidence of Tradition* (Grand Rapids: Baker, 1980), 112.

Critical scholarship concerned with the date of the Muratorian Fragment gives this passage a great deal of attention. My interest here is in the observation that once again a premium is placed on antiquity; or, in the case of the Shepherd of Hermas, the *lack* of antiquity. The value of this popular writing is acknowledged by the author of the Fragment, and so "it ought indeed to be read." But because it is of *recent* vintage (whether literally so, if the Fragment is second century; or fictitiously, if the Fragment is fourth century), "it cannot be read publicly...in church"; that is, because the Shepherd of Hermas lacks canonical authority it cannot be read in church services.

We also have very important testimony in Jerome's brief paragraph celebrating the life of Pamphilus (c. 240–309), student of Origen and patron of Eusebius. Jerome reports that Pamphilus

> was so inflamed with love of sacred literature, that he transcribed the greater part of the works of Origen with his own hand and these are still preserved in the library at Cæsarea. I have twenty-five volumes of Commentaries of Origen, written in his hand, *On the twelve prophets* which I hug and guard with such joy, that I deem myself to have the wealth of Croesus... He wrote an *Apology for Origen* before Eusebius had written his and was put to death at Cæsarea in Palestine in the persecution of Maximinus. (*De viris illustribus* 75)[32]

This is a remarkable statement. Jerome (c. 342–420) claims that the copies made by Pamphilus, who was martyred in 309 during the persecution of Maximinus, "are still preserved in the library at Caesarea." This means that at the time Jerome writes, these copies would be about a hundred years old. More remarkable is what Jerome says next: "I have twenty-five volumes of Commentaries of Origen, written in his hand [*viginti quinque* ἐξηγήσεων *Origenis volumina manu ejus*]." These copies would have to be at least 150 years old (if "his hand" refers to Origen), or 100 years old (if "his hand" refers to Pamphilus), at the time of writing *De viris illustribus*. Jerome knows full well their value and because he possesses them regards himself as having "the wealth of Croesus," the legendary king of Lydia said to have been fabulously wealthy. Jerome also remarks that the copies made by Pamphilus remain at the library at Caesarea. These copies, and possibly a few manuscripts that had belonged to Origen, remained in the library of Caesarea until it was destroyed by

---

32. Translation based on E. C. Richardson, "Jerome and Gennadius. Lives of Illustrious Men," in *A Select Library of Nicene and Post-Nicene Fathers of the Christian Church*, Vol. III, ed. H. Wace and P. Schaff (Oxford: James Parker, 1892), 377.

Arabs in the seventh century.³³ By that time the copies made by Pamphilus would have been some 300 years old. If there were any of Origen's manuscripts still in the library, they would have been 350 years old.

I conclude this section with a comment by Augustine of Hippo (354–430). In his dispute (397–398) with Faustus the Manichean over allegations of spurious insertions in Scripture, Augustine recommends, "And if any uncertainty remained, we should consult the original text [*praecedens lingua*]" (*Contra Faustum Manichaeum* 11.2). Augustine may be referring to the original language (that is, the *lingua*, whether Greek or Hebrew), as opposed to Augustine's native Latin, but he may also be assuming the antiquity of Christianity's sacred books, which will include old copies in Greek (though not of course autographs, which by this time are no longer extant). These old copies, Augustine rightly believes, will not contain the suspect insertions.

The polemics of early Christian writers clearly presuppose the antiquity of at least some New Testament manuscripts; otherwise, their arguments against heretics and the newness of their alternate and competing versions of Scripture would carry no weight. The recognition of the importance of antiquity would have strongly encouraged Christians, especially scholars and clergy, to preserve and protect New Testament autographs, even as non-Christians safeguarded and revered their books. It is hard to believe that the autographs and early copies of Christian Scripture would not have been cared for and, in time, venerated as holy relics (as evidently attested in Bishop Peter's Paschal homily).

Of course, the apologetic interests of these Church Fathers are obvious, so it must be admitted that there may sometimes be exaggeration, naïvete, or perhaps outright falsehood. There is no justification, however, for a blanket rejection of their testimony. This is especially so in light of other relevant factors that will soon be taken into consideration. I turn now to the testimony of late antique non-Christian writers, whose interests are for the most part quite different from the interests of the Church Fathers and where in most cases no apologetic seems to be in play.

Late Antique Non-Christian Claims of Longevity

Late Antique non-Christian writers also remark on the longevity of literary books. Their comments have nothing to do with apologetics, as is often the case with respect to Christian writers, but some of their concerns

---

33. "Pamphilus," in *The Oxford Dictionary of the Christian Church*, ed. F. L. Cross and E. A. Livingstone, 3rd edn (Oxford: Oxford University Press, 2005), 1221. The date of destruction is estimated to have been the year 638.

(such as determining a proper reading or finding an old copy) are similar. The non-Christian testimony is especially important because there is often greater detail with regard to the history and ownership of old books, including complaints concerning theft and careless treatment of ancient and valuable books.

In reference to the library assembled by Peisistratus (d. 527 BCE), Aulus Gellius (c. 125–c. 190 CE) tells his readers that

> …later Xerxes, when he took possession of Athens and burned the entire city except the citadel [480 BCE], removed the whole collection of books and carried them off to Persia. Finally, a long time afterwards, king Seleucus, who was surnamed Nicanor, had all those books taken back to Athens. (Gellius, *Noctes Atticae* 7.17.2; cf. Isidorus, *Etymologiae* 6.3.3-5)

In 480 BCE Xerxes captured Athens and seized the "whole collection of books," taking them to Persia. Seleucus I Nicanor (r. 305–281 BCE) had "all those books taken back to Athens." It is assumed that they are the same books, not copies, looted in 480. If so, the books had been in Persia for about 180 years. We should assume that many of them were old at the time Xerxes seized them. Accordingly, many of the recovered books would have been more than two hundred years old when they were returned to Athens. In what condition they were we are not told, but we should assume Seleucus I would not have bothered had the books been reduced to detritus.

Gellius relates another relevant story in *Noctes Atticae* 18.5.1-12, in which he recounts an occasion when he and his colleagues discussed an unlikely reading in an old copy of *Annals* by Quintus Ennius (239–169 BCE). In the course of conversation one Apollinaris remarks, "I procured at great trouble and expense, for the sake of examining one line, a copy of heavy and venerable antiquity, which it was almost certain had been edited by the hand of Lampadio [*librum summae atque reverendae vetustatis, quem fere constabat Lampadionis manu emendatum*]" (18.5.11). The copy in question had been owned and annotated by Octavius Lampadio (c. 190 BCE) and was still available for study in the late second century CE. If we accept the testimony of Gellius, then the manuscript in question was about 350 years old.[34] The manuscript, evidently, was copied when the autograph itself was still relatively new.

---

34. The passage is discussed in G. W. Houston, *Inside Roman Libraries: Book Collections and Their Management in Antiquity*, Studies in the History of Greece and Rome (Chapel Hill NC: The University of North Carolina Press, 2014), 21.

Another relevant example comes from Strabo (c. 63 BCE–c. 24 CE) and is repeated in part by Plutarch (before 50 CE–after 120 CE). It concerns Sulla's celebrated theft of a collection of books that once belonged to Aristotle. It is necessary to quote a lengthy portion of the story in order to follow its somewhat convoluted sequence:

> From Scepsis came the Socratic philosophers Erastus and Coriscus and Neleus the son of Coriscus, this last a man who not only was a pupil of Aristotle and Theophrastus, but also inherited the library of Theophrastus, which included that of Aristotle. At any rate, Aristotle bequeathed his own library to Theophrastus, to whom he also left his school; and he is the first man, so far as I know, to have collected books and to have taught the kings in Egypt how to arrange a library. Theophrastus bequeathed it to Neleus; and Neleus took it to Scepsis and bequeathed it to his heirs, untrained people, who kept the books locked up and not even carefully stored. But when they heard how zealously the Attalic kings[35] to whom the city was subject were searching for books to build up the library in Pergamum, they hid their books underground in a kind of trench. But much later, when the books had been damaged by moisture and moths, their descendants sold them to Apellicon[36] of Teos for a large sum of money, both the books of Aristotle and those of Theophrastus…immediately after the death of Apellicon, Sulla, who had captured Athens, carried off Apellicon's library to Rome, where Tyrannion the grammarian, who was fond of Aristotle, got it in his hands. (Strabo, *Geographica* 13.1.54; cf. Plutarch, *Sulla* 26.1-2)[37]

The library originated with Aristotle (384–322 BCE), which he bequeathed to his colleague Theophrastus, who succeeded the famous philosopher as headmaster (*scholarch*). The latter bequeathed his books and those of Aristotle to Neleus the son of Coriscus. The books that make up this library are listed in Diogenes Laertius (early third century CE) and are said to comprise some "232,808 lines [στίχων]" (Diogenes Laertius, *Vitae philosophorum* 5.42-50). By ancient standards this private library was very large. Diogenes Laertius also quotes from the will of Theophrastus: "All my books (I give) to Neleus [τὰ δὲ βιβλία πάντα

---

35. Strabo refers here to Eumenes II (r. 197–159 BCE).
36. Died c. 84 BCE. More on this person below.
37. Translation from H. L. Jones, *The Geography of Strabo*, LCL 223 (Cambridge MA: Harvard University Press; London: William Heinemann, 1924), 6:109–13. For a recent study of the story of Aristotle's library, see F. Tutrone, "Libraries and Intellectual Debate in the Late Republic: The Case of the Aristotelian Library," in *Ancient Libraries*, ed. J. König, K. Oikonomopoulou, and G. Woolf (Cambridge: Cambridge University Press, 2013), 152–66, esp. 160–5.

Νηλεῖ]" (Diogenes Laertius, *Vitae philosophorum* 5.52). Judging by the provisions in the will, we perhaps should assume that Theophrastus had intended that this collection of books remain in the school (to which Theophrastus made a number of bequests) and not be taken to another city.[38]

At some point and for whatever reason, Neleus eventually took the library "to Scepsis and bequeathed it to his heirs, untrained people [ἰδιώταις ἀνθρώποις],[39] who kept the books locked up and not even carefully stored [οὐδ' ἐπιμελῶς κείμενα]."[40] Fearing confiscation and knowing the great value of the library, the descendants of Neleus "hid their books underground in a kind of trench," where they were "damaged by moisture and moths."[41] Still later the books were sold to Apellicon of Teos "for a large sum of money." Not long after the death of Apellicon the library was seized by Sulla, in about 86 BCE, and taken to Rome.[42]

If I may digress, we find a colorful description of this man Apellicon in Athenaeus of Naucratis (c. 170–c. 230 CE). It is related that

> D...Apellicon of Teos...had become a citizen of Athens and...lived a most whimsical and ever-changing course of life. For at one time he was a philosopher, and collected all the treatises of the Peripatetics, and the whole

---

38. It is speculated that Theophrastus assumed that Neleus himself would be named as the new headmaster. The appointment of Strato, instead, may have led to Neleus's decision to relocate. (Aristotle quit Plato's academy apparently for the same reason.) The will of Theophrastus apparently "did not anticipate that Neleus might leave the community." So C. Jacob, "Fragments of a History of Ancient Libraries," in König, Oikonomopoulou, and Woolf (eds.), *Ancient Libraries*, 57–81, here 68–9.

39. The use of ἰδιώτης here refers to a person not properly trained, in this case not trained in the care of manuscripts. The failure of the heirs of Neleus to store properly the library of Aristotle and Theophrastus is evidence of this lack of training.

40. Note 2 Macc. 8:31: "Collecting the arms of the enemy, they stored them all carefully [ἐπιμελῶς] in strategic places..."

41. In the old Palatine Anthology we are reminded that the worm, or "page-eater" (σελιδηφάγος), is "the worst enemy of the Muses" (*Anthologia palatina* 9.251), in that worms and rot will eventually destroy a book.

42. For discussion of the history of this library, see Jacob, "Fragments of a History of Ancient Libraries," 66–74. The long survival of these books, despite their poor care, is cited by T. C. Skeat as evidence of durability and longevity of papyrus. See T. C. Skeat, "Early Christian Book Production: Papyri and Manuscripts," in *The Cambridge History of the Bible*. Vol. 2, *The West from the Fathers to the Reformation*, ed. G. W. H. Lampe (Cambridge: Cambridge University Press, 1969), 54–79; repr. in T. C. Skeat, *The Collected Biblical Writings of T. C. Skeat*, intro. and ed. J. K. Elliott, NovTSup 113 (Leiden: Brill, 2004), 33–59, here 38–9.

library of Aristotle [τὴν Ἀριστοτέλους βιβλιοθήκην], and many others; for he was a very rich man; ᴱ and he had also stolen a great many original copies of decrees of the ancients out of the *Metroon* [τὰ τ' ἐκ τοῦ Μητρῴου τῶν παλαιῶν αὐτόγραφα], and whatever else there was ancient [παλαιόν] and rare in other cities... (Athenaeus, *Deipnosophistae* 5.214d-e)[43]

It is tantalizing to speculate how old the "great many original copies," or autographs [αὐτόγραφα], were, as well as the "whatever else" that was "ancient" (παλαιόν). Apellicon seems to have had a taste for the ancient and rare, and he was not above theft.

Most of the books in the Aristotle-Theophrastus library, probably including autographs, were about 250 years old at the time they fell into Sulla's hands. There is not a hint in Strabo's account that the great longevity of this library was unusual. What was remarked upon, however, was the damage done to the books because of their storage underground. Perhaps it is not surprising that Plutarch comments that the books of Aristotle and Theophrastus "came into the hands of careless and untrained [ἀφιλοτίμους καὶ ἰδιώτας] people" (Plutarch, *Sulla* 26.2).[44] The implication is that had these bookrolls been properly cared for, they would have been in good condition, despite their great age and their existence in Greece. Had this library been stored in warm, arid Egypt, the damage described by Strabo likely would not have occurred.

Strabo's account of the history of Aristotle's library documents the great value placed on books, how books and whole libraries were sought after, sometimes violently, how books and libraries were bequeathed to colleagues and heirs,[45] how books and libraries survived for generations, and how books and libraries did not always receive the care they needed to avoid decay and damage. The latter was especially important in wet climates, in contrast to the much drier climates of Egypt and parts of the Middle East.

At his death, Strato, the headmaster who succeeded Theophrastus, bequeathed his library: "I leave the school to Lyco...I also give and

---

43. Translation from C. D. Yonge, *The Deipnosophists*, 3 vols. (London: Henry G. Bohn, 1854), 1:341.

44. Plutarch enlarges upon the criticism of the heirs of Neleus by describing them not only as "untrained" (ἰδιώτας), as stated in Strabo's account, but also as "careless" (ἀφιλοτίμους), which implies that these people lacked ambition to do what was expected and proper.

45. I should mention that at his death in 78 BCE, the library of Sulla passed on to his son Faustus and may have eventually gone to Lucullus in the 50s (Plutarch, *Lucullus* 4.4).

bequeath to him all my books [τὰ βιβλία πάντα], except those that we (i.e., I) have written [γεγράφαμεν]" (Diogenes Laertius, *Vitae philosophorum* 5.62).

I should note that the Church Father Origen also inherited old books. According to Eusebius: "And memoirs too of Symmachus are still extant... These, along with other interpretations of the Scriptures by Symmachus, Origen indicates that he had received from a certain Juliana, who he says received the books by inheritance from Symmachus himself [παρ' αὐτοῦ Συμμάχου τὰς βίβλους διαδέξασθαι]" (*Historia ecclesiastica* 6.17.1). Symmachus, either a Samaritan or a Jewish proselyte, flourished in the second century. An otherwise unknown woman named Juliana inherited his books and she in turn passed them on to Origen. These books may have been a hundred years old when Origen acquired them.[46]

The story of the library of Aristotle and Theophrastus is an unusual one, to be sure; in part because of the great value placed on it. But the practice of keeping a library intact was not unusual. On this point George Houston comments that "there is good reason to suspect that book collections frequently retained their essential shape and character over a period of two or three generations, and the most likely mechanism for such a phenomenon would be inheritance, either within the family or by a friend or student."[47] Houston limits his study to non-Christian book culture, but as we have seen, the same appears to apply to Christian practice as well.

In a lengthy passage on the manufacture of papyrus, Pliny the Elder (c. 23–79 CE) discusses the durability of this material, which allows "records to last a long time." He then cites a few first-hand examples to justify his claim: "At the house of the poet and most distinguished citizen Pomponius Secundus I have seen documents in the hand of Tiberius and Gaius Gracchus [*Tiberi Gaique Gracchorum manus*] written nearly two hundred years ago; while as for autographs of Cicero, of his late majesty Augustus, and of Virgil, we see them constantly" (*Naturalis historia* 13.83).[48] As Pliny says, the Gracchi autographs in his time were almost two centuries old. In the time of Pliny the autographs of Cicero (106–43

---

46. See W. A. Johnson, *Readers and Reading Culture in the High Roman Empire: A Study of the Elite Communities*, Classical Culture and Society (Oxford and New York: Oxford University Press, 2010), 189 n. 27: "We do know of bookrolls in antiquity that are passed along with an estate, which is hardly a surprise given the value of the artifact."

47. Houston, *Inside Roman Libraries*, 31.

48. Translation adapted from H. Rackham, *Pliny: Natural History IV. Books XII–XVI*, LCL 370, rev. edn (London: Heinemann/Cambridge University Press, 1968), 149.

BCE) would be a century old or more. The autographs of Augustus would only be forty or fifty years old. It should not be overlooked that Pliny claims that he and his colleagues "constantly see" (*saepenumero videmus*) autographs of these illustrious (and prolific) people. Apparently autographs, even a hundred years old, were not rare. I remind readers that these old writings circulated *in Italy* (as opposed to Egypt) and so were occasionally exposed to damp weather; yet even so, they survived for many generations.

Pliny also relates the story of the discovery of papyrus books found in the sarcophagus of Numa Pompilius (d. 673 BCE), second king of old Rome (*Naturalis historia* 13.85-88).[49] The discovery was made in the consulship of Publius Cornelius Cethegus (c. 181 BCE). The papyrus books, evidently treated with citrus oil and waxed, were about five hundred years old. It was not uncommon in antiquity to place books in tombs and sarcophagi. Pliny quotes his source as saying that "people wondered how those books could have lasted so long" (13.86). Indeed, they had reason to wonder. The survival of books two or three centuries above ground and properly cared for was one thing; five centuries underground was something else! It is clear that this kind of longevity, in Italy, and in these conditions, was viewed as very unusual.

In a discussion of books available for medical research Galen (c. 129–199 CE) tells his readers that "some also had desired to find very old volumes, written three hundred years ago, which I had at Pergamum, of which part were preserved in rolls, part on papyrus [χάρτοις], and part on excellent lime-tree bark [φιλύραις]" (*In Hippocratis* 18.2). In another context Galen complains of old books not well cared for: "These (books), then, did not cause me small pain when copying them. As it is, the papyri are completely useless, not even able to be unrolled because they have been glued together by decomposition, since the region is both marshy and low-lying, and, during the summer, it is stifling" (*De indolentia* 19).

What we learn from Galen is consistent with the testimony of Strabo. If cared for properly, books, whether written on papyrus (χάρτης) or on lime-tree bark (φιλύρα), could last a long time, even three centuries or more. With respect to texts written on wooden tablets, one thinks of the one thousand or so tablets recovered thus far from Vindolanda, in northern England. The oldest of these reach back to the late first century.[50] If not well cared for, as in the case of the books of Aristotle and Theophrastus

---

49. Pliny credits the story to Cassius Hemina, *Annals* 4.
50. On the Vindolanda Tablets, see A. K. Bowman, *Life and Letters on the Roman Frontier: Vindolanda and its People*, rev. edn (London: British Museum, 2003). Several hundred of these tablets have been published to date (T.Vindol. 1–4).

and the books about which Galen complains, damage occurs, usually because of damp. The damage that Galen describes was seen over and over again in the recovery of papyri at Oxyrhynchus, Egypt. Whereas near the surface of the sandy trash mounds the papyri were dry and usually well preserved, papyri three to five meters below the surface almost always were damp and badly damaged.

Late Antique Claims Regarding the Value and Cost of Books

The great value placed on books has already been observed in the above review of late antique testimony. The autograph, or at least what was believed to be the autograph, of the Gospel of John was revered by Christians in Ephesus. Jerome treasured the books written in the hand of Origen. He regarded them as priceless. In the story recounted by Aulus Gellius, his acquaintance Apollinaris claims to have purchased an old copy of *Annals* by Ennius "at great trouble and expense." The convoluted story of the library of Aristotle reflects the great value of these books. Indeed, this library was looked upon as loot, to be seized if found. Unfortunately, hiding this valuable collection resulted in damage.

Originally libraries were little more than archives, often under the authorities of rulers. These archives primarily consisted of financial records, agreements, laws, and annals, some of which were little more than propaganda boasting of the ruler's achievements, victories, and the like. Archives of this nature date back to the third millennium BCE. These written records have survived two millennia or more because they are written or painted on stone, plaster (inside tombs), or baked clay. One thinks of the several thousand tablets recovered from Ebla. Texts such as these survive as long as they do because they are unaffected by moisture and worms.

At some point in antiquity it became fashionable to acquire books. As collections grew it became necessary to construct buildings to house and protect the books. Literary remains provide us with the oldest references to book collecting.[51] One especially ancient testimony comes from soldier, adventurer, and statesman Xenophon of Athens (c. 430–354 BCE). He relates a conversation between Socrates and the youthful dreamer Euthydemus. The latter, we are told, "had formed a large collection of books [γράμματα πολλά] of the works of celebrated poets and professors" (Xenophon, *Memorabilia* 4.2). When Socrates inquires about this collection of books, Euthydemus assures the great philosopher, "I am

---

51. In what follows I rely on Jacob, "Fragments of a History of Ancient Libraries," 57–81.

still adding to it, to make it as complete as possible." Without reviewing the whole dialogue or the point that Socrates was attempting to impress on young Euthydemus, what is clear is the conviction that possession of books was very much to one's advantage.[52]

According to Gellius, "the philosopher Plato...bought three books of Philolaus the Pythagorean for ten thousand denarii... Aristotle too according to report, bought a very few books of the philosopher Speusippus, after the latter's death, for three Attic talents, a sum equivalent in our money to seventy-two thousand sesterces" (Gellius, *Noctes Atticae* 3.17; cf. Diogenes Laertius, *Vitae philosophorum* 4.5).

It has been a long-held belief that the establishment of libraries in Rome began in 168 BCE,[53] thanks to the victory of Aemilius Paulus over the Macedonians and the capture of the royal library. We are told that Aemilius won fame for not seizing for himself the gold and silver from the royal treasuries. Rather, "he handed them over to the quaestors for the public chest. It was only the books of the king [τὰ βιβλία τοῦ βασιλέως] that he allowed his sons, who were devoted to learning, to select from for themselves" (Plutarch, *Aemilius Paulus* 28.11).[54] From the much later Isidorus Hispalensis of Seville, Spain (c. 560–636 CE), we hear that "Aemilius was the first to bring a copious supply of books [*librorum copiam*] back to Rome after defeating Perseus the king of Macedonia" (*Etymologiae* 6.5.1).

Michael Affleck rightly challenges the assumption that there were no libraries in Rome prior to 168 BCE. From the comment by Isidorus, Affleck plausibly suggests that the captured Macedonian library was the first *large* collection of books to find its way to Rome, which is how Isidorus should be understood.[55] Affleck also cites a passage in Polybius (c. 200–c. 118 BCE) that shows that libraries were in existence and in use by the middle of the second century BCE. In a context in which the importance of consulting eyewitnesses is emphasized, Polybius concedes that consulting books saves time and expense, and can avoid danger too: "Inquiries from books [ἐκ τῶν βυβλίων] may be made without any danger or hardship, provided only that one takes care to have access to a city rich

---

52. Socrates, of course, challenges the naïve assumption that the mere possession of a library provides an education.

53. M. Affleck, "Priests, Patrons, and Playwrights: Libraries in Rome before 168 BC," in König, Oikonomopolou, and Woolf (eds.), *Ancient Libraries*, 124–36.

54. Translation based on B. Perrin, *Plutarch, Lives: Dion and Brutus, Timolean and Aemilius Paulus*, LCL 98 (Cambridge, MA: Harvard University Press, 1918), 431.

55. Affleck, "Priests, Patrons, and Playwrights," 125–6.

in documents [ὑπομνημάτων πλῆθος] or to have a library [ἢ βυβλιοθήκην] near at hand" (*Historiae* 12.27.4). The implication is that whereas many cities have libraries, not all do. This could hardly have been the case at the time Polybius writes, if libraries only began with the Macedonian royal library seized by Aemilius and taken to Rome.

Plutarch sings the praises of Lucius Licinius Lucullus of Tusculum (118–56 BCE), soldier and administrator, for not only establishing a large library but for generously making its many volumes available to those who wished to read and study:

> But what he did in the establishment of a library [τὴν τῶν βιβλίων κατασκευήν] deserves warm praise. He got together many (books) [πολλά], and they were well written [γεγραμμένα καλῶς], and his use of them was more honourable to him than his acquisition of them. His libraries [τῶν βιβλιοθηκῶν] were thrown open to all, and the cloisters surrounding them, and the study-rooms, were accessible without restriction to the Greeks, who constantly repaired to them as to an hostelry of the Muses, and spent the day with one another…" (Plutarch, *Lucullus* 42.1)[56]

Lucullus and his library are mentioned favorably by Cicero. A few years after the death of Lucullus, Cicero visited the late man's home and library, which now belonged to his son. When he arrived, he found Cato "sitting in the library, surrounded by many books of the Stoics [*in bibliotheca sedentem multis circumfusum Stoicorum libris*]" (*De finibus* 3.7).[57] Cicero himself was interested in seeing some commentaries by Aristotle (*De finibus* 3.10), which might have been given to Lucullus by his friend Sulla.

The example of Lucullus, who made public his books, may have influenced other Roman benefactors. For example, Suetonius tells his readers that Julius Caesar (100–44 BCE) wished "to make public [*publicare*] the biggest possible Greek and Latin libraries [*bibliothecas Graecas Latinasque*]" (Suetonius, *Iulius* 44). Perhaps following Caesar's lead, Asinius Pollio (76 BCE–4 CE) also "made public [*publicavit*] both Greek and Latin libraries" (Isidorus, *Etymologiae* 6.5.2). Pliny, writing much earlier and with greater detail, says: "The library [*bibliotheca*] which was made public at Rome [*publicata Romae est*], (was) the first in the world, by Asinius Pollio from his booty" (Pliny, *Historia naturalis* 7.115; cf. 35.10:

---

56. Translation based on B. Perrin, *Plutarch, Lives: Themistocles and Camillus, Aristides and Cato Major, Cimon and Lucullus*, LCL 47 (London: Heinemann; Cambridge, MA: Harvard University Press, 1914), 605.

57. For discussion of this passage and the library of Lucullus, see Tutrone, "Libraries and Intellectual Debate in the Late Republic," 157–60.

Placing portraits of authors in libraries "was the invention of Asinius Pollio at Rome, who was the first to make the genius of men public property by dedicating a library").[58] The language of "making public" (*publicare*), in reference to books, statues, and portraits, becomes commonplace in the latter part of the first century BCE and on into the first century CE.

No one benefitted more from these public libraries than Pliny. Large collections of books made it possible for scholars to write their histories and treatises touching various topics. This point is made by Pliny the Elder who says that "by perusing about two thousand volumes [*voluminum circiter duorum milium*]…we have collected in thirty-six volumes 20,000 noteworthy facts obtained from one hundred authors that we have explored, with a great number of other facts in addition…" (*Historia naturalis praef.* 17). Collections such as those on which Pliny depended had grown so large that finding ways of housing them became a pressing problem. For this reason, Pliny reminds his readers of what Domitus Piso once said: "It is not books but store-houses that are needed!" (ibid.).

Of course, many libraries remained private. The wealthy poet Persius (34–62 CE) bequeathed a large amount of money and "about seven hundred volumes of Chrysippus or his entire library [*libros circa septingentos Chrysippi sive bibliothecam suam omnem*]" to his friend and philosopher Lucius Annaeus Cornutus (Suetonius, *Vita Persi*).[59] Cornutus accepted the books but refused the money.

A few generations later we hear from Athenaeus that Larensis, a wealthy Roman, who funds the scholarly gatherings,

> owned so many ancient Greek books [βιβλίων…ἀρχαίων Ἑλληνικῶν] that he surpassed all who have been celebrated for their large libraries, including Polycrates of Samos…the kings of Pergamum…Aristotle the philosopher, Theophrastus, and Neleus, who preserved the books of the two last named…. [O]ur King Ptolemy, surnamed Philadelphus, purchased them all and transferred them with those which he had procured at Athens and at Rhodes to his beautiful capital, Alexandria. (Athenaeus, *Deipnosophistae* 1.4)[60]

---

58. For discussion of these and other related texts, see M. Nicholls, "Roman Libraries as Public Buildings in the Cities of the Empire," in König, Oikonomopoulou, and Woolf (eds.), *Ancient Libraries*, 261–76.

59. Latin text and English translation from J. C. Rolfe, *Suetonius*, Vol. II, LCL 38, rev. edn (Cambridge, MA: Harvard University Press, 1997), 472–3. Suetonius is given credit for this brief *Vita Aulis Persi Flacci*, but Suetonian authorship is doubtful (ibid., 470).

60. Translation from C. B. Gulick, *Athenaeus: The Deipnosophists. Books I–III.106e*, LCL 204 (Cambridge, MA: Harvard University Press, 1969), 11; Jacob, "Fragments of a History of Ancient Libraries," 78.

This passage shows how ambitious some could be in expanding their collections of books. Private citizen Larensis possessed a huge collection, while Ptolemy the king of Egypt purchased the collections of whole libraries from cities around the Mediterranean.

We are told that Gordian II, who in 238 CE was Roman emperor for all of three weeks, took his studies very seriously as a boy. When his tutor died, "he left the young Gordian all the books [*omnes libros*] that had belonged to his father, Serenus Sammonicus, and these were estimated at 62,000. And this raised him to the seventh heaven, for being now possessed of a library of such magnitude and excellence, thanks to the power of letters he became famous among men" (*Historia Augusta: Gordiani tres* 18.2-3).[61]

From statements such as these we hear about libraries collected by scholars, by the wealthy, and by kings. Whole collections were purchased, to augment and expand new or existing libraries, such as the library at Alexandria.

The cost of making books in late antiquity varied. For the most part, the cost of a book depended on the quality of the paper, the quality of its collation and binding, and the skill of the scribe. Only the wealthy could afford high-end books and only the wealthy could assemble a large collection of books. People of more modest means could afford books, but not as many and not of high quality.

We do possess some data about the prices of books and the payment of scribes. Epictetus (c. 55–c. 135 CE) chastises a student who imagines that he is making great progress because he has read and understood a small book and now can talk about it: "Do not confine yourself to expounding your books, but go and write some of the same kind yourself. And what will you gain thereby? Do you not know that the whole book costs only five denarii [ὅλον τὸ βιβλίον πέντε δηναρίων]? Is the expounder of it, then, think you, worth more than five denarii?" (Epictetus, *Diatribai* 1.4.16).[62] Five denarii appears to be a conventional price for a small book in the first and second centuries.

---

61. Translation from D. Magie, *The Scriptores Historiae Augustae II*, LCL 140 (London: Heinemann; Cambridge, MA: Harvard University Press, 1924), 413. For discussion of this passage and the problem of storing large collections of books in antiquity, see P. L. Tucci, "Flavian Libraries in the City of Rome," in König, Oikonomopolou, and Woolf (eds.), *Ancient Libraries*, 277–311, here 307–9; idem, *The Temple of Peace in Rome*. Vol. 1, *Art and Culture in Imperial Rome* (Cambridge: Cambridge University Press, 2017), 188–90.

62. Translation based on W. A. Oldfather, *Epictetus*, LCL 131 (London: Heinemann; Cambridge, MA; Harvard University Press, 1925), 31, 33. The small book alluded to is Chrysippus, *On Choice* (cf. Epictetus 1.4.6, 7, 9, 14).

We hear the same in Martial (c. 40–c. 103 CE): "Ask for Atrectus (that being the name of the shop's proprietor), and he will hand you from the first or second pigeonhole a Martial, shaved with pumice [*rasum pumice*] and smart with purple, for five denarii [*denaris quinque*]" (Martial, *Epigrammata* 1.117.13-17).[63] The small book is not especially expensive but it is made well. Papyrus was rubbed with pumice to prepare the surface for writing. The purple adds a touch of class. In a second passage Martial declares: "The whole multitude of mottos contained in this thin little book [*in hoc gracili…libello*] will cost you, if you purchase it, four small coins [*nummis quattuor*]. If four is too much, perhaps you may get it for two, and the bookseller, Trypho, will even then make a profit" (Martial, *Epigrammata* 13.3.2).[64] A small book of Martial's epigrams may have contained only about 262 lines; hence the possibility of getting it for half price.

In one of the Petaus papyri (second century CE) we hear of renting bookrolls for the purpose of copying them: "When Deios was with us, he showed us the six parchments [μεμβράνας]. We did not take any of these, but we made collations [ἀντεβάλομεν] against eight others, for which I paid 100 drachmas on account" (P.Petaus 30, 3–7).[65] If renting eight parchments cost 100 drachmas, one wonders how much the purchase cost would have been.

In Lucian of Samosata (c. 120–192 CE) we hear of a case where an affluent elderly man is tricked into paying a handsome price for a forgery. Lucian mockingly praises a con man who forged a work on rhetoric which he attributed to the well-known rhetorician Tisias[66] and sold it to a gullible man for a king's ransom: "You yourself composed (it)…thus robbing that stupid old man…for because of Tisias's name he paid seven hundred and fifty drachmas for the book, gulled into it [κατασοφισθείς] by you" (*Pseudologista* 30). This incident shows that not only were books highly prized, but if they were linked to a celebrity author they were potentially worth a great deal of money.[67] We should assume that Christians likewise

---

63. Translation based on D. R. Shackleton Bailey, *Martial, Epigrams*, Vol. I, LCL 94 (Cambridge, MA: Harvard University Press, 1993), 131.

64. Translation based on W. C. A. Ker, *Martial, Epigrams*, Vol. II, LCL 95 (Cambridge, MA: Harvard University Press, 1920), 391.

65. For discussion of P.Petaus 30, see Johnson, *Readers and Reading Culture in the High Roman Empire*, 184; Houston, *Inside Roman Libraries*, 227–8.

66. Tisias (fifth century BCE) is referenced in Plato, *Phaedrus* 267A.

67. In this case it may have been a swindle, but it does demonstrate that, as William Harris puts it, "750 drachmas is an imaginable price for a rare book." Harris, *Ancient Literacy*, 225 n. 254.

would have placed a great deal of value on old copies of New Testament Scripture, especially autographs.

The late T. C. Skeat estimated that the cost of producing the New Testament papyrus codex $\mathfrak{P}^{45}$, which contains the four Gospels and the book of Acts,[68] in the first half of the third century would have been about 44 drachmas (24 drachmas for the scribe and 20 for the papyrus).[69] Although this is not a heavy expense, it does represent about seven weeks' wages (on the assumption that a day's wage was one drachma[70]), which would have been only a minor expense for the wealthy.

It will be worthwhile to consider the cost of a few libraries and collections. Cicero, a bibliophile if there ever was one, begged his friend Atticus not to sell his library to anyone but him. The library, however, was costly and Cicero needed time to round up enough money for the purchase. He tells Atticus: "I am putting all my little gleanings aside to pay for this standby for my old age" (*Epistulae ad Atticum* 1.10.4). Cicero was affluent, so we must assume that the library of Atticus was worth a lot of money.

Pliny the Younger (c. 61–c. 112 CE) writes to Baebius Macer, expressing his delight that his friend has enjoyed reading his late uncle's books. Pliny explains that, among other things, he inherited from his uncle (Pliny the Elder) 160 notebooks, "written in a minute hand on both sides" of the papyrus rolls, which means that he has inherited the equivalent of more than 300 books. Pliny relates further, "He used to say that when he was serving as procurator in Spain he could have sold these notebooks to Larcius Licinius for 400,000 sesterces" (*Epistulae* 3.5.17). This amount of money was a fortune (400,000 sesterces = 100,000 denarii). Larcius Licinius was *legatus iuridicus* in Spain c. 73 CE. If we assume that only 150 notebooks had been written by 73 CE (and the number may have

---

68. $\mathfrak{P}^{45}$ is in the Chester Beatty Library in Dublin, Ireland. It is estimated that the surviving fragments represent about 14 percent of the original codex.

69. T. C. Skeat, "A Codicological Analysis of the Chester Beatty Papyrus Codex of Gospels and Acts (P 45)," in *The Collected Biblical Writings of T.C. Skeat*, introduced and edited by J. K. Elliott, NovTSup 113 (Leiden: Brill, 2004), 141–57, here 157. The study originally appeared in *Hermathena* 155 (1993): 27–43.

70. Greek soldiers were paid one drachma per day. Roman soldiers were paid 225 denarii per year. In the first century CE Emperor Domitian increased the annual salary of legionaries to 300 denarii. Depending on skill, workers could earn more than one drachma or denarius per day. According to Aristophanes (*Wasps* 300–302), jurors were paid a half-drachma per day, just enough for subsistence. Recall too the parable of the Workers in the Vineyard (Matt. 20:1-16), where the men are offered one denarius for the day's work. For more on the subject, see D. Schaps, "What Was Money in Ancient Greece?" in *The Monetary Systems of the Greeks and Romans*, ed. W. V. Harris (Oxford: Oxford University Press, 2010), 38–48.

been smaller), which was six years before the death of Pliny the Elder, then Larcius was offering more than 2,500 sesterces (= 625 denarii) for each notebook. This was an enormous price. Pliny was a respected author, and no doubt his friend Larcius admired him; but Pliny was no Plato or Aristotle.

And finally we should remember the effect the Apostle Paul's evangelizing had on the people of Ephesus. Evidently the failure of the seven sons of Sceva to exorcize a powerful demon resulted in the name of Jesus becoming well known and respected (Acts 19:11-17). As it turns out, a number of people became Christians and gave up their magic books: "And a number of those who practiced magic arts brought their books together and burned them in the sight of all; and they counted the value of them and found it came to fifty thousand pieces of silver" (19:19). We should probably assume that these silver coins are drachmas or denarii.[71] Unfortunately, we are not told the number of the books that were destroyed. Accordingly, we have no idea what the values were for individual books themselves. Nevertheless, we have reason to believe that books of magic were greatly prized in late antiquity.

The value of books and personal libraries sometimes lay in ostentation, rather than in a genuine interest in learning. Seneca (4 BCE–65 CE) laments the wealthy who pretend to scholarship and interest in great learning by acquiring and shamelessly displaying books by famous scholars. Some of these people, says Seneca, "have countless books and libraries, whose titles their owners can scarcely read through in a whole lifetime" (*De tranquillitate animi* 9.4). Still on a roll, Seneca holds in contempt the man

> who seeks to have book-cases of citrus-wood and ivory, who collects the works of unknown or discredited authors and sits yawning in the midst of so many thousand books... [I]t is in the houses of the laziest men that you will see a full collection of orations and history with the boxes piled right up to the ceiling; for by now among cold baths and hot baths a library also is equipped as a necessary ornament of a great house..., these collections of the works of sacred genius with all the portraits that adorn them are bought for show and a decoration of their walls. (9.6-7)[72]

In reading Seneca's description of a wealthy man's well-appointed mansion, especially the reference to a library "as a necessary ornament,"

---

71. For other references to money in Luke-Acts, see Luke 15:8; 19:15, 23; 21:2; Acts 7:16.

72. Translation based on J. W. Basore, *Seneca II. Moral Essays II*, LCL 254 (London: Heinemann; Cambridge, MA: Harvard University Press, 1932), 247, 249.

one cannot help but think of the famous "Villa of the Papyri" (Italian: *Villa dei Papiri*) of ancient Herculaneum, buried under the volcanic ash of Mount Vesuvius in 79 CE. Excavated 250 years ago, the villa was found to contain some 1,800 papyrus bookrolls preserved through carbonization.[73] This library, which clearly favors Epicurean works, includes books by Greek and Latin authors. Epicurean authors include Metrodorus of Lampsacus, Colotes of Lampsacus, Carneiscus, Philodemus, Polystratus, Demetrius of Laconia, Lucretius, and perhaps Lucius Manlius Torquatus, in addition to Epicurus himself. Non-Epicurean authors include Chrysippus, Ennius, and Caecilius Statius.[74] Most bookrolls remain unidentified. Given their fragility, very few have been read, though progress is being made through highly sophisticated technologies.

Was the owner of this grand villa guilty of ostentation, along the lines articulated by Seneca? Perhaps, perhaps not. The collection is sophisticated and evidently well focused. The owner may well have been a genuine man of letters. Scholars have speculated that the villa was owned at one time by Philodemus (c. 110–c. 35 BCE) himself, or Lucius Calpurnius Piso Caesoninus (c. 100–43 BCE), the father-in-law of Julius Caesar. Who owned the villa when Vesuvius erupted in 79 CE is unknown. Whatever his education and whatever his motives, the library that the villa's owner had acquired would have been very valuable. Indeed, a great many of the bookrolls of this library had been packed in boxes, ready for evacuation to a place of safety. But the sudden onrush of hot gas and ash from the volcano cut short the operation.

Leaving aside his criticism and sarcasm, Seneca provides some useful information regarding the collection, care, and value of books. He alludes to bookcases made "of citrus-wood and ivory" (*citro atque ebore*). Citrus-wood (*citrus*) was used in making furniture, usually of great quality (Pliny, *Naturalis historia* 16.66, 231). It was valued also because it resisted rot (13.101: "virtually everlasting, being proof against all causes of decay"). High-end furniture included ivory (*eboreus*), sometimes as a veneer (16.232). Bookcases made of citrus-wood would be both beautiful, enduring, and protective of the bookrolls they held.

---

73. Not all of the villa has been excavated. It is possible more bookrolls will be discovered.

74. For a list of authors and works thus far identified, see J. T. Fitzgerald, D. D. Obbink, and G. S. Holland, "Introduction: Philodemus and the Papyri from Herculaneum," in *Philodemus and the New Testament*, ed. J. T. Fitzgerald, D. D. Obbink, and G. S. Holland, NovTSup 111 (Leiden: Brill, 2004), 1–12, here 7–12; Houston, *Inside Roman Libraries*, 90–8, 280–6.

The important point is that here again we have evidence of how greatly valued books were in late antiquity. Not all owners of books were scholars and some collectors of books may have done so out of vanity. Whatever the motive and whatever the purpose that lay behind their acquisition, books were valued. Relatively inexpensive books from a wealthy man's perspective were, nevertheless, expensive for most people. Rare books and books of great quality, well out of reach for all but the very wealthy, could command extravagant prices. It is not surprising that books—even inexpensive ones—were well cared for and were passed on as treasure to family and students.

Before concluding this section we should briefly consider the cost of papyrus and the fees paid to scribes and copyists. Scribes were typically paid according to the number of lines copied. Rates of payment were based on the quality of the scribe's handwriting (P.Lond. 7.2110; Diocletian, *Edictum de pretiis rerum venalium* 7.41-43). The cost of the paper also varied, according to the quality of its make and the purpose for its use (Pliny, *Naturalis historia* 13.74-78). William Harris explains that in Egypt papyrus would have cost "four drachmas a roll, and a single sheet might cost two obols… [T]he real price of papyrus would have been much higher in Greece or Italy, not to mention Spain or Britain, than in Egypt… And actual finished books written on papyrus were very expensive for most of the inhabitants of the Roman Empire."[75] He further notes that the "books that were available were often poorly produced" and so did not cost a great deal. Nevertheless, for most people, who of course were not wealthy, these modest books "were likely to be quite expensive."[76]

Late Antique Claims Regarding Loss of Books

In late antiquity books and whole libraries were lost to theft, fire, and confiscation (either for the purpose of being added to another library or for the purpose of destruction). Fires could be accidental or deliberate (i.e., "book-burning"). Thefts might involve a single volume or a whole collection. Books that were old and in poor condition, or books that for whatever reason had lost their value, might be thrown out as trash or recycled (e.g., for use as cartonnage). Other books, through neglect and improper storage, were badly damaged by rot and worms.

---

75. Harris, *Ancient Literacy*, 195.
76. Ibid., 225.

The greatest danger to books and libraries was fire. Half of the city of Rome was destroyed by fire in 64 CE. Several libraries and countless books were destroyed.[77] According to Suetonius the fire burned for "six days and seven nights…the houses of leaders of old were burned, still adorned with trophies of victory…and whatever else interesting and noteworthy had survived from antiquity" (*Nero* 38.2).[78] Tacitus adds that among the losses were "the primitive and uncorrupted memorials of literary genius" (*Annales* 15.41).[79] Livy speaks of the loss of almost all of the "public and private archives [*publicis privatisque…monumentis*]" (Livy, *Ab urbe condita* 6.1.2). We should assume that many of the grand houses, temples, and other structures dedicated to various victories and achievements that were destroyed in the fire contained books, some quite old. Most, if not all, of these books were lost.

Roman libraries suffered damage a second time in 80 CE. This fire, says Dio Cassius, "consumed the temple of Serapis, the temple of Isis, the Saepta, the temple of Neptune, the Baths of Agrippa, the Pantheon, the Diribitorum, the theatre of Balbus, the stage building of Pompey's theatre, the Octavian buildings together with their books [μετὰ τῶν βιβλίων], and the temple of Jupiter Capitolinus with its surrounding temples" (Dio Cassius, *Historia romana* 66.24.1-2).[80] Dio goes on to remark that many other buildings were destroyed also. He specifically mentions the books in the Octavian buildings, because they housed libraries. We should assume that several of the other buildings did also.

Fire struck Rome yet again in 192 CE. Galen mentions the destruction, naming a number of books lost in the libraries on the Palatine (*De indolentia* 13).[81] The implication is that several libraries and their contents were either badly damaged or completely destroyed. Among these libraries would have been the Greek and Latin libraries built by Augustus, as part of his temple of Apollo (Suetonius, *Augustus* 29.3).[82] According to the

---

77. For a survey of Rome's libraries, see E. Bowie, "Libraries for the Caesars," in König, Oikonomopoulou, and Woolf (eds.), *Ancient Libraries*, 237–60.

78. Translation from Rolfe, *Suetonius*, Vol. II, 149, 151.

79. Translation from J. Jackson, *Tacitus V: Annals Books 13–16*, LCL 322 (Cambridge, MA: Harvard University Press, 1937), 277. In n. 5 Jackson comments that the "natural inference, though direct evidence is lacking, is that the Palatine Library had suffered in the fire." This is explicitly stated, however, with reference to the fire in 192 CE.

80. Translation based on E. Cary, *Dio Cassius Roman History Books 71–80*, LCL 177 (Cambridge, MA: Harvard University Press, 1927), 309.

81. Houston (*Inside Roman Libraries*, 247) discusses the Palatine libraries mentioned by Galen.

82. See Tucci, "Flavian Libraries in the City of Rome," 286–91.

not-always-reliable fourth-century *Historia Augusta*, Emperor Commodus (ruled 180–192 CE) "ordered the burning of the city" (*Historia Augusta*: *Commodus Antoninus* 15.7: *urbem incendi iusserat*), but in his earlier and more detailed account Dio Cassius (c. 150–c. 235 CE) says nothing about the emperor's involvement. He says, rather, "a fire that began at night in some dwelling leaped to the Temple of Peace…whence the flames, borne aloft, entered the palace and consumed very extensive portions of it, so that nearly all the state records [τὰ γράμματα] were destroyed" (*Historia romana* 73.24.1-2).[83]

Great libraries elsewhere in the classical period were destroyed. The magnificent library of Alexandria caught fire in 48 BCE when Julius Caesar fought for control of the harbor. According to Plutarch, the fire "spread from the dockyards and destroyed the great library [τὴν μεγάλην βιβλιοθήκην…διέφθειρε]" (Plutarch, *Caesar* 49.3). Dio Cassius speaks of the destruction of "storehouses of grain and of books [τῶν βίβλων]" (*Historia romana* 42.38.2). Writing in the early fifth century CE Orosius says the number of books lost in the fire was 400,000 (*Historiae adversum Paganos* 6.15.32). But this number may reflect legends, not realistic data.

That there was damage and loss of many books in this fire is not in doubt, but Plutarch probably exaggerates when he says that the great library was *destroyed*. Seneca says 40,000 books were lost in the fire (*De tranquillitate animi* 9.5). This is a large number but it probably represents only a portion of the library's holdings.

We hear more about the history of the library of Alexandria in the pseudonymous *Letter of Aristeas to Philocrates* (c. 170 BCE), which dates itself to the reign of Ptolemy II of Egypt (ruled 285–247 BCE). According to this work, Demetrius of Phalerum (c. 350–c. 280 BCE) was appointed "keeper of the king's library" and began aggressively acquiring books (*Aristeas* 9). Epiphanius (c. 315–403 CE) reports that Demetrius added some 54,800 volumes (*De mensuris et ponderibus* 269-270). The total collection, we are told, reached 200,000 volumes, but the king declared that he wanted 500,000! (*Aristeas* 10). Indeed, elsewhere we are told that Ptolemy ordered that all ships that docked at Alexandria be searched for books and that copies be made of them (Galen, *In Hippocratis* 3.17a.605-606). Athenaeus remarks that there is no need to mention the "number of books"! (*Deipnosophistae* 5.36-37, 203e). Ammianus Marcellinus

---

83. Translation based on Cary, *Dio Cassius Roman History Books 71–80*, 121. Dio Cassius claims that Commodus arrived after the fact and offered to assist in putting out the fire (73.24.3). The libraries of the Temple of Apollo were once again damaged by fire in the fourth century (Ammianus, *Historiae* 23.3.3).

(c. 330–395 CE), the last great historian of classical Rome, claims that the library's holdings reached 700,000 volumes (*Historiae* 22.16.3), which I confess is hard to imagine.[84]

Whatever the true extent of the damage and whatever the actual number of books in its possession (and over time no doubt this number varied), the library of Alexandria continued to function for many generations to come. In 41 BCE Marc Antony removed 200,000 books from libraries at Pergamum and gave them to Cleopatra to compensate for the loss (Strabo, *Geographica* 13.4.2; Plutarch, *Antonius* 58.5; Gellius, *Noctes Atticae* 7.17). This gift may well have played a major role in restoring the library. We are told that Emperor Domitian (ruled 81–96 CE) ordered books lost in libraries of Rome (in the second fire, mentioned above) to be replaced by making copies of or making comparison with the books in the library of Alexandria (Suetonius, *Domitianus* 20). Such an order presupposes that the library of Alexandria possessed a goodly number of books. The ongoing function of the library at Alexandria seems confirmed when at the end of the second century CE Tertullian, the north African, says "to this day…the libraries of Ptolemy are to be seen" (*Apologia* 18.8).

The fate of a few other libraries can be mentioned briefly. The library of Pantainos (or Pantaenus), located in the Agora in Athens and founded c. 100 CE, was destroyed in 267 CE when the Germanic Heruli tribe sacked Athens.[85] The library was well known for its inscription: "No book is to be taken out, because we have sworn an oath [βύβλιον οὐκ ἐξενεχθήσεται, ἐπεὶ ὠμόσαμεν]. (The library) is to be open first hour until the sixth" (SEG 21.500).[86] An unpublished inscription from Rhodes expresses the same restriction: "No one is permitted to take the books

---

84. See R. S. Bagnall, "Alexandria: Library of Dreams," *Proceedings of the American Philosophical Society* 146 (2002): 348–62. For more on the library of Alexandria, see M. Hatzimichali, "Ashes to Ashes? The Library of Alexandria after 48 BC," and M. W. Handis, "Myth and History: Galen and the Alexandrian Library," in König, Oikonomopoulou, and Woolf (eds.), *Ancient Libraries*, 167–82 and 364–76, respectively; M. Berti, "Greek and Roman Libraries in the Hellenistic Age," in *The Dead Sea Scrolls at Qumran and the Concept of a Library*, ed. S. W. Crawford and C. Wassen, STDJ 116 (Leiden: Brill, 2016), 33–54, here 33–47. For important bibliography, see 46 n. 50.

85. J. M. Hurwit, *The Athenian Acropolis: History, Mythology, and Archaeology from the Neolithic Era to the Present* (Cambridge: Cambridge University Press, 1999), 283.

86. For an image of the SEG 21.500 inscription, see Agora Image 2008.20.0059. For a number of excellent studies on the history, function, and fate of ancient libraries, see König, Oikonomopoulou, and Woolf (eds.), *Ancient Libraries*.

outside [τὰ βυβλία...μηθενὶ ἐξέστω ἐκφέρειν ἔξω]" (line 7).[87] These prohibitions reflect the value of the books. We should assume, moreover, that the oath in the Pantainos Library inscription involved swearing to the gods.[88] Protection of the library's holdings was taken very seriously. There is evidence that other libraries took steps to secure their precious bookrolls.[89] Even so, in many cases destruction could not be avoided. The library of Celsus in Ephesus was destroyed by earthquake and fire in 262 (perhaps also a Gothic invasion), the library in Antioch was destroyed by fire in 364,[90] and, as already mentioned, the library of Caesarea Maritima was destroyed in the seventh century.

Loss of books through theft and violence was sometimes very personal. Cicero informs an official in Illyricum about the theft of some of his valuable books: "My slave Dionysius, who has been managing my book collection—which is worth quite a lot—stole a large number of manuscripts and then, when he thought he would probably be caught, he fled. He is in your province" (*Epistulae ad familiares* 13.77.3).[91] The orator Libanius (314–c. 393) relates that someone stole from him a rare copy of Thucydides. The book was eventually recovered and returned (Libanius, *Orationes* 1.148-150).

One of the most violent examples concerns Georgius, bishop of Alexandria, who in 361 was murdered, and his library seized shortly after by the Roman emperor Julian "the Apostate" (d. 363). Ammianus Marcellinus tells us during a riot in Alexandria "all the populace...made for Georgius and seized him, maltreating him in diverse ways and trampling upon him; then they dragged him about...and killed him" (*Res Gestae* 22.11.8). Hearing of his death, Julian takes steps to acquire Georgius's library.[92] Writing to the prefect of Egypt, the emperor requests:

87. Houston, *Inside Roman Libraries*, 250.

88. ὀμνύω is commonplace in the papyri, usually in legal contexts (e.g., P.Oxy. 483: "I swear [ὀμνύω] by the gods Augusti...and my ancestral gods..."; 108 CE). Books are so valuable that those granted access to the library take an oath not to remove any of the books. The library inscription is a reminder of that solemn oath.

89. Houston, *Inside Roman Libraries*, 230–1.

90. For more on the libraries at Antioch (and Pergamum), see Berti, "Greek and Roman Libraries in the Hellenistic Age," 47–51. For a concise entry the libraries of the classical period, see S. Hornblower, A. Spawforth, and E. Eidinow (eds.), *The Oxford Companion to Classical Civilization*, 2nd edn (Oxford: Oxford University Press, 2014), 454–6.

91. Here I follow the translation in Houston, *Inside Roman Libraries*, 249.

92. For more on the library of Georgius and how Julian was acquainted with it, see H. Y. Gamble, *Books and Readers in the Early Church: A History of Early Christian Texts* (New Haven: Yale University Press, 1995), 175–6.

> Therefore grant me this personal favor, that all the books that belonged to Georgius [πάντα τὰ Γεωργίου βιβλία] be sought out. For there were in his house many on philosophy, and many on rhetoric; many also on the teachings of the impious Galileans. These latter I wish to be utterly annihilated [ἠφανίσθαι πάντῃ], but for fear that along with them more useful works may be destroyed by mistake, let all these also be sought for with the greatest care.[93] (Julian, *Epistulae* 23 [to Ecdicius])

The books "on the teachings of the impious Galileans [τῆς τῶν δυσσεβῶν Γαλιλαίων διδασκαλίας]" are Christian books and probably include New Testament writings.[94] These books Julian wanted "utterly annihilated" (lit. "made to disappear").

Julian's actions reflect once again the great value placed on books. Although he is the emperor of Rome, he is not above ordering the governor of Egypt to oversee a salvage operation with hopes of recovering most of a late Church leader's library (many of them had been stolen when the bishop's house was looted and vandalized). The Christian books are to be destroyed, but great care is to be taken, lest non-Christian books are inadvertently destroyed along with them.

Protective measures above and beyond the norm were sometimes taken in late antiquity to guard against theft or destruction. This is not the least surprising, given the calamities that have been observed. Galen relates that he and others rented imperial warehouses near the Palatine, for storage of their books. These buildings were chosen because they were guarded and the only wood in the structures was in the doors (Galen, *De indolentia* 8-10).[95]

Late Antique Book Burning

Many books in antiquity were destroyed deliberately, either by mobs or, more often, by authorities. We see this in the just-mentioned story involving Emperor Julian. Although the lynching of Bishop Georgius had little or nothing to do with his books and Julian's interest in his books was positive—in that he valued and coveted them—nevertheless, the incident

---

93. Translation based on W. C. Wright, *The Works of Emperor Julian*, III, LCL 13 (London: Heinemann; New York: Macmillan, 1913), 73.

94. Julian apparently called Christians "Galileans." He authored a work entitled *Contra Galilaeos*, which has not survived, apart from quotations, most of which are found in a refutation authored by Cyril (d. 444), patriarch of Alexandria.

95. Houston, *Inside Roman Libraries*, 251.

did give the emperor the opportunity to destroy books deemed Christian and, in the opinion of the emperor, harmful to the empire. We will see that the deliberate act of destroying the late bishop's Christian books was in fact in accord with long-standing Roman practice.

Before looking at other examples of Rome's acts of book burning, I should mention the earlier Seleucid effort to destroy Jewish sacred books in the second century BCE. During the pogroms of Antiochus IV Epiphanes (ruled 175–164 BCE), Jewish Torah scrolls in Israel, if not whole libraries, were destroyed. This is stated explicitly in 1 and 2 Maccabees. The relevant passage in the former reads: "The books of the law which they found they tore to pieces and burned with fire [τὰ βιβλία τοῦ νόμου, ἃ εὗρον, ἐνεπύρισαν ἐν πυρὶ κατασχίσαντες]" (1 Macc. 1:56).[96] It is a matter of conjecture what was exactly meant by "the books of the law." It is possible that other books of Scripture, as well as the five books of Moses, were in view.

The question is important because of what the author of 2 Maccabees says in reference to the restoration and reassembly of books lost during the war with Antiochus IV. We read in 2 Macc. 2:13-15:

> ἐξηγοῦντο δὲ καὶ ἐν ταῖς ἀναγραφαῖς καὶ ἐν τοῖς ὑπομνηματισμοῖς τοῖς κατὰ τὸν Νεεμιαν τὰ αὐτὰ καὶ ὡς καταβαλλόμενος βιβλιοθήκην ἐπισυνήγαγεν τὰ περὶ τῶν βασιλέων βιβλία καὶ προφητῶν καὶ τὰ τοῦ Δαυιδ καὶ ἐπιστολὰς βασιλέων περὶ ἀναθεμάτων. [14] ὡσαύτως δὲ καὶ Ιουδας τὰ διαπεπτωκότα διὰ τὸν γεγονότα πόλεμον ἡμῖν ἐπισυνήγαγεν πάντα, καὶ ἔστιν παρ' ἡμῖν· [15] ὧν οὖν ἐὰν χρείαν ἔχητε, τοὺς ἀποκομιοῦντας ὑμῖν ἀποστέλλετε.
>
> The same things are reported in the records and in the memoirs of Nehemiah, and also that he founded a library and collected the books about the kings and prophets, and the writings of David, and letters of kings about votive offerings. [14] In the same way Judas also collected all the books that had been lost on account of the war which had come upon us, and they are in our possession. [15] So if you have need of them, send people to get them for you.

It is not clear what the "records and memoirs of Nehemiah" were. The claim that "he founded a library and collected" books lacks support from ancient sources. The relevant Old Testament literature does not itself say this. It has been plausibly suggested that it would have been assumed that as re-founder and restorer of Jerusalem and the temple,

---

96. According to Josephus, "a certain soldier finding the sacred book of the law, tore it to pieces, and threw it into the fire [ἔνθα τῶν στρατιωτῶν τις εὑρὼν ἔν τινι κώμῃ τὸν ἱερὸν νόμον διέρρηξέν τε τὸ βιβλίον καὶ εἰς πῦρ κατέβαλεν]" (*J.W.* 2.229).

Nehemiah, like other Hellenistic kings, would also assemble archives and a library.[97] Josephus tells us that the Jewish temple in fact did possess archives (*Contra Apionem* 1.28-36)[98] and that in the event of their destruction they were restored and that the priests played a key role in this restoration of records (1.34-36).[99]

According to the narrative in 2 Maccabees, Judas Maccabeus "collected all the books that had been lost on account of the war which had come upon" (v. 14) the Jewish people. The adjective πάντα in v. 14 refers to the βιβλία of v. 13. (The noun βιβλία does not appear in v. 14, but it is assumed.) The library has been restored; readers of 2 Maccabees (principally those in Egypt) are invited to visit Jerusalem and review these records. This is no mere courtesy, it is a challenge: The history recounted in 2 Maccabees is backed up by reliable sources; skeptics can examine these records for themselves.[100] Surely more is in view here than only the five books of Moses. Of what the new library in Jerusalem comprised and how it functioned are two important questions scholars have addressed in recent years.[101]

---

97. D. R. Schwartz, *2 Maccabees*, Commentaries on Early Jewish Literature (Berlin: de Gruyter, 2008), 166. See also A. van der Kooij, "The Canonization of Ancient Books Kept in the Library of Jerusalem," in *Canonization and Decanonization: Papers Presented to the International Conference of the Leiden Institute for the Study of Religions, Held at Leiden 9–10 January 1997*, ed. A. van der Kooij and K. van der Torn, SHR 82 (Leiden: Brill, 1998), 17–40; idem, "Canonization of Ancient Hebrew Books and Hasmonean Politics," in *The Biblical Canons*, ed. J.-M. Auwers and H. J. de Jonge, BETL 163 (Leuven: Leuven University Press, 2003), 27–38.

98. "…these records have been written all along down to our own times with the utmost accuracy…" (1.29).

99. "…those priests that survive them compose new tables of genealogy out of the old records [ἐκ τῶν ἀρχαίων γραμμάτων]…we have the names of our high priests, from father to son, set down in our records [ἐν ταῖς ἀναγραφαῖς], for the interval of two thousand years…" (1.35-36).

100. So rightly Schwartz, *2 Maccabees*, 167.

101. A. Lange, "2 Maccabees 2:13-15: Library or Canon?" and S. Schorch, "The Libraries in 2 Macc 2:13-15, and the Torah as a Public Document in Second Century BC Judaism," in *The Books of the Maccabees: History, Theology, Ideology: Papers of the Second International Conference on the Deuterocanonical Books. Pápa, Hungary, 8–11 June, 2005*, ed. G. Xeravits and J. Zsengellér, JSJSup 118 (Leiden: Brill, 2007), 155–67 and 169–80, respectively. Schorch tries to distinguish between library and archive and thinks only an archive is in view in 2 Macc. 2:13-15. Lange, rightly in my view, disagrees.

I will not address this question in the present study in any detail, but I think we can say that the books collected under the authority of Judas and his successors evidently included at the very least most if not the whole of the Hebrew Bible. I say this not only because of the continuity of Hebrew Scripture, inside and outside the land of Israel, but because at Qumran we have recovered fragments, some substantial, of all of the books of the Hebrew scriptures, with the apparent exception of the book of Esther (whose absence from Qumran's library may have been intentional).

Although it is true that most of the Hebrew scrolls from Qumran post-date the pogroms of Antiochus IV, a few of them antedate the Seleucid ruler. Among these are 4QExod-Lev^f (4Q17), 4QpaleoDeut^s (4Q46), 4QSam^b (4Q52), and 4QpaleoJob^c (4Q101), which are dated to the third century BCE, while 4QLev-Num^a (4Q23), 1QIsaiah^a, and 4QPs^a (4Q83) are dated to the mid-second century BCE. Approximately 40 scrolls, many of them Bible scrolls, were one hundred to two hundred years old—and evidently still in use—when the community was destroyed in the first century CE.[102] All of these scrolls survived the Roman destruction of the community; several of them evidently survived the earlier Seleucid war. If nothing else, placing the scrolls in jars and then hiding them in wilderness caves—in the face of an approaching enemy—demonstrates the Jewish people's commitment and ingenuity in the protection of their sacred books. Indeed, we are told that Jewish Christians did this very thing, hiding their sacred books in wine jars during times of persecution (Epiphanius, *De mensuris et ponderibus* 18).

The confiscation and destruction of the sacred books of Christians should be understood in the context of Roman practice.[103] The motivations for the destruction of sacred books were several. Romans were by and large superstitious. Of great concern to them was maintaining the *pax deorum*, the "peace of the gods." Rituals and religious books that were foreign to them were viewed with suspicion. Books of magic—not necessarily aligned with a particular religion or cult—were from time to time

---

102. On the dates of the scrolls, see F. M. Cross, "The Oldest Manuscripts from Qumran," *JBL* 74 (1955): 147–72; idem, "Palaeography and the Dead Sea Scrolls," in *The Dead Sea Scrolls after Fifty Years: A Comprehensive Assessment*, ed. P. W. Flint and J. C. VanderKam, 2 vols. (Leiden: Brill, 1998–99), 1:379–402.

103. D. Sarefield, "The Symbolics of Book Burning," in *The Early Christian Book*, ed. W. E. Klingshirn and L. Safran (Washington, DC: Catholic University of America Press, 2007), 159–73; D. Rohmann, *Christianity, Book-Burning and Censorship in Late Antiquity: Studies in Text Transmission*, AKG 135 (Berlin: de Gruyter, 2016).

ordered destroyed. This was done out of fear, fear that the sorcerers and owners of books of magic could harm people.[104] The destruction of the books of magic, described in Acts 19:19, is exceptional in that the owners of these books destroyed them themselves; the books were not confiscated and destroyed by the state. Romans also feared that foreign cults, supported and encouraged by their sacred writings, might undermine the state and perhaps, by offending Rome's official gods, bring calamity.

Roman opposition to magic, astrology, and soothsaying (or fortune-telling) reaches back to ancient times.[105] The fifth-century BCE *Twelve Tables*, the earliest known Roman laws, proscribe chanting incantations (*Duodecim Tabulae* 8). Why ancient Roman society was opposed to magic is unclear, but the grounds for suppression of magic and related arts become very clear in later centuries.

Roman authority actively suppressed foreign rites, especially if practiced openly and in a time of crisis. One such crisis was Hannibal's invasion of Italy in 213 BCE. The senate ordered the confiscation of books, such as those of "divination or forms of prayers or sacrificial ritual" (Livy, *Ab urbe condita* 25.1.6-12). Acting on orders, officers were "seeking out and burning all books of pretended prophecies, and abolishing ritual, except what was in keeping with Roman practice" (39.16.9; cf. 4.30.9-11: "The aediles were instructed to see to it that none but Roman deities were worshipped").

So spooked of foreign religion were the Romans, that they even destroyed many of the previously mentioned ancient books recovered from the tomb of Numa, one of Rome's ancient kings, despite their enormous antiquarian value (Livy, *Ab urbe condita* 40.29; Valerius Maximus, *Facta et dicta memorabilia* 1.1.12: the books were burned "in the sight of the people"). This event took place in 181 BCE, a few years after the senate outlawed the Dionysiac cult of the Bacchae and other foreign rites.[106] Rome

---

104. As is well illustrated in J. G. Gager, *Curse Tablets and Binding Spells from the Ancient World* (New York and Oxford: Oxford University Press, 1992).

105. For a very convenient compilation of the relevant texts, see D. Ogden, *Magic, Witchcraft, and Ghosts in the Greek and Roman Worlds: A Sourcebook*, 2nd edn (Oxford: Oxford University Press, 2009), 275–99.

106. The senate's edict has been found in a lengthy inscription, in archaizing Latin, on a bronze tablet recovered at Bruttium (now Calabria, southern Italy), dated to 186 BCE. The inscription (*ILS* 18) reads in part: "Let none of them aspire to maintain a Bacchanal… No one is to aspire to perform rites either in secret, or in public, or in private, or outside the city, unless he has approached the city praetor, and he has given permission… you will proclaim this decree in assemblies…" For historical commentary on the senate's edict, see Livy, *Ab urbe condita* 39.8-14.

feared that foreign, non-Roman religion and rites could harm the state. The thinking of Antiochus IV, who was in Rome during this approximate time, may have been similar.[107] Whatever his motives in his vendetta against the Jewish people, his goal in part was to alter their religious thinking, and to do that required the destruction of their sacred books.

In 139 BCE Jews and Chaldean astrologers were expelled by the praetor Cornelius Hispalus. They were charged, says Valerius Maximus (c. 26 CE), with "trying to corrupt Roman morality with their cult" (Valerius Maximus, *Facta et dicta memorabilia* 1.3.3). In 33 BCE Marcus Vipsanius Agrippa (c. 63–12 BCE), friend and supporter of Emperor Augustus, drove out astrologers and sorcerers (Dio Cassius, *Historia romana* 49.43.5). In 29 BCE Agrippa advises Augustus: "You should hate and punish those who introduce foreign elements into our religion, not just for the sake of the gods…but because men of this sort, by importing new powers [δαιμόνια], persuade many people to take up foreign customs…" (Dio Cassius, *Historia romana* 52.36.1-2).

In 13/12 BCE, when Augustus assumed the office of *pontifex maximus* (that is, "high priest"), "he collected whatever prophetic books of Greek or Latin origin [*librorum Graeci Latinique generis*] were in circulation anonymously or under the names of authors of little repute, and burned more than two thousand [*supra duo milia…cremavit*] of them, retaining only the Sibylline books and making a choice even among those…" (Suetonius, *Augustus* 31.1).[108] Augustus's social and political cleansing included reviving "some of the ancient rites which had gradually fallen into disuse" (Suetonius, *Augustus* 31.4). In 11 CE Augustus banned divination (Dio Cassius, *Historia romana* 56.23). Evidently Augustus, taking his role as high priest very seriously, heeded Agrippa's advice.

Tiberius (r. 14–37 CE) seems to have followed in the footsteps of his stepfather Augustus. Suetonius tells us that the emperor banned divination: "He forbade the consultation of soothsayers in secret and without witnesses" (Suetonius, *Tiberius* 63.1). Early on in his administration "the senate decreed that astrologers be expelled from Italy" (Tacitus, *Annales* 2.32). In 52 CE, before he became emperor, Nero (r. 54–68)

---

107. As suggested by J. Goldstein, *I Maccabees*, AB 41 (Garden City: Doubleday, 1976), 125.

108. Translation based on J. C. Rolfe, *Suetonius*, Vol. I, LCL 31, rev. edn (Cambridge, MA: Harvard University Press, 1998), 197. Part of the emperor's motivation was to purge literature that seemingly offered prophecies relating to himself. We should assume that some of these prophecies were negative, even threatening. Rohmann, *Christianity, Book-Burning*, 242: "to bar unwanted prophecies about his reign from circulation." Accordingly, Augustus wanted these prophecies destroyed.

expelled astrologers for attempts to predict his death (Tacitus, *Annales* 12.52). In 69 CE Vitellius summarily executed any astrologer accused of speaking against him (Suetonius, *Vitellius* 14). In 198 CE the praefect of Egypt ordered district governors to suppress divination, including related writings (P.Yale 299: "...through oracles or writings...").[109]

Hostility toward magic, soothsaying, and foreign rites is clearly expressed in Roman law. In Justinian's Digest a legal ruling attributed to Modestinus, a third-century CE Roman jurist and student of Ulpian, declares: "By *senatus consultum* the man who performs or organizes evil sacrifices [*mala sacrificia*] is ordered to be condemned to the penalty of this statute" (*Digesta* 48.8.13). The third-century collection of *Sententiae*, fictitiously attributed to Julius Paulus, a late second-century CE Roman jurist who is frequently cited in the Digest, rules that magicians are to be thrown to wild animals or crucified. The text adds: "[If] books on the craft of magic [*libros magicae artis*]" are found in a man's house, his property is to be confiscated and the books "burned in public [*ambustis his publice*]" (Ps.-Paulus, *Sententiae* 5.23.17-18).

Books of magic and foreign rites were burned, but books were sometimes burned for other reasons. During the reign of Tiberius charges were brought against one Cremutius Cordus after publishing a controversial account, in which the assassins of Caesar are eulogized. After Cremutius concludes his speech before the senate, with the emperor presiding, Tacitus tells us: "The Fathers ordered his books to be burned by the aediles [*libros per aediles cremandos censuere patres*]; but copies remained, hidden and afterwards published" (Tacitus, *Annales* 4.35).[110]

Tacitus also relates the story of a political critic, whose books Nero ordered burned. The case came to a head when the accused claimed that the emperor sold offices: "This last count decided Nero to take the case into his own hands. He convicted Veiento, banished him from Italy, and ordered his books to be burned. These, while they were only to be procured at a risk, were (now) anxiously sought and widely read" (*Annales* 14.50).[111]

In the time of Emperor Domitian (r. 81–96), charges were brought against one Senecio, who had written a controversial biography. The senate ordered "the destruction of the books in question," but Senecio's wife "managed to save them when her possessions were confiscated, and took them with her into exile" (Pliny, *Epistulae* 7.19.6).[112] It is ironic

---

109. J. Rhea, "A New Version of P. Yale Inv. 299," *ZPE* 27 (1977): 151–6.
110. Translation based on Jackson, *Tacitus Annals Books 4–6, 11–12*, 63.
111. Translation based on ibid., 187.
112. Translation based on B. Radice, *Pliny I: Letters and Panegyricus I*, LCL 55 (London: Heinemann; Cambridge, MA: Harvard University Press, 1969), 527.

that the attempts by Tiberius, Nero, and Domitian to destroy the books of controversial authors ultimately failed, for copies survived and public interest in the prohibited literature was increased.

Roman book burning took place for a variety of reasons, but the most common was in connection with the suppression of magic and foreign rites. It is in this context that we should understand Roman suppression of the Christian movement. As Christianity exited the synagogue and increasingly seemed no longer part of the Jewish people—who enjoyed religious freedom in the Roman Empire—it was increasingly vulnerable to the charge of being a foreign cult or superstition. This is implied in the oft-cited passage in Tacitus, where Christianity is described as a "deadly superstition" and "disease" (Tacitus, *Annales* 15.44: *exitiabilis superstitio...malus*). Tacitus said this in reference to the persecution of Christians in the aftermath of the fire in 64 CE.

The fire in Rome was viewed by some as an expression of divine displeasure. According to Tacitus, "means were sought for appeasing the gods [*petita dis piacula*], and application was made to the Sibylline books," which presumably would be those Sibylline volumes that survived the aforementioned purge under Augustus. We are told that "public prayers were offered" to various gods and "ritual banquets and all-night vigils" were held, yet "all modes of placating Heaven [*deum placamentis*]" failed to "stifle scandal or dispel the belief that the fire had taken place by order" (Tacitus, *Annales* 15.44).

Whatever Nero's true motives and however the general public perceived the religious activities that the emperor undertook, all of this reflected Rome's convictions that it was essential to maintain the *pax deorum*. The fire suggested that this *pax* had been broken. The pogrom against the Christians must be interpreted in this light. They were convenient scapegoats, not simply because they were an easy target or were disliked "for (their) hatred of the human race [*odio humani*]," as Tacitus puts it. They were targeted because their religious convictions and practices were both foreign and disrespectful of the Roman gods, sacrifices, and rituals. Indeed, in time Christians will be accused of "destroying the gods."[113] Burning Christians, presumably to appease Rome's gods, was fully in

---

113. People shout against Polycarp (c. 69–c. 155 CE): "This is the teacher of Asia, the father of the Christians, the destroyer of our gods [ὁ τῶν ἡμετέρων θεῶν καθαιρέτης], who teaches many not to sacrifice or worship" (*Martyrdom of Polycarp* 12:2). Teaching Greeks and Romans "not to sacrifice or worship" their gods is precisely what will unsettle the *pax deorum*. The charge against Polycarp was anticipated a century earlier in Acts 16:20-21, where it is said of Paul and his companions, "[T]hey are disturbing our city. They advocate customs which it is not lawful for us

step with Rome's long-standing policy. Although Christian books are not mentioned by Tacitus, what he describes in 64 CE adumbrates the violent suppression of Christianity in the second century, which included burning Christians *and their books*.

Nero's actions against Christians in the aftermath of the fire might not have included the destruction of Christian books, possibly because Roman authority was not aware of the importance of Christian books at that time. A half century later holy books apparently played no role in Pliny's interrogation, torture, and execution of Christians in Asia Minor (Pliny, *Epistulae* 10.96). But in the middle of the second century books do play a role.

Lucian of Samosata (c. 120–c. 185) provides early evidence of pagan awareness of the importance of sacred books for Christians. In his satirical account of Peregrinus, a religious-philosophical dabbler who for a time associated with Christians, Lucian says the man "was a prophet, cult leader, head of the congregation, and everything, all by himself. He interpreted and explained some of their books, and wrote many himself [τῶν βίβλων τὰς μὲν ἐξηγεῖτο καὶ διεσάφει, πολλὰς δὲ αὐτὸς καὶ συνέγραφεν]" (Lucian, *De morte Peregrini* 11). All mockery aside, Lucian's comments strongly suggest that he was quite aware that books were very important to Christians.[114] Lucian rightly understood that to interpret "their books" and even to write a few himself proved that Peregrinus had indeed risen to a prominent position among the childish Christians. To possess and to exegete books, so it is implied, are essential activities of Christians, especially their leaders.

A close link between Christians and sacred Scripture is seen in the story of the Numidian Christian martyr named Speratus, who, along with others, in the late second century CE was brought before Saturninus, the Roman proconsul of Africa.[115] Speratus confesses, "I am a Christian" (*Passio Sanctorum Scillitanorum* 10). The proconsul then asks Speratus, "What sort of things do you have in that case [*capsa*] of yours?"[116] Speratus said,

---

Romans to accept or practice"; and in 19:26, where it is said of Paul, "[T]his Paul has persuaded and turned away a considerable company of people, saying that gods made with hands are not gods."

114. Rightly perceived by Sarefield, "The Symbolics of Book Burning," 164 n. 22, 165–6.

115. I depend on H. Musurillo, *The Acts of the Christian Martyrs* (Oxford: Clarendon Press, 1972), 86–9; and Sarefield, "The Symbolics of Book Burning," 165.

116. A *capsa* was a box for holding books and papers. They were usually made of wood or canvas, though some were made of metal and even had locks. In the Catacombs of Domitilla in Rome the Apostle Paul is depicted with a *capsa*,

"Books and letters of Paul [*libri et epistulae Pauli*], a righteous man" (*Passio Sanctorum Scillitanorum* 12). Speratus is given a chance to recant, but he continues to confess, "I am a Christian." The proconsul pronounces judgment on Speratus and the other Christians with him: "…in spite of the opportunity given to them to return to the Roman way of life, they have stubbornly persisted in maintaining theirs, I have decided that they be put to the sword" (*Passio Sanctorum Scillitanorum* 14b).[117] Speratus and the others were taken away and decapitated (*Passio Sanctorum Scillitanorum* 17). We are not told what was done with the "the books and letters of Paul," but it is most probable that they were destroyed.

It is important to note that Saturninus sees Christianity as contrary to the "Roman way of life [*ad Romanorum morem*]." The Roman way of life, of course, is in concert with the will of the gods. It is also interesting that Speratus brought with him Christian books (Gospels?) and Pauline epistles.[118] Did he do this for protection (as an amulet)? For moral and spiritual strength, so as not to recant under pressure? It is possible too that Speratus knew that to be in possession of Christian writings confirmed that he was indeed a Christian. Rather than hiding these writings (as some Christians and clergy did, especially during the Diocletian persecution), he openly presented and acknowledged them at his trial. It was as if to say, "I am a Christian and I have the books to prove it." In the pogroms against sorcerers it was often the possession of books of magic that proved guilt (Tacitus, *Annales* 2.30; Ps.-Pauli, *Sententiae* 5.23.18).[119]

Even as those accused and convicted of sorcery were burned alive (Ps.-Pauli, *Sententiae* 5.23.17: "Actual magi, however, are burned alive [*vivi exuruntur*]"), so some Christians, during the great persecution in Lugdunum (Lyons) in 177 CE, were burned alive and after death

containing what appear to be five bookrolls, presumable his own letters. In the Catacombs of Peter and Marcellinus in Rome a Christian is depicted holding a codex. Both paintings date to the third century.

117. The proconsul's policy reflects imperial law at this time: "For Caesar had written that they should be tortured to death, but that if any recant they should be let go" (Eusebius, *Historia ecclesiastica* 5.1.47).

118. According to our sources, the Christians of Scilli quote or allude to Matthew, Acts, and four of Paul's letters. For more on this question, see A. Smarius, "Rome versus de christenen: de zaak tegen de christenen uit Scilli," *Lampas* 42 (2009): 26–41; and idem, "Roman Persecution of Christians: The Scillitan Martyrs," *Ancient History Magazine* 2 (2016): 47–51. Codex Parisinus Latinus 2179 reads *libri evangeliorum*, "books of Gospels."

119. Sarefield, "The Symbolics of Book Burning," 162; Ogden, *Magic, Witchcraft, and Ghosts*, 279.

incinerated (Eusebius, *Historia ecclesiastica* 5.1.22, 38, 52, 62: their corpses were "burned and turned to ashes"). Again it is important to note that the persecution in Lugdunum was driven by the desire to cleanse the city of a foreign cult that threatened the *pax deorum*. This thinking is what lies behind statements such as "they thought that in this way they would vindicate their gods" (5.1.31) and "efforts were made to force them to swear by their idols" (5.1.53).

Under Emperor Messius Quintus Decius (r. 249–251) inhabitants of the empire were compelled to swear allegiance and perform sacrifice to the Roman gods in the presence of a Roman magistrate, from whom they would receive a signed *libellus*, or certificate.[120] Many Christians died or were imprisoned for refusing to obey the new policy; among them were Fabian, bishop of Rome, Alexander, bishop of Jerusalem, and Babylas, bishop of Antioch (Eusebius, *Historia ecclesiastica* 6.39.1-4). Origen, the great biblical scholar, was imprisoned and tortured in 250, eventually dying in 254 (6.39.5). A number of Christians, many of them leaders, were dragged through the streets, beaten, stoned, and burned to death (6.41.4, 7-8, 15-18, 21). The houses and goods of many were looted and possessions were burned (6.41.5-6). Although it is probable that Christian literature, including New Testament writings, was destroyed during the Decian persecution, there is nothing that indicates that Christian literature was specifically targeted. This will change a generation later.

The first widespread attempt to destroy Christian literature took place under Emperor Diocletian (r. 284–305; died c. 312). The emperor wished to eradicate Christianity from the empire as part of his reforms, which included returning to the traditional gods. He believed that "traditional expressions of piety to the Roman gods (were) beneficial to himself and the state."[121] To accomplish his goals, Diocletian ordered the destruction of churches and the confiscation and burning of Christian books. The pogroms got under way on 23 February 303, the day Romans celebrated

---

120. A few of these *libelli* are extant, e.g., P.Oxy. 4.658: "It has ever been my custom to make sacrifices and libations to the gods, and now also I have in your presence in accordance with the command poured libations and sacrificed and tasted the offerings... I therefore request you to certify my statement. The 1st year of the Emperor Caesar Gaius Messius Quintus Traianus Decius..." See also P.Oxy. 41.2990 ("...I saw you sacrificing and tasting...") and P.Mich. 3.158 ("...we, Aurelius Serenus and Aurelius Hermas, saw you sacrificing..."), as well as SB 6.9084 and PSI 7.78. See also J. Knipfing, "The *Libelli* of the Decian Persecution," *HTR* 16 (1923): 345–90. Knipfing's study is dated but still worth consulting.

121. Sarefield, "The Symbolics of Book Burning," 166.

the festival of the Terminalia, a sacred festival believed to date back to the time of the ancient king Numa. This festival, focused as it was on boundaries, readily accommodated the doctrine of the *pax deorum*. What better day to launch an attack against the pernicious Christian superstition that shamelessly held the Roman gods in contempt?

Eusebius, who lived through the persecution and later wrote about it in his history, accesses a number of sources and adds his own comments. Eusebius reports that the "imperial letter was everywhere promulgated, ordering the razing of the churches to the ground and the destruction by fire of the Scriptures [τὰς δὲ γραφὰς ἀφανεῖς πυρὶ γενέσθαι]" (*Historia ecclesiastica* 8.2.4). A second letter ordered church leaders to be imprisoned and then coerced into offering sacrifice to the Roman gods (8.2.5). Eusebius recounts many stories of martyrdom, including being burned to death (8.8; 8.10.10; 8.11.1; 8.12.1-2, 6-7, 10) and crucified (8.8).[122] Many bishops were either imprisoned and tortured (as, for example, the aforementioned Peter, bishop of Alexandria; 8.13.7) or executed (8.13.1-8).[123]

Eusebius provides an eyewitness account of the destruction of churches and Christian Scripture:

> [W]e saw with our own eyes [ἐπείδομεν ὀφθαλμοῖς] the houses of prayer thrown down to the very foundations, and the divine and sacred Scriptures committed to the flames in the midst of the market-places [τὰς δὲ ἐνθέους καὶ ἱερὰς γραφὰς κατὰ μέσας ἀγορὰς πυρὶ παραδιδομένας αὐτοῖς], and the shepherds of the churches basely hidden here and there, and some of them captured ignominiously, and mocked by their enemies. (8.2.1)[124]

Other sources state that some church leaders attempted either to hide Scripture or, as a dodge, surrender to authorities defective texts, heretical writings, or pagan writings of one sort or another (Augustine, *Breviculus collationis cum Donatistis* 3.13.25; *Contra Cresconium* 3.27.30).[125] Other

---

122. Note the epitaph in the catacombs of Rome: "Lannus, Martyr of Christ, rests here. He suffered under Diocletian [*sub Dioclisiano passus*]." Cited and discussed in W. Ingraham Kip, *The Catacombs of Rome: As Illustrating the Church of the First Three Centuries*, 4th edn (New York: Daniel Dana, 1859), 94; W. H. Davenport Adams, *The Catacombs of Rome: Historical and Descriptive* (London and New York: T. Nelson & Sons, 1877), 64.

123. Additional accounts are found in Eusebius, *De martyribus Palaestinae*; and Lactantius, *De mortibus persecutorum*.

124. Translation from Oulton, *Eusebius Ecclesiastical History II*, 257.

125. Cited and discussed by Sarefield, "The Symbolics of Book Burning," 168 and nn. 42–3.

leaders flatly refused to surrender their copies of Scripture and were executed for refusing to do so (e.g., Felix, a bishop in Africa).[126] Indeed, in the case of one Euplus (Latin: Euplius) we are told that he proved himself to be a Christian by presenting to the authorities his copies of "the holy Gospels [τὰ ἄχραντα εὐαγγέλια]" (*Acts Eupli* 1.1 [Greek recension]). When asked what the books are, Euplus explains that they are the Gospels of Matthew, Mark, Luke, and John (1.4 [Greek recension]). The Roman governor asks him, "Why did you retain these writings, which the emperors (Diocletian and Maximian) have forbidden? Why did you not give them up?" Euplus replies, "Because I am a Christian and it (is) forbidden to give them up... Whoever gives them up loses eternal life" (2.1-2 [Latin recension]). The idea here is that to give up the Scriptures is tantamount to denying what they proclaim.

Euplus's refusal to obey the imperial edict and surrender Scripture runs parallel to Christians' refusal to offer sacrifice to the Roman gods, for to do so is to violate the plain teaching of Scripture. This reasoning is made explicit in one of the examples of martyrdom provided by Eusebius: "... without hesitation they gladly went to their death. For they knew what had been prescribed for us by the sacred Scriptures. For he says, 'He who sacrifices to other gods shall be utterly destroyed' (Exod. 22:20); and 'You shall have no other gods except me' (Exod. 20:3)" (*Historia ecclesiastica* 8.10.10).[127] As expected, Euplus is condemned. The official takes the book of the Gospels, fastens it to the neck of the martyr, and cries out: "Behold Euplus the Christian, an enemy of our emperors and our gods [*inimicus deorum et imperatorum*]!" (*Acta Eupli* 3.3 [Latin recension]).[128]

As one would expect, in the city of Nicomedia, where Diocletian was residing, "when the Scriptures were found they were burned [*scripturae repertae incenduntur*]" (Lactantius, *De mortibus persecutorum* 12.2).

In the *Gesta apud Zenophilum* we find a detailed account of an interrogation, where state officials in Numidia attempt to find, identify, and confiscate Christian books of Scripture. I will only present a few lines of this interesting material.[129] It begins with the mayor approaching the

---

126. According to the *Acta S. Felicis Episcopi* (*PL* 8.680-83). Cited by Sarefield, "The Symbolics of Book Burning," 168 n. 44.

127. Translation from Oulton, *Eusebius Ecclesiastical History II*, 285.

128. Sarefield, "The Symbolics of Book Burning," 169, following Musurillo, *The Acts of the Christian Martyrs*, 319.

129. J. Stevenson (ed.), *A New Eusebius: Documents Illustrating the History of the Church to AD 337*, rev. W. H. C. Frend (Grand Rapids: Baker Academic, 2013), 287–9. The Latin text will be found in CSEL XXVI, pp. 186–8. For discussion, see Gamble, *Books and Readers in the Early Church*, 145–7.

local Christian bishop, demanding: "Bring out the writings of the law and anything else you have, according to the order, so that you may obey the command." The bishop replies, saying that the "readers have the scriptures, but we will give you what we have here." A search gets under way. Finally, "one very large volume" is surrendered. Deacons or subdeacons are called upon to assist the mayor in finding books said to be in possession of the readers. The mayor and his officers track down the "readers" and receive from them another four books. Their homes are searched; the wife of one reader "produced his books." The search over, the mayor warns the subdeacons: "If there has been any omission, the responsibility is yours."

Elsewhere in the empire the new laws of Diocletian against the Christians and their books were enforced with less severity. We are told that Caesar Constantius in Gaul and Britain only confiscated Christian Scripture and property and so avoided creating martyrs through executions (Lactantius, *De mortibus persecutorum* 15.7–16.1). Even so, some officials may have tortured and executed Christians who were non-compliant.

Because of ill health Diocletian was forced to step down in 305. The violence against the Christians lessened but did not end. Many Christians suffered imprisonment, confiscation of property, torture, and execution. Among these was Peter, the bishop of Alexandria, who was executed in 311. Eventually under Constantine (r. 306–337) the pogroms ended, and in 313 an agreement was reached (the so-called Edict of Milan), which legalized Christianity and other religions.[130] Christians enjoyed peace for the next fifty years.

Constantine encouraged and subsidized the production of fifty copies of Scripture, perhaps as compensation for the loss of books of Scripture during Diocletian's campaign against the Church. The order for these copies is found in Constantine's letter to Eusebius, which Eusebius presents in his biography of Constantine: "We make known to you that you are to commission fifty volumes which are to be bound in leather, easy to read and (for convenience) portable. They are to be written by craftsmen who are both calligraphers and used to working accurately. They are to be copies (σωμάτια) of the divine Scriptures (τῶν θείων δηλαδὴ γραφῶν), which you well know must be available for reading in church" (*Vita Constantini* 4.36.2). Eusebius comments: "Thus the emperor instructed. Action immediately followed word, as we sent him

---

130. For the edict, see Eusebius, *Historia ecclesiastica* 10.5.1-14. Nevertheless, Christians still faced difficulties with Licinius in the east. Licinius abdicated in 324; thereafter, Constantine ruled alone.

threes and fours [τρισσὰ καὶ τετρασσά] in curiously worked bindings" (4.37.1).[131]

Scholars have been intrigued by the meaning of "threes and fours" (τρισσὰ καὶ τετρασσά). Some have wondered if the language is in reference to the format of the codices that were produced, that is, in three-column and four-column books. If so, then the great codices Vaticanus (formatted in three columns) and Sinaiticus (formatted in four columns) could be two of these fifty copies of Scripture.[132] But a number of scholars have raised objections to this interpretation. The words τρισσὰ καὶ τετρασσά seem to modify the action "we sent," that is, "We sent the emperor copies of Scripture in batches of threes and fours."[133]

There are other reasons why the great codices Vaticanus and Sinaiticus might not be two exemplars of these fifty copies. One, it is not clear that the entire Bible is in view.[134] The books envisioned may only have been Gospels and perhaps Paul's letters. Second, Vaticanus and Sinaiticus may have been produced somewhat after Constantine's death (and so are not early enough); and, third, they are quite ornate. On this last point, David Parker notes that the instructions in Constantine's letter "suggest that the interest is in useful rather than in impressive books: they are to have leather bindings (for durability), to be easily legible, and to be portable."[135] The instruction that the scribes be καλλιγράφοι ("calligraphers") does not necessarily indicate a beautiful, ornate writing style; rather, it may only mean that their penship is professional and therefore quite legible.

And finally, Parker also reminds us that other emperors commissioned copies of Scripture. Athanasius of Alexandria recounts producing and sending copies of Scripture to Emperor Constans: "I sent to him bound volumes of the holy Scriptures [τῶν θείων γραφῶν], which he had ordered me to prepare for him" (Athanasius, *Apologia ad Constantium* 4.2).[136]

---

131. I have followed the translation offered in D. C. Parker, *Codex Sinaiticus: The Story of the World's Oldest Bible* (London: The British Library; Peabody, MA: Hendrickson, 2010), 19–20.

132. B. M. Metzger and B. D. Ehrman, *The Text of the New Testament: Its Transmission, Corruption, and Restoration*, 4th edn (Oxford: Oxford University Press, 2005), 15: "Codex Vaticanus and Codex Sinaiticus…may have been among those ordered by Constantine."

133. Gamble, *Books and Readers in the Early Church*, 159.

134. T. D. Barnes, *Constantine and Eusebius* (Cambridge, MA: Harvard University Press, 1981), 123: "It could be that Eusebius' fifty Bibles contained the New Testament alone."

135. Parker, *Codex Sinaiticus*, 21.

136. Ibid., 22.

Vaticanus and Sinaiticus could well be ornate presentation copies. In any event, they fit better a time somewhat later than that described by Eusebius.

This peace was briefly interrupted in 363 when Julian, known as "the Apostate" (r. 361–363) and nephew of Constantine, began promoting the restoration of pagan temples and rites. His premature death brought his re-paganization of the empire to an end. The story of the seizure of the books from the house of Georgius, bishop of Alexandria, in which the emperor ordered the non-Christian books preserved and the Christian books destroyed, has already been described. How much more of this activity took place is uncertain. Had Julian lived longer, it is possible that the pogroms enacted under Diocletian sixty years earlier might have been repeated.

Archaeology and Climate

An important indication that collections of books in fact remained in use for one or two centuries, sometimes longer, is seen in observations made by the British scholars Bernard Grenfell and Arthur Hunt and later by Evaristo Breccia in their work at Oxyrhynchus. I refer here to discoveries of collections of bookrolls or small libraries found more or less intact. Through paleography the bookrolls could be dated, as well as the stratum in which the collection was unearthed. From these observations an approximation of the longevity of the bookrolls could be determined. George Houston has worked through the relevant publications and reports.[137]

Four private libraries have been recovered from the sandy trash mounds of Oxyrhynchus. Referencing the oldest book in each collection at the time of discarding, Houston sums up accordingly: (1) The library from Grenfell and Hunt's first find has a bookroll about 175 years old; (2) the library from Grenfell and Hunt's third find, which Breccia completed several years later, contained a bookroll between 200 and 300 years old; (3) the oldest book in the Aurelius collection is somewhat less than 100 years old; and (4) Grenfell and Hunt's second find includes a book almost 500 years old.[138] A fifth library, the one preserved at the Villa of the Papyri

---

137. For the most recent and detailed statement on this topic, see Houston, *Inside Roman Libraries*, 130–79. One will also want to see G. W. Houston, "Grenfell, Hunt, Breccia, and the Book Collections of Oxyrhynchus," *GRBS* 47 (2007): 327–59.

138. See the tabulation in Houston, *Inside Roman Libraries*, 175. The old reports by Grenfell and Hunt have been conveniently collected and reprinted in A. K. Bowman, et al. (eds.), *Oxyrhynchus: A City and Its Texts*, Graeco-Roman Memoirs

in Herculaneum, thanks to the eruption of Mount Vesuvius in 79 CE, has also yielded important chronological data. Houston finds that most of the bookrolls in the villa's collection "were some 120 to 160 years old," when the villa was buried under ash. However, a number of bookrolls in this library were much older: three were copied in the third century BCE and six in the third or second century BCE. This means that a few of the bookrolls in this impressive collection were anywhere from 250 to 350 years old at the time of eruption.[139]

In the conclusion of his study, under the heading of "The Life Span of a Book Roll," Houston states:

> The identification of such collections, and of the manuscripts within them, provides new evidence on an old question: how long did a papyrus roll last? The evidence from our collections indicates that a usable lifetime of about 100 to 125 years was common and can reasonably be considered the norm; a small but significant number of manuscripts were still usable some 300 years after they were first created; and on rare occasions a manuscript might last, it seems, for half a millennium.[140]

I referenced some of these data in my earlier study.[141] A few scholars have objected, stating that the longevity of bookrolls in Egypt, in the region of the Dead Sea, and in the unusual conditions of Herculaneum would not apply to manuscript longevity in non-arid regions, such as Asia Minor, Greece, Macedonia, and Italy. This is a strange objection, given what has just been observed with respect to the library recovered at the Villa of the Papyri. As just mentioned, these bookrolls ranged in age from 120 to 350 years old *before Vesuvius* erupted. They did not exist in an arid climate; and they are extant today, almost two thousand years after their burial, because they were carbonized.

I must emphasize the same point with respect to the several testimonials and narratives reviewed above, concerning very old books in one collection or another, books two or three hundred years old, some of them suffering from rot and worms thanks to the indifferent care of

---

93 (London: Egypt Exploration Society, 2007), 345–68. For Breccia's reports, see E. Breccia, "Fouilles à Oxyrhynchos et à Tebtunis," in *Le Musée Gréco-Romain d'Alexandrie 1925–1931* (Bergamo: Istituto Italiano d'arti grafiche, 1932), 60–3; idem, "Fouilles d'Oxyrhynchos," in *Le Musée Gréco-Romain d'Alexandrie II 1931–1932* (Bergamo: Istituto Italiano d'arti grafiche, 1933), 36–47.

139. Houston, *Inside Roman Libraries*, 120–1.
140. Ibid., 257.
141. Evans, "How Long Were Late Antique Books in Use?" 25–29.

their owners. All of these books were circulated, stored, and in use in the non-arid climes of Asia Minor, Greece, Italy, or Caesarea Maritima. The literary data we have, the testimony we have, often from first-hand sources, claim that bookrolls, if given proper care, were expected to survive and be usable for two hundred years and more. Highly valued books, such as autographs of celebrated figures, were very likely to enjoy a longer life.

The significance of the arid climates of the Dead Sea region and much of Egypt lies in the fact that written material can last two or three *thousand* years, that is, the written material lasts long, long after it has been discarded, and even reaches our own time. The chronological data recovered from the trash mounds in Oxyrhynchus in modern times would not have been possible, had the climate been damp. Of course, however dry the surface may have been in Oxyrhynchus and elsewhere in Egypt, papyrus buried deep and exposed to moisture was in very poor condition. To be sure, the arid climate of Egypt and the region of the Dead Sea made it easier for the people of late antiquity, who lived in those regions, to care for manuscripts, but people who lived in the non-arid regions I have mentioned were also able to preserve manuscripts for centuries.

In the non-arid climes of Europe many books exist today that are more than one thousand years old. Many of them have suffered damage from mold and worms. Their storage and care were not always as they should have been. Yet, they have survived. Vaticanus and Sinaiticus are almost 1,700 years old. Bezae is at least 1,600 years old; Washingtonianus and Alexandrinus are almost as old. Thousands of Medieval books, Christian or otherwise, have survived the damp winters and stifling summers of Europe for a millennium or more.[142] Why should we think that books of late antiquity, whose owners treasured and cared for them, could not survive for more than a generation or two? Ancient testimony, both Christian and non-Christian, says they in fact did survive for a century or more, which the results of archaeology appear to confirm.

So what happened to the autographs and early copies of the writings that eventually came to make up the New Testament? The most probable explanation is that autographs and early copies, which in some cases came

---

142. In private communication Ken Dark of the University of Reading draws to my attention the *St. Cuthbert Gospel*, which is a copy of the Gospel of John produced in damp northern England in the late seventh century. This book was placed in St Cuthbert's coffin in 698 when it was in Lindisfarne. The book was retrieved, in good condition, when the coffin was opened at Durham Cathedral in 1104 some four centuries later.

to be venerated, were either accidentally or deliberately destroyed. Little speculation is needed here. We have detailed accounts of Diocletian's aggressive campaign designed specifically to destroy the physical artifacts of Christianity: their churches and their books of Scripture. Failure to surrender these books meant arrest, imprisonment, torture, and death. Eusebius claims to have seen books of Scripture burned, and he passes on the testimony of others. Other sources pass on similar accounts. Christian books may have been destroyed in the late second century, during the kind of pogroms that took place in north Africa and at Lugdunum, France, and during the rule of Decian in the mid-third century as well, but in Diocletian's pogroms thousands of Christian books were destroyed, and some of these may have been quite old.

It is in the Diocletian persecution that the old copy of the Gospel of John, venerated by Christians in Ephesus, could have been destroyed. However, according to the testimony of Bishop Peter, this "autograph" (ἰδιόχειρον) existed "up to this day" (that is, c. 306). Its preservation, says Peter, has been "by the grace of God" (χάριτι τοῦ θεοῦ). What does he mean? Is he implying that God's grace has prevented the manuscript from suffering decay and disintegration, or from being destroyed during Diocletian's persecution? Given all the testimony that has been reviewed in this essay, I should think the latter option is the more likely.

By the beginning of the fourth century the autograph of John, or, if not an autograph, at least a very old copy of John, apparently was still in existence in Ephesus, where it was venerated by Christians. Given its notoriety and perhaps its value for apologetic purposes, it would have been difficult to hide it from authorities during the persecutions that began in 303. Yet, in a Passover homily dated to 306, one year after Diocletian was forced to abdicate, Peter, bishop of Alexandria, makes reference to the autograph of the Gospel of John, saying that it "up to this day has by the grace of God been preserved." The most natural understanding of Peter's comment is that the precious autograph survived Diocletian, and the faithful of the church of Ephesus still venerate it.

The autograph, or very old copy, of John may have survived, but many other manuscripts—old and new alike—did not. Lost among the old copies may have been an autograph or two. Apart from a remarkable discovery, we shall never know. Given the testimony of Tertullian, Peter, and others, and given the testimony of non-Christian scholars and book collectors, the possibility, perhaps even probability that at least a few New Testament autographs and first copies survived for two centuries should be entertained.

Summing Up

As I was bringing this essay to a conclusion, Timothy Mitchell, a doctoral student at the University of Birmingham, courteously sent me a paper soon to be published in a collection of studies concerned with the text of the New Testament. In this paper he voices a number of objections against the view that I have taken here, objections that correspond at points with some of the objections and criticisms that have been expressed in cyberspace.[143] I welcome the opportunity to engage his objections here at the conclusion of my paper. I also look forward to the appearance of the volume itself, which no doubt will contain some interesting and helpful studies.

Mitchell begins his essay with references to appeals made to biblical autographs in debates centered on the inspiration and inerrancy of Scripture. He then quotes a pastor and popular writer who affirms his confidence in the reliability of the New Testament text because "it's more than a little likely that the originals…would have been preserved and used to make countless new copies over decades or even centuries before they were lost."[144] As it so happens, the pastor learned of the possibility of the longevity of New Testament autographs from Craig Blomberg, a New Testament scholar in Denver, who in one of his recent books cites me.[145]

Now all of this is interesting, to be sure. But I also want to make it crystal clear that my investigation of the longevity of late antique manuscripts—both Christian and pagan—has nothing to do with an apologetic agenda and nothing to do with debates about the inspiration or inerrancy of the text of Scripture. As I will explain shortly, my investigation is largely in response to an interesting comment by Professor Frederik Wisse a number of years ago.

---

143. T. N. Mitchell, "Myths about Autographs: What Were They and How Long Did They Survive?" in E. Hixson and P. J. Gurry (eds.), *Myths and Mistakes in the New Testament Textual Criticism* (Downers Grove, IL: InterVarsity, forthcoming").

144. G. Gilbert, *Why Trust the Bible?* (Wheaton, IL: Crossway, 2015), 48; cited by Mitchell.

145. C. L. Blomberg, *Can We Still Believe the Bible? An Evangelical Engagement with Contemporary Questions* (Grand Rapids: Brazos, 2014), 34. I should explain that Professor Blomberg heard me give the paper at a conference a few years before its publication in the *Bulletin for Biblical Research*. Gilbert acknowledges his dependence on Blomberg in *Why Trust the Bible?*, 43.

The next point of criticism raised by Mitchell has me somewhat confused. Reminding readers that I conclude from the evidence that it is probable that "the autographs and first copies circulated and were in use for one century or longer" and that therefore there is no justification for supposing that the "text of the NT writings underwent major changes in the first and second centuries,"[146] Mitchell cites the recent study of Matthew Larsen, whose work, we are told, stands "in contrast to the optimism of Evans." Yet, what Mitchell quotes from Larsen does not address the longevity of autographs or first copies, or even textual stability for that matter. For the convenience of the reader I provide that part of Larsen's study that Mitchell quotes:

> [W]e can no longer simply assume that a text was finished and published, especially texts that are not high literature. Unless we can determine that a text was finished, closed and published, which would exclude many of the texts now called the New Testament, traditionally conceived modes of textual criticism may be a square peg for a round hole.[147]

Larsen's caution is well taken. I suspect most of the New Testament letters were dispatched as "finished and published," but in the case of the Gospels it is very much an open question. I am not sure all textual critics will agree with Larsen, but I do think he makes a good point and the discussion that will ensue will no doubt be an interesting one. My own work on the Synoptic Gospels runs along lines that in some ways correlate with Larsen's perspective.

I make my views clear in two recent essays that appeared in a book that critically examines four approaches to solving the Synoptic Problem.[148] In my first essay, in which I argue for the Two Source Hypothesis, I caution that all attempts at resolving the Synoptic Problem will run into some difficulties because "we do not know how many 'editions' of each Gospel were produced (e.g., which edition of Mark did Matthew use?)," etc.[149] In my second essay, in which I respond to the other contributors, I state that the "likelihood that the Synoptic Gospels were produced in stages and

---

146. And here Mitchell is quoting from Evans, "How Long Were Late Antique Books in Use?" 37.

147. M. D. C. Larsen, "Accidental Publication, Unfinished Texts and the Traditional Gospels of New Testament Textual Criticism," *JSNT* 39 (2017): 362–87, with quotation from 379–80.

148. C. A. Evans, "The Two Source Hypothesis" and "Two Source Hypothesis Response," in *The Synoptic Problem: Four Views*, ed. S. E. Porter and B. R. Dyer (Grand Rapids: Baker Academic, 2016), 27–45 and 113–25, respectively.

149. Ibid., 44.

under the influence of the oral tradition throughout the first century is a factor that must be taken into account," etc.[150] At the end I say that "all three Synoptic Gospels were 'published' in two or more recensions," etc.[151] Given what I say here, I am not sure how Larsen's study works against my optimism that autographs and first copies remained in circulation for many years and by doing so helped maintain the stability of the text. I should mention too that I am fully aware of the difficulty in speaking of autographs in the sense of one, final text. This is why I say "autographs and first copies."

What we don't know is the degree to which the respective evangelists maintained control over their written work. Late antique authors sometimes complain of this very problem. That a number of writers produced new Gospels and Gospel-like writings in the second and third centuries cannot be denied. But did they offer new versions of the first-century Gospels? Marcion apparently produced a truncated version of Luke, but it was identified as such. Did anyone else attempt this? The *Gospel of Peter* might count as a drastically altered and embellished recension of Matthew. But the excerpt that we have does not provide enough text to determine this. If we had larger samples of the Ebionite Gospels, which some believe are recensions of the Gospel of Matthew, we might have a better idea. As it is, however, the stability of the text of the four Gospels suggests that at some stage a particular edition came to be recognized as the "finished" version. This would explain why, for example, the Gospel of John that we find in $\mathfrak{P}^{66}$ is the same as the Gospel of John that we find in $\mathfrak{P}^{75}$. The texts are not identical, of course, but $\mathfrak{P}^{66}$ and $\mathfrak{P}^{75}$ are nonetheless copies of the same document, the Gospel of John.

We simply do not have two recensions of Matthew, two recensions of Mark, and so forth, the way we do in the case of other writings. This was the point I was trying to make in my earlier study in comparing the New Testament Gospels to some of the Gnostic writings. The *Apocryphon of John* provides a very helpful example. We have four copies of this writing. Two of these copies represent a "short recension" (NHC III, *1* and BG 8502, *2*), the other two represent a "long recension" (NHC II, *1* and IV, *1*). There are many discrepancies, some quite major, among these texts. Ascertaining the "autographic" text, or even an *Ausgangstext*, of this work is impossible. The same can be said of several other writings.[152]

---

150. Ibid., 114. See also my comment in n. 3.
151. Ibid., 124.
152. In the bulk of his essay Mitchell defines the meaning of "autograph," cites a number of papyri, including the much talked about and very relevant P.Oxy. 2192, and

I come now to what Mitchell says about longevity of late antique manuscripts.[153] He briefly reviews the findings of Grenfell and Hunt and summarizes the recent work of George Houston.[154] Mitchell regards the longevity averages identified by Houston as "best case scenarios." This is because, Mitchell tells us, "[p]apyrus did not fare well in the more humid environments of the rest of the Mediterranean world."[155] To prove this, he cites Galen's comment in *De indolentia* 19, in which he complains of the poor condition of old bookrolls because of the marshy, stifling conditions in which they had been kept.[156]

Galen's complaint, however, presupposes that the old bookrolls could have and should have been better cared for, especially in view of the marshy environment and the stifling heat of summer. That Galen's description is not typical of the care and longevity of bookrolls in Italy, Asia Minor, Greece, Macedonia, etc. is clear when one considers the implications of the library uncovered in the Villa of the Papyri in Herculaneum. We know the year this library ceased being in use: it was the year 79. What we should bear in mind is that, unlike the collections of books found in Egypt, the books in the library of the Villa of the Papyri *were still in use*; its bookrolls had not been retired and thrown out. As already noted, many of these bookrolls were more than one hundred

---

discusses writing, editing, and manuscript circulation in late antiquity, the problems of plagiarism, copying, and circulating works without the author's permission, and so forth. Experts know all of this, but many readers will find it useful.

153. Mitchell, "Myths about Autographs," 13–16.

154. Mitchell does not make it clear that Grenfell and Hunt, with Breccia some years later completing one of the digs, produced results for four book collections at Oxyrhynchus. Houston discusses these four collections and then discusses the library at the Villa of the Papyri. Curiously, Mitchell remarks that "Grenfell and Hunt did not reveal how they ascertained the date these collections were discarded" (ibid., 14). Actually they did. They did it through stratigraphy, that is identifying and dating the layer in which the book collection was found. Throughout their reports Grenfell and Hunt talk about various layers (Byzantine, Roman, Greek, etc.). Their report of the fifth season (1905–1906) contains a very clear example. After describing the various layers in the mound they excavated, they say: "The evidence of documents found below the literary texts shows that the latter must have been thrown away in the fifth century; but the MSS themselves are chiefly of the second or third century." See Bowman, et al. (eds.), *Oxyrhynchus: A City and Its Texts*, 362. All will want to read carefully Houston's assessment of these reports and those of Breccia, in Houston, *Inside Roman Libraries*, 130–79.

155. Mitchell, "Myths about Autographs," 14.

156. Ibid., 15. See my discussion of Galen, *De indolentia* 19 above.

years old at the time of the eruption and some were two hundred and even three hundred years old—and they were still in use! Had the eruption not occurred, these bookrolls would have been read, copied, and studied for many years to come.

And, of course, Herculaneum is in Italy. It is not in arid Egypt or the region of the Dead Sea. Galen may describe the area, where the poorly cared for books were stored, as "marshy and low-lying" and he may remark that summers are "stifling." But Italy, Greece, Asia Minor, etc. are part of the Mediterranean world and as such have what meteorologists call a "Mediterranean climate." The climate is in fact semi-arid; it is not tropical and it is not humid.[157]

Houston's longevity findings based on the four collections in Egypt and the large collection in the villa in Herculaneum are not "best case scenarios," implying that elsewhere longevity is less. Houston's averages are averages that probably do apply throughout the Greco-Roman world. That this is likely correct is supported by the Christian and non-Christian testimonies regarding the great longevity of manuscripts, including autographs, that have been reviewed above.

In reference to the discovery of several New Testament manuscripts in the trash mounds of Oxyrhynchus, Mitchell comments: "This reveals that Christians sometimes threw away biblical manuscripts after a period of use, likely after being replaced with a new copy, rather than being retained for hundreds of years."[158] The problem with this statement is that Mitchell does not know how long "a period of use" is. Some manuscripts may have been discarded after a few years, as he surmises; others may have been confiscated and pitched out; still others may have been in use for a century or two, then thrown out. Unless we have stratigraphy and from stratigraphy chronological data, we simply do not know. Should we assume that the Egyptian archives and collections of literature that were thrown out were copied before being thrown out? What the circumstances were with regard to isolated manuscripts, lacking context and lacking chronological data, are unknown. For all we know, some of the Oxyrhynchus New Testament manuscripts may have been read, studied, and copied for

---

157. The *Encyclopedia Britannica* defines "Mediterranean climate" as "characterized by hot, dry summers and cool, wet winters and located between about 30° and 45° latitude." The accompanying map shows what would approximate most of the Greco-Roman world. It includes Spain, Italy, Greece, Asia Minor, the Mediterranean islands, western Syria, and western Israel. Eastern Israel and north Africa, including Egypt, are in arid climate zones.

158. Mitchell, "Myths about Autographs," 15–16.

long periods of time before being thrown out. And in any case, given the value placed on autographs attributed to important figures, as seen in both Christian and non-Christian authors, it is most unlikely that an autograph, as Mitchell says,[159] would be discarded. In fact, it flies in the face of the testimony—Christian and non-Christian alike. Who would throw out as trash a Pauline autograph?

Mitchell concludes his essay by suggesting that the ongoing survival and circulation of an autograph would likely not have influence on the text. Why that is so is not clear. What I have suggested closely corresponds to the arguments of second-century Christian apologists: because they possess autographs and early copies, they know their form of the text is original.

To make the case that autographs were not valued, did not survive long, and would not in any case have had much influence on the text, Mitchell appeals to the interesting example of the two final columns of text at the conclusion of book 18 of the Κεστοί ("Embroidered Girdles") of Julius Africanus (c. 160–c. 240 CE) found at Oxyrhynchus (P.Oxy. 412).[160] When the copy under review was about fifty years old, it was re-used. This tells Mitchell that the book "was not valued for long by its owners."[161] And, moreover, although the copy itself is good quality, several lines of an incantation in the first column of the extant fragment are corrupt. Mitchell believes that these two data—disuse of the original text after only fifty years and textual corruption—refute my argument that New Testament autographs probably survived a long time and that their lengthy survival contributed to a stabilized text.

Mitchell's inferences and conclusions are gratuitous. First, it is most unlikely that the original owners were still living fifty years after acquiring this book, so the book's subsequent re-use tells us nothing about the value the original owners placed on it and it tells us nothing about the book's later owners and the circumstances at the time the book was re-used. The first owners were probably Christians; who the last owners were, we have no idea. And in any case, this book was a treatise on miscellaneous topics by a third-century Church Father; it was not an autograph or early copy of one of the New Testament Gospels or one of Paul's letters. Why should we expect Christians to assign the same value and respect to a writing by Africanus that they would to a Gospel or apostolic letter?

159. Ibid., 16.
160. Ibid., 16–17.
161. Ibid., 16.

Second, a few garbled lines of an incantation tell us nothing about the influence New Testament autographs and early copies would have and did have in the copying and circulation of New Testament writings. I might add that the accurate transmission of the text of the New Testament did not require the existence of ancient autographs and first-century copies. My only point is that the evidence—both testimonial and artifactual—suggests that at least some of the autographs and early copies did last a long time.

Possessing old copies of Scripture, if not in some cases autographs themselves, worked well in Christian apologetic, especially in countering "heretical" writings, which Christian apologists describe as recent and as lacking support from old MSS, on which they are supposedly based. If Christian manuscripts typically lasted only one generation or so, as a few modern critics seem to think, then the argument of the Christian apologists would have carried little weight. Preserving the autographs and early copies comports with early Christian book culture and apologetic, as well as devotion.

By the end of the first century and beginning of the second we hear expressions of the recognition of the authority of Christian writings, even regarding them as on par with Israel's ancient Scriptures. For example, the scriptural or quasi-scriptural status of Paul's letters appears to be attested in 2 Peter. The author says in reference to Paul's letters: "There are some things in them hard to understand, which the ignorant and unstable twist to their own destruction, as they do the other scriptures [τὰς λοιπὰς γραφάς]" (2 Pet. 3:16). Here λοιπάς is probably better translated "remaining." Although a number of scholars date 2 Peter to the first half of the second century, Richard Bauckham makes a strong case for dating the letter no later than the last decade of the first century.[162] Bauckham and others rightly think the author of 2 Peter views Paul's letters as Scripture on par with Old Testament Scripture.[163] We should assume, moreover, that this thinking predates the composition and circulation of 2 Peter.

The author of 1 Tim. 5:18 introduces and quotes Deut. 25:4 and Luke 10:7 (cf. Matt. 10:10; *Did.* 13:1) with the formula "for the scripture says" (λέγει γὰρ ἡ γραφή). The reference to γραφή suggests that the author is not thinking of free-floating sayings but *writings*, in this case

---

162. R. J. Bauckham, *Jude, 2 Peter*, WBC 50 (Dallas: Word, 1983), 158.
163. Ibid., 333. So does C. Bigg, *A Critical and Exegetical Commentary on the Epistles of St. Peter and St. Jude*, ICC (Edinburgh: T. & T. Clark, 1901), 302: αἱ γραφαί "cannot here mean anything but scripture."

Deuteronomy and either Matthew or Luke (or perhaps Q). If 1 Timothy was written at the end of the first century, or perhaps in the first two or three decades of the second century, the author may well have had in mind either Matthew or Luke.[164]

Another early reference to New Testament writings as "Scripture" is found in *2 Clement*. *2 Clement*, which is not a letter at all but a sermon, is dated roughly between 100 and 140 CE.[165] At 2:4 the author quotes from the Gospel of Mark: "And another scripture says [ἑτέρα δὲ γραφὴ λέγει], 'I have not come to call the righteous, but sinners'" (= Mark 2:17; cf. Matt. 9:13; *Barn.* 5:9).[166] Elsewhere the author of this sermon introduces and abridges Ezek. 14:14-20 with the same formula: "And the Scripture [ἡ γραφή] also says" (*2 Clem.* 6:8). For the writer of *2 Clement*, it would seem, passages from both Mark and Ezekiel may be quoted and referred to as γραφή.

The author of the pseudepigraphal letter of *Barnabas*, writing sometime before 130 CE, introduces and quotes Exod. 34:28 with the words, "For the Scripture says [λέγει γὰρ ἡ γραφή]" (*Barn.* 4:7), then a few verses later quotes and introduces Isa. 5:21 the same way: "For the Scripture says [λέγει γὰρ ἡ γραφή]" (4:11). A few verses after that, the author quotes Matt. 22:14, introducing it, "as it is written [ὡς γέγραπται]" (4:14; cf. 5:2, "It is written [γέγραπται] concerning him… 'He was wounded because of our transgressions,'" etc.). The author of *Barnabas* apparently regards Matthew as γραφή.[167]

---

164. Pauline authorship of the Pastorals is accepted by Luke Timothy Johnson. For this reason, he wonders in what sense Paul can refer to a dominical saying as "Scripture." See L. T. Johnson, *The First and Second Letters to Timothy: A New Translation with Introduction and Commentary*, AYB 35A (New Haven and London: Yale University Press, 2001), 278. Even if 1 Timothy was composed by Paul and therefore was composed sometime in the 60s, it is possible that many dominical sayings were circulating in written form (again, perhaps Q) and by virtue of being *dominical* could be regarded, even as early as the 60s, as written Scripture on par with Old Testament Scripture.

165. The date options are reviewed in J. B. Lightfoot, J. R. Harmer, and M. W. Holmes, *The Apostolic Fathers*, rev. edn (Grand Rapids: Baker, 1989), 65–7.

166. J. B. Lightfoot, *The Apostolic Fathers: Clement, Ignatius, and Polycarp*. Part One: *Clement*, vol. 2 (London: Macmillan, 1889), 215: "Thus the Gospel, treated as a written document, is regarded as Scripture like the Old Testament." See also H. Köster, *Synoptische Überlieferung bei den apostolischen Vätern*, TU 65 (Berlin: Akademie-Verlag, 1957), 71, 139, 144.

167. There are approximate parallels to Matt. 22:14 in *4 Ezra* 8:3 and 9:15. However, the quotation in *Barn.* 4:14 matches Matt. 22:14 more closely. For discussion, see Köster, *Synoptische Überlieferung*, 126–7.

And finally, in Polycarp's letter to the Philippians, Ps. 4:5 and Eph. 4:26 are referenced as "these Scriptures." The passage reads: "I am convinced that you are well trained in the sacred Scriptures [*in sacris literis*] and that nothing is hidden from you... [A]s it is said in these Scriptures [*ut his scripturis*], 'be angry but do not sin' (Ps. 4:5), and 'do not let the sun set on your anger' (Eph. 4:26)" (Polycarp, *Phil.* 12:1).[168] It is probable that Polycarp recognizes that he is quoting two texts—Ps. 4:5 (which is quoted in Eph. 4:26a) and Eph. 4:26b—because of the way he presents his quoted material in two distinct parts, saying *his scripturis*. In other words, he is not simply quoting Eph. 4:26, unaware that part of the passage is actually a quotation of Ps. 4:5.[169] If so, we have here another instance in which an apostolic writing is cited, along with an Old Testament text, as Scripture.

These references to New Testament writings as γραφή bear witness to early appreciation and respect for their authority. These examples are not in reference to specific manuscripts, of course, but they are consistent with a mindset in which autographs and early copies would be valued and preserved. It is hard to imagine early Christian communities throwing out apostolic autographs, even after new copies have been made. One would think that Christians would have made every effort to safeguard the autographs and early copies as treasures of the Church. Given the patristic testimony noted earlier in this study, that indeed seems to have been the thinking and the practice, a thinking and practice clearly attested in non-Christian late antique writings.

My interest in the question of the longevity of the autographs and first copies of the New Testament writings grew out of my involvement with the Coptic Gnostic codices from Nag Hammadi, beginning in my doctoral studies back in the 1970s. I well recall the frustration from time to time voiced over the uncertainty of the Coptic text, given the substantial variations in cases where we had two or more copies of a given writing. The *Apocryphon of John*, which I mentioned above, was an especially vexatious example.

My interest was aroused again when thirty years ago the late William Petersen published a collection of conference papers on the text of the Gospels in the second century.[170] The paper that caught my eye was the

---

168. Much of Polycarp's letter, including the part that I have cited, is extant only in Latin translation.

169. For discussion, see Köster, *Synoptische Überlieferung*, 113.

170. W. L. Petersen (ed.), *Gospel Traditions in the Second Century: Origins, Recensions, Text, and Transmission*, Christianity and Judaism in Antiquity 3 (Notre Dame, IN: University of Notre Dame Press, 1989).

one by Professor Frederik Wisse of McGill University, who was one of the contributors to the Nag Hammadi project that resulted in the publication of the Nag Hammadi codices and related writings.[171]

Wisse begins his essay by directly confronting an assumption held in some circles thirty years ago:

> It is widely taken for granted in Biblical scholarship that early Christian texts were extensively redacted during the first century of their transmission. These redactional changes are thought to have served mainly theological purposes, i.e., to change or augment the theological outlook of a writing in order to make it conform to changes in the beliefs or practices of a particular community… Since this view has for many the status of a virtual fact, one would expect that it is based on clear textual evidence. However, this is not the case.[172]

What Wisse objects to is the claim that the texts were "extensively redacted." He of course knows that minor editing, as well as the usual scribal errors and corrections, took place and are everywhere in evidence. This is not in dispute. His point is that there simply is no evidence of significant and widespread redaction, including interpolations of new material, or the excision of original material. The only substantial interpolations—the long ending of Mark and the *pericope adulterae*—seem to have crept into the text at a later time and, in any event, do not alter or add anything to Christian beliefs and teaching.[173] Even the majority of the minor interpolations are late, not early.[174]

In notable contrast to Wisse's perspective, Helmut Koester regards it as a truism that "serious corruptions occur" in the first hundred years or so

---

171. J. M. Robinson (ed.), *The Nag Hammadi Library* (Leiden: Brill; San Francisco: Harper & Row, 1977 and subsequent editions). Fred Wisse's principal contribution was the translation and introduction of the *Apocryphon of John* (pp. 98–116).

172. F. Wisse, "The Nature and Purpose of Redactional Changes in Early Christian Texts: The Canonical Gospels," in Petersen (ed.), *Gospel Traditions in the Second Century*, 39–53, with quotation from p. 39.

173. Wisse, "The Nature and Purpose of Redactional Changes in Early Christian Texts," 47–8. See also L. W. Hurtado, "The *Pericope Adulterae*: Where from Here?" in *The Pericope of the Adulteress in Contemporary Research*, ed. D. A. Black and J. N. Cerone, LNTS 551 (London and New York: Bloomsbury T & T Clark, 2016), 147–58.

174. Wisse, "The Nature and Purpose of Redactional Changes in Early Christian Texts," 48–50.

of the transmission of a text.¹⁷⁵ By its very nature such a claim is almost immune from verification, for it is rare that more than small fragments of a literary work are extant from such an early period of its existence. With respect to most classical literature, there are gaps of many centuries, sometimes a millennium, between original composition and our earliest surviving manuscripts, including fragments.¹⁷⁶ It is true that sometimes classical authors complained of alterations to their writings. As we have seen, Church Fathers also sometimes complained of alterations to New Testament texts. But these instances seem to be the exception, not the rule; and, in any case, the altered texts were spotted and recognized for what they are. We should remember too that textual criticism was in fact practiced by late antique copyists and scholars. The ancients were not as naïve and uncritical as we moderns sometimes assume. Indeed, in several of the testimonies reviewed above, the whole point of acquiring autographs and ancient copies was for the purposes of ascertaining the original reading of the text. Both non-Christians and Christians valued autographs and ancient copies for this reason.

There are at least four problems with the assumption that "serious corruptions" occurred in the first century or so of the transmission of New Testament manuscripts, corruptions, we apparently should assume, that remain present and undetected in the text. First, New Testament writings were copied and distributed, quickly reaching several locations and regions. Wide distribution of copies early on would make it difficult to introduce interpolations and alterations in enough texts in enough regions to gain acceptance as the authentic text. The mere fact of sending a letter to one city, in a given region, and retaining a copy in another city, possibly in a different region, would immediately make it problematic for a copyist to introduce a significant corruption, whether intentional or inadvertent, that would escape detection and become widely accepted. Recall too that some of the New Testament writings were probably intended to circulate from the beginning and so may have been sent out to several destinations as multiple original copies (e.g., the letter to the churches of Galatia, perhaps also Ephesians, James, one or more of the Gospels). If so, how could a given copyist introduce a change that was then able to work its way into enough copies and succeed in reshaping the text?

175. H. Koester, "The Text of the Synoptic Gospels in the Second Century," in Petersen (ed.), *Gospel Traditions in the Second Century*, 19–37, with quotation from p. 19.

176. For several examples, see F. G. Kenyon, *Handbook to the Textual Criticism of the New Testament*, 2nd edn (London: Macmillan, 1926), 5.

Second, I wonder if there is an unconscious anachronism lying at the heart of hypothetical scenarios in which copyists are imagined to have introduced theologically motivated changes. We must ask how early copyists—those who copied New Testament writings in the first century of their existence—would know what theological directions to take? Should the humanity of Jesus be enhanced? Or his divinity? Surely late first-century and early second-century copyists could not anticipate Nicene Christology, could they? Another question asks how early copyists would know which Christian writings would in fact become authoritative and form the basis of Christian theology and ethics? I think it is very probable that early copyists respected the authority of apostolic writings and writings assumed to be apostolic, but that does not mean that they could have known that these writings and not others would make up a canon of Scripture. Not knowing what books would become canonized (or that a New Testament canon would ever materialize) or what nuances of theology would become "orthodox" undercuts motives for redacting New Testament texts.

Third, why should we assume that most of the copyists were Christians, with theological interests? A recent study makes a good case that most of the copyists were professional copyists and that few of them were in fact Christians.[177] If so, these copyists would have had no motivation at all to redact the text. Simply put: They had no theological dog in the fight. The copyists were paid to copy the text before them and to copy it legibly and accurately. Some of these copies would have been proof-read by a διορθωτής. If so, most errors, intentional or not, would have been corrected.

A fourth and final point is consistent with the three previous points: We are now in possession of some 139 Greek New Testament papyri, several of which date to the late second century and first half of the third century, and there are no textual surprises. Surely, if what Koester claims is true, we should expect the papyri to exhibit a few surprises, to give some indication of significant textual corruption that crept into the text in its first hundred years of transmission. But they do not. And that is Wisse's point: the text of the New Testament is stable. There simply is no evidence in our oldest extant fragments of "serious corruptions." Indeed, Eldon Jay Epp, veteran textual critic and former student of Koester, has remarked that "the textual variants of the Oxyrhynchus New Testament papyri, relatively speaking, are unremarkable and unlikely to foment

---

177. A. Mugridge, *Copying Early Christian Texts: A Study of Scribal Practice*, WUNT 362 (Tübingen: Mohr Siebeck, 2016).

revolutionary changes in our critical text."[178] In reference to all of the New Testament papyri, Epp adds, with some understatement, that they "are not conspicuous for furnishing a mass of new, meaningful variant readings."[179] No, indeed not.

In view of the evidence, Wisse concludes his essay by affirming that

> the claim of extensive ideological redaction of the Gospels and other early Christian literature runs counter to all of the textual evidence. This lack of evidence cannot be explained away by speculations about an extensively interpolated "standard" text which was imposed by the orthodox leadership late in the second century, and the successful suppression of all non-interpolated copies. The Church certainly lacked the means and apparently also the will to do this... If indeed the text of the Gospels had been subjected to extensive redactional change and adaptation during the second century, the unanimous attestation of a relatively stable and uniform text during the following centuries in both Greek and the versions would have to be considered nothing short of a miracle.[180]

I heartily concur with Wisse; other textual critics do also.[181] Of course, there is no need to appeal to miracles. The text of the New Testament did not suffer "extensive redactional change and adaptation during the second century." Rather, the text of the New Testament writings remained stable because the writings were respected and, as I have argued in this paper, the respected, even venerated autographs and first copies in all probability remained in circulation as long as did other highly valued autographs and copies of literature in this period of time. Autographs and first copies were

---

178. E. J. Epp, "New Testament Papyri and the Transmission of the New Testament," in Bowman, et al. (eds.), *Oxyrhynchus: A City and Its Texts*, 315–31, with quotation from 319.

179. E. J. Epp, "Are Early New Testament Manuscripts Truly Abundant?" in *Israel's God and Rebecca's Children: Christology and Community in Early Judaism and Christianity. Essays in Honor of Larry W. Hurtado and Alan F. Segal*, ed. D. B. Capes, et al. (Waco, TX: Baylor University Press, 2007), 77–107, with quotation from 106.

180. Wisse, "The Nature and Purpose of Redactional Changes in Early Christian Texts," 52–3. It is important to recall that Wisse has worked with the various recensions of the *Apocryphon of John*. He is well acquainted with a text that exhibits extensive interpolations and corruptions.

181. L. W. Hurtado, "The New Testament in the Second Century: Text, Collections and Canon," in *Transmission and Reception: New Testament Text-Critical and Exegetical Studies*, ed. J. W. Childers and D. C. Parker (Piscataway, NJ: Gorgias Press, 2006), 3–27.

not only highly treasured, they could be consulted, even as non-Christian scribes and authors consulted the autographs and old copies that they valued.[182]

I have argued for the longevity of the New Testament autographs and first copies for several reasons. First, two Church Fathers, Tertullian and Bishop Peter of Alexandria, explicitly speak of autographs in existence in their respective times. Other Fathers, such as Theophilus and Gaius, argue against new texts and altered texts on the basis of the apparent existence of old, if not autographic texts. Second, late antique non-Christian writers speak of the existence of very old copies of literature, including autographs. Their testimony, along with the testimony of Christian Fathers, strongly supports the possibility that books in late antiquity could and did last for two hundred years or more and were seen as valuable for study, copying, and textual criticism. Great longevity should not surprise, for books in late antiquity were greatly valued.

Third, the recovery of four libraries from Egypt, where chronological data were acquired through paleography and stratigraphy, provides physical evidence of the great longevity of literary manuscripts. The longevity of the books from these libraries ranges from just under one century to three centuries. The recovery of a fifth library, the one from the Villa of the Papyri in Herculaneum, provides evidence that longevity of two hundred and even in some cases three hundred years was possible in the Mediterranean world outside of arid Egypt and the region of the Judean wilderness. This physical evidence lends important support, if not confirmation, to the veracity of the Christian and non-Christian testimony that has been reviewed.

Fourth, I have suggested that New Testament autographs and first copies that enjoyed great longevity were probably deliberately destroyed by Roman authorities, especially in the Great Persecution under Emperor Diocletian at the beginning of the fourth century, a persecution that specifically targeted Christian literature and churches, where Christian literature would have been kept in storage, especially precious artifacts such as autographs and very old copies. It is of course possible that some New Testament autographs and first copies were destroyed in the late second century and in the middle of the third century, again during

---

182. Long ago Kenyon spoke of the evangelist Luke "having prepared two originals, one for Theophilus and one for the public." The latter would serve as "the archetype from which the transcripts for general circulation would be made." Kenyon, *Handbook to the Textual Criticism of the New Testament*, 33. This would most likely apply to all of the New Testament writings.

times of persecution. Indeed, it is possible that some old copies of New Testament writings were destroyed in the brief period of persecution during the reign of Julian the Apostate.

And finally, I have argued that the longevity of New Testament autographs and first copies may help explain in part the evident stability of the text of the New Testament, a stability that was not brought about by ecclesiastical controls, for no such controls existed. It is admitted that autographs and ancient copies were not necessary for the transmission of a stable text, but longevity would facilitate such transmission. If autographs and early copies did enjoy longevity of a century or more, as the evidence seems to suggest, then it is very likely that these old books would have been copied and studied for as long as they were available, thus adding stability to the text.

3

GREEK WRIT PLAIN:
VILLAGE SCRIBES, Q, AND THE PALAEOGRAPHY
OF THE EARLIEST CHRISTIAN PAPYRI

Gregg Schwendner

Who compiled, composed, and copied the source material (Q) of the Synoptic Gospels? Kloppenborg's theory that village scribes living in northern Galilee could have done so has been supported by recent work by Bazzana, who draws on comparative evidence from Ptolemaic and Roman Egypt.[1] This article, in three parts, is a papyrological perspective on the question raised by their work.[2] The first part concerns what we know about the educational levels in villages in Egypt, especially in the Fayum, and the role played by sub-literary texts. In the second part of the study I will briefly treat the evidence of copying the *Acta Alexandrinorum*; and in the third part I will consider informal or plain writing. I conclude with a palaeographical question: Why were so many early Christian texts written in a plain, non-cursive documentary script, rather than in book scripts? There follows a palaeographical appendix examining the similarities between the plain documentary style of writing and how early Christian papyri were written.

1. *Village Education*

In Roman Egypt, three sites in the Fayum can be cited to illustrate the scope of village literacy: Soknopaiou Nesos and Tebtynis, temple-centered communities, and Karanis, a large agricultural village (although still designated a κώμη).

---

1. John S. Kloppenborg, *The Formation of Q: Trajectories in Ancient Wisdom Collections* (Harrisburg: Trinity Press International, 1987), and Giovanni Bazzana, *Kingdom of Bureaucracy: The Political Theology of Village Scribes in the Sayings of Gospel Q*, BETL (Leuven: Peeters). I owe thanks to Lincoln Blumell for asking me to speak at the SBL panel on this question in San Antonio in 2016, and to Brent Nongbri for careful reading of an early difficult draft.

2. All abbreviations for papyrological editions are according to the Online Checke list of Editions of Greek, Latin, Demotic and Coptic Papyri, Ostraca and Tablets.

Soknopaiou Nesos is a small village (16.75 ha.)[3] on the northern edge of the Fayum depression, whose residents were almost entirely Egyptian priests and their families. The population is estimated at 1,100, until the Antonine plague in 179 CE.[4] It was founded in the third century BCE, was abandoned at some point in the mid-third century CE, and reoccupied in the fifth century.[5] It may be considered roughly equivalent to the site of Capernaum, for all its difficulties.[6]

In the Ptolemaic period Egyptian texts (Demotic, Hieratic) far outnumber Greek (70 percent), but in the first century this ratio is reversed (75 percent Greek); in the second century 94 percent of texts are in Greek.[7] Soknopaiou Nesos was administered by the usual village officials: *komogrammateus*, *praktor argurikon*, and *nomographos*, and there was, consequently, a *grapheion*.[8]

Many of the Greek literary texts found there from the Roman period are the type we associate with a basic education: Sententiae (LDAB 2446, 2448), Math (LDAB 1273, 5144, 5346, 4953, 4930, 4929) and Geometry problems (4397), Plato's *Apology* (LDAB 3756), and Homer (LDAB 1427, 1467, 2315). Some texts indicate readers with a level of rhetorical training: an anonymous persuasive speech (LDAB 4401), and possibly

---

3. Paola Davoli, Ivan Chiesi, Simone Occhi and Nicola Raimondi, "Soknopaiou Nesos Project: The Resumption of the Archaeological Investigation: The Settlement and its Territory," in *Proceedings of the Twenty-Fifth International Congress of Papyrology*, ed. Traianos Gagos, American Studies in Papyrology (Ann Arbor: University of Michigan, 2010), 149–64.

4. Willy Clarysse, "Soknopaiou Nesos," in *A Gazateer of the Fayum Area*, part of the K.U.Leuven Fayum project @ Trismegistos.org: "According to the poll-tax register SB XVI 12816 there were 244 adult males in the village in September 178, but this number was reduced to 169 by August 179, perhaps due to the great plague."

5. Following Peter van Minnen's assessment in "Bookish or Boorish? Literature in Egyptian Villages in the Fayum in the Greco-Roman Period," *JJP* 28 (1998): 151–2.

6. No more than 17 ha., more likely between 6-10 ha.: Jonathan L. Reed, *Archaeology and the Galilean Jesus: A Re-examination of the Evidence* (Harrisburg, PA: Trinity Press International, 2002), 83 and 152 respectively; see also John Dominic Crossan, *The Birth of Christianity* (Edinburgh: T. & T. Clark, 1999), 220, for a breakdown of the problem.

7. A list of texts is available at: https://www.evernote.com/l/ADvttFg6NURMNou3LOsQXAx9LDR1azkB-6k. This follows the pattern observed by Brian Muhs, "The Grapheion and the Disappearance of Demotic Contracts in Early Roman Tebtynis and Soknopaiou Nesos" in *Tebtynis und Soknopaiu Nesos: Leben in Römerzeitlichen Fajum*, ed. Sandra Lippert and Maren Schentuleit (Wiesbaden: Harrassowitz Verlag, 2005), 93–104.

8. I list of officials can be found at https://www.evernote.com/l/ADtx7QYhYCZBRK8wBRU9bJ7RAqx4u9UNYME.

two orators: Demosthenes (LDAB 607, 627), and Isocrates (LDAB 2472), although their provenance is uncertain.⁹

Throughout the first century CE, documents here were written mostly in Greek and Demotic: of 101 documents with Demotic writing, 55 are bilingual (Demotic contracts required a precis in Greek), 46 are Demotic only; 169 are written in Greek only, of which 12 are translations of Demotic documents.¹⁰

When documents were written, or signed on behalf of, declarants who claimed themselves unlettered or literate only in Egyptian, 17 are Greeks, and 37 are Egyptians.¹¹ Village officials more often bear Egyptian names than Greek (4 of 16 village scribes, 2 of 4 nomographoi).

In Soknopaiou Nesos, there had been a long period of Greek rule (300 years) under the Ptolemies for Egyptians to come to terms with bilingual administration, so evidence of literacy, probably bilingual, given that we are dealing with a priestly village, is not a surprise. The proportion of Demotic to Greek texts in the second century CE is the opposite from the early Roman period: 26 documents are in Greek, 9 of which are bilingual; 111 are Demotic only.¹² This village is an important comparison with the situation in Galilee because the majority of writers in Soknopaiou Nesos were Egyptians, not Greek colonials, or Roman officials.

As a control, the site of **Tebtynis**¹³ in the southern part of the Fayum depression shows a pattern of literary finds similar to Soknopaiou Nesos. Here we see Roman-period finds of literary papyri, including works by Homer (*Iliad* 30; *Od.* 2)¹⁴ and Hesiod,¹⁵ along with Herodotus,¹⁶

---

9. See Mario Capasso, "Libri, Autori, e Pubblico a Soknopaiou Nesos," in Lippert and Schentuleit (eds.), *Tebtynis und Soknopaiu Nesos*, 1–17. Special care needs to be taken for literary texts from Soknopaiou Nesos, since in some collections (especially the Aberdeen papyri and in the Nationalbiblotek, Wien) the attribution is often ambiguous or unreliable.

10. https://www.evernote.com/shard/s59/nl/1685401911/17b9f68b-a8f4-4071-be3d-2073ade0a843/

11. Search on PN s.v. κωμογραμματ, (and s.v. πρακτ) Provenance: Soknopaiou Nesos, Date 27 BCE–250 CE.

12. https://www.evernote.com/l/ADvttFg6NURMNou3LOsQXAx9LDR1azkB-6k.

13. Larger than Soknopaiou Nesos (57 ha., population 4,000–5,000—A. Bowman, "Ptolemaic and Roman Egypt: Population and Settlement," in A. Bowman and A. Wilson, *Settlement, Urbanization, and Population*, OSAE [Oxford: Oxford University Press, 2012], 337), but less important religiously (50 priests).

14. Search LDAB: Author: Homerus, book *Ilias*, Date 1 and 201, provenance Tebtynis, and Author: Homerus, book *Odyssea*, Date 1 and 201, provenance Tebtynis

15. LDAB 1220 (TM 60106).

16. LDAB 1162 (TM 60048)

Xenophon,[17] Demosthenes,[18] and Menander,[19] and another document written on the back of a Demotic text.[20] There are a number of school texts, and a narrative summary of the works of Callimachus.[21] Medical (9)[22] and astronomical (4)[23] texts normally associated with Egyptian priests also were found.

Karanis,[24] the largest of these three villages (about the size of Tiberias or Sepphoris),[25] shows a similar pattern, with the difference that there are no (published) Demotic finds from the site,[26] although there is one Hieratic fr. (unedited)[27] and a third-century Coptic version of Job.[28] Latin is a little more prevalent, due to the number of Roman veterans who retired there.[29]

17. LDAB 4188 (TM 62996) Symposium, LDAB 4192 (TM 63000) Oeconomicus.

18. LDAB 637 (TM 59535), LDAB 656 (TM 59554) both de falsa Legatione, LDAB 4774 (TM 63565) sententiae.

19. LDAB 2644 (TM 61497), LDAB 2655 (TM 61508) sententiae copied as a school exercise.

20. LDAB 2627, P. Lund 1 4 R°, on the back of which is an unedited Demotic text, TM 142489.

21. LDAB 470 (TM 59371) Diegesis.

22. Search LDAB: Book: medical; Language/Script: Greek; Provenance Tebtynis.

23. Search LDAB: Book: astronomical, Language/Script: Greek; Provenance Tebtynis.

24. 60 ha., population: 3,600, Bowman, "Ptolemaic and Roman Egypt," 337.

25. Karanis was local, rather than a regional administrative center which Sepphoris and Tiberias both were in their turn. The archives (Hebrew ʿarkhei ha-yeshanah; ἀρχεῖα in Josephus) for Galilee were moved from Sepphoris to Tiberias sometime during the reign of Tiberias, 14–37 CE and were then moved back to Sepphoris c. 67 CE, or, at minimum, were no longer kept in Tiberias. These archives can be assumed to contain records of debt; cf. Josephus, *War* 2.427, where the contracts of the lenders and collectors (τὰ συμβόλαια τῶν δεδανεικότων καὶ τὰς εἰσπράξεις) in the archives (τὰ ἀρχεῖα) in Jerusalem were burned at the beginning of the revolt and marriages (Stuart S. Miller, *Studies in the History and Traditions of Sepphoris* [Leiden: Brill, 1984], 53–6). Similar Jewish archives were kept in Alexandria: BGU 4.1151, verso ↓ = C.Pap.Jud. 2.143 (P.Berol. inv. 13049) verso: καθ' ἣν ἔθετο διαθήκ(ην) διὰ τοῦ τῶν Ἰουδαίων |⁸ ἀρχείου.

26. There are a number of unpublished Demotic ostraca from the excavation.

27. "Hieratic Fragments from Karanis: An Egyptian Religious Handbook among the Greek Papyri" presented in the American Society of Papyrologists panel, American Philological Association Annual Meeting, New York, 29 December 1996.

28. *Pap.Castr.* 7.2 (LDAB=TM 107779).

29. R. Alston, *Soldier and Society in Roman Egypt: A Social History* (London-New York: Routledge, 1995), 117–42. There are 18 published Latin texts, two of which are literary / school texts (TM 63274, 63851): search TM Language/Script: Latin; Provenance Karanis, date between 1 and 250.

Greek literary texts found or excavated at the site include, inter alia, Homer Iliad (15), Odyssey (2), Hesiod (2),[30] Hypotheses of Euripides,[31] Menander, Epitrepontes,[32] Demosthenes,[33] Isocrates,[34] and Callimachus.[35]

Somewhat out of the ordinary, a fragment of a novel was found there,[36] a tragedy with musical notation,[37] and a very early copy of the Homeric lexicon of Apollonius Sophista.[38] The part of the site that has garnered most interest is structure B17 (Fig. 1).

Figure 1. B17, Karanis

The problem is that papyri that were found in houses did not fare well. What survives are mostly tattered, tiny pieces, unless they had been deliberately stored in a cupboard or a pot.[39] Papyri survive best in dumps at Karanis, where they seem to have remained untouched. A favorite

30. LDAB 1169 (TM 60055), LDAB 1178 (TM 60054).
31. Prose summaries: LDAB 10028 (TM 68753).
32. LDAB 2643 (TM 61496).
33. Olynthiacs: LDAB 653 (TM 59551), In Aristocratm: LDAB 655 (TM 69553).
34. LDAB 6596 (TM 61362).
35. LDAB 477 (TM 59378), LDAB 10733 (TM 98079), TM=LDAB 14439.
36. LDAB 542, TM 59443.
37. LDAB 4761, TM63552.
38. LDAB 295 (TM 59200).
39. See W. Graham Claytor, "The Threshold Papyri of Karanis," https://www.trismegistos.org/archive/25; papyri found in jars, e.g. the Archive of Milon Praktor https://www.trismegistos.org/archive/141.

location for a neighborhood dump was an abandoned house. With the owner dead, or absconded, the doors and roof beams being wooden and therefore valuable, were taken, and the remaining roofless shell was used as a dump. Sometimes, as the street levels rose, new houses would be built on top of the old, sealing the site, but just as often the location remained abandoned. When a house changed hands, the belongings of the previous residents were deemed worthless, and old books, papers, broken furniture or toys were cleared out. In B17, none of the texts were found stored, but as part of the fill.[40] Identified by Gagos and van Minnen[41] as the house of a village official responsible for collecting taxes owed in money, Sokrates, son of Sarapion, it goes beyond the evidence to say that B17 was Sokrates' home. So much material was found in B17, which must have been looted before Michigan excavated it in 1927, and so many well-preserved papyri, it is possible B17 should be considered the dump site where Sokrates' papers ended up.

The non-documentary texts found in B17 are interesting: a play of Menander,[42] a grammatical treatise on the use of the definite article,[43] and a text that appears to be in the same genre as the *Acta Alexandrinorum*.[44]

---

40. The location of what would become B17 in the Michigan excavation seems to have been looted, since papyri that likely belong among Socrates' papers came into the hands of two private collectors in Berlin: Rudolf Mosse (d. 1920), and the Egyptologist Heinrich Karl Brugsch (d. 1894), both collections now in the Neues Museum, Berlin. Looted papyri from B17 are in Goodspeed Manuscript Collection at the University of Chicago, Aberdeen University, the Cairo Egyptian Museum, and the University of Michigan, including two of the three Karanis Tax Rolls that were purchased before excavation a began.

41. <Traianos Gagos>, Peter van Minnen, "House-to-House Enquiries: An Interdisciplinary Approach to Roman Karanis," *ZPE* 100 100 (2994): 227–51. Due to a mistake, Gagos' name was omitted from this paper, but I can bear witness to the fact that the research it reports was a truly collaborative effort. It is regrettable, therefore, that Traianos' name is not as closely connected with Karanis research as it should be.

42. LDAB 2643 (TM 61496).

43. LDAB 4674 (TM 63555).

44. LDAB 19 (TM 58920). Natalia Vega Navarrete includes this text in the latest edition of the Acta: Pap.Colon. XL 4.2.2. following Chris Rodriguez's discussion of the P.Mich.inv. 4800 in "Le P.Mich.inv.4800: un témoignage du conflit de 38–41?" *JJP* 39 (2009): 161–97. P.Mich.inv. 4800 falls into the same pattern often found in copies of the literary Acta Alex.: it is written on the verso ↓ where the recto → is a document, and the papyrus is found in an official context.

2. Copying of the Acta Alexandrinorum

The Egyptian *Acta Alexandrinorum*, or more precisely, the literary genre of Acta,[45] is analogous to Q in that it is an anonymous, quasi-historical, anti-establishment text. It was written with several features of documentary copying not found in book production: abbreviations and display script (or enlarged letters). Copies have been found in both Karanis and Soknopaiou Nesos.

The documentary transcripts, or summaries, of judicial proceedings which the literary Acta imitate follow a simple format: there is an introductory section, giving the date of the proceedings and the source of the document, followed by questions by one rhetor, answered by the rhetor for the defense. That is, narration is minimal; the Acta are comprised for the most part of speeches and dialogue. "Q," by contrast, gives no dates at all, and does not mention the source of its material. Q would not have resembled a quasi-historical document in the same sense as the Acta do, but would have looked more like collections of *Chreiae*, and example of which is given in Figure 2.[46]

> Ἀριστίππος ὁ Κυρη[ναῖ]ος ὁ φι[λόσοφος, ἐρωτηθεὶς διά τί
> Τιμόθεος ὁ αὐλή[τη]ς παρὰ μ[ὲν τοῖς αὐληταῖς
> μει, παρὰ δὲ τοῖς ἄ[λλ]οῖς οὐ πάνυ ἔφη ὅτι .... μά-]
> γειρον οὐ τοῖς μαγ[εί]ροις ἀλ[λὰ τοῖς ἄλλοις
> -κεῖν.[47]

> Aristippos the Cyre[nai]an phil[losopher, having been asked why
> Timotheos the flute player among flute players
> but among others, not at all, he said
> a cook not to other cooks, bu[t....[48]

Notice how the formatting of this chreia, if applied to a document like Q, would have facilitated the act of reading, selecting, and copying particular sayings.[49]

---

45. For the difficulties of distinguishing Acta (the written record of trial proceedeings) as a literary genre from copies/versions of the specific work we call "Acta Alexandrinorum," see Natalia Vega Navarrete, *Die Acta Alexandrinorum im Lichte Neuerer und Neuester Papyrusfunde* (Paderborn: Ferdinand Schöningh, 2017), 9–15.

46. This follows the point made by John S. Kloppenborg, *Excavating Q: The History and Setting of the Sayings Gospel* (Minneapolis: Fortress Press, 2000), 160–3.

47. LDAB 341 (TM 59245). The illustration is of P.Mich. inv. 25.

48. Translation from Ronald F Hock and Edward N. O'Neil (trans. and ed.), *The Chreia and Ancient Rhetoric: Classroom Exercises*, Vol. 2 (Leiden: Brill, 2002), 18.

49. This from a remark by Prof. Kloppenborg in the discussion of this paper. Other chreiae in the same format: PSI 1.85, verso ↓; BGU 9.162 (sententiae or chreiae?).

Figure 2. *Chreia*

The level of rhetorical skill necessary to produce the speeches we read in the Acta, even more so those delivered in actual court cases, must be considered relatively high: although, at times, the dialogue in the literary Acta seem more suitable to a mime performance than a court proceeding. Q, on the other hand, is much less rhetorical, and might have required a writer who had studied the Progymnasmata, but was otherwise without rhetorical schooling.

A second important form, the narrative (*diegesis, narratio*), is common to both stages of education. Narrative summaries abstracted from longer, usually poetic material are found in villages (hypotheses of Euripides and Homer for example, were used as beginning reading material, to judge from Quintilian)

We see both forms applied when scribes were called upon to draw up a petition. They were highly formulaic in nature, although not really what we would call boilerplate.

1. address 2. statement of wrong 3. narrative 4. appeal.

Of these, the narrative section was the least formulaic.

The *Acta* bear evidence of both forms (given the number of texts written on the back of documents).[50] Something else that adds to the

---

50. A partial list: Pap.Colon. XL 3.3.2 (C.Pap.Jud. 2.156c, P.Berol. inv.8877, verso ↓; LDAB 33. TM 58938) recto → doc.ined.; Pap.Colon. XL 4.1.1 (P.Oxy. 20.2264, verso ↓; LDAB 25. TM 95830); recto → a 2nd c. land register, ined.; Pap.Colon. XL

impression that these texts were written by, and in some respects for, a readership familiar with secretarial conventions of the time is their use of display script, normally eschewed in book production (Fig. 3).⁵¹

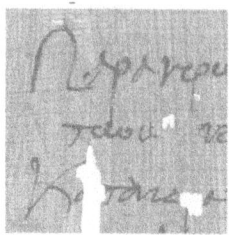 

Figure 3. *Display script/style: large letters, sometimes in a distinct script*

Comparable use of display script is found in Jewish texts in Greek, e.g. the Greek Minor Prophets Scroll (8HevXIIgr, Figs. 4 and 5) found in the Cave of Horrors near the Dead Sea. One puzzling feature of this manuscript is the use of display script at the beginning of a line and after a pause, a feature encountered again in P.Oxy. 65.4443, LXX Esther (first–second century CE: below, Fig. 6).⁵²

3.4 (P.Harr. 2.240; LDAB 45, TM 58950) verso ↓; recto → account ined; Pap.Colon. XL 3.3.1.1 (BGU 2.511, inv. 7118; LDAB 30, TM 58935) verso ↓; recto → accounts (*Rechnungen, ined.*) with a marginal note in a second hand referencing the reign of Marcus Aur. and Verus (161–169 CE); Pap.Colon. XL 3.5 (P.Oxy. 10.1242, verso ↓; LDAB 36, TM 58941); recto → doc. (described), reign of Antoninus Pius; Pap.Colon. XL 2.3 (P.Oxy. 42.3021, verso ↓; LDAB 8632, TM 67315) recto → doc.ined.

51. An exception to this rule is the occasional use of display script in initial titles and end-titles, where they are in the same hand as the text (GMAW², 13–14): P. Lond.Lit. 30, Francesa Schironi, ΤΟ ΜΕΓΑ ΒΙΒΛΙΟΝ: *Book-Ends, End-Titles, and Cornonides in Papyri with Hexametric Poetry*, American Studies in Papyrology XLVIII (Durham, NC: American Society of Papyrologists, 2010), cat.no. 17, p. 119 (ΟΔΥΣΣΕΙΑC [Γ], 1st c., LDAB 1382, TM 60262); P. Lond.Lit. 11, Schironi cat.no 14, p.113 (ΙΛΙΑΔΟC Δ, 1st c.; LDAB 1957, TM 60829);

Schironi cat.no. 13 (ΙΛΙΑΔΟC B, 1st c.; LDAB 1380, TM 60260); P.Lond.Lit. 27, Schironi cat.no. 12 (ΙΛΙΑΔΟC Δ, First Century; LDAB 2283, TM 6144); P.Lond.lit. 132, the Arden papyrus (LDAB 2423, TM 61281) see in Wm. Johnson, *Bookrolls and Scribes of Oxyrhynchus* (Toronto: University of Toronto Press, 2004), pll. 16-17.

52. Peter Parsons analysis of the use of Capital (what I am calling "display") letters in the Minor Prophets roll concludes that it "may suggest that the Christians inherited the practice, rather than inventing it; the problem remains, why Greek-speaking Jews should have adopted it in the first place," in Emanuel Tov (ed.), *The*

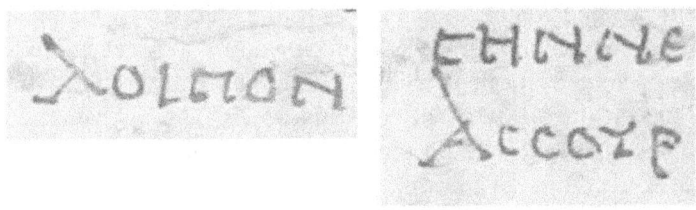

Figures 4 and 5.

Figure 6.

Abbreviations for the titles of government officials, e.g., υ),[53] γυ[μ],[54] αρχι[δ],[55] are another documentary convention used in copies of the Acta but not usually in books. The speaker's name in the Acta is never abbreviated, as far as I can see, but their inclusion at all is anomalous, change of speakers in prose conventionally being signalled by a paragraphos and a dicolon.[56]

Greek Minor Prophets Scroll from Nahal Hever (8HevXIIgr), Discoveries in the Judean Desert 8 (Oxford: Oxford University Press, 1990), 24.

53. ὑ(πέρ) is extremely common in documents (1–100 CE, PN search s.v. #υ)°, 72 ×. The scribe of P.Oxy. 3.471 uses the documentary form of this abbreviation, υ), rather than one of those conventional in literary or sub-literary texts: υ', υπ, ὑ, ὐ, υ[π]. See Kathleen McNamee, *Abbreviations in Greek Literary Papyri and Ostraca*, BASP Supplement 3 (Chico, CA: Scholars Press, 1981), svv., 101–2.

54. Examples from documents: P.Mil.Vogl. 6.264 (Tebtynis, 127 CE), SB 16.12520.19, 25 (Theadelphia, 141–142 CE), P.Theon 27.2 and 29.37 (both from Oxyrhynchus, 161 CE); P.Oxy. 62.4336 (169–73 CE).

55. Found in 31 texts dating from the second century CE, both for the noun γυμ(νασίαρχος), and the participial form γυμ(νησιαρῆσας)· PN search sv. γυμν°.

56. Eric G. Turner and P. J. Parsons, *Greek Manuscripts of the Ancient World*, rev. edn, BICS Supplement 46 (London: Institute of Classical Studies, 1987), 13: "The speakers of tragic and comic verses are marked in desultory fashion by writing their name in shortened form or as a monogram." Speakers' names in the Acta genre are

A change of speaker is indicated in trial proceedings by the formula subject + verb, e.g.: "the rhetor said" followed by a direct quote.[57]

The use of abbreviations is also a distinctive feature of Christian texts, although the origin of the practice is unknown. The abbreviation of the name Jesus as a speaker would make sense as a labor-saving device, and was done in accounts of various kinds. This of course cannot account the distinctive Christian style of abbreviation, i.e. maintaining the final letter of the word. The only similar style in Greek is found in marginal comments on a papyrus of Plato's *Republic*, which incorporate both stenographic signs and seemingly extemporaneous abbreviations, such as θ^c for θ(εό)ς.[58]

3. *Plain Writing*

The earliest Christian texts are not written in formal book hands popular in the first-second centuries, but in informal hands, rather styleless and plain. The similarity between these informal hands and the plain writing sometimes encountered in Greek documentary texts is evident in the term "reformed documentary" used by C. H. Roberts.[59] The best terminology is by Cavallo, who considered the script to be a forerunner of Alexandrian Majuscule, based on the visual similarities of particular graphic features.[60]

---

sometimes written on a new line, the speech beginning on the following line: Pap. Colon. XL 3.3.1.1 (BGU 2.511, inv. 7118; LDAB 30, TM 58935), col. I 2, 6, col. II 11, 14; Herbert Musurillo, *Acta Alexandrinorum 1: Acta Alexandrinorum* (Leipzig: Teubner, 1961), no. 1, col. II 21 (PSI 10.1160, the "Boule Papyrus," not included in Pap.Colon XL. LDAB 13, TM 58918). The phrase "Καῖσαρ εἶπεν is only found in *Acta Alex.* and in historians: Appian 3.12.14, Plutarch, *Caes.* 62.5, Cassius Dio 50.31; Appian 5.3.29: εἶπεν ὁ Καῖσαρ, item Plutarch, *Moral.* 794 10; Τιβέριος ὁ Καῖσαρ ἔλεγε, Appian 5.9.77.

57. ρητ = ῥήτ(ωρ) ὑπὲρ Πασίωνος εἶπ(εν) BGU 3.969.8 (P.Berol. inv. 6982, 139 CE); ρ = ῥ(ήτωρ) seems not to occur before 200 CE: P.Oxy. 41.2955.3, 5, 7 (218 CE), cf. P.Oxy. 63.3117 (235 CE), etc. see PN search: ρ°τωρ.

58. P. Oxy. 15.1808, written in a third-century hand; see Kathleen McNamee, *Annotations in Geek and Latin Texts from Egypt*, American Studies in Papyrology 45 (Oxford: Oxbow Books, 2007), 353 (LDAB 3780, TM 62595).

59. Colin H. Roberts, *Manuscript, Society and Belief in Early Christian Egypt* (Oxford: Oxford University Press, 1977), 14.

60. In brief, see Guglielmo Cavallo, "Greek and Latin Writing in the Papyri," in *The Oxford Handbook of Papyrology*, ed. Roger Bagnall (Oxford: Oxford University Press, 2009), 129–31, and Pasquale Orsini and Willy Clarysse, "Early New Testament Manuscripts and Their Dates: A Critique of Theological Palaeography," *ETL* 88, no. 4 (2012): 452–3. The terminology remains a problem: Alexandrian Stylistic Class

Documentary examples, such as private letters, petitions, and court documents, may have been written plainly because, to reach a broader audience, there was a greater need for clarity. This was attained by writing most letters in the form that would have been familiar to someone of limited education, and spacing them far enough apart. Plain writing was useful if the intended reader had only a basic education, but could also be a necessity if the writer was unable to write very fluidly.

Why not write in cursive?[61] The majority of Greek documents from the first–second centuries are written cursively. Cursive allows the writer to limit the number of pen-lifts by altering or abbreviating letter shapes, and to string groups of letters together either by a direct ligatures or by using entrance and exit strokes between letters.

Replacing familiar letter forms with unfamiliar allographs was bound to confuse the inexpert reader. Sometimes cursive writing devolved into a *Verschleifung* pattern, where graphic features are assimilated to one another, often leaving their meaning ambiguous. Entrance and exit strokes between letters tend to mask the vertices by which the letter forms are recognized: so, in Figure 7, the stroke that attaches pi and the next letter renders it ambiguous: it could be γ, ε, ν, π, or τ.

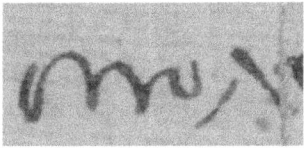

Figure 7. πτολ-

Figure 8. γεν

is still in use, but is either avoided or qualified by other palaeographers, including Cavallo himself. A less opaque term would be something like "proto-Alexandrian Maj."

61. The term cursive is used in connection with Greek writing on papyri to mean everything from handwriting in which adjacent letters touch, although the stroke sequence between them is discontinuous (i.e. the scribe lifts his pen between the first and second letters)—a pseudo-ligature in Cavallo's terminology, to two or three letters made in one sequence (Turner and Parsons, *Greek Manuscripts of the Ancient World*, 1), to writing in which is fully joined up, with breaks between words.

The same is true of the way graphic features of letters are abbreviated or altered. In Figure 9, the (interior) angle of the vertex where the vertical and horizontal strokes of gamma join, which is typically 90° from vertical, is pitched downward at something close to 40°.

Figure 9. γεν

Epsilon is abbreviated by omitting the top stroke (the top half of the curve), and altering the interior vertex, the angle where stokes 1 and 3 meet, from 90° from vertical to closer to 40°, as with gamma. The final letter of the sequence, nu, is again abbreviated, making it resemble <n> more closely than <N>. The result is a script that is easier to write than read, a conclusion supported by current neurological research into how the brain recognizes objects.[62]

By way of analogy, in mid-seventeenth-century England, there was a demand for texts to be copied in Italic, rather than the traditional Secretary script, because Italic was easier to read. Italic contained, for example, far fewer allographs and abbreviations.

> The greater legibility of italic made it suitable for readers whose limited literacy might not have extended to decoding the more complex secretary, which up to the 1620s remained the preferred everyday hand of the highly educated functionaries who performed the actual work of the government.[63]

By the end of the second century, a chancery (i.e. bureaucratic) script begins to replace plain writing, just as the rounded book hands of the second century are replaced by the more angular Biblical Majuscule and the *Severe* (in the sense of undecorated, austere) *Style*. We do know why this shift in taste occurred, but two major events provide the background for the discontinuity. The Antonine plague caused high death rates in

---

62. This is known as the Biederman effect; see Stanislas Dehaene, *Reading in the Brain: The New Science of How We Read* (New York: Penguin Press, 2010), 139.

63. Harold Love, *The Culture and Commerce of Texts: Scribal Publication in Seventeenth-Century England* (Amherst: University of Massachusetts Press, 1993), 108.

Egypt,[64] which would have relaxed the grip of tradition by reducing the number of competent scribes trained in the old way. Second, there was a change with the ascendancy of the Severans in 193, notable especially because Septimius Severus' reign seems to have seen the introduction of a new bureaucratic script, which displaces plain writing during the course of the third century.

If one surveys the literary papyri in Greek[65] from the first three centuries CE, they fall into several broad categories: (1) books that were formally produced which usually contained classical literature, or commentary on it. These would have been written by scribes concerned with formatting and trained to write calligraphic scripts. (2) Books written in a quicker, less formal way, as one would write a letter, especially, but not exclusively[66] non-classical literature and personal copies of classical texts. (3) The sort of cursive, professional writing one sees in Roman-period documents; however, this is rarely if ever encountered in literary texts.

By genre, the most predictably formal texts are classical literature, especially the poets who make up the bulk of grammar school reading; prose texts, philosophy, history, which are often written less formally; post-classical literature, which was written with the least formality, for example novels, mimes (with exceptions), quasi-historical works like the Alexander Romance and the Acta Alexandrinorum, and genres specific to grammatical education, especially sententiae and glossaries.

So, according to this typology, early Christian texts were informally produced primarily because they were post-classical, and not read in schools. But there is a secondary point to be made here that is perhaps relevant to our question. Sometimes it can be surmised that the appearance of the text was designed to reflect the content, viz., quasi-historical genres had a documentary appearance that was claimed for the content.

---

64. Estimates as high as 20% for 166, in W. Rathbone's estimate: D. W. Rathbone, "Villages, Land and Population in Graeco-Roman Egypt," *Proceedings of the Cambridge Philological Society* 36 (1990): 114–19. There is a good summary of recent scholarship by Christer Bruun, "The Antonine Plague and the 'Third Century Crisis,'" in *Crises and the Roman Empire: Proceedings of the Seventh Workshop of the International Network Impact of Empire*, ed. Olivier Hekster, Gerda de Kleijn, and Daniëlle Slootjes (Leiden-Boston: Brill, 2007), 201–18.

65. I carried out such a survey for this paper, using a sample of about 750 texts from the most easily accessible collections, namely those in Berlin, Vienna, and Michigan, as well as Oxyrhynchus texts still in the Sackler library in Oxford.

66. See below concerning the Oxyrhynchus scribe #A3, copyist of an elegant roll of Aeschylus.

The Alexander Romance has a large epistolary component, sometimes preserved in the formatting by the scribe. In PSI XII 1285 v, the valedictory greeting, ἔρρωσο is isolated on a single line, as it would be in an actual letter (Fig. 10):

Figure 10.

The literary Acta also has a dramatic setting in court, well-suited to a documentary script-type, imitative of genuine court proceedings.

What, if anything, does this imply for early Christian books? It would seem that for some reason, readers expected Christian books to be written in a quasi-documentary style. There may be several reasons for this. Q preserves the *logia*, or sayings of Jesus, with a minimum of narration, a structure very similar to the Acta. So perhaps one could explain the use of a quasi-documentary script as suitable for this aspect of the subject matter: to make it appear what it purports to be, namely the sayings of Jesus.

A second possibility, touching on theory of "village scribes" or the like, is that if the original version of Q were written in a bureaucratic style, subsequent copies might adhere to the format and the writing style of the original. Compare the transmission of the Pauline Epistles. It is hard to imagine that these letters were written in anything other than the plain script scribes tended to use for correspondence. It is unsurprising therefore that 𝔓⁴⁶ is written in the same type of script, albeit in a later style. By the third century, many more Christian texts were written in book hands than not (as are copies of the literary Acta), although occasionally papyri are found in written third-century script that replaced plain script, Severan chancery.[67]

4. Conclusion

In conclusion, there is surprising support for the Q-scribe theory among details of literacy in rural Roman Egypt. The typology of Q seems closest to that of *chreia*, whose form and conventions any professional writer would be acquainted with and would be able to imitate.

In terminology and topicality, a grapheion or its Galilean corollary would fit well as the point of origin. The (theoretical) script-type and formatting conventions, the use of display script in particular, also point to scribes using documentary forms at the point of origin, which could then be imitated in subsequent copies to bolster their claim to authenticity.

Appendix:
Examples of Christian Papyri in Plain Writing

This list includes plainly written texts and some examples of stylized versions of plain writing to show some of the similarities and differences between the two. I focus here on the specific sub-type of plain writing that uses loops to simplify the ductus of some letters, notably α, μ, υ, and ω. This feature afforded the writer a cursive stroke pattern (ductus) that did not abbreviate or elide any of the vertices essential for letter recognition, and could be written more quickly, once mastered. During the reign of Hadrian,[68] this way of writing gained prestige among documentary script types, which may help explain its use in books.

---

67. NT P37 (P.Mich. 3.137): see Orsini and Clarysse, "Early New Testament Manuscripts and Their Dates," 459.

68. See especially Orsini and Clarysse, "Early New Testament Manuscripts and Their Dates," 458, and Guglielmo Cavallo, "Greek and Latin Writing in the Papyri," in Roger S. Bagnall (ed.), *The Oxford Handbook of Greek Papyrology* (Oxford: Oxford University Press, 2009), 129.

Stylized letters (alpha with a hook entrance stroke).

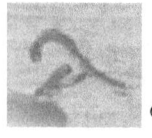 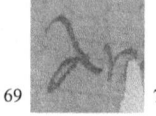  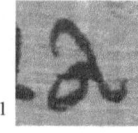

Two graphic features in this plainest of styles seem an attempt by the scribe to upgrade his writing. Alpha with a hook-serif entrance stroke is typical of some forms of display lettering in documents, but is extremely rare in the body of the text. In early Christian books, however, it is not at all uncommon to find it used both for display and in the body of the text. The second is bilinear rho, i.e. having only a shortened descender or none at all. This form of rho occurs in documents, but rarely. It is used in some places for no apparent reason, but in others, the context seems to the writer to require as much formality as possible.[73] For many writers, this form of rho must have been a part of their grammatical education, since it is also found in documents produced by unskilled writers: e.g. in private letters and subscriptions.

 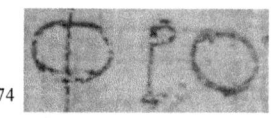

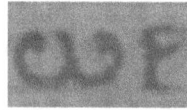 

69. SB 18.13786.7, 94 CE (=P.Tebt.Wall 5; P.Tebt. 2.483 descr.): Αρποχρασ (line-initial).
70. P.Oxy. 51.3606.19, 230-35: Αυρη^λ.
71. Rahlfs 967 Esther IV.1.
72. 𝔓^52 P.Ryl. 3.457.
73. 1. P.Oxy. 41.2987 (78/79), BGU 3.823 (176-179 CE): petitions to the Prefect; 2. official correspondence; BGU 1.73 (135): an Archidikastes writing to a strategos; BGU 5.1210, "Der Gnomon des Idios logos" (after 140); Judicial Proceeding: P.Oxy. 42.3016 (148 CE); P. Köln 8.351 (190 CE): an official letter in "Chancery Script" is used by palaeographers of Greek documents to refer to a stylized script emanating from high government officialdom in Alexandria, such as the Archidikastes, the "chief justice," or the Prefect (ἔπαρχος); both were of the equestrian order and appointed by the Emperor. In the case of P.Köln 8.351, it can be assumed the Prefect was the author because of the chrematistic valediction: ἔρρωσθαι ὑμᾶς βούλομαι.
74. BGU 5.1210 "Regulatory Code of the Private Account."
75. 78/79 CE —P.Oxy. 41.2987: Petition to Prefect C. Aeternius Fronto.
76. 𝔓^46.

By comparing dated examples of plainly written documents to one another,[77] this approach aims at creating a chronological typology of graphic or formatting features, or at least such clues as can be discerned regarding how handwriting production changes over time. Comparing these to similarities in the handwriting of early Christian texts would violate the admonition to compare *simila cum similibus* (documents with documents, book hands with book hands), but such a violation is inevitable,[78] given the fact that sometimes scribes writing Christian books seem better acquainted with documentary writing styles than book hands.

A tentative typology of several elements of plain style writing will play a role in the prima facie dates discussed in what follows. These include using loops to simplify the ductus of some letters, which begins to flourish in Hadrian's reign, notably under the governorship of Petronius Mamertinus (133–137 CE). Its popularity persists more or less unchanged until the death of M. Aurelius (March 17, 180 CE), when it is largely replaced by a modified version in the reign of Septimius Severus (April 14, 193).[79] These modifications include: (i) the use of a contextual form[80] of alpha.

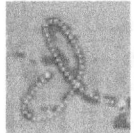 

(ii) the use of "prominent" letters (letters that are noticeably larger), typically, kappa and beta, that are used consistently, not only as display letters;

77. Https://www.academia.edu/35937755/Greek_Documents_in_Plain_Writing_Catalogue_Raisonnée.

78. Most recently Stanley Porter, "Recent Efforts to Reconstruct Early Christianity on the Basis of its Papyrological Evidence," in *Christian Origins and Greco-Roman Culture: Social and Literary Contexts for the New Testament*, ed. Stanley E. Porter and Andrew W. Pitts (Leiden: Brill, 2013), 81.

79. Earlier examples of this type are: P.Tebt. 2.286 (131–138 CE), 318 (166 CE), PSI 7.961 (176–178 CE), SB 8.9923 (P.Oslo inv. 1096, 175/176 CE), P.Tebt. 2.328 (181–192 CE).

80. A "contextual form" of a letter refers to an allograph whose shape is altered to accommodate the following or, less commonly, a preceding letter (cf. "connected" letter forms in Syriac or Arabic).

(iii) mu, omicron, and omega float above the baseline.

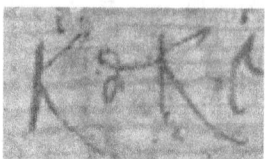

The date range during which the Hadrianic looped style flourished seems to be about 50 years (say 133–180), on present knowledge. Finer chronological distinctions cannot be supported unless some other indications are present. In a document, these would generally be prosopographical, especially government officials whose dates are known. It is difficult to say what might date a literary text written in a documentary style more precisely. A dated document on the other side would provide a terminus, either ante or post quem; an undated document would be just as imprecise as the literary text written in a documentary style. Furthermore, we must suppose one transitional period to account for its gradual adoption and another for the decline in its popularity.

How long such a period of transition might have been we cannot know, given the state of our evidence generally, and the preliminary state of the evidence I am using here. However, comparing one case study of the transitional to proto-gothic from Caroline scripts in Europe is instructive: Eric Kwakkel calculated that between 1100 and 1120, certain proto-gothic features were found in only 15 percent of the dated mss. he studied, but by 1120, these features were found in 75 percent of mss.[81]

For comparison, I include excerpts from three documentary papyri, one from the reign of Hadrian and the governorship of Petronius Mamertinus, another from Septimius Severus, and a petition by the father of Aur. Isidorus (298). I also include here a sample of the handwriting of the Oxyrhynchus scribe designated A3 by E. G. Turner.[53]

---

81. Eric Kwakkel, "Decoding the Material Book: Cultural Residue in Medieval Manuscripts," in *The Medieval Manuscript Book: Cultural Approaches*, ed. Michael Johnston and Michael Van Dussen (Cambridge: Cambridge University Press, 2015), 61–3.

example A: Oxyrhynchus Scribe #A3[82], roll of Aeschylus' plays							
$\alpha^1 / \alpha^2 / \alpha^3$	η	κ	μ	ρ	υ	ω
α^1						ω^1
α^2						ω^2
α^3						

OBSERVATIONS The handwriting of this scribe is described by Turner as a "less formal example of the round calligraphic hand,"[83] α^1 (with an allograph, α^3, in two strokes), along with μ, υ, and ω^1, in one movement (i.e. with no pen lift); ρ has a rather short descender or is bilinear, like κ. More often than not, the scribe conceals with a loop at the apex of alpha (α^2) giving the impression that the faster form (with the loop, and no pen lift) was considered less suitable for a book.

example B: BGU 20.2863 (133–137 CE)[84]						
α^4 / α^5	η	κ	μ		υ	ω
α^4					υ^1	
α^5					υ^2	

OBSERVATIONS: α^4, along with μ, υ^{1-2}, and possibly ω, in one movement (with no pen lift); α^5 with a tear-drop bowl and a straight back oblique is also used. The arms of κ are made in a single motion; η in two strokes, 1, 2+3; ρ has a descender.

82. E. G. Turner, "Scribes and scholars of Oxyrhynchus," in *Akten des VIII. Internationalen Kongresses für Papyrologie*, ed. H. Gerstinger, MPER 5 (Vienna: R. M. Rohrer, 1956), 146.

83. Turner and Parsons, *Greek Manuscripts of the Ancient World*, cat. no. 24 (p. 54).

84. 133–137 CE, the years of the governorship of Petronius Mamertinus.

example C: P. Oxy. 51.3614 (200 CE)							
α	η	μ	ν	π	υ	ω	

	Observations: although clearly a continuation of the Hadrianic "looped" (*occhiellata*) style (α, μ, υ, ω in one movement), by the time of Septimius Severus (193–211 CE), there are notable differences. The loop-allograph of alpha has a contextual form, i.e. in certain contexts, its axis is turned so that the third (ballistic) stroke ends well above the baseline, the exact angle depending on what letter follows. The line format is two-tiered: α (δ?) λ, ε, η, υ are typically above tau height (H_τ). Prominent letters are used: β, κ; two letters (ω, ο) float above the baseline, as μ often does too.
 α per se 1 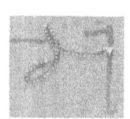 contextual form of α 1	

floating μ, ω (ημων) 1

1. P. Egerton 2 + P. Köln 6.255[85] 150–250 CE[86]; non-canonical gospel (codex); TM 63527 (LDAB 4736)						
α⁶ / α⁷	η	μ	ν	π	υ	ω

Observations: Looped features: α⁶- α⁷ along with μ and ω, in one movement (with no pen lift). Rho has a shortened descender, probably an attempt at stylization. Line format is strictly bilinear (with some exceptions).[87] Display letters are used in line-initial position, and sometimes at the beginning of a new clause: line 53* →: εληλυθας Αγαρποιεις line 31* →: απενευσεν. Display α often has a contextual form, although the axis tilt is not as extreme as in fast cursive.

85. I have adjusted the brightness and contrast of the images
86. P. Malik and L. R. Zelyck, "Reconsidering the Date(s) of the Egerton Gospel," *ZPE* 204 (2017): 55–64.
87. → line 7]κονταταρχη The underlined letters are above tau-height. The scribe, by these admittedly slim indications, is making a conscious effort to keep to a strictly bilinear format, which is not the usual way he/she wrote.

2. P.Oxy. 60.4009
"Second century" *ed. pr.*; "300–350" Orsini; non-canonical gospel (codex); TM 63663 (LDAB 6872)

α⁶ / α⁷ / α⁸	η	μ	ν	π	υ	ω
1 α⁶						
2 α⁷						
3 α⁸						

OBSERVATIONS: looped features: α⁶, μ, ω, in one movement. α⁷-α⁸ both were produced in two movements: α⁷ has a straight oblique, as in documents; α⁸ begins the oblique stroke with a hook entrance stroke, typical of some forms of display script in documents, best understood as an attempt at stylization here. η is written in three movements (multi-stroke), rather than two, more usual in documents. ω floats above the baseline.

3. 𝔓²⁰ (codex),
P. Oxy. IX 1171; "Third century"; Ep. James TM 61618 (LDAB 2768)

α⁹ / α¹⁰	η	μ	ν	π	υ	ω
α⁹						
α¹⁰						

OBSERVATIONS: looped features, α⁹⁻¹⁰, μ, ω, in one movement (cursive). Pi in three movements (multi-stroke); flick serifs at the base of some hastas (π, τ). The contextual alpha and the way omega floats above the baseline favor the third-century date assigned in the *ed. pr.*

Both should be considered stylized features. Serifs are not uncommon in documentary plain writing.

4. P.Oxy. 4.656 ; "second–third" century; LXX Genesis (codex) ; Rahlfs 905; TM 61937 (LDAB 3094)						
α	η	κ	μ	ρ	υ	ω

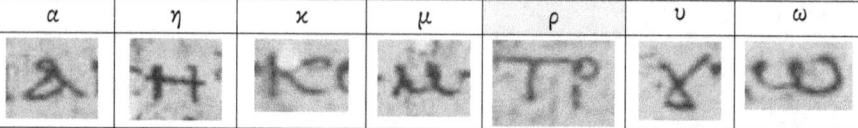

OBSERVATIONS: looped features: υ, ω, in one movement, μ in two; α the oblique has a hook entrance stroke. There are display letters in line-initial position. No stylized features are evident, apart from the alpha already mentioned.

5. P.Oxy. 4.654 ; "Third" century; Gospel of Thomas (re-used roll, ↓) ; TM 704964 (LDAB 4030)						
α¹¹ / α¹² / α¹³	η	κ	μ	ρ	υ	ω

1. α^{11}

2. α^{12}

3. α^{13}

OBSERVATIONS: α^{11} is sharp nosed and the oblique begins with hook entrance stroke, and is used both as a display letter (line initial: lines 4, 18, 29) and in the body of the text; α^{12} is made in one motion, without a pen lift, with a visible loop at the apex. In α^{13} the writer seems to try to conceal the loop at the apex, as the Oxyrhynchus Scribe A3 does (α^{12}, example A above).

Why so many allographs of alpha in a single column of text? The writer may be a novice, not yet capable of consistently producing the graphic effect he/she is aiming for, α^{11}.

The writer produces α^{12} out of habit, and tries to minimize the mistake with the α^{13} form. Or else, since this seems to be a personal copy (written on the back of a documentary roll), consistency is not so important to the writer. NB that the contextual form of α^{12} and sometimes α^{13} is an indication of a date after the accession of Septimius Severus (193 CE).

Another stylized features is υ in the form γ. The scribe struggles somewhat with this graphic feature, which he/she produces in non-standard and unsteady ways.

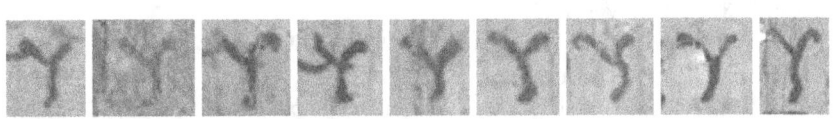

Other display letters in line-initial position are common, as well as marking a new section: Λεγει Ιης (lines 9, 27, 36), and for the heading: ΟΙΤΟΙΟΙ ΟΙΛΟΓΟΙ ΟΙ[(line 1). The size of χ and β are prominent. The line format has a two-tiered body height ($H_{b1} = H_{r}$, $H_{b2} = H_{e}$), but the baseline is ragged, with hardly three letters together sharing the same basis, typical of the contrastive style in which the size and width of letters are variable.

6. 𝔓^{52} P.Ryl. 3.457;
"125–175 CE" Clarysse-Orsini "late second-early third century"; G.John (codex) TM 61624 (LDAB 2774)

$α^1/α^2$	η	χ	μ	ρ	$υ^3 - υ^4$	ω
$α^{14}$					$υ^3$	
$α^{15}$					$υ^4$	

OBSERVATIONS: looped features: $α^{15}$, μ, ω, $υ^4$ in one movement, η in two (strokes 2 and 3 combined by a loop). The two other allographs of alpha are the same as in no. 2 above (P.Oxy. 60.4009). The use of the looped alpha ($α^{15}$) and the straight-backed ($α^{14}$) allograph in the same text is not unusual, e.g. 133–137—BGU 20.2863. It seems likely the scribe is trying to stylize an ordinary alpha by preferring the hook-serif entrance stroke, reserved in documents for use as a display letter.

7. a. Rahlfs 816 P.Schøyen 1.23
"175–225 CE" Orsini; LXX Joshua, (codex) TM 66869 (LDAB 8119)
and b. Rahlfs 0830 P. Schøyen 2.26
175–225 "175–225 CE" Orsini; LXX Leviticus, (codex) TM 66870 (LDAB 8120)

α	η	κ	μ	ρ	υ⁵ - υ⁶	ω

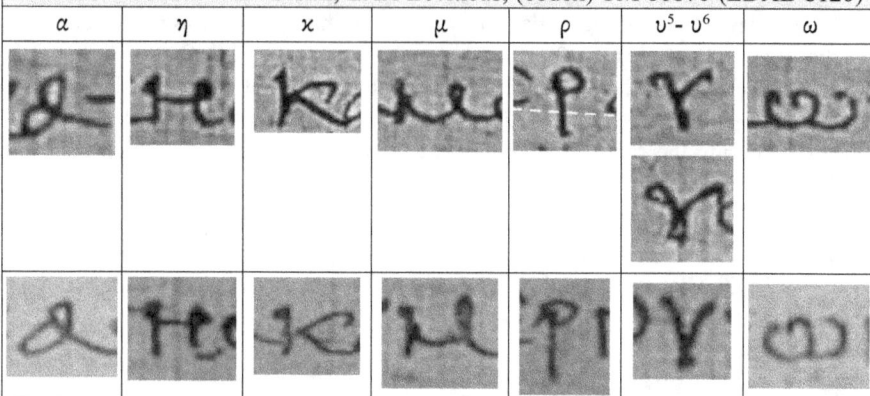

OBSERVATIONS: α υ are produced in one motion; η and μ in two (both combining strokes 2 and 3); upsilon is V-form, and is high-waisted. Display letters are used at the beginning of a new line, and after pauses in writing, after the spaces left around *nomina sacra* (Josh. 10:12) ν, line 11: πολεμωΤοτε; ibidem, line 13. οθc Τοναμορραιον, the former (11) with the force of punctuation or a paragraphos, and the latter (13) comes mid-sentence, the scribe's response to starting again after the vacat.

8. Rahlfs 970; P. Bad. 4.56 (Heidelberg P. G. 1020 a +608);
"Second CE"; LXX Exodus 8, Deuteronomy 28–30 (codex); TM 61929 (LDAB 3086)

α	η	κ	μ	ρ	υ⁵ - υ⁶	ω

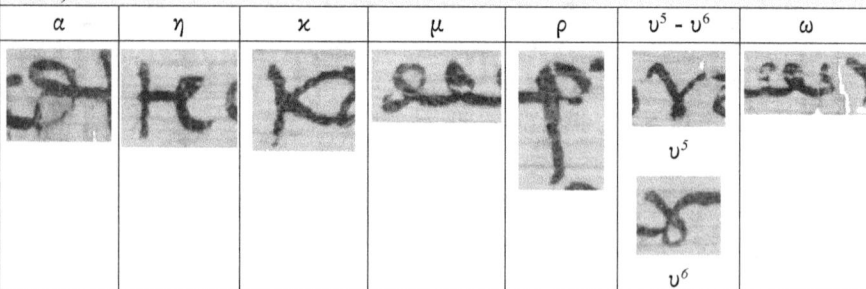

OBSERVATIONS: looped features: α, μ, sometimes ω and υ⁴, without a pen lift. Some extenders imitate Old Roman Cursive, specifically ν, χ and sometimes υ, but there are no other stylized features. The line format is roughly bilinear: ο and ω tend to float above the baseline; beta is prominent. Display letters are only occasionally used in line-initial position, and once at the beginning of a new clause: Exod. 8:12, fr. a (cod.verso, →) κcΕιπεδεκcπροc.

9. P.Beatty 7.9-10 + PTA 5, 10, 21, + P.Monts.Roca 4.47, + Princ.Stud.Pap. III "175-250 LDAB"; LXX Daniel, Esther; Rahlfs 967; (codex) TM 61933 (LDAB 3090)

α¹⁶ / α¹⁷	η	χ	μ¹ / μ²	ρ	υ⁹ / υ¹⁰	ω
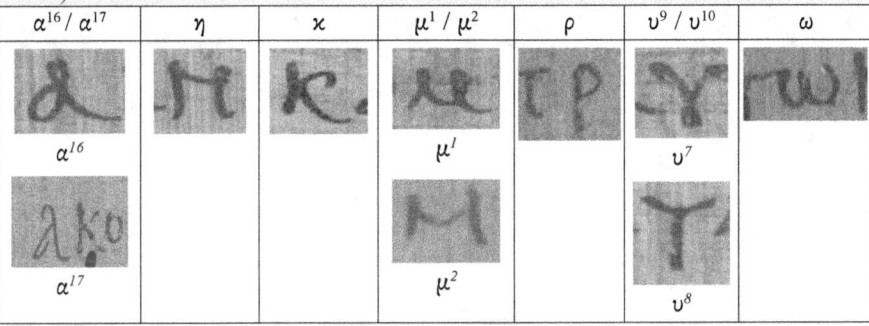						
α¹⁶			μ¹		υ⁷	
α¹⁷			μ²		υ⁸	

OBSERVATIONS α¹⁶, μ, υ⁵, ω written with a loop feature in one motion (no pen lift). χ is large (either beginning above the body height or finishing below the baseline, sometimes both); ρ has a short descender, which may be taken as an attempt at stylization/formality. In the last pages of Esther. The allograph α¹⁷ has a hook entrance stroke. υ⁶ is a modified Y-form, a stylized feature sometimes used by notaries in the Fayum,[88] but also in the formal Severe Style.

9.a LXX: Ezechiel The same codex as no. 10, but written in a more formal script.

α	η	χ	μ	ρ	υ	ω
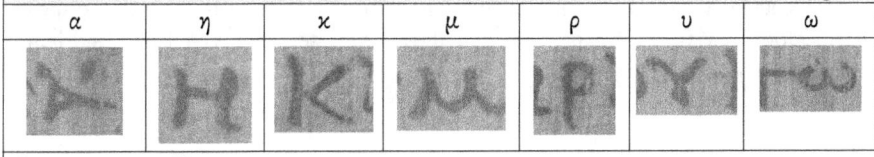						

OBSERVATIONS: Sharp nose α;

10. P.Köln 4.170;
"200–250 CE"; Philemon; 𝔓⁸⁷; (codex) TM 61857, (LDAB 3013)

α¹⁸ / α¹⁹	η	χ	μ	ρ	υ	ω
α¹⁸						
α¹⁹						

OBSERVATIONS: α¹⁸ and α¹⁹ has the hook-entrance stroke typical of display letters in documents; α¹⁸ has the sharp nosed form, also found in documents.[89] Otherwise the letters are produced with a slower ductus (e.g. multistroke ω, μ, υ).

88. SB 8.9923 (P.Oslo inv. 1046; 175/176 CE).
89. P.Oxy. 60.4059, col. II 3, 9, 13 (159–163 CE); BGU 15.2471 (158 CE).

11. P.Beatty 2²; "c. 200 CE"; Pauline Epistles; 𝔓⁴⁶ (codex) TM 61628 (LDAB 2778)							
α^{20} / α^{21}	η	κ	μ	ρ	υ	ω	
α^{20}							
α^{21}							

OBSERVATIONS: Slowly written, with a bilinear ρ and Y-form υ. Serifs are both produced at the onset/finish of a stroke, and added secondarily (after pen lift), sometimes clumsily. Alpha has both a short-oblique form (α^{20}) and a hook-entrance stroke form, (α^{21}) the latter used both as a display letter, usually line-initial. ω and ο sometimes float above the baseline, but not always. Both nos. 12 and 13 are considered by Orsini and Clarysse to belong to the "Alexandrian Stylistic Class," considered to be an outgrowth, and stylization of the Hadrianic "chancery" type. What that means here is that the letter forms of nos. 12-13 resemble those of the looped type examined here, but they are a step removed from Hadrianic documentary scripts.

12. 𝔓⁶⁶ P.Bodmer 2 "c. 200 CE," G.John., (codex) TM 61627 (LDAB 2777)						
α	η	κ	μ	ρ	υ	ω

OBSERVATIONS: α, υ, ω are made in one movement; η and κ combine strokes 1 and 2 with a visible loop; ρ has a short descender. μ is constructed by three individual strokes. Display letters are rare, even in the title, but are observable in John 1:3 εγενετο · Και. In short, this hand has more in common with the looped style than not, and shows none of the features of the later second century. Turner's assessment is right, though not in every particular: "Whenever possible, the scribe makes letters in a single sequence (e.g. α, η, κ, μ, υ)."⁹⁰ And although our scribe has taken care to conceal this feature, one can see the way this scribe's loops at the apex of α, the middle arm of ω, and at the base of the first hasta of η, κ, and the base of υ differ in appearance from the anchor points of μ (a, pts BC, b pts. DE) and the anchor points of η, strokes AB and CD, and κ, strokes AB+CD. This ductus η and κ is not typical of documents: for κ, one would usually join CD+EF; and for κ, CD and EF would typically be one continuous curve, beginning at the top arm, curving inward towards the hasta, and usually touching it, and then curving outward towards the foot of the leg. Therefore the connection between usual documentary practice and the handwriting of this scribe is more tenuous than it first appears. The line formatting is two-tiered bilinear although H_e is shorter than is typical perhaps to not detract from the bilinear effect.

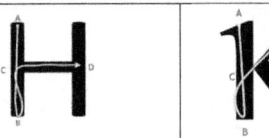

17. P.Oxy. 83 *forthcoming*; second century; Romans

---

90. E.g. Turner and Parsons, *Greek Manuscripts of the Ancient World*, cat. no. 62 (p. 108).

Conclusion to the Appendix

	looped (*occhiellata*) α, μ, υ, ω,	Stylized forms	Bilinearity — strict Hb = Hτ[91]	Bilinearity — two-tiered Hb1 = Hτ, Hb2 = Hε[92]	Display letter	large letters	format α = contextual form of alpha
A. Oxy. scribe A3	α, μ, υ, ω	ρ			line initial: Ὑπατοις	β (mod.)	
B. BGU 20.2863	α, μ, υ, ω			α δ λ / ε η υ		β	
C. P.Oxy 51.3614	α, μ, υ, ω			α δ λ / ε η υ		β ι χ	α / float. ω, ο
1. "Egerton Gospel"	α, μ, υ, ω				line initial, §-break		α (only 2x)
2. GPeter P.Oxy. 60.4009	α, μ, υ, ω	α			line initial,		vac. = phrase boundary
3. 𝔓20 P.Oxy. 9.1171	α, υ, ω			α δ λ / ε η υ	post paus.		α, float. ω, ο
4. Rahlfs 905 P.Oxy. 4.656	μ,* υ, ω						
5. GThomas P.Oxy. 4.654	α12-13 μ,* ω	α ρ υ		α - λ / ε η -		χ β	α

91. Body height (x-height) = the height of a tau;
92. The second, taller body height (x-height) = the height of epsilon etc. (typically α δ λ ε η υ).

6. 𝔓52 P.Ryl. 3.457	α15 η*·μ· υ4 ω	α14 υ3		α η χ	post paus.	
7. Rahlfs 816 P.Schøyen 1.23 Joshua	α η* μ* υ			α δ λ	line initial	serifs
7.a Rahlfs 830 P. Schøyen 2.26 Leviticus						
8. Rahlfs 970 P.Bad. 4.46	α η* μ υ ω			α λ η^sh		α
9. Rahlfs 967 P.Beatty 7.9-10 Esther	α16 η* μ5 υ5 ω	α17 μ2				β
9.a Ezechiel	υ?	α			line initial	β floating o, ω
10. 47 P.Beatty 3		α		α δ λ / ε η υ		
11. 87 P.Koeln 4.170		α				
12. 46 P.Beatty 22		α, ρ		α δ λ inconsistently	line initial / post paus.	β δ
13. 66 P.Bodm. 2	α η* μ υ ω			α δ λ / ε η υ		
14. P.Oxy. 83 forthcoming						

Hb1 = tau height

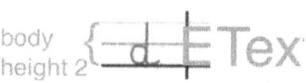

Hb2 = medial stroke of epsilon = tau height

contextual letter form	an allograph whose shape is altered to accommodate the following or, less commonly, a preceding letter (cf. "connected" letter forms in Syriac or Arabic).
chancery	an official hand, indicative of a high level of bureaucracy (Alexandria or Rome), or its imitation
cursive letter	a letter whose ductus is simplified to eliminate pen-lifts
cursive script	"joined up" writing, where pen lifts between letters are eliminated to varying degrees.
display letters	enlarged letters (litterae notabiliores, or capitals) typically at the beginning of a line or after a pause in writing.
entrance stroke	

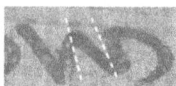

Figure 6. δια delta with an exaggerated, Latinesque entrance stroke.

exit stroke

Figure 7. υς with the exit stroke of υ between dotted lines

fast cursive — "joined up" writing, where letter shapes are abbreviated or altered to accommodate the entrance stroke of the following or preceding letter.

fashion cycle: This point is only of conceptual importance for paleography of papyri, since our evidence is too incomplete typically to derive such statistics. For the sake of example, I use figures from a Bell curve.

1. innovation beginning of the cycle, few examples: in a Bell curve, 2.5 percent of the total.
2. early adopters the second standard deviation from the mean at the beginning of the cycle (2σ), about 13.5 percent.
3. floruit the main period of a style's popularity, in a Bell curve, one standard deviation from the mean ($1\sigma = 68.2$ percent)

    4. decline the conservative end of the cycle, the 16 percent who maintain a style after it is no longer fashionable.

floating letter	a letter written above, not on, the baseline
line initial	the beginning of a line at the left margin
looped ductus (occhiellata)	A letter form in which loops are substituted for pen-lifts between strokes.
stylized letter	the ductus of a letter that is altered to appear more like a book hand.
vacats	spaces left by the scribe between letters or words to aid the reader (punctuation), or as part of the writing process (the scribe stops writing momentarily, upon restarting leaves space between the last letter and the next).

4

My Lord and Protector:
Papyri and *Skepē* Patronage in Sirach and *3 Maccabees**

Christopher J. Cornthwaite

1. Introduction

The Wisdom of Sirach, composed in Hebrew between c. 195 and 180 BCE, was translated into Greek by the author, Ben Sira's grandson, in Alexandria in the late second century BCE.[1] While the grandson completed a relatively wooden translation, he appears to have inserted material at some points.[2] One apparent addition, Sir. 22:23-26, offers us a

---

* I would like to thank the members of the Colloquium for Religions of Mediterranean Antiquity in the Department for the Study of Religion (University of Toronto) for their valuable comments on this chapter, especially Ryan Olfert for his formal response. Thanks also to the participants in the Papyrology and Early Christian Backgrounds section of the 2016 SBL Annual Meeting for their helpful comments. Finally, I wish to thank John Kloppenborg for his insights at various stages of this research and Peter Arzt-Grabner for his assistance with the papyrological material. This work was supported by a generous grant from the Social Sciences and Humanities Research Council of Canada (SSHRC).

1. John J. Collins, *Jewish Wisdom in the Hellenistic Age*, OTL (Louisville, KY: Westminster John Knox Press, 1997), 23–41; Benjamin G. Wright, "Sirach (Ecclesiasticus)," in *T&T Clark Companion to the Septuagint*, ed. J. K. Aitken (London: Bloomsbury T&T Clark, 2015), 410–24.

2. Henry J. Cadbury, "The Grandson of Ben Sira," *HTR* 48 (1955): 219–25; Benjamin G. Wright, *No Small Difference: Sirach's Relationship to Its Hebrew Parent Text*, SCS 26 (Atlanta, GA: Scholars Press, 1989); Antonino Minissale, *La versione greca del Siracide. Confronto con il testo ebraico alla luce dell'attività midrascica e del metodo targumico*, AnBib 133 (Rome: Pontificio Istituto biblico, 1995), 29–30, 153–71. Minissale provides a list of the contents of the Hebrew MSS of Sirach; see also Alexander A. Di Lella, *The Hebrew Text of Sirach: A Text-Critical and Historical*

glimpse into the social world of the translator, especially his ideas about friendship (I include vv. 20-22 in italics for context):

> 20. *He who throws stones at birds scares them off, and he who insults a friend dissolves a friendship.*
> 21. *If you draw a sword on a friend, do not despair, for a way back is possible.*
> 22. *If you open your mouth against a friend, be not concerned, for reconciliation is possible—with the exception of reproach and arrogance and revealing a secret and a treacherous blow—in these cases any friend will flee.*
> 23. Gain your fellow's trust in poverty so that in his prosperity you may be filled as well; in a time of distress stay with him so that in his inheritance you may be a joint heir.[3]
> 24. Preceding a fire there are a furnace's vapor and smoke; so preceding bloodshed are abuses.
> 25. I will not be ashamed to shelter a friend, and from before him I will never hide.
> 26. And if bad things will happen to me on his account, everyone who hears will guard against him (Sir. 22:20-26 [NETS]).[4]

The text of 22:23-26 does not appear in any extant Hebrew manuscript. In fact, the one manuscript from the Cairo Genizah archive which does include our text, MS C, omits 22:23–23:10 and the Hebrew text proceeds directly from 22:22–23:11.[5]

Study, SCL 1 (Hague: Mouton, 1966), 23–105; Israel Levi, *The Hebrew Text of the Book of Ecclesiasticus* (Leiden: Brill, 1969); Bradley Gregory, *Like an Everlasting Signet Ring: Generosity in the Book of Sirach* (Berlin: de Gruyter, 2010), 13–19; Conleth Kearns, "The Expanded Text of Ecclesiasticus: Its Teaching on the Future Life as a Clue to Its Origin," in Conleth Kearns, *The Expanded Text of Ecclesiasticus: Its Teaching on the Future Life as a Clue to Its Origin* (Berlin: de Gruyter, 2011), 23–316.

3. GK II adds here: "for one should not always despise the outline, nor is a rich person admirable when he has no purpose" (NETS).

4. Greek excerpts for comparison: v. 23. πίστιν κτῆσαι ἐν πτωχείᾳ μετὰ τοῦ πλησίον, ἵνα ἐν τοῖς ἀγαθοῖς αὐτοῦ ὁμοῦ πλησθῇς· ἐν καιρῷ θλίψεως ἰάμενε αὐτῷ, ἵνα ἐν τῇ κληρονομίᾳ αὐτοῦ συγκληρονομήσῃς… 25. φίλον σκεπάσαι οὐκ αἰσχυνθήσομαι καὶ ἀπὸ προσώπου αὐτοῦ οὐ μὴ κρυβῶ, 26. καὶ εἰ κακά μοι συμβήσεται δι' αὐτόν, πᾶς ὁ ἀκούων φυλάξεται ἀπ' αὐτοῦ.

5. For a comparison of the OG text in comparison to the Syriac MSS and the Vulgate, see Johannes Marböck, "Gafährdung und Bewährung: Kontexte zur Freundschaftsperikope Sir 22, 19-26," in *Freundschaft bei ben Sira: Beiträge des Symposions zu Ben Sira Salzburg 1995*, ed. Friedrich V. Reiterer (New York: de Gruyter, 1996),

If this is an insertion, why is it included? What does it add to Sirach's already exhaustive commentary on friendship (below)? In fact, I will suggest in this chapter that these brief verses and their discussion of friendship betray something vitally important which is entering the work from the Egyptian milieu of the translator. It is not immediately obvious, but a comparison of the language of this pericope with papyri shows that the grandson is incorporating the unique system of Egyptian patronage into his discussion of friendship, a fact that is signaled by his use of admonition to gain a neighbor's trust in poverty (v. 23: πίστιν κτῆσαι ἐν πτωχείᾳ μετὰ τοῦ πλησίον) and his acceptance of sheltering a friend (v. 25: φίλον σκεπάσαι οὐκ αἰσχυνθήσομαι).

To properly appreciate the addition of the pericope and what it might mean, it is first necessary to move the discussion beyond ancient friendship and towards the ways in which indebtedness and protection were uniquely constructed in late Ptolemaic and early Roman Egypt. Papyri from this period show that there were singular practices of what we might call patronage in Egypt, although they were vastly different from both Roman patronage and the Greek euergetism. These constructs of protection are especially grouped around two word roots in papyri. The first, the noun σκέπη and the related verb σκεπάζω, refers to the covering or shelter offered by one party to another in a variety of social contexts, including *asylia*, withdrawal, protection, favoritism, and opportunity. The second, πίστις and the verb πιστεύω, was used as a description for the trust, protection, and financial aid which that relationship of *skepē* provided. This, I argue, is the social setting which is refracted into Sirach (both in translation and in the insertion mentioned above), as well as in *3 Maccabees*, and is even visible elsewhere in the translations of the Septuagint (LXX). In what follows, I will outline the social practices of *skepē* protection from the papyrological record and then draw connections to Judaean literature. In doing so, I will show that the social practice of *skepē* influenced the translation of the LXX, and that original Greek material composed in Egypt bears its marks, Sirach through justifying skepē practices of protection and debt and *3 Maccabees* through incorporating skepē language to explain the divine protection of God.

98–102; also Pancratius Cornelis Beentjes, *The Book of Ben Sira in Hebrew: A Text Edition of All Extant Hebrew Manuscripts and a Synopsis of All Parallel Hebrew Ben Sira Texts*, VTSup 68 (Leiden: Brill, 1997).

2. *Egyptian* Skepē *in Context*

In 1975, the same year that Paul Veyne's landmark study on Greek *euergetism*, *Le pain et le cirque*, was released, a small book was published that outlined a unique system of patronage that was witnessed in Egyptian papyri and nowhere else: Marta Piątkowska's *La ΣΚΕΠΕ dans l'Égypte ptolémaïque*.[6] While Veyne's work prompted a hunger for understanding benefaction in ancient Greece, and a near-renaissance of associated work in Greece, Rome, and beyond, Piątkowska's doctoral thesis on the same subject in papyri went mostly unnoticed. She drew upon an observation first made by the father of papyrology Ulrich Wilcken, and developed by Friedrich von Woess, that there were certain places in Egypt, most notably temples, which were called places of shelter (*skepē*) in the Ptolemaic and early Roman papyri.[7] Michael Rostovtzeff had expanded this claim that debtors fleeing imprisonment at the hands of their creditors could go to temples for protection, suggesting also that there were powerful households at play in Ptolemaic Egypt, especially in the second century BCE, and individuals who attached themselves to these, even as debtors, were given a great deal of personal and economic protection.[8] Piątkowska's study came a year after Dorothy Thompson showed from a case study in Soknopaiou Nesos (BGU 1.23 [207 BCE]) that the last vestiges of the *skepē* were used to challenge the new Roman system as an appeal to a dying tradition for legitimacy.[9] Another contribution from Thompson showed that the numerous complaints against the officials in Ptolemaic Egypt belied the notions of good rulers that are prominent in the sycophantic pretense of petitions; the *skepē* was a protection offered from such abuses.[10] Most recently, Sitta von Reden has placed the *skepē* firmly

---

6. Marta Piątkowska, *La ΣΚΕΠΕ dans l'Égypte ptolémaïque*, Polska Akademia Nauk Komitet Nauk O Kulturze Antycznej: Archiwum Filologiczne 32 (Warszawa: Zaklad Narodowy im. Ossolińskich, 1975).

7. Ulrich Wilcken (ed.), *Grundzüge und Chrestomathie der Papyruskunde*, 2 vols. (Leipzig: B. G. Teubner, 1912), 2:323–4; Friedrich von Woess, *Das Asylwesen Ägyptens in der Ptolemäerzeit und die spätere Entwicklung, eine Einführung in das Rechtsleben Ägyptens besonders der Ptolemäerzeit*, ed. Eduard Schwartz, Münchener Beiträge zur Papyrusforschung 5 (Munich: C. H. Beck, 1923), 100.

8. Michael Ivanovitch Rostovtzeff, *The Social and Economic History of the Hellenistic World*, 3 vols. (Oxford: Clarendon Press, 1941), 325, 901–6; also Horst Braunert, *Die Binnenwanderung: Studien zur Sozialgeschichte Ägyptens in der Ptolemäer- und Kaiserzeit.* (Bonn: L. Röhrscheid, 1964), 87.

9. Dorothy Crawford, "*Skepē* in Soknopaiou Nesos," *JJP* 18 (1974): 169–75.

10. Dorothy Crawford, "The Good Official of Ptolemaic Egypt," in *Das ptolmäische Ägypten: Akten des Internationalen Symposions 27.-29. September 1976 in*

where it belongs, within the context of credit and lending: "permanent work relationships bound employees into relationships of patronage and protection (*skepē*) which created favourable conditions for lending and borrowing."[11]

The *skepē* thrived in a world in which the effects of significant social inequities on the individual could be mitigated through connections to people of higher status. While inequality was hardly unique to Egypt, the Egyptian response does seem unparalleled. Rostovtzeff describes a class of aristocrats with enormous wealth in Ptolemaic Egypt and, especially as the crown weakened in the second century BCE, these people became extraordinarily powerful; alignment with them could pay dividends in social opportunities and protection from prosecution, financial loss, and assaults from others with more social power.[12] A *skepē* from a person of the same social status as these intimidating figures often meant that individuals would be afforded some degree of protection from tormentors. This relationship of protection was often called a *pistis*, which was a connection of deep trust between two parties which entailed mutual obligations. The necessary conditions for physical protection existed within this confidence as well as, vitally, the ability to do business on credit. So, lending and trading, shipping and contract-work, were all bound in a moral framework of honorability, trustworthiness, and loyalty.

Entering into *skepē* often seems a *de facto* result of a work or loan agreement, as we shall see below. However, we do have an example of someone entering the protection of the *skepē* in a letter of request from Pnepheros son of Paous (a beer and natron tax farmer). Around 117 BCE he writes to the king's scribe in Kerkeosiris and acknowledges that those living in the village claim this scribe's protection and expresses the same

---

Berlin, ed. Herwig Maehler and Volker Michael Strocka (Mainz: Philipp von Zabern, 1978), 195–202.

11. Sitta von Reden, *Money in Ptolemaic Egypt: From the Macedonian Conquest to the End of the Third Century BC* (Cambridge: Cambridge University Press, 2007), 227.

12. Rostovtzeff, *The Social and Economic History of the Hellenistic World*, 903. In Dorothy Crawford's compilation of the virtues that a good official should have (such as ἐπιμέλεια, εὔονοια, πρόνοια), she shows that these virtues were universally extolled for leaders, yet the complaints in papyri show that officials "oppressed the people of Egypt using force and violence, whips and torture, knives and cudgels, practicing extortion and illegal exaction and accepting bribes from those who they terrorized…but apart from the perpetual petition appealing to the interest of the king, compliance and payment were the only escape for their victims." See "The Good Official of Ptolemaic Egypt," 199.

desire: ἀντέχεσθαι τῆς σῆς σκέπης. He also indicates that when this is done he will be able to pay his dues.[13] In another example, the entry into protection seems to come by recommendation. Here someone writes a letter to Zenon, thanking him for acting on his behalf in some way, and he proudly announces that he is being taken into full *pistis* by someone with more social power.[14] This is the creation of a *skepē*. But just as this relationship could be initiated, in theory it could also be terminated, and we also have evidence of patrons growing tired and frustrated with their clients and choosing to end the relationship.[15]

One of the most clear purposes of the *skepē* is physical protection. An example of this is found in a papyrus from Kerkeosiris (c. 100 BCE) from the crown tenants and the komarch of the village to Kronios, the commander of the guards (ἀρχιφυλακίτης), complaining that Marres the *topogrammateus* keeps bringing armed bands to the town…

> …with the utmost insolence making continual attempts at extortion upon the wives of some of us and of others, disregarding the pledges (*pisteis*) which we have obtained from Lysanios, the (king's) cousin and *strategos*; therefore many of us, having had our suspicions aroused, have retired to the neighboring villages. For these reasons we are hindered in the collection of the sums owed for both rent and crowns; and we therefore present to you this petition in order that you may give instructions in the proper quarter, so that Marres may be sent for and made to refund his extortions and may receive suitable punishment, and that we being undisturbed may be enabled to attend to the collection of the revenues and the interests of the king may suffer no harm… (P.Tebt. 1.41.1-27 [105–90 BCE])[16]

---

13. P.Tebt. 1.40 (c. 117 BCE).

14. P.Col. 4.64.4 (257–55 BCE): προαγήγοχεν ἡμᾶς εἰς πᾶσαν πίστιν.

15. P.Tebt. 3.758 (199–175 BCE); Crawford, *The Good Official*, 200 (P.Tebt. 1.11 [119 BCE]); also P.Hib. 1.95 (Aug. 15, 257 BCE).

16. Translation is by the editors. The Greek text reads: Κρονίωι ἀρχιφυλακίτηι Κερκεοσίρεως παρὰ Ἁρμιύσιος κωμάρχου καὶ τῶν ἐκ τῆς αὐτῆς βασιλικῶν γεωργῶν. Πυκνό|τερον Μαρρείους τοπογραμματέως 5. σὺν ἄλλοις πλείοσι ἐν μαχαίραις παρ[α] γινομένου εἰς τὴν κώμην καὶ [μ]ετὰ τοῦ παντὸς σκυλμοῦ συνεχεῖς ἐπιλήψεις ποιου|μένου τινῶν ἡμῶν καὶ ἑτέρων 10. γυναικῶν διασείειν, οὐ στοχασά|μενος ὧν ἔχομεν παρὰ Λυσανίου τοῦ συγγενοῦς καὶ στρατηγοῦ πίστεων, καὶ ἐκ τοῦ τοιούτου ἱκανῶν ἡμῶν ὑπόπτως ἐχόντων ἀνακεχωρή| 15. καμεν εἰς τὰς περιοίκας κώμας. ὧν χάριν ἐμποδιζόμενοι τῆι εἰσαγωγῆι τῶν ὀφειλομένων (οφειλημενων) πρός τε τὴν μίσθωσιν καὶ τοὺς στεφάνους διὸ ἐπιδίδομέν σοι τὸ ὑπόμνημα 20. ὅπως ὑποτάξῃς οἷς καθήκει ἵνα τοῦ Μαρρείους κατασταλέντος καὶ εἰσπραχθέντος τὰ σείσματα τύχῃ τῆς ἁρμοζούσης ἐπιπλήξεως, αὐτ[οί] τε ἀπαρενόχλητοι ὄντες 25. δυν[ώ]μεθα ἀντέχεσθαι τῆς εἰσαγωγῆς καὶ οὐθὲν τῶι βασιλεῖ διαπέσῃι.

Apparently the crown tenants and the komarch expect that Kronios will intervene on their behalf, their protection being safeguarded by promises from the king's cousin.[17] It is not clear whether Marres does not know about the *pisteis* or is simply choosing to ignore them. This example highlights two of the most salient features of *skepē*. First of all, we have the call for protection, but secondly we can see the financial ramifications of this relationship. It is in the protector's self-interest to offer this safeguarding, since doing so ensures the flow of money. Another example of this type of protection from a similar context is found in a letter from an Alexandros to a commander of the guards, Philon, in which he appends copies of correspondence with his agent named Aniketos. The aim of all of the correspondence is to request that several people be given protections (*pisteis*) to continue their current work until he can come to hear their petitions.[18] Both of these examples include the physical protection from violence or extortion, but they also betray the interests of the protectors who safeguard a debtor for their labor or revenues.[19]

Furthermore, the patron would occasionally act within their own social networks to protect their clients, shown in a letter from Tebtunis:

> Philoxenos to Apollos his brother, greeting and good health. As soon as you receive this letter go with Horos son of Kotys to see Hermias the village scribe about the person he has arrested, and to Chairemon the collector; and let him be released and not be troubled by anybody, for Demetrios has written to me about him, saying that he is under his protection (*skepē*), and his tenant. I am therefore writing to you to give them instructions. (P.Tebt. 1.34 [c. 100 BCE])[20]

---

17. See also P.Lond. 3.897 (p. 206; 84 CE) in which someone asks for protection for travelling.

18. P.Tebt. 3/1.741 (187/6 BCE): …δο[θήτωσαν] 10 τοῖς διασαφουμέν[ο]ις αἱ πίστεις καὶ γινέσθωσαν π[ρὸς τῆι] ἐγκεχειρισμένηι χρείαι μέχρι τοῦ ἐπιβαλόντας [ἡμᾶς] ἐπὶ [το]ὺς τόπους τὴ[ν] προσήκουσαν ἐπι[στροφὴν] ποήσ[α]σθαι ὑπὲρ ὧν διασαφοῦσι; see also UPZ 1.119 (Aug. 16, 156 BCE).

19. Protectors were also aware that they created economic stability. In P.Hib. 1.35 (250 BCE), the temple slaves of the goddess Theoris petition their protector, a certain Sonnophris, observing that by his current protection (*skepē*) they are able to pay their tributes to the temple and that in the future they will also be so protected (5. διατελο[ῦ] μεν τοὺς φόρους εὐτακτοῦντες εἰς τὸ ἱερὸν διὰ τὴν παρ' ὑμῶν σκέ[π]ην, καὶ νῦν καὶ ἐν τοῖς ἔμπροσθε χρόνοις ὑπὸ ὑ| [μῶ]ν σκεπαζόμε[θ]α).

20. Editors' translation (l.10: διὰ τὸ γεγραφηκέναι ἡμῖν Δητριος \περὶ αὐτοῦ/, ὄντα δὲ αὐτοῦ ὑπὸ σκέπην καὶ γεωργό(ν). γράφω σοι δὲ διαστολὰς αὐτοῖς δοῦναι).

In this example, Demetrios is drawing upon his social networks to act in the interests of both his client and himself,[21] and in other examples these same networks could be leveraged for opportunities for the client's social advancement.[22] As stated above, these sorts of relationships made the economy work, and became the foundation for money lending, advanced payments for goods, and work contracts.[23]

Beyond physical protection offered by a patron, the protection given by a particular place of *asylia* is also often called *skepē*. Woess' initial recognition that *skepē* was sometimes (he thought always—above) connected to buildings shows the connection of the practice with that of *asylia*, a widespread phenomenon in the Greek world. The formal practice of *asylia* in Egypt appears in documents from the first century BCE.[24] Kent Rigsby suggests that the Ptolemies' practices of *asylia* had little in common with

21. Piątkowska, *La ΣΚΕΠΕ dans l'Égypte ptolémaïque*, 15 (P.Cair.Zen. 3.59384, et al.); As Crawford says "...a brother and friends in high places were all that a man needed to escape prosecution," see "The Good Official of Ptolemaic Egypt," 201.

22. This represents cases in which the patron could use their connections to provide gainful employment and social improvement for their clients. Sometimes this was through the protective structure of the household, in which case the letter might be introduced with οἱ ἐν οἴκῳ, see Clinton W. Keyes, "The Greek Letter of Introduction," *AJP* 56 (1935): 28–44; In an example from Arsinoites, someone named Sisouchos writes to Zenon to ask that a certain Ptolemaios receive a clerk's position, P.Cairo.Zen 3.59342 (Jan. 31, 246 BCE): 4 ἐὰν οὖν σοι φαίνηται, καλῶς ποιήσεις γράψα[ς . . . .] οἷ ἂν σὺ δοκιμάζηις, ἵνα κατα|ταγῆι πρὸς γράμμασιν [ἑτέρῳ] δὲ μηθενὶ μέρει προσαχθῆι, ὀψώνιον δὲ τὸ καλῶς ἔχον λαμβ[άνηι]. ἔρρωσο. (ἔτους) λθ, Χοίαχ ι. This papyrus provides insight into possibilities for advancement and hiring created by one's network of trust, and in this case Zenon's word has a great deal of influence for his client. Piątkowska gives another example where the introduction of a young man to the king caused his career to advance quickly (*La ΣΚΕΠΕ dans l'Égypte ptolémaïque*, 17). In another instance that she cites, one Zoilos of Aspendos has been ordered by the god Serapis to build a temple for him in Alexandria. He writes to Apollonios for help and says that he was introduced to him by a friend of the king (P.Cair.Zen 1.59034 [257 BCE]); therefore he is in the circle of king's friends.

23. PSI 6.666 (263–229 BCE): τὴν δὲ πίστιν σοι δώσομεν (a surety on a money advance); P.Princ. 2.26 (154 CE) is a *pistis* guarantee from Philadelphia on a shipping contract by a certain Didymus (πίστ<ε>ι Διδύμου, 1.5). The same man guarantees another shipper's receipt to the *sitologos* in the same year at Philadelphia, P.Warr. 5 (Nov. 28, 154). P.Oxy. 3.508.11 (Aug. 23, 102 CE) is a *pistis* guarantee on a loan from Oxyrhynchus; see Reden, *Money in Ptolemaic Egypt*, 199–200.

24. Kent J. Rigsby, *Asylia: Territorial Inviolability in the Hellenistic World* (Berkeley and Los Angeles: University of California Press, 1997), 540. He argues that the Ptolemies initiated the practice of *asylia* around 100 BCE, although it was based on a much older Egyptian custom. For a full list of *asylia* references, see pp. 542–4.

the Greek world, but rather that they "granted asylum in the sense the Romans understood it, religious immunity from civil law; and surely it is from Egypt that the Latin word *asylum* comes, consistent in form and meaning with what we see in Egypt."[25] One of the best known locations for *asylia* is undoubtedly the Serapeion, and we have numerous references to people taking refuge there.[26] However, any place could be made a site of *asylia*, as seen in a priest's request that his house be given *asylia* priveleges[27] or the well-known example of a Judaean *proseuchē*, perhaps at Leontopolis, being granted the same.[28] Places of *asylia* were meant to provide safe haven from those searching for a person, especially to collect on debts or reneged contracts.[29] We have ominous records of surety-holders promising to deliver an individual if they are seen outside of a "temple, altar, *temenos*, or any other place of *skepē*."[30] These documents suggest that the *skepē* could operate like a protection racket, with figures lurking in the shadows waiting to do harm to those out of the protection of either place or person.

The papyrological evidence suggests that some of the practices of *skepē* created economic instability, since a loan or work contract was useless if the weaker party could simply skip into a place of shelter when things got difficult. Withdrawal became so common that Rostevtzoff suggested that it was crippling to the Ptolemaic economy, as refugees hid in temples "while government was in urgent need of their labour."[31] In one

25. Ibid.
26. P.Cair.Zen 4.59620 (248–239 BCE): Here a certain Eutychos takes refuge in the Serapeion at Memphis; in UPZ 1.64 (156 BCE) a guard is offered money in exchange for telling those chasing asylum seekers in the Serapeion when the targets emerged; also UPZ 1.4 (164 BCE). Rigsby observes that the oldest mention of *asylia* in Egypt was in the case of a slave girl being recaptured after running away; she is described as being "out of asylia" (ibid., 542).
27. UPZ 1.119 (Aug. 16, 156 BCE).
28. William Horbury and David Noy, *Jewish Inscriptions of Graeco-Roman Egypt* (Cambridge: Cambridge University Press, 1992), 125; Rigsby, *Asylia*, 571–3.
29. BGU 2.451 (I–II CE); 6.1247 (149/8 BCE); 8.1829 (52/1 BCE).
30. In addition to being called places of *asylia*, or *skepē*, they were also occasionally called places of help, using words with *boēth*-roots; see SB 3.6301 (Aug. 4, 226 BCE): παρέξομα[ι] αὐτὸν ἐμ[φανῆ ἔξω ἱ]εροῦ καὶ βωμοῦ καὶ [τε]μένους κα[ὶ σκέπης] πάσης; also P.Hib. 1.93.4-5 (c. 250 BCE). Here the person securing the debt promises to produce the debtor if they are seen "out of the temple or of any other protection" (ἔξω ἱεροῦ κα[ὶ πάσης] σκέπης).
31. Rostovtzeff, *The Social and Economic History of the Hellenistic World*, 903. See also Jean Bingen, *Le Papyrus Revenue Laws: tradition grecque et adaptation hellénistique* (Opladen: Westdeutscher Verlag, 1978), 38; Hélène Cuvigny,

example of this, a certain Panakestor writes to the *dioiketes*, Apollonios, through Zenon, describing how a group of farmers refused to agree to a tax valuation and refused any contract:

> They said that after having deliberated for a while they would give us an answer and, after four days, taking up residence in the temple they said they did not want to agree to any valuation, be it fair or unfair, but preferred to renounce their right to the crop. For they alleged there was an agreement between you and them that they would pay one third of the produce...[32]

Here the temple and the asylum that it offered seem to operate similarly to a modern strike, since withdrawal is providing leverage in disputes. The increasing number of people disappearing into temples rather than paying debts or finishing contracts caused some difficulty with economic stability, and it led to a well-recognized novelty within the contracts themselves: the workers or debtors swore an oath that they would not disappear. As an example of this, we have the contract of a thresher named Goirēnios from Philadelphia who,

> ...being a thresher from Philadelphia in the Arsonoite nome hand wrote an oath that he swore to work for Semtheus of Teos while staying out of the temple or any other protection (*skepē*) for thirty days...[33]

Presumably here Goirēnios must swear this oath in order to work, and his promise not to resort to a temple or any other *skepē* is telling; why would this be included in a contract unless workers disappearing was a fairly regular occurrence? The thirty day inclusion here is seen elsewhere, and often in the form of a *pistis* letter. This was a letter, which was apparently carried around at all times by a debtor or worker, which they could produce to show that they were in the protection of some recognized figure when they were apprehended by debt-collecting goons.[34] These

---

L'arpentage par espèces dans l'Égypte ptolémaïque d'après les papyrus grecs (Bruxelles: Fondation Égyptologique Reine Élisabeth, 1985), 120.

32. PSI 5.502 (July 7, 257 BCE) (John L. White [trans.], *Light from Ancient Letters*, FF [Philadelphia: Fortress Press, 1986], 18).

33. PSI 5.515 (251 BCE): 8. ὅρκον ὃν ὤμοσον καὶ ἐπεχειρογρά|φησεν Γοιρήνιος Πετεσούχου 10. ἐκ τοῦ Μεμφίτου Θοτεῖ Ἀρυώ|του τοῦ παρὰ Ζήνωνος ποή|σειν ἡμέ(ρας) λ' ἀλοῶντα ἐμ Φι|λαδελφείαι τοῦ Ἀρσι[νοίτου] | νομοῦ ὑπὲρ Σεμθοῦς Τεῶ| 15. τος ἔξω ἱ\ε/ροῦ βωμοῦ σκέπης πάσης. εὐορκοῦντι μέν μοι εὖ εἴη, ἐφιορκοῦντι μέν μοι εὖ εἴη, ἐφιορκοῦντι δὲ ἔνοχός εἰ|μι τῆι ἀσεβείαι.

34. BGU 8.1810 (51–50 BCE): [Σέλ]ευκος Ἡρακλείδηι Εὐτυχίδου [καὶ τ]ῆι τούτου θυγατρὶ Εἰρήνηι δέδονθ' ὑμῖν πίστεις ἀπὸ τῆς [ὑ]ποκειμένης πρὸς ἡμέρας 5. τριάκοντα, ἐν

prohibitions on contracts became so common that by the early Imperial period we have a standardization of a clause which appears in numerous loan contracts, mostly recovered from Alexandrian mummy cartonnage. Yet these additions to contracts went far back to the so-called "Persians of the *Epigone*," and they were attached to loans to prevent losses to the lender in the event that the debtor disappeared into a *skepē* and was consequently impossible to prosecute for the debt.[35] The formula from the Roman period is as follows:

> ...the same loan will be guaranteed from all danger, and he (the loan receiver) shall not flee for refuge on a *pistis* nor into the temple nor upon a petition of supplication, nor upon the command of the order for payment by benefactors or of a guild nor to a place of asylum nor common shelter, nor anywhere else of absolute protection (*skepē*)... (BGU 4.1053 2 [Apr. 2, 13 BCE])[36]

A significant part of this formalization for the present question became the way of nullifying a contract if any *pisteis* of any *skepē* was threatened

---

αἷς ὑπ' οὐδενὸς [περισπασ]θήσε[σθε]. (ἔτους) ᾳ' Μεχείρ; see also BGU 8.1811 (47–46 BCE); 16.2609 (Sept. 28, 7 BCE). In P.Alex. 30 (undated) the *pisteis* is given for 60 days; the multiple of 30 implies that these times were standard. In P.Dion. 11 (Oct. 12, 108 BCE), a petitioner requests a *pistis* from his *strategos*; this was also the limit to which the individual could carry a *pistis*, which in this case was also letter of guarantee; see P.Tebt 3/2.895.38, 117, 124 (c. 175 BCE); 1.112.41 (112 BCE). See also later examples, BGU 4.1120.44 (Nov. 24, 5 BCE); 1126.20 (Nov. 13, 9 BCE); 1156.25 (16–15 BCE).

35. See n. 30. Also Rigsby, *Asylia*, 543; Rostovtzeff, *The Social and Economic History of the Hellenistic World*, 905–6; The *agōgimos* clause was initially applied to the middle status people, the so-called "Persians of the *Epigone*," in order to limit their ability to seek asylum; see Aryeh Kasher, *The Jews in Hellenistic and Roman Egypt: The Struggle for Equal Rights*, TSAJ 7 (Tübingen: Mohr Siebeck, 1985), 90–1. It was adopted through Ptolemaic and Roman times to limit the ability "to avoid legal responsibility in commercial affairs" (91). On the related issue of the *kathaper ek dikes* (καθάπερ ἐκ δίκης) clause in contracts, see José Luis Alonso, "Juristic Papyrology and Roman Law," in *The Oxford Handbook of Roman Law and Society*, ed. Paul J. du Plessis, Clifford Ando, and Kaius Tuori (Oxford: Oxford University Press, 2016), 62; Reden, *Money in Ptolemaic Egypt*, 153–5 (esp. n. 5); and some discussion in S. R. Llewelyn and R. A. Kearsley (eds.), *New Documents Illustrating Early Christianity: A Review of the Greek Inscriptions and Papyri Published in 1980–81*, vol. 6 (New South Wales: The Ancient History Documentary Research Centre: Macquarie University, 1992), no. 13, esp. 91–2.

36. 10–11: μηδ' ἐπ' ἄλ|λην μηδεμίαν ἁπλῶς σκέπην... (two sheets affixed together).

(πίστεων πασῶν σκέπης πάσης).³⁷ If a worker tried to escape the contract, presumably they would have no defense if they were apprehended, since they had sworn their rights away at the beginning of that contract. These types of promises were often accompanied by oaths not to enter places of *asylia*, of which we have examples in Greek and Demotic.³⁸ Upon swearing the oath connected to this contract, the debtor would become powerless to undertake any form of protection, and elsewhere it is made clear that they would have no legal recourse if the case was brought to trial, an extension of the *kathaper ek dikēs* clause.³⁹ Such were the practices of *skepē* and *pistis* which appear in the Egyptian papyri. It is not clear whether they were limited to Egypt or not—we lack the sort of written documents (ie. papyri) from elsewhere to judge—but for the purposes of the discussion below I focus primarily on material with an Egyptian connection. The *skepē* entered a slow decline during the Roman period, and by the third century it had all but disappeared.

3. *The* Skepē *and Judaean Literature*

Having outlined the basic social practices around the *skepē* in Egypt, it is now possible to evaluate some examples where Judaean literature may have come in contact with these. This must be a tentative venture, since *skep-* words occur relatively frequently, and *pist-* words are, of course, common. Since the *skepē* is visible from the Ptolemaic period to its dying dregs in the third century CE, we have a significant time period through which it may have impacted literary texts. However, attempting to identify these is difficult enough with literature composed in Greek, but those which are translated from the Hebrew add an extra level of difference. Finally, genre provides a difficult barrier to good social history, since the ambiguity which is so treasured in poetry and wisdom literature makes the task more difficult.

To make a convincing case that the *skepē* influenced Graeco-Judaean writings we must rely on discrepancies introduced into the translations, as well as the language and social context of Greek writings composed in Egypt. In the examples below, this includes a neologism that seems drawn from the *skepē*. Space does not permit an exhaustive overview of

37. BGU 4.1147 (14 BCE); 1149 (13 BCE); 1150 (13 BCE); 1166 (13 BCE), et al.

38. Rigsby, *Asylia*, 543. Also in financial exchange the double *pistis* was occasionally employed, of which we have examples beyond Egypt; see Peter Arzt-Grabner, *Philemon*, Papyrologische Kommentare zum Neuen Testament 1 (Göttingen: Vandenhoeck & Ruprecht, 2003), 54–5.

39. I.e. BGU 4.1161 (24/3 BCE).

the uses of *skepē* words in the LXX, nor would such a task be judicious. There are clearly many uses of *skepē* language in the translation which refer to shelter,[40] whether offered by shade,[41] under wings,[42] in the shelter of a rock[43] or of a tent.[44] All of these intimate some level of protection, and often are metaphorical indications of God's protection, but are hardly evidence of a unique Egyptian milieu.[45] The shifts which I suggest are displayed at various points in the LXX translation and especially in Sirach and *3 Maccabees* are as follows: the semantics of *skep-* words expand when dealing with the protection offered by one person to another or from God to a person or group of people; we have the introduction of a new noun to describe God as the protector (*skepastēs*); and we begin to see direct lines drawn between the action of trusting (*pisteuō*) and the action of being protected. The use of *skepazō* as a verb marks a shift from the Hebrew in which protection is metaphorical, to a direct act of protecting. We also find *skepē* language incorporated into translation in a way that does not reflect the original meaning of the Hebrew text.

Before turning to the examples of Sirach and *3 Maccabees*, which display these shifts clearly, some examples from the LXX illustrate the impact of *skepē* language on LXX translation. First, we can see the incorporation of the verb *skepazō* with a direct meaning of "to protect." The divine mockery of those who sought the shelter of Pharaoh in LXX Isa. 30:2–3 creates a juxtaposition with the articular infinitive of the verbal forms of βοηθέω and σκεπάζω.

οἱ πορευόμενοι καταβῆναι εἰς Αἴγυπτον ἐμὲ δὲ οὐκ ἐπηρώτησαν τοῦ βοηθηθῆναι ὑπὸ Φαραω καὶ σκεπασθῆναι ὑπὸ Αἰγυπτίων, ἔσται γὰρ ὑμῖν ἡ σκέπη Φαραω εἰς αἰσχύνην καὶ τοῖς πεποιθόσιν ἐπ' Αἴγυπτον ὄνειδος.

The Hebrew text reads:

² הַהֹלְכִים לָרֶדֶת מִצְרַיִם וּפִי לֹא שָׁאָלוּ לָעוֹז בְּמָעוֹז פַּרְעֹה וְלַחְסוֹת בְּצֵל מִצְרָיִם:
³ וְהָיָה לָכֶם מָעוֹז פַּרְעֹה לְבֹשֶׁת וְהֶחָסוּת בְּצֵל־מִצְרַיִם לִכְלִמָּה:

40. Esth. 4:14; Isa. 16:4; also *Let. Aris.* 140.
41. Judg. 9:15; 1 Kgdms 25:20.
42. Pss. 16(17):8; 35(36):8; 60(61):5; 62(63):8.
43. Prov. 2:14.
44. Job 21:28.
45. 1 Macc. 3:3, here Judah Maccabee protects a camp (σκεπάζων); 1 Macc. 11:16, Alexander flees to Arabia to find protection (σκεπασθῆναι); 2 Macc. 5:9, looking for protection from the Spartans because of kinship (ὡς διὰ τὴν συγγένειαν τευξόμενος σκέπης); 2 Macc. 13:17, Judah and his troops successfully raid the camps of Antiochus Eupator (διὰ τὴν ἐπαρήγουσαν αὐτῷ τοῦ κυρίου σκέπην).

The English translation of the LXX reads,

> ² who set out to go down to Egypt
>   without asking for my counsel,
> to take refuge in the protection of Pharaoh,
>   and to seek shelter in the shadow of Egypt;
> ³ Therefore the protection of Pharaoh shall become your shame,
>   and the shelter in the shadow of Egypt your humiliation. (Isa. 30:2-3 [NETS])

Here we can see some interesting things arising from the translation into Greek. The Hebrew, וְלַחְסוֹת בְּצֵל מִצְרָיִם, does literally refer to trusting the shadow of Egypt, but requires the *bēth* preposition for the sense of the noun *ṣl*. The Greek translation requires no such construction, instead the passive infinitive of the verb *skepazō* intimates being given protection. Furthermore, in verse 3, מָעוֹז פַּרְעֹה (lit. "the strength of Pharaoh"), is translated as *skepē*, while the בְּצֵל־מִצְרַיִם is now translated with the verb πείθω, which does refer to "trust."⁴⁶ I suggest that the reference to a shadow in the NETS translation is unnecessary. Both the verb and noun signal to the reader the common practice of sheltering, just as the use of *skepazō* in contemporary papyri likewise signals an act of protection.⁴⁷ The same phenomenon occurs in the translation of Deut. 13:9 in the description of how to treat a friend who tries to lead you into idolatry. The Hebrew suggests that the friend should be killed and that no one should cover over the friend: עָלָיו וְלֹא־תְכַסֶּה. In this case, the Hebrew כָּסָה with the עַל seems to have the sense of protection, and is appropriately translated as: οὐδ' οὐ μὴ σκεπάσῃς αὐτόν. Yet the other occurrences of עַל כָּסָה are translated using the verb καλύπτω.⁴⁸ The unique appearance of *skepazō* here signals that the LXX translator(s) have a *skepē* context in mind, using the verb to indicate protection rather than simple covering. Therefore,

---

46. This same passage from Isaiah is quoted by Justin Martyr in his *Dialogue with Trypho* (79.3).

47. This is the case of the *hierodouloi*, mentioned above: διατελο[ῦ]μεν τοὺς φόρους εὐτακτοῦντες εἰς τὸ ἱερὸν διὰ τὴν παρ' ὑμῶν σκέ[π]ην, καὶ νῦν καὶ ἐν τοῖς ἔμπροσθε χρόνοις ὑπὸ ὑ|10[μῶ]ν σκεπαζόμε[θ]α... (P.Hib. 1.35.10 [250 BCE]); P.Gen. 3.92, frs. A.1.9 & B.2.19 (165 BCE): τῶν σκεπαζομένων ("those who are protected"); P.Tar. 5, Fr. G.2, l. 5-6 (c. 189 BCE): αὐτοὺς σκεπαζομένους ὑπό τινων ἡγουμένων... ("those who are protected by some authorities"); SB 12.10845.3 (204 BCE): τῶν σκεπαζομένων γεω[ρ]γῶν; SB 20.14106.17 (95–4 BCE): μηδὲ κώμας σκεπάζε[ιν], et al.

48. 2 Chron. 5:8 συνεκάλυπτεν (Cherubim covering the ark); Num. 16:33, ἐκάλυψεν (the earth covered them); Prov. 10:11: καλύψει ἀπώλεια (conceal violence).

the incorporation of the *skep-* root in both of these cases suggests that its meaning of protection simplifies the Hebrew idiom.

Another example of creative translation comes from the arrangements for the Passover as given to Moses and Aaron in Exodus 12. In this case, the verb and preposition combination of פָּסַח עַל is twice translated with *skepazō*. In Exod. 12:13, the famous promise is given: "when I see the blood I will pass over you."[49] From the Hebrew וּפָסַחְתִּי עֲלֵכֶם, the Greek translator has rendered ὄψομαι τὸ αἷμα καὶ σκεπάσω ὑμᾶς, changing the second verb to a promise of protection. The translator uses the same language after the ritual of Passover is established, at Exod. 12:27, in which the participants are required to tell their children that the LORD passed over them (פָּסַח עַל-). The LXX renders this: ἐσκέπασεν τοὺς οἴκους τῶν υἱῶν Ισραηλ. In both of these cases, a semantic shift has occurred, and the Greek adopts language of divine protection as opposed to being spared divine judgement, a subtle but significant change. Yet the פָּסַח עַל construct also appears in verse 23: וּפָסַח יְהוָה עַל־הַפֶּתַח. Here the translator does not use the verb *skepazō* but renders the phrase as παρελεύσεται κύριος τὴν θύραν. The identical Hebrew construction is translated in two different ways. When the translator uses the verb *skepazō* they clearly have protection in mind, yet when it comes to describing the actual passing over of the door the verb παρέρχομαι is used instead.[50] The translation has been updated to reflect Egyptian social practice. The subtle theological shift to God as protector will become important below. These few examples suggest that the incorporation of *skep-* words by the translator(s) are pregnant with local context and meaning which justify a lack of adherence to the Hebrew.

I would like to focus the remainder of the chapter on two books in particular which give us examples of composition in Hellenistic Egypt: Sirach and *3 Maccabees*. Measuring a *skepē* influence on Sirach is difficult because of the combination of translation and additions and an incomplete Hebrew manuscript tradition.[51] However, in the introduction I suggested that Sir. 22:20-26 is probably an insertion:

---

49. NRSV

50. Note the other occurrence of פָּסַח in Isa. 31:5, where *skepē* is not used in the translation.

51. N.B. most references to the noun *skepē* in Sirach refer to shade or protection from the elements: Sir. 6:29 (wisdom is a strong shelter; 14:26 (wisdom is shelter like a tree); 29:22; 34:16 (here the eyes of the Lord are a shelter from the heat of the day); 48:12.

23. Gain your fellow's trust in poverty so that in his prosperity you may be filled as well; in a time of distress stay with him so that in his inheritance you may be a joint heir.[52]
24. Preceding a fire there are a furnace's vapor and smoke; so preceding bloodshed are abuses.
25. I will not be ashamed to shelter a friend, and from before him I will never hide.
26. And if bad things will happen to me on his account, everyone who hears will guard against him. (Sir. 22:20-26 [NETS])

Read through the lens of *skepē*, we can suggest a social context for the addition in which the grandson in his translation is attempting to legitimize protection practices. In this case, the pericope and its construction seems to consider gaining a neighbor's *pistis* as somehow related to the practice of protecting a friend. It encourages establishing a close bond with the neighbor, but it is clearly a friendship rooted in some form of financial exchange (as Benjamin Wright has captured in the NETS translation). In this case bringing the neighbor into *pistis* implies a relationship of trust with debt attached to it; the text is recommending a sort of financial speculation on a neighbor's well-being so that one will prosper (lit. "to be filled" [πίμπλημι]) when the neighbour does. While perhaps vulgar to modern sensitivities, in which a friendship based on money seems no friendship at all, it may be quite normal in terms of ancient fiscal relationships.[53] Furthermore, we should not consider this advice to be recommending taking soulless advantage of a neighbor's vulnerability; it is reasonable to suggest that the grandson's view of fiscal friendship was quite charitable. The ominous εἰ κακά μοι συμβήσεται δι' αὐτόν may not refer to the *philos* acting wickedly, but to evil which might befall the protector through those who would harm her friend; in this case διά would have the sense of "on account of," and the reference to others "guarding against him" (φυλάξεται ἀπ' αὐτοῦ) may refer to keeping away from that friend. We might translate this: "If evil should fall to me on account of (my protection of) him, everyone who hears about it will keep away from him (i.e., so evil does not fall to them)." However, in light of the cautions against false friends in Sirach (5:15–6:1; 19:8-9; 29:6) it may make more sense to read the meaning of this as it stands; protect a friend unless they hurt you. Regardless of whether this pericope was in the

---

52. GK II adds here: "for one should not always despise the outline, nor is a rich person admirable when he has no purpose" (NETS).
53. Gregory, *Like an Everlasting Signet Ring*, 143. He says that loans across economic positions are common to Sirach and not only from the very wealthy.

original composition or whether it is part of an evolving wisdom tradition around Sirach, it fits with the theme of the book. Ben Sira is approving of wealth as long as one does not hoard it.⁵⁴ Bringing a neighbor into debt also aligns with Sirach's debt-positive attitude at 8:12-13, where readers are warned not to lend to someone more powerful, this done in the context of warnings about dealing with people who have more social power. Chapter 29, on the other hand, has a much more expanded discussion of debt, ordering generosity to the poor (vv. 8-13) and to those of lower social status, as well as approval of loans to a neighbor in verses 1-7 and guaranteeing a neighbor's debts in verses 14-20 (29:14, being an ἔγγυος).⁵⁵ However, it is absent from the Hebrew manuscript tradition, and may also reflect an addition to the original material.

While the focus of this chapter is not *pistis*, the aligning of *pistis/ pisteuō* language with protection is an interesting development in Sirach. Dieter Lührmann suggested that this was the introductory point for the understanding of *pistis* which would dictate later Christian belief.⁵⁶ Dennis Lindsay's study of *pist-* words in Sirach identifies 48 instances of the words, of which 22 appear only in Greek without a comparable Hebrew text. He suggests that the noun *pistis* is normally a translation of the Hebrew אמן-rooted nouns, although only two Hebrew comparisons exist; the verb *pisteuein* is often a representation of the hiphil אמן,

---

54. Benjamin G. Wright and Claudia Camp, "Who Has Been Tested by Gold and Found Perfect? Ben Sirah's Discourses of Riches and Poverty," *Henoch* 23 (2001): esp. 155–8; Maurice Gilbert, "Prêt, aumône et caution," in *Der Einzelne und seine Gemeinschaft bei Ben Sira*, ed. Renate Egger-Wenzel and Ingrid Krammer, BZAW 270 (Berlin: de Gruyter, 1998), 179–81. He shows that Ben Sira does not exist in a world in which the state gives loans, and the individual being wound up in fiscal exchanges is considered perfectly normal (187–8).

55. Gregory, *Like an Everlasting Signet Ring*, 128–69. Sitta von Reden suggests that loans were first sought among family and neighbours, before moving outwards into other social relationships, such as employee/employer and landlord/tenant, *Money in Ptolemaic Egypt*, 251.

56. Dieter Lührmann, "Pistis im Judentum," *ZNW* 64 (1973): 33–4. His argument rests on Sirach's introduction of a theologically charged πιστεύειν κυρίῳ or νόμῳ in the place of the Hebrew אמן, as well as using *pistis* to translate a wide variety of Hebrew words. He thinks that the uses of *pistis* in Sirach are thus Hebraisms and not reflective of common Hellenistic use; also Gerhard Barth, "Pistis in Hellenistischer Religiosität," *ZNW* 73 (1982): 110–26, who offers a Hellenistic context for *pistis*. For an overview of the history of interpretation of *pistis*, see Benjamin Schliesser, *Abraham's Faith in Romans 4: Paul's Concept of Faith in Light of the History of Reception of Genesis 15:6* (Tübingen: Mohr Siebeck, 2007), 7–73.

although Sirach is unique in including it as a translation of בטח ("to trust") and שמר ("to guard, keep"); and both *empisteuō* and *pistos* either match or deviate significantly from the translations in the LXX.[57]

> Sirach stands with one foot firmly planted in the normal LXX use of the word group but begins to take a further step with his use of πιστ-, and especially with the verb (ἐμ)πιστεύειν. Sirach employs the Greek word group to represent Hebrew expressions other than ones represented by the root אמן—a use unprecedented elsewhere in the LXX.[58]

Since Sirach's use of the Hebrew text employs some novelties, it is important to discern whether there is a difference between the employment of *skepē* language in translation and the grandson's composition. Some such language is employed, for example, in the discussion of a faithful (*pistos*) friend:

> Faithful friends are a sturdy shelter[59]
>   whoever finds one has found a treasure.
> Faithful friends are beyond price;
>   no amount can balance their worth.
> Faithful friends are life-saving medicine;
>   and those who fear the Lord will find them.
> Those who fear the Lord direct their friendship aright,
>   for as they are, so are their neighbors also. (Sir. 6:14-17)

The first line here in Greek reads: φίλος πιστὸς σκέπη κραταιά ὁ δὲ εὑρὼν αὐτὸν εὗρεν θησαυρόν, and the strong *skepē* of a *pistos* friend seems replete with economic possibility, especially given that a friend is a storehouse (*thēsauros*); a *filos pistos* is consequently called "beyond price," valuable, and "life-saving medicine" (6:15-17).[60] However, despite using this language to translate the Hebrew, the sense of the text does not actually endorse friendship in exchange for gain, but merely emphasizes the

---

57. Dennis R. Lindsay, *Josephus and Faith: "Pístis" and "Pisteúein" as Faith Terminology in the Writings of Flavius Josephus and in the New Testament*, AGJU 19 (Leiden: Brill, 1993), 39–43.

58. Ibid., 43.

59. Jeremy Corley, *Ben Sira's Teaching on Friendship*, BJS 316 (Providence, RI: Brown Judaic Studies, 1996), 37. Gregory (*Like an Everlasting Signet Ring*, 27 n. 3) suggests that the Hebrew, אוהב, in MS A is a mistake for אוהל.

60. Gregory, *Like an Everlasting Signet Ring*, 27–8. On the value of friendship in financial terms, see Corley, *Ben Sira's Teaching on Friendship*, 58–9.

value of that friendship, albeit in heightened language in comparison to the Hebrew. In Hebrew, הון ("treasure") becomes a θησαυρόν in Greek, a "storehouse." The Hebrew תקוף (AII r) or perhaps מגן תיוף (CII v) is rendered as σκέπη κραταιά for "strong shield."

It is not clear that friendship without fiscal implications is ever completely possible in antiquity, given that what Sitta von Reden calls "a deeply rooted culture of credit, by which the social imperative of helping one's friends, neighbours and fellow-citizens was transmitted, formed the background of an extensive monetary credit economy throughout classical antiquity."[61] Therefore, in the grandson's justification of potentially exploitative friendship, I disagree with Lindsay's interpretation that, at Sir. 22:23, gaining the *pistis* of a neighbor is "obviously an admonition to faithfulness and steadfastness, and is directly parallel to 'stand by him [in the time of trouble]' in the second part of this verse... [I]t becomes obvious that friendship itself is a 'sacred' relationship and that *pistis* in these contexts cannot be fully appreciated simply at the profane level."[62] Much more accurate is John J. Collins' assessment that this is "enlightened self-interest."[63] In fact, for those readers of Sirach who were familiar with *skepē* practices, the pericope spiritualizes these and justifies them as protection and help, granting licence for the reader to enter into protective relationships with client debtors who might otherwise be "ashamed" to participate in the *skepē*.

There are two other linguistic moves in Sirach which likely signal that the grandson is familiar with *skepē* practice. The first is not unique to Sirach, but occurs elsewhere in the LXX as in *3 Maccabees* (below), namely, the use of a new title for God: ὁ σκεπαστής:

---

61. Sitta von Reden, *Money in Classical Antiquity* (Cambridge: Cambridge University Press, 2010), 122.

62. Ibid., 44; For Sirach's attitude towards the poor, see Pancratius Cornelis Beentjes, "'Sei den Waisen wie ein Vater und den Witwen wie ein Gatte'. Ein kleiner Kommentar zu Ben Sira 4,1-10," in *Der Einzelne und seine Gemeinschaft bei Ben Sira*, ed. Renate Egger-Wenzel and Ingrid Krammer, BZAW 270 (Berlin: de Gruyter, 1998), 51–64.

63. Collins, *Jewish Wisdom in the Hellenistic Age*, 75. See also Seth Schwartz, who argues that Sirach is uncomfortable with the reality of social reciprocity given the admonitions of Torah to charity, and so he is "trying to provide a Jewish, Torah-based justification for a set of social and cultural norms that in reality were radically at odds with the norms and ethos of the Torah." *Were the Jews a Mediterranean Society? Reciprocity and Solidarity in Ancient Judaism* (Princeton: Princeton University Press, 2010), 45–79, esp. 77–8.

...for you have been my protector (*skepastēs*) and helper (*boēthos*)
and have redeemed my body from destruction
and from a trap of a slanderous tongue,
from lips that fabricate a lie,
and against those who stand by
you have been a help (*boēthos*)... (Sir. 51:2)

Here we see the actions of God, as a helper (*boēthos*), but also as a protector (*skepastēs*). The noun *skepastēs* only appears in Graeco-Judaean texts, where it is usually applied to God as the protector.[64] Thus the language of protection between humans is echoed for the divine, who takes on a *skep-* rooted title. The second thing which must be highlighted in light of the discussion of *skepē is* a brief but interesting relationship between *skep-* and *pist-* words among a group of woes in Sirach 2. At Sir. 2:13-14 we see the verbs *pisteuō* and *skepazō* closely related, again in reference to divine protection:

13 Woe to a faint heart, because it does not have faith;
Therefore it will not be sheltered.
14. Woe to you who have lost endurance.
And what will you do when the Lord makes his reckoning? (NETS)

Here there is a direct link between trust and protection (ὅτι οὐ πιστεύει διὰ τοῦτο οὐ σκεπασθήσεται), and a lack of one leads to a lack of the other.[65] In this case, the exchange between trust and protection mirrors *skepē* language. To conclude the discussion of Sirach, the unique developments in friendship in the Greek text seems to draw upon fiscal relationships, and the grandson's positive view of debt allows him to endorse *skepē* relationships in his wisdom teaching in dealing with humans, while also using *skepē* language to refer to God. Therefore, the translation of Sirach,

---

64. Also in LXX Exod. 15:2: βοηθὸς καὶ σκεπαστὴς is used to translate עָזִּי וְזִמְרָת (lit. "my strength and song"); For other uses of *skepastēs*, see Jdt 9:11; 3 Macc. 6:9 (below); *Odes Sol.* 1:2; Ps. 70(71):6 (here σκεπαστής seems to be translated for גוֹזִי בְּךָ). The term is completely absent in most Greek literature after the LXX until its appearance in Origen, i.e. *Comm. Jo.* 13.28.168. Adjectival forms of *skepast-* are witnessed from classical literature: Aesch., *Tetr.* 29, B, fr. 292b; Thuc. 5.71.1; Arist., *De gen. anim.* 719b.17, et al.; as well as the word *skepazō* (Hipp., *Aquis et locis* 8.14).

65. Teresa Morgan, *Roman Faith and Christian Faith: Pistis and Fides in the Early Roman Empire and Early Churches* (Oxford: Oxford University Press, 2015), 194–5. Occasionally, trust (*pisteuō*) also comes with the promise of earthly reward in Sirach (2:8; 51:30), what Benjamin Schliesser calls a "divine economy"; see Schliesser, *Abraham's Faith in Romans 4*, 174–5.

likely with insertions by the grandson, bears the marks of its Egyptian milieu (though some imprint of Egyptian influence may even have been upon the Hebrew original as well[66]).

The story of *3 Maccabees*, written in Alexandria around 100 BCE, records the persecution of Judaeans in Egypt under Ptolemy IV Philopator (221–204 BCE).[67] The reason for the king's hatred towards Judaeans, the story says, is that he was barred from entry into the holiest of holies at the Jerusalem temple after the Battle of Raphia (1:8-29; 3:16-19) and that the Judaeans in Egypt had failed to observe Dionysiac rituals (2:28-30). The work dramatically describes how they are brought to the hippodrome to meet their fate under the feet of Ptolemy's war elephants, but God intervenes. The author knows Daniel (*3 Macc.* 6:6) and the text appears to have a narrative and structural relationship to Esther.[68] It seems to have been written to a Judaean audience, either to encourage particularism in the diaspora (ie. against the Dionysiac cults) and celebrate past accomplishments, or perhaps to demonstrate continuity between the steadfastness of those in Jerusalem and in the diaspora.[69]

---

66. For a comparison of the Egyptian wisdom tradition's influence on Ben Sira, see Jack T. Sanders, *Ben Sira and Demotic Wisdom* (Chico, CA: Scholars Press, 1983), esp. 61–106.

67. H. Anderson, "3 Maccabees," in *The Old Testament Pseudepigrapha*, ed. James H. Charlesworth, 2 vols. (New York: Doubleday, 1985), esp. 2:510–12. Josephus has the Ptolemy here as IX Physcon (*Ap.* 2:5). Moses Hadas (*The Third and Fourth Books of Maccabees* [New York: Harper for Dropsie, 1953], 3, 19–22) argues that it was composed at the Roman takeover, 24 BCE, with the threat to the Jewish position in the new administration. He places the composition at the Roman conquest of Egypt given the presence of the *laographia* in the work (2:28), which he says shows Jewish anxiety about changing status and new tax requirements under the Romans. However, the *laographia* and opposition to it is not strictly a product of Roman times, and I follow here Sara Raup Johnson, *Historical Fictions and Hellenistic Jewish Identity: Third Maccabees in Its Cultural Context* (Berkeley: University of California Press, 2004), 134–9, who argues for a date around 100 BCE based on similarities to LXX Esther and Aristaeas; see also John J. Collins, *Between Athens and Jerusalem: Jewish Identity in the Hellenistic Diaspora*, 2nd edn (Grand Rapids: Eerdmans, 2000), 125–6; N. Clayton Croy, *3 Maccabees*, Septuagint Commentary Series (Leiden: Brill, 2006), xi–xii; Sara Raup Johnson, "3 Maccabees," in *T&T Clark Companion to the Septuagint*, ed. J. K. Aitken (London: Bloomsbury T&T Clark, 2015), 292–305.

68. Noah Hacham, "3 Maccabees and Esther: Parallels, Intertextuality, and Diaspora Identity," *JBL* 126 (2007): 765.

69. J. R. C. Cousland, "Reversal, Recidivism, and Reward in 3 Maccabees: Structure and Purpose," *JSJ* 34 (2003): 81. He shows an astonishing number of interesting

Throughout the work, *skepē* language is employed rhetorically to show the helplessness of the Judaeans and then the mighty protection of God by contrast. First, when the Greeks living in Alexandria who were their friends and neighbors hear of what is about to befall them, they offer them pledges (πίστεις ἐδίδουν); here the *pisteis* given are guarantees to protect (3:10).[70] Chapter 3 presents a letter from Ptolemy to his soldiers and generals which relates the situation in Jerusalem and the Judaean's disrespect towards his benevolence (v. 20: φιλανθρώπως). It reports that they have rejected the citizenship that was offered. Finally, it ends with a threat:

> But whosoever shelters any of the Judeans (ὃς δ' ἂν σκεπάσῃ τινὰ τῶν Ἰουδαίων), from the old to the young, even infants, will be executed with degrading torments, along with their entire household. As for those who are willing to inform, they will receive the property of the one incurring the punishment, as well as a thousand drachmas from the royal treasury, and they will be honored with the crown of freedom. Any place where a Judean is discovered being sheltered in any way, however, is without exception to become untrodden and scorched; it will become altogether worthless to every mortal creature for all time. (*3 Macc.* 3:27-29 [NETS])[71]

The verb *skepazō* is used here for giving protection and the same verb is repeated two verses later with a warning to places sheltering Judaeans (σκεπαζόμενος Ἰουδαῖος). The letter also paints an ominous picture of people being rewarded for turning in their neighbors and the interesting

---

reversals in the Aristotelian *peripeteiac* tradition (pp. 44–5); On the creation of continuity with Palestine, see David S. Williams, "3 Maccabees: A Defense of Diaspora Judaism?" *JSP* 7 (1995): 17–29; Noah Hacham, "Is Judaism the ΕΥΣΕΒΕΙΑ of Alexandria? 3 Maccabees 2:31a Revisited," *CP* 109 (2014): 72–9.

70. Various forms of *pist*- appear in the work: 2:7—τοὺς δὲ ἐμπιστεύσαντας; 3:21—τὰ πεπιστευμένα; 4:19—πιστωθῆναι. *3 Macc.* 5:44 does seem to refer to the *skepē* with the use of *pistis*, referring to those close to the king, οἱ φίλοι καὶ συγγενεῖς μετὰ πίστεως.

71. Croy, *3 Maccabees*, 65–72, provides a full overview of the decree and its issues. Further on the authenticity of the Ptolemaic letter, see Adolf Deissmann, *Bible Studies: Contributions Chiefly from Papyri and Inscriptions to the History of the Language, the Literature, and the Religion of Hellenistic Judaism and Primitive Christianity*, trans. Alexander Grieve (Edinburgh: T. & T. Clark, 1901), 341–5. He says that the reliability of the decree is questionable, but that it certainly matches Ptolemaic decrees formally (he compares it with UPZ I 121[156 BCE], a warrant for the arrest of some runaway slaves). On the issue of citizenship and the military implications of *3 Maccabees*, see Joseph Modrzejewski, *Troisième livre des Maccabées*, La bible d'Alexandrie 15.3 (Paris: Éditions du Cerf, 2008), 76–82.

promise that they will be given freedom (τῇ ἐλευθερίᾳ στεφανωθήσεται).[72] We have two threats of destruction, therefore, first to people and secondly to places which shelter Judaeans. As we have already seen, the papyri show that this type of protection could be by an individual or a specifically designated place. N. Clayton Croy suggests that the threat of destruction to the place of shelter may be hyperbole; however, the complete destruction of a place of *skepē* is not outside of the realm of imagination, and would coincide with it losing its right to be a place of *asylia* (above).[73] The point here is that the king threatens people and places of *skepē* for any role in sheltering Judaeans, serving the rhetorical purpose of emphasizing their helplessness. In fact, several chapters later the author reports that it seemed to the gentiles "that the Jews were without any other aid," as the NRSV translates it:

οἱ δὲ πάσης σκέπης ἔρημοι δοκοῦντες εἶναι τοῖς ἔθνεσιν Ιουδαῖοι διὰ τὴν πάντοθεν περιέχουσαν αὐτοὺς μετὰ δεσμῶν ἀνάγκην...

But the Judaeans, who to the nations seemed to be bereft of all defense on account of the constraint of their chains that confined them on every side...
(*3 Macc.* 5:6 [NETS])

The description of them as being apart from any help, represented by the use of the genitive πάσης σκέπης, is familiar to us from the *skepē* papyri.[74] In fact, this exact genitive construction appears over thirty times in extant papyri as a blanket prohibition against taking refuge in any place of protection. Although most of these come from Alexandrian cartonnage

---

72. Literally "he/she shall be crowned with freedom" (τῇ ἐλευθερίᾳ στεφανωθήσεται). MS Alexandrinus has καὶ τῆς ἐλευθερίας στεφανωθήσεται. Hugo Grotius first suggested that this may be a corruption of the dative plural (τοῖς ἐλευθερίοις στεφανωθήσεται), which would indicate being crowned at the Dionysiac Eleutheria, *loc ad.* in Adolf Deissmann, *Bible Studies: Contributions Chiefly from Papyri and Inscriptions to the History of the Language, the Literature, and the Religion of Hellenistic Judaism and Primitive Christianity*, trans. Alexander Grieve (Edinburgh: T. & T. Clark, 1901), 342–3 (Deissmann hesitates to accept this given the absence of record of an Eleutheria in Egypt, but it is supported by Anderson, "3 Maccabees," 2:522 [note e]). Deissmann interprets is as referring to Jews who inform on fellow Jews who will be spared from judgement; they will be released from their slave (*3 Macc.* 2:28) status (p. 345).

73. Croy, *3 Maccabees*, 72 (he cites Dan. 3:29; Esth. 3:13; 8:11; Add Esth. 8:12x[16:24]).

74. P.Hib. 1.93.1; BGU 4.1161.25; above nn. 33 and 37.

of the imperial period,⁷⁵ several examples from around 200 BCE suggest that, even by that time, these two words were standard ways to indicate taking shelter in any other place that might offer it beyond the temples and sanctuaries.⁷⁶ The language would be clear to those who were familiar with these loan documents and would illustrate to the readers the severity of the Judaeans' circumstance, since they literally had no possible place of protection, indicating the hopelessness of their situation. These two uses of *skep-* words, once in a royal letter and once perhaps echoing language from contracts, suggests that the author is drawing on the common social imagery of the *skepē,* perhaps even both as direct quotations.

Yet now, having portrayed the helplessness of the Jews and their complete lack of *skepē,* the author invokes one last *skep-* word, after describing how they cry out to God to help them (5:25: αὐτοῖς βοηθῆσαι), who then provides aid (5:35: βοήθεια):

καὶ νῦν μίσυβρι πολυέλεε τῶν ὅλων σκεπαστά⁷⁷ τὸ τάχος ἐπιφάνηθι τοῖς ἀπὸ Ισραηλ γένους ὑπὸ ἐβδελυγμένων ἀνόμων ἐθνῶν ὑβριζομένοις

And now, you who hate insolence, abounding in mercy, Protector of the universe, swiftly manifest yourself to those of the race of Israel, who are now suffering outrages at the hands of detestable and lawless nations. (*3 Macc.* 6:9 [NETS])

In contrast to the fact that nobody could provide them shelter, God is now called the protector (*skepastēs*) of all (6:9) in the vocative, drawing again on that title which is unique to Judaean writings. The message is clear: the *skepē* which the Jews have is not human; in fact, when all else seemed lost, God became their *skepastēs.*⁷⁸ This dramatic reversal reaffirms the power and control of God, and completely erases any possibility of human agency in facilitating the rescue of the Judaeans. Therefore, it makes *skepē* a theological lesson in the protection of God in contrast to hopelessness.

75. BGU 4.1145.18 (5 BCE); 1147.33 (14–13 BCE); 1149.37 (13 BCE), et al.
76. SB 3.6277 + 6301.11–13 (226 BCE): ἐφ' ὧι παρέ|ξομα[ι] αὐτὸν ἐμ[φανῆ ἔξω ἱ]εροῦ καὶ βωμοῦ καὶ [τε]μένους κα[ὶ σκέπης] πάσης... (N.B. the reading is certain because of the duplicate which fills in the lacuna); see also P.Hamb. 1.28.11 (199–150 BCE); P.Hib. 1.93 (250 BCE); PSI 5.515.15–6 (251 BCE): ἔξω ἱ\ε/ροῦ βωμοῦ σκέπης πάσης; and above, n. 29.
77. Alexandrinus and other witnesses include *skepasta* here.
78. Ashley Bacchi, "God as Kingly Foil in 3 Maccabees," *Zutot* 11, no. 1 (2014): 57–69, argues something similar, that the author deliberately chooses to give them no early help in an attempt to make God the ultimate helper.

4. Conclusion

The use of *skepē* language for protection occurs in other Graeco-Judaean literature in works like Judith,[79] Wisdom,[80] Testament of Benjamin,[81] and eventually moved into early Christian writings (they are mostly absent in Philo, who prefers to use *skepē* as covering in opposition to nakedness[82]). In the parable of the willow tree, in the Shepherd of Hermas, this mighty tree casts its shadow (*skepē*) over all who are called "by the name of the Lord" (*Sim.* 8.1.1–2). The work uses both meanings of "shadow" and "protection," shown in the interpretation of the parable which reads:

> "Listen," he says; "this great tree which overshadows (τὸ σκεπάζον) plains and mountains and all the earth is the law of God which was given to the whole world; and this law is the Son of God preached unto the ends of the earth. But the people that are under the shadow (ὑπὸ τὴν σκέπην) are they that have heard the preaching, and believed (πιστεύσαντες) on Him." (Herm. *Sim.* 8.3.2)[83]

As in Sirach, Hermas gives us a connection between *pisteuō* and being under protection, albeit in a metaphor. He goes on to say that those *episkopoi* and *philoxenoi* who sheltered (ἐσκέπασαν) those who needed it will be forever under the Lord's *skepē* (*Sim.* 8.104.2-3).[84] This use of the preposition *hypo* here aligns with several similar examples in the papyri of being under protection,[85] and Hermas uses *skepazō* for both divine protection and human protection. The use of *skepē* in Hermas which uses a physical shadow as a metaphor for protection (presumably offered by

---

79. Jdt 8:15: "For unless he be willing to come to our aid (βοηθῆσαι ἡμῖν) within the five days, he has the power, within the course of the days he wishes, either to shield or destroy us before the eyes of our enemies (σκεπάσαι ἡμέραις ἢ καὶ ὀλοθρεῦσαι ἡμᾶς)."

80. Wis. 5:16: "Therefore they will receive a glorious crown and a beautiful diadem from the hand of the Lord, because with his right hand he will cover them, and with his arm he will shield them."

81. *T. Benj.* 3:4; 4:3. *skepazomenos*.

82. Every occurrence of *skep-* in Philo refers to coverings, not protection—*Leg.* 2.53 (vice and virtue are coverings of the soul); *Leg.* 3.252 (clothes are the covering of the body); *Cher.* 126 (shelter of a house); *Sacr.* 843 (a soul without covering during sacrifice); *Spec.* 1.83 (clothing for a covering); *Praem.* 99 (shelter).

83. J. B. Lightfoot (trans.), *The Apostolic Fathers* (London: Macmillan & Co., 1891), modified.

84. …οὗτοι οὖν πάντες σκεπασθήσονται ὑπὸ τοῦ κυρίου διαπαντός.

85. P.Tebt. 1.34 (100 BCE); P.Lond. 3.897.5–6 (p. 206; 84 CE): ἐὰν δὲ δύνημαι σκεπάσαι ἢι ὑπὸ σκέπην τινα γενέσθαι.

salvation) aligns with Origen, who contrasts being under the shadow of the law with the shadow of Christ; these two are then contrasted with the shadow of death.

> But the shadow (*skepē*) of Christ, under which we now live among the Gentiles, that is to say, the faith of his incarnation, affords complete protection… Yet the period of this shadow too is to be fulfilled at the end of the age… (*Song of Songs Comm*. III.5)[86]

Here again *pistis* is linked to protection, and Origen locates believers under it. Therefore, the loaded meaning of *skepē* as both a shadow and as protection, the choice of translators and writers, would be mediated through the LXX and would influence the way that God's protection and human salvation were perceived for centuries to come.

In fitting with the theme of this volume, the incorporation of *skepē* language and practices into translation indicates that the translators and writers of the LXX were familiar, to some extent, with *skepē*. In some cases, translators have apparently used the language to completely change the sense of the Hebrew original, likely in order to update or adapt it to their social context. We can see the Hebrew metaphors of protection being solidified into the simple action verb in the Greek, and occasionally complete departures from the original Hebrew meaning to more familiar local language (Exod. 12:13). Moreover, I have made the case that in Sirach the instructions on friendship are actually updated with new material that justifies giving *pistis* to a neighbor and *skepē* to a friend. *3 Maccabees* uses *skepē* as an evocative juxtaposition of the helplessness of the Judaeans and the protection offered by God. The work either records or creates a letter from Ptolemy which includes reference to both persons and places offering *skepē*, and borrows from the standard, threatening formula by which a debtor either may be delivered for judgement or is prohibited from entering any other place of *skepē*. In this case, we have a strong indication that the writer is familiar with these loan contracts. Finally, the title of God as the *skepastēs* enters into translation and composition.

---

86. Origen, *The Song of Songs: Commentary and Homilies*, trans. R. P. Lawson, ACW 26 (London: Longmans, 1957), 184.

5

Hilarion's Letter to His Wife, Child Exposure, and Early Christianity

Jeremiah J. Johnston

The chance discovery of Hilarion's letter to his wife Alis (P.Oxy. 4.744), in which he commands her to throw out her soon-to-be-born infant if it turns out to be a girl, provides a graphic touch of reality to the discussion of infant exposure in late antiquity. It also clarifies aspects of early Christian criticism of the practice of exposure, on the one hand, and morbid accusations leveled against Christians, on the other. I begin with Hilarion's letter. Greek text, notes, and translation are as follows:[1]

1. The *editio princeps* appears in B. P. Grenfell and A. S. Hunt (eds.), "744. Letter of Ilarion," in *The Oxyrhynchus Papyri*, Part IV (London: Egypt Exploration Fund, 1904), 243–4. For transcriptions, translations, and brief notes, see also G. Milligan, *Selections from the Greek Papyri* (Cambridge: Cambridge University Press, 1910), 32–3 + frontispiece; W. Schubart, *Ein Jahrtausend am Nil: Briefe aus dem Altertum verdeutscht und erklärt* (Berlin: Weidmann, 1912), 122, no. 40; idem, *Ein Jahrtausend am Nil: Briefe aus dem Altertum. Zweite Auflage. Mit 4 Lichtdrucktafeln und 35 Textabbildungen* (Berlin: Weidmann, 1923), 65–6, no. 46; S. Witkowski, *Epistulae Privatae Graecae quae in Papyris aetatis Lagidarum servantur*, 2nd edn (Leipzig: B. G. Teubner, 1912), no. 72; A. Laudien, *Griechische Papyri aus Oxyrhynchos* (Berlin: Weidmann, 1912), no. 1; A. S. Hunt and C. C. Edgar, *Select Papyri I*, LCL 266 (Cambridge, MA: Harvard University Press; London: Heinemann, 1932), 294–5, no. 105; W. H. Davis, *Greek Papyri of the First Century* (London and New York: Harper, 1933), 1–7; J. G. Winter, *Life and Letters in the Papyri*, Jerome Lectures 1 (Ann Arbor: University of Michigan Press, 1933), 56; A. C. Johnson, *Roman Egypt to the Reign of Diocletian* (Baltimore: Johns Hopkins University Press, 1936), 281, no. 170; J. Finegan, *Light from the Ancient Past: The Archaeological Background of Judaism and Christianity*, 2nd edn (Princeton: Princeton University Press, 1959), 406–7 + pl. 140; H. Metzger, *Nachrichten aus dem Wüstensand: Eine Sammlung von Papyruszeugnissen* (Zurich: Artemis, 1974), no. 46; N. Lewis, *Life in Egypt under Roman Rule* (Oxford: Clarendon Press, 1983), 54; D. Braund, *Augustus to Nero: A Sourcebook on*

Greek Text

recto

Ἱλαρίωνα[a] Ἄλιτι τῆι ἀδελφῆι[b] πλεῖστα χαί
ρειν καὶ Βεροῦτι τῇ κυρίᾳ μου καὶ Ἀπολλω-
ναριν[c]. γίνωσκε ὡς ἔτι καὶ νῦν ἐν Ἀλεξαν
δρέᾳ[d] σμεν[e]· μὴ ἀγωνιᾷς ἐὰν ὅλως εἰσ
5 πορεύονταί[f], ἐγὼ ἐν Ἀλεξανδρέᾳ[g] μενῶ[h]
ἐρωτῶ σε καὶ παρακαλῶ σε ἐπιμελη
θι[i] τῷ παιδίῳ καὶ ἐὰν εὐθὺς ὀψώνι
ον λάβωμεν ἀποστελῶ σε[j] ἄνω. ἐὰν
πολλὰ πολλῶν τέχῃς ἐὰν ἦν ἄρσε
10 νον ἄφες, ἐὰν ἦν θήλεα ἔκβαλε.
εἴρηκας δὲ Ἀφροδισιάτι[k] ὅτι μή με
ἐπιλάθῃς· πῶς δύναμαί σε ἐπι-
λαθεῖν; ἐρωτῶ σε οὖν ἵνα μὴ ἀγω-
νιάσῃς.
15 (ἔτους) κθ Καίσαρος Παῦνι κγ.
verso
Ἱλαρίων Ἄλιτι ἀπόδος.

Apparatus

[a]r.1. Ἱλαρίων (as in verso line 1)
[b]r.1. ἀδελφῆι previous editions; on iota adscript, see Davis, *Greek Papyri*, 2.
[c]r.2-3. Ἀπολλω|ναρίῳ

Roman History, 31 BC–AD 68 (Kent, UK: Croom Helm, 1985), no. 723; R. K. Sherk, *The Roman Empire: Augustus to Hadrian*, Translated Documents of Greece and Rome (Cambridge: Cambridge University Press, 1988), 245; H. Kloft, *Wirtschaft der griechisch-römischen Welt* (Darmstadt: Wissenschaftliche Buchgesellschaft, 1992), 74; J. Rowlandson, *Women and Society in Greek and Roman Egypt* (Cambridge: Cambridge University Press, 1998), 230; H.-J. Drexhage, H. Konen, and K. Ruffing, *Die Wirtschaft des Römischen Reiches (1.-3. Jahrhundert)* (Berlin: Akademie-Verlag, 2002), 281; R. Burnet, *L'Égypte ancienne à travers les papyrus* (Paris: Flammarion/Pygmalion, 2003), no. 199; J. A. Straus, *L'Égypte gréco-romaine révélée par les papyrus: L'esclave*, Entretiens sur l'Antiquité gréco-romaine 26 (Liège: Université de Liège, Sciences de l'Antiquité, Langues et Littératures Classiques, 2004), no. 1; G. Messeri, "Donne dell'Egitto greco-romano attraverso i papiri," *Atene e Roma* 51 (2006): 75–96, at 94; B. Palme, "Papyrologie und Mentalitätsgeschichte der Antike," in K. Strobel (ed.), *Von Noricum nach Ägypten: Eine Reise durch die Welt der Antike. Aktuelle Forschungen zu Kultur, Alltag und Recht in der römischen Welt*, Akten des 1. Klagenfurter Papyrologentages (Klagenfurt and Ljubljana: no publisher, 2007), 193–220; J. Lenaerts, "Vieux papiers à lettres," *Disciplina* 23 (2011): 46–50. This bibliography is selective; P.Oxy. 744 is cited in many other studies.

^dr.3-4. Ἀλεξαν|δρε<ί>ᾳ
^er.4. ἔσμεν
^fr.4-5. εἰσ|πορεύωνται
^gr.5. Ἀλεξανδρε<ί>ᾳ
^hr.5. μένω previous editions
ⁱr.6-7. ἐπιμελή|θ<ητ>ι
^jr.8. σοι
^kr.11. Ἀφροδισιάδι; Ἀφροδισιᾶτι previous editions

Translation

recto

Hilarion to his sister Alis, many greetings, also to my lady Berous and Apollonari[o]n. Know that we are still in Alexandria; and do not worry if they all come back, I remain in Alexandria. I ask you and entreat you, take care of the child, and if we receive our pay soon, I will send it up to you. If perhaps you bear a child and it is male, let it be; if it is female, throw it out. You have told Aphrodisias, "Do not forget me." But how can I forget you? So I ask you not to worry.
The 29th year of Caesar, Pauni 23.

verso

Hilarion to Alis, deliver.

Description

The letter proper appears on one side of the papyrus (the recto, as would be expected). The papyrus itself measures 25 × 14.7 cm (or about 10 inches high and 6 inches wide). The papyrus has deteriorated in places on the left side of the recto, creating minor lacunae in lines 8-12. For the most part, restoration is not too difficult. There is a two-line gap between lines 14 and 15, thus drawing attention to the last line of the recto, which provides the date, "29th year of Caesar, Pauni 23," which is 17 June 1 BCE. The single line on the verso directs the courier to deliver the letter to Alis. Given its shocking content, it is not surprising the letter has been much discussed.[2]

---

2. For commentary and extended notes, see A. Deissmann, *Light from the Ancient East* (London: Hodder & Stoughton; New York: George H. Doran, 1927), 167–70 + fig. 26; J. L. White, *Light from Ancient Letters*, Foundations and Facets (Philadelphia: Fortress Press, 1986), 111–12, no. 72; E. Specht (ed.), *Alltägliches Altertum*

Critical Issues

In a recent study Stephanie West suggests that it is not Hilarion's wife who is pregnant, but Apollonarion, who may have been a slave or a single mother.³ Hilarion presumably feels little attachment to this infant and, in any case, recognizes the problem of having another mouth to feed. West proposes understanding the difficult πολλαπολλων as a nickname for Apollonarion mentioned in lines 2–3.⁴ Paul McKechnie finds her proposal convoluted and unnecessary.⁵ I agree. There is nothing cryptic or clever about this letter. There is no reason to think that the command to expose an unwanted infant is directed to anyone other than Alis, to whom the letter is in fact addressed. "Hilarion quite simply told his wife to throw her new baby out if it was a girl."⁶

McKechnie wonders why Hilarion *asks* and *entreats* his wife "to take care of the child." He speculates that perhaps Alis more than Hilarion was "inclined to drastic family limitation measures."⁷ That is, the existing child is to be cared for and the baby to come is to be kept—unless it is a girl. Accordingly, Hilarion asks and entreats Alis to care for the child. Perhaps too this is why Hilarion impresses upon Alis that he most certainly will not forget her. McKechnie's speculation is plausible.

As for the difficult phrase ἐὰν πολλὰ πολλῶν, which is also much discussed in the literature,⁸ McKechnie draws our attention to a sentence

---

(Frankfurt am Main: Peter Lang, 1998), 167–71, no. 2; S. West, "Whose Baby? A Note on P. Oxy. 744," *ZPE* 121 (1998): 167–72; P. McKechnie, "An Errant Husband and a Rare Idiom (P. Oxy. 744)," *ZPE* 127 (1999): 157–61; K. Strobel (ed.), *Von Noricum nach Ägypten: Eine Reise durch die Welt der Antike. Aktuelle Forschungen zu Kultur, Alltag und Recht in der römischen Welt*, Altertumswissenschaftliche Studien Klagenfurt (Klagenfurt: Hermagoras, 2007), 200–205.

3. West, "Whose Baby?" 167–72.

4. In making this suggestion West follows the lead in Grenfell and Hunt ("Letter of Ilarion," 244), who wondered if it was Apollonarion who was pregnant and if the obscure πολλαπολλων in fact alluded to her. The suggestion requires reading τέκῃ ("she give birth"), instead of τέκῃς ("you give birth"), in line 9. But the sigma seems clear enough.

5. McKechnie, "An Errant Husband," 157–61.

6. Ibid., 161.

7. Ibid., 159.

8. W. B. Sedgewick, "Πολλὰ πολλῶν (P. Oxy. IV, 744)," *Classical Review* 46 (1932): 12; G. Zuntz, "ἐὰν πολλὰ πολλῶν," *Symbolae Osloenses* 12 (1933): 94–5; E. Heikel, "Πολλὰ πολλῶν," *Eranos* 17 (1917): 91–6; Davis, *Greek Papyri*, 5; D. Tabachovitz, "Πολλὰ πολλῶν," *Eranos* 59 (1961): 45–8. The words also puzzled Grenfell and Hunt.

in Plato, where the meaning seems clear enough: "So, Socrates, don't be surprised if *perhaps* [ἐὰν...πολλὰ πολλῶν] we remain unable to develop an account of the gods, and the origin of everything, which is in every way self-consistent and perfectly precise" (*Timaeus* 29c4). "Most likely," says McKechnie, "πολλὰ πολλῶν was a colloquial and rare phrase for 'perhaps'," whose meaning is as obscure for us moderns as it was for native-speaking Greeks a few centuries after the composition of Hilarion's letter.[9]

The remaining spelling and grammatical solecisms in Hilarion's letter are not especially problematic.

Commentary

The letter begins on a tender note:

> Hilarion to his sister Alis, many greetings, also to my lady Berous and Apollonarion.

Hilarion addresses his wife, Alis, as "sister," an expression of endearment that suggests that Hilarion truly loved Alis.[10] (Marriages in antiquity were often arranged and did not always result in love between the spouses.) The "lady Berous" could be Alis's mother or sister,[11] while Apollonarion may be Berous' sister (or a child of Alis and Hilarion). The greeting (χαίρειν) is commonplace in late antique letters. It also occurs a few times in New Testament letters (James 1:1; 2 John 10, 11; cf. Acts 15:23; 23:26; letters of Ignatius). Berous is addressed as "my lady" (τῇ κυρίᾳ μου), which is a mark of respect. It appears in 2 John 1, 5. In P.Oxy. 14.1679 (third century CE) and P.Lips. 1.110 (c. third–fourth century CE) it is used in addressing a mother.

---

9. McKechnie, "An Errant Husband," 161. For this insight McKechnie gives credit to Tabachovitz, "Πολλὰ πολλῶν," 45–8. McKechnie states: "By collating *Timaeus* 29c4 with P.Oxy. 744, Tabachovitz made sense of both." I agree.

10. Grenfell and Hunt, "Letter of Ilarion," 243: "no doubt his wife." See Davis, *Greek Papyri*, 2; R. Helbing, *Grammatik der Septuaginta* (Göttingen: Vandenhoeck & Ruprecht, 1907), 72–3. Deissmann (*Light*, 168 n. 4) takes sister literally. Sometimes a wife addressed her husband as "brother." See P.Lond. 42 (168 BCE): "Isias to her brother Hephaestion greeting." Older family friends might be addressed as "mother" or "father." Although blood brothers and sisters sometimes married in late antique Egypt, there is no reason here to think Hilarion and Alis were related by blood.

11. Addressing Berous as "my lady" was a mark of courtesy. See P.Lips. 1.110, as well as 2 John 5.

Hilarion and others in his work party are in Alexandria, Egypt, about two hundred miles north of his home in Oxyrhynchus. He wants to assure his wife, pregnant with their child, that she should not worry about his well-being:

> Know that we are still in Alexandria; and do not worry if they all come back, I remain in Alexandria.

Sarah Pomeroy has suggested that Hilarion is a soldier,[12] but it is much more likely that he is a migrant worker, perhaps employed either on a building project in Alexandria or in shipping produce or other goods from Oxyrhynchus to Alexandria. In any event, Hilarion has the opportunity to prolong his stay in Alexandria, in all probability to work a bit longer and earn more money. Because of the extension of his stay he has hired a scribe to pen a letter to his wife. The scribe is adequate for the task;[13] he is not highly trained but rather is a scribe that a migrant worker like Hilarion could afford.

> I ask you and entreat you, take care of the child, and if we receive our pay soon, I will send it up to you.

In all probability, Alis was several months pregnant when Hilarion left Oxyrhynchus for work up north in Alexandria. Because of his decision to remain in Alexandria longer than originally planned, he realizes his wife could give birth before his return. He assures Alis that he will send his wages to her as soon as he receives them. This is important, for Alis, who probably is herself employed, will likely be unable to work for some time after she gives birth. The family income will be reduced. Hilarion wishes to allay her fears. He promises to send Alis his wages as soon as they are received.[14]

> If perhaps you bear a child and it is male, let it be; if it is female, throw it out.

---

12. S. Pomeroy, "Infanticide in Hellenistic Greece," in *Images of Women in Antiquity*, ed. A. Cameron and A. Kuhrt (London: Routledge, 1983), 207–19, at 208. McKechnie ("An Errant Husband," 158 n. 8) finds the suggestion unpersuasive.

13. The penmanship is just barely workmanlike; there are also a few slips, e.g., the accusative σε ("you") in line 8, where it should be the dative σοι ("to you"). The same grammatical slip will be found in P.Oxy. 1.119.4–5. In line 9 ἦν should be ἦ. On both, see Davis, *Greek Papyri*, 5.

14. On wages (ὀψώνιον), see Luke 3:14; 1 Cor. 9:7. For metaphorical usage, see Rom. 6:23.

That is, if Alis gives birth before Hilarion returns home, she knows what is expected of her: She is to keep the infant, if it is male; if it is female, it is to be thrown out. Hilarion (or his scribe) uses the verb ἔκβαλε, which strikes a harsh note, for it is a verb that is often used in reference to throwing out debris or casting out evil spirits.[15] Normally the verb used in reference to the exposure of infants is ἐκτίθημι.[16]

Hilarion's command to expose the infant if it is a girl reflected a common practice among Greeks and Romans in late antiquity. Girls, as well as boys, did go to work at young ages and help the family get by. Still, unwanted girls and infants with birth defects and deformities were routinely cast out to die of exposure either to the elements or to wild animals. In some cases, unwanted children were later sold into slavery or prostitution. (I will say more on this topic below.) The most probable reason for Hilarion's command is that the family could not afford another mouth to feed and/or the dowry that would be expected when his daughter was given in marriage.

Interestingly enough, Hilarion's instructions to Alis remind us of Pharaoh's policy of infanticide directed against the Hebrew people, only in reverse: "Then the king of Egypt said to the Hebrew midwives… [16]'When you serve as midwife to the Hebrew women, and see them upon the birthstool, if it is a son, you shall kill him; but if it is a daughter, she shall live [ἐὰν μὲν ἄρσεν ᾖ, ἀποκτείνατε αὐτό, ἐὰν δὲ θῆλυ, περιποιεῖσθε αὐτό]'" (Exod. 1:15-16). In its own perverse way, Pharaoh's command reflects the values presupposed in Hilarion's instructions; that is, boys are more valuable than girls.

After all of this, Hilarion's letter to Alis closes with affection, responding to a message evidently conveyed to Hilarion by a neighbor or friend:

> You have told Aphrodisias, "Do not forget me." But how can I forget you? So I ask you not to worry.

Aphrodisias is either a friend of the family or perhaps a member of the family. Alis has asked him to exhort her husband not to forget her (μή με ἐπιλάθῃς).[17] Hilarion assures his wife that he will not forget her and

---

15. See, for example, Matt. 15:17, where excrement is thrown (ἐκβάλλεται) into the latrine. In Mark 12:8 ἐξέβαλον is used in reference to the corpse of the murdered man thrown out of the vineyard.

16. See M. Huys, "Ἔκθησις and ἀπόθησις: The Terminology of Infant Exposure in Greek Antiquity," *L'Antiquité Classique* 58 (1989): 190–7; West, "Whose Baby?" 170.

17. For biblical parallels, see LXX Jer 14:9 "O Lord…do not forget us [μὴ ἐπιλάθῃ ἡμῶν]!"; LXX Ps. 73:19 "do not forget the life of your poor forever [μὴ ἐπιλάθῃ εἰς τέλος]."

therefore she need not worry. His earlier assurance that his wages will be sent to her in due course is part of the reason she need not worry.[18]

Deissmann is much offended by Hilarion's tone and wonders if the man is only making excuses for not returning with the others, or at least for having not already sent Alis his wages. Deissmann even remarks on the name *Hilarion*: "Is he, as his name implies, a gay dog, a good-for-nothing?"[19] I think this is a bit much. Deissmann is reacting as a man of the late nineteenth/early twentieth century, outraged by the command to throw out a baby girl. Given the culture in which Hilarion and Alis lived, the contents of the letter as a whole provide us with no grounds for thinking of Hilarion as a faithless husband. His respect and concern for his wife seem genuine, notwithstanding his command to expose an infant daughter.

Exposure and Infanticide in Late Antiquity

In P.Oxy. 4.744 it is Hilarion who orders the exposure of the infant. But one should not infer from this one example that only men called for the exposure of unwanted infants; women sometimes did too.[20] In a legal document dating to 8 BCE, a woman claims the right to expose the child

---

18. For another epistolary exhortation not to worry, see P.Oxy. 1296, lines 5–8: "Do not be anxious, father, about my studies; I am industrious and take relaxation. All will be well with me." See also Phil. 2:28, where Paul inquires of the Philippian Christians "that I may be less anxious"; and in 4:6 he enjoins them, "Have no anxiety about anything."

19. Deissmann, *Light*, 170. The name Hilarion derives from the adjective ἱλαρός ("happy" or "cheerful").

20. Legally of course in Greco-Roman antiquity men possessed the authority, or *potestas*, of life and death over their children. See W. K. Lacey, "*Patria Potestas*," in *The Family in Ancient Rome: New Perspectives*, ed. B. Rawson (Ithaca, NY: Cornell University Press, 1987), 121–44, at 133–5. Birth itself did not guarantee a newborn's place in the family. In essence the father approved the infant's admission into the family: "On the eighth day, the father would 'raise up' (*tollere*, Latin) the child and so accept it into the household." C. B. Horn and J. W. Martens, *"Let the Little Children Come to Me": Childhood and Children in Early Christianity* (Washington, DC: The Catholic University Press of America, 2009), 20. In Jewish tradition, the newborn male is circumcised eight days after birth (Gen. 17:12; Lev. 12:3) and, as implied in Luke 1:57-60 (cf. 2:21), he may also have been named at that time. In Greco-Roman tradition infants were "purified" and named eight (or nine) days after birth (Suetonius, *Nero* 6.2; Macrobius, *Saturnalia* 1.16.36). The eighth (or ninth) day is the "day of purification" (*dies lustricus*), because, according to Varro, newborn "children…are pure" (*apud* Censorinus, *De die natali* 14.2: *pueros…sint puri*).

she is carrying, if that is required in order for her to marry another man.[21] She needs this "right" in writing, because normally a man would decide the matter.

The practice of exposure and infanticide in the Greco-Roman world was widespread and ancient.[22] The Roman *Law of the Twelve Tables*, which may date in its earliest form to the fifth century BCE, required fathers to put to death any child who was deformed. One of these laws reads: "A notably deformed child shall be killed immediately."[23] We must not infer from this, however, that infanticide was primarily limited to female infants or deformed infants.[24] Aristotle (384–322 BCE) recommends abortion and infant exposure, lest the quality of the Greek population decline (*Politica* 1334b–1335b).[25] The philosopher believed that it was necessary to prune or cull the population, so to speak. Plutarch (c. 50–120 CE), historian and moralist, tells us that the ancient Spartans put this recommendation into practice. For example, they cast the unhealthy and deformed infant into a ravine, since such an infant, they believed, was "of no advantage either to itself or to the state" (*Lycurgus* 16.1–2). First-century Roman writer Seneca tells his readers: "Unnatural progeny we destroy [*portentosos fetus exstinguimus*]; we drown even children who at birth are weak or abnormal [*debiles, monstrosique*]" (*De ira* 1.15.2).[26] Aristotle would have approved.

Infanticide was not simply about unwanted girls or deformities. As Cornelia Horn and John Martens point out, "Infanticide could be linked to economics, superstition, the health of the child, the belief that one

---

21. BGU 1104: "although she is pregnant, she will make no claim regarding [the expense of] her childbed, since she has been satisfied [monetarily] for that, but she retains the right to expose the infant [τὸ βρέφος ἐκτίθεσθαι] and to unite herself to another man."

22. Horn and Martens, *"Let the Little Children Come to Me,"* 18–21.

23. *Leges Duodecim Tabularum*, Table IV.1.

24. E. Scott, "Unpicking a Myth: The Infanticide of Female and Disabled Infants in Antiquity," in *TRAC 2000: The Proceedings of the Tenth Annual Theoretical Roman Archaeology Conference Held at the Institute of Archaeology, University College of London, April 6–7, 2000* (Oxford: Oxbow Books, 2001), 143–51; M. Golden, "Demography and the Exposure of Girls at Athens," *Phoenix* 35 (1981): 316–31.

25. M. Lu, "Aristotle on Abortion and Infanticide," *International Philosophical Quarterly* 53 (2013): 47–62.

26. W. V. Harris, "The Theoretical Possibility of Extensive Infanticide in the Graeco-Roman World," *Classical Quarterly* 32 (1982): 114–16; idem, "Child-exposure in the Roman Empire," *JRS* 84 (1994): 1–22.

had too many children, the suspect parentage of a child, or, indeed, to gender or deformation. More significant than the reasons per se was the acceptance of exposure or infanticide as methods of birth control or household management."[27] As an example of superstition, the birth of twins was believed to be a bad omen. Consequently one of the twins was thrown out.[28]

Regarding the economics of infant exposure, Musonius Rufus (c. 30–100) comments: "What seems most strange to me is not that some people who have poverty to offer as an excuse, but that those who have an abundance of things and some who are even wealthy nevertheless have the boldness not to rear children born to them, in order that those previously born might be more prosperous" (*Reliquiae* 15B). Plutarch (c. 48–122) provides a somewhat different explanation: "Poor people do not bring up their children, because they are afraid that they, having been brought up less well than is proper, will become servile and uneducated and will lack all the good qualities. Considering poverty to be the worst evil, they cannot bear to share it with their children, as if it were a dangerous, serious disease" (*Moralia* 497E). When Plutarch says the poor "do not bring up their children," he means they either have given them away or exposed them.

Consistent with Hilarion's command to expose the infant if it is a female is evidence that females were in fact cast out in much great numbers than were males. The practice of exposing female infants had the unintended effect of slowing population growth and in some instances may have actually caused a decrease in population.[29] The reasons for infant exposure may have varied, but the negative effects were significant and tragic.[30]

Rescuing exposed infants could entail various disadvantages. In the mid-second-century *Codes and Regulations* we find the following rule: "If an Egyptian brings up a child exposed on a dung heap and adopts him, a fourth of his estate is confiscated at death" (§41). Besides the risk of being rescued for servitude and/or prostitution, the infant that survives exposure, even if raised by a good family, faces social disadvantages. Again appealing to *Codes and Regulations*, we read: "(A child exposed)

---

27. Horn and Martens, *"Let the Little Children Come to Me,"* 20.
28. Scott, "Unpicking a Myth," 148–9.
29. The evidence is reviewed in R. Bagnall, "Missing Females in Roman Egypt," *Scripta Classica Israelica* 16 (1977): 121–38; D. Engels, "The Problem of Female Infanticide in the Roman World," *Classical Philology* 75 (1980): 112–20; Pomeroy, "Infanticide in Hellenistic Greece," 207–19.
30. Horn and Martens, *"Let the Little Children Come to Me,"* 18–21.

on a dung heap cannot become a priest" (§92).[31] Survivors of exposure may well have been disqualified from other professions and areas of service or employment.

Striking a happier note, one Asiaticus, freedman of Augustus and procurator of the Assuritanian region, dedicates a tomb inscription "to his devoted and well-deserving foster-son" Hypnus, who died at the age of 23 (*ILS* 1485, Carthage). Found a number of times on North African tombs, "foster-son" (*alumnus*) usually implies a rescued infant.

There may also have been some human sacrifice, involving infants and young children, practiced in Egypt in the Roman period. One thinks of Wis. 14:23, where killing children "in their initiations" and in "secret mysteries" probably refers to Greek mystery religions, especially the cult of Dionysius, whose followers at one time supposedly ripped their victims apart and ate them raw. The author of the Wisdom of Solomon condemns the "ruthless slayers of their own children" (Wis. 12:5). In the ostensible literary setting of this apocryphal work, it is King Solomon who speaks, and so perhaps would be understood as referring to the pagan practice of child-sacrifice that took place in the ancient Near East. But in the time of the writing of the Wisdom of Solomon (first century BCE), child sacrifice was rare. It may be that the author was alluding to abortion and infant exposure as practiced by contemporary Greeks and Romans. What was not rare was the disposal of unwanted infants in the settings of brothels. One thinks of the horrifying archaeological discovery at Ashkelon, in Israel, of the skeletons of some one hundred infants who had been dropped into a sewer.[32]

Although Jews, so far as we know, did not rescue pagan infants that had been cast out, they did not themselves practice abortion or infanticide. Jewish apologist and allegorist Philo of Alexandria (c. 20 BCE–50 CE), appealing to Exod. 21:22, condemns exposure of infants and all forms of infanticide.[33] His younger contemporary, Josephus, does the

---

31. Greek: κηπριάρτῳ οὐκ ἐξὸν ἱερᾶσθαι... The spelling of κηπριάρτῳ ("on a dung heap") is odd. In §41 we find the more conventional spelling of the cognate κοπρίας. In §92 the implied subject is βρέφος, νήπιος, or τέκνον. For the Greek text of §41 and §92, see BGU 5.1210.115-16, 210. The text was recovered in Theadelphia.

32. L. E. Stager, "Eroticism and Infanticide at Ashkelon," *BARev* 17 (July–August 1991): 34–53; Patricia Smith and Gila Kahila, "Bones of a Hundred Infants Found in Ashkelon Sewer," *BAR* 17 (July–August 1991): 47.

33. "This ordinance carries with it the prohibition of something else more important, the exposure of infants [βρεφῶν ἔκθεσις], a sacrilegious practice which among many other nations, through their ingrained inhumanity, has come to be regarded with complacence" (*Spec. Laws* 3.110; cf. 3.111-119). See A. Reinhartz, "Philo on Infanticide," *Studia Philonica Annual* 4 (1992): 42–58.

same.³⁴ Notwithstanding the testimony of Philo and Josephus, some contend that Jewish practices were almost as bad as pagan practices. In a recent study Daniel Schwartz convincingly refutes this contention.³⁵ The comments of Roman historian Tacitus (c. 56–118 CE), who was no friend of the Jewish people, confirms the claims of Philo and Josephus. According to Tacitus, Jews "take thought to increase their numbers; for they regard it as a crime to kill any ineligible child" (*Historiae* 5.5).³⁶ By "ineligible" (*agnatus*) is meant a child not eligible to inherit. Such a child in late antiquity was far more in danger of exposure.³⁷ The implication of course is that if the Jews do not kill ineligible children, they certainly will not kill those that are eligible to inherit the family name and fortune.

That infant exposure in the Greco-Roman world was widespread is also attested by explicit condemnation of the practice in early Christian texts. The *Didache* (early second century) commands: "Do not murder a child by abortion, nor kill it at birth" (*Did.* 2:2b). The same proscription is found in the *Epistle of Barnabas* (mid-second century): "Do not murder a child by abortion, nor, again, destroy that which is born" (*Ep. Barn.* 19:5c). The *Didache* also speaks of those "who persecute the good, who hate truth, who love falsehood…who do not show mercy to a poor person, who are not distressed by [the plight of] the oppressed, who do not know him who made them, [who are] child murderers, who destroy what God has formed" (*Did.* 5:2). The clear implication is that because the wicked do not know God, who created humanity in his own image (cf. Gen. 1:26), they think nothing of murdering children and destroying what God forms in the womb. According to the *Letter to Diognetus*, Christians "marry like

---

34. "The Law orders all the offspring to be brought up, and forbids women either to cause abortion or to make away with the foetus; a woman convicted of this is regarded as an infanticide, because she destroys a soul and diminishes the race" (*Ag. Ap.* 2.202).

35. D. R. Schwartz, "Did the Jews Practice Infant Exposure and Infanticide in Antiquity?" *Studia Philonica Annual* 16 (2004): 61–95.

36. Other Jewish texts from late antiquity confirm the claims of Philo and Josephus. See Ps.-Phocylides, *Sentences* 184-185 ("Do not let a woman destroy the unborn babe in her belly, nor after its birth throw it before the dogs and the vultures as prey"); *Sib. Or.* 2:280-282 ("as many as aborted what they carried in the womb, as many as cast forth their offspring wickedly"); 3:765-766 ("Rear your own offspring and do not kill it, for the Immortal is angry at whoever commits these sins"). See A. Lindemann, "'Do Not Let a Woman Destroy the Unborn Baby in Her Belly': Abortion in Ancient Judaism and Christianity," *Studia Theologica* 49 (1995): 253–71.

37. Strabo claims that Egyptians "bring up all children that are born. They circumcise the males, and spay the females, as is the custom among the Jews" (*Geographica* 17.2.5).

everyone else, and have children, but they do not expose their offspring" (5:6). The author of the *Apocalypse of Peter* (late second or early third century CE) condemns infanticide, including abortion. The eighth chapter of this apocalypse provides a graphic description of hell and the awful fate awaiting those guilty of infanticide and abortion.[38]

Christian condemnation of infanticide may have roots in Dominical tradition as well as in Judaism. In a recent study Loren Zelyck argues that the "little ones" of Matt. 18:1-14 are not new or young disciples in the Church but are children, even infants. On the basis of comparative study of Matt. 5:27-30, *Apoc. Pet.* 8, and *b. Nid.* 13b, Zelyck suggests that the σκανδαλίζειν of which Jesus speaks is the exposure and sexual abuse of children. Many exposed infants—male and female alike—were "rescued" by pimps and slave merchants and sold into prostitution. Jesus warns his disciples of the fearful judgment that will befall those who exploit and abuse children in this way.[39]

Anti-Christian Slander and Persecution

Acting on Jesus' teaching of the great value of children, Christians not only refused to practice abortion and infant exposure, they rescued those cast out as unwanted. But this practice, along with the celebration of the Eucharist, in which Jesus likens the bread to his body, left early Christians vulnerable to the charge that they rescued exposed infants and other unwanted children, either to abuse them sexually (as was common in the Greco-Roman world) or to eat them in religious ceremonies. Consequently, Christians were accused of cannibalism and strange sexual practices, among other things.

Justin Martyr, a Christian apologist executed in 165 CE, alludes to pagan claims that Christians indulged in "promiscuous intercourse and eating human flesh" (*1 Apologia* 26.7). Justin adds that some pagans think a Christian is one "who counts it good to feast on human flesh" (*2 Apologia* 12.1). Indeed, says Justin mockingly, "We slay a man and... drink our fill of blood" (12.5).[40] Christians "are assailed in every kind of way" (12.6).

---

38. For critical discussion, see P. Gray, "Abortion, Infanticide, and the Social Rhetoric of the *Apocalypse of Peter*," *Journal of Early Christian Studies* 9 (2001): 313–37.

39. L. Zelyck, "Matthew 18,1–14 and the Exposure and Sexual Abuse of Children in the Roman World," *Bib* 98 (2017): 37–54.

40. Justin argues that Christians are (falsely) accused of doing the very things that some pagans in fact do in their perverse worship of Jupiter and other gods. In

Accusing Christians of cannibalism was not hard to do. After all, the eating of raw flesh, even human flesh, was supposedly the practice of some pagan mystery cults. Among these, the cult of Dionysius was especially well known.[41] Moreover, precedent had already been established, for pagans sometimes accused Jews of cannibalism (and the horrifying story of the starving Jewish woman who ate her infant during the Roman siege of Jerusalem in 70 CE would only have confirmed the slander[42]).

Christian observation of Eucharist, or the Lord's Supper, made the accusation of cannibalism especially easy. "This is my body which is for you," said Jesus to his disciples. "This cup is the new covenant in my blood" (Matt. 26:26-29; Mark 14:22-25; Luke 22:14-23; 1 Cor. 11:23-25). Even worse is what Jesus said on the occasion of multiplying the loaves and fishes: "He who eats my flesh and drinks my blood has eternal life" (John 6:54). The whole passage (i.e., John 6:48-58), if taken literally, could be construed in terms of cannibalism. Pagan critics of the early Christian movement were more than willing to do so.

Critics of Christianity had a lot of fun with the Words of Institution and the utterance in John 6. Commenting on Jesus' strange saying, arch-critic Porphyry remarks: "Truly this saying is not merely beast-like and absurd, but it is more absurd than any absurdity, and more beast-like than

---

Apologeticus 9.1 Tertullian levels the same charge. On this topic, see J. B. Rives, "Human Sacrifice among Pagans and Christians," *Journal of Roman Studies* 85 (1995): 65–85, here 75–6. The Pagan practice is also criticized by Tatian, Justin's disciple. See Tatian, *Oratio ad Graecos* 29.1. It is described by the Pagan Dionysius of Halicarnassus, *Antiquitates* 4.49.2-3. Educated Greeks and Romans viewed cannibalism with horror, as we see in Juvenal, *Satirae* 15.78-83; Porphyry, *De abstinentia* 3.17.3; 4.21.4 (in reference to barbaric Scythians); cf. Tertullian, *Apologeticus* 9.9.

41. Graphically portrayed, for example, in Euripides, *Bacchae*, esp. lines 1122–1147, where Agaue, possessed by the spirit of Dionysius, rips apart and devours portions of her son Pentheus. Another popular myth concerns the feast served to Thyestes, guilty of adultery against his brother Atreus. After he eats his dinner, his brother informs him that he has devoured the flesh of his own sons (Aeschylus, *Agamemnon* 1590–1599; Seneca, *Thyestes*). A similar legend is told of one Harpagus, who unwittingly "feasted on the flesh of his dearest" (as related in Macarius Magnes, *Apocriticus* 3.15).

42. The story is recounted in Josephus, *Jewish Wars* 6.201-213. On pagan slander against the Jewish people, see P. W. van der Horst, "The Myth of Jewish Cannibalism: A Chapter in the History of Antisemitism," in *Studies in Ancient Judaism and Early Christianity* (Leiden: Brill, 2014), 173–87. The accusation of cannibalism was not uncommon in contexts of slander. See A. McGowan, "Eating People: Accusations of Cannibalism against Christians in the Second Century," *Journal of Early Christian Studies* 2 (1994): 413–42.

any fashion of a beast, that a man should taste human flesh, and drink the blood of members of the same tribe and race, and that by doing this he should have eternal life" (Macarius Magnes, *Apocriticus* 3.15).[43]

The allegations of these critics were taken very seriously and sometimes led to harsh interrogation, even torture and execution of Christians. An example of this is found in Pliny the Younger's correspondence with Emperor Trajan (reigned 98–117 CE). Dispatched at the rank of legate to Bithynia and Pontus in Asia Minor (modern Turkey), Pliny set to work to restore law and order. The principal problem is that the temples were largely deserted, sacrifices were not being offered, and the gods were not being honored. The culprits, it seems, were members of a strange new superstition. They were called "Christians," so named after their founder. Pliny had them brought before him. If they refused to recant, they were executed. If they were Roman citizens, they were sent to Rome for trial. Exasperated by their obstinacy (it seems, the governor discovered, that true Christians simply will not recant), Pliny interrogated/tortured them and discovered, among other things, that the Christians assembled together "to take food of an ordinary, harmless [*innoxium*] kind" (*Epistulae* 10.96.1-10, here 10.96.7).[44]

Governor Pliny's description of "ordinary, harmless" food was in reference to the widespread rumor that Christians were cannibals. Although in his time as governor (c. 110–112) Pliny found no truth in the ugly allegation, the accusation of cannibalism persisted. Almost a half century later Justin Martyr would still be fending off the charge.

The charge apparently was based not only on the Words of Institution but on the Christian practice of rescuing infants and young children who were cast out. Justin speaks to this as well. "We have been taught that to expose the newborn is wicked." It is wicked not only because many of those exposed died, but those rescued by pagans almost always "were reared for sexual immorality," that is, for prostitution. Although this was the fate of most females who were cast out, males too were recovered

---

43. The passage is cited in full and discussed in J. G. Cook, *The Interpretation of the New Testament in Greco-Roman Paganism*, Studies and Texts in Antiquity and Christianity 3 (Tübingen: Mohr Siebeck, 2000), 202–5. Although the "Greek" critic in the *Apocriticus* is not explicitly identified, it is believed that he is Porphyry (234–305 CE).

44. For a discussion of Pliny's mission to Bithynia and Pontus, see C. A. Evans, "Christian Demographics and the Dates of Early New Testament Papyri," in *The Language and Literature of the New Testament: Essays in Honour of Stanley E. Porter's 60th Birthday*, ed. L. K. Fuller Dow, C. A. Evans, and A. W. Pitts, BibInt 150 (Leiden: Brill, 2017), 201–17, here 205–10.

by pagans for the purpose of prostitution (Justin Martyr, *1 Apologia* 27.1; 29.1; cf. Tertullian, *Apologeticus* 9.17). The practice was hateful to Christians.

A generation later, Tertullian (c. 160–225), a North African Latin-speaking Christian apologist, complains that pagan critics continue to slander Christians with regard to infanticide and cannibalism: "Monsters of wickedness, we are accused of observing a holy rite in which we kill a little child [*infanticidii*] and then eat it; in which, after the feast, we practice incest... This is what is constantly laid to our charge, and yet you take no pains to elicit the truth of what we have been so long accused" (*Apologeticus* 8.1). Tertullian then rails against the pagan practices of infanticide, including killing "by drowning, or by exposure to cold and hunger and dogs" (9.6-9). Not until Christianity swept the Roman and Byzantine Empires did the practice of abortion and infanticide become illegal.[45]

Concluding Remarks

The documentary papyri from late antiquity continue to shed light on everyday life in the Greco-Roman world. These writings can also shed light on matters of philosophy, theology, politics, and ethics that were once matters of dispute and sharp disagreement. Hilarion's letter to his wife Alis presupposes a custom among Greeks and Romans that was not controversial. Parents could decide to expose a newborn for almost any reason.[46] Whatever his reason—and we can only guess at it—Hilarion ordered his wife to throw out her newborn if it turned out to be a girl. Jews and Christians found the practice abhorrent and criticized it.

---

45. For discussion on the change in thinking brought on by the Christianization of Europe and Mediterranean world, see M. J. Gorman, *Abortion and the Early Church: Christian, Jewish and Pagan Attitudes I the Greco-Roman World* (Downers Grove, IL: InterVarsity Press, 1982); O. M. Bakke, *When Children Became People: The Birth of Childhood in Early Christianity* (Minneapolis: Fortress Press, 2005).

46. The practice of infant exposure among Greeks and Romans was so commonplace it became a popular theme in drama and tragedy. On this interesting point, see D. Ogden, *Greek Bastardy: In the Classical and Hellenistic Periods* (Oxford: Oxford University Press, 1990); M. Huys, *The Tale of the Hero Who Was Exposed at Birth in Euripidean Tragedy: A Study of Motifs* (Leuven: Leuven University Press, 1995); D. Munteanu, "The *Nothos*: Between Tragic and Comic, between Hero and Social Outcast," *Aevum Antiquum* 4 (2004): 439–51. The *nothos* (νόθος), or "bastard," often emerges as a hero in dramatic literature.

Because Christians actually did something about the pagan custom of infant exposure—they rescued exposed and unwanted children—they were accused of cannibalism. Because in their sacred meal, the Eucharist, the words of Jesus identified bread and wine with his body and blood, accusations of cannibalism were easy to make. Some may have accused Christians of sexually abusing the children they rescued, even as these unfortunate little ones were abused and exploited by pagan pimps and sex-traffickers.

Hilarion's letter thus finds itself at the intersection of diverse ethics and cultures in sharp conflict. It is a letter that provides dramatic and shocking evidence of a practice that was commonplace and uncontroversial in the world prior to the emergence of the Jesus movement and the Christian Church.

6

Fetishizing the Word: Literacy, Orality, and the Dead Sea Scrolls*

Ian C. Werrett

Tout objet historique est fétiche
—Maurice Merleau-Ponty[1]

As a scholar working in the field of Qumran Studies, I have told the story of the discovery of the Dead Sea Scrolls countless times. The effect this narrative has on audiences is palpable, which is no doubt why it is a ubiquitous feature of television documentaries and introductions on the Scrolls. Not only is it a tale filled with colorful characters and intrigue; it is set in an exotic land during a tumultuous and violent decade. But of all the fascinating moments in this story, the one that elicits the biggest response from audiences is when they hear that Muhammed Ahmed el-Hamed, the Bedouin shepherd credited with discovering the Dead Sea Scrolls, once contemplated using the leather from these ancient texts to repair the straps

---

* I would like to thank my Dead Sea Scrolls class at Saint Martin's University (fall 2016) for their questions, insights, and observations during the preliminary stages of this paper's creation. I would also like to thank Dr. Liv Ingeborg Lied and the members of the Hebrew Scriptures and Cognate Literature section for inviting me to present an earlier draft of this piece during the Society of Biblical Literature's annual meeting in San Antonio, Texas, in 2016. Finally, I would like to thank Dr. Jeremiah Johnston and Dr. Craig Evans for the invitation to participate in this volume and for their thoughtful editorial suggestions. The feedback and encouragement I have received from these individuals, and groups, was invaluable and rewarding on numerous levels. Any remaining errors, of course, are mine and mine alone.

1. Maurice Merleau-Ponty, *Le Visible et L-invisible*, abrégé VI (Paris: Gallimard, 1964), 328.

of his sandals.² Reactions to this part of the narrative range from audible gasps to laughter and I have to confess that I have taken great pleasure in conveying this part of the story over the years. Recently, however, I have started to think more critically about the meaning of these responses and, in doing so, I find that I have become increasingly uncomfortable with the idea of presenting Muhammed Ahmed el-Hamed and his Bedouin companions as unwitting rubes.

In an interview with el-Hamed conducted on October 23, 1956, a resident of Bethlehem by the name of Najib Khoury succeeded in obtaining a rare first-hand account of the shepherd's miraculous discovery. The Arabic transcript of this interview, and its English translation, were subsequently published by William Brownlee in 1957.³ Although there are many interesting details in this interview, four things stand out: First, el-Hamed claims to have found the Scrolls in 1945, rather than in late 1946 or early 1947, which means that he may have held on to the texts for upwards of two years before their discovery was announced to the general public; second, he refers to the scrolls as "rolled leather with scrawling on it" or "leather," never as "writings" or "texts"; third, he validates the rumor that his initial thought was to repair his sandal straps and those of his companions with the leather; and fourth, the interviewer signs the transcript on behalf of el-Hamed by using the Bedouin's nickname rather than his given name: "'Muhammad ed-Deeb,' One of the Arabs of Ta'amireh."⁴

The lack of formal education among the Ta'amireh Bedouin is well-documented and need not be recounted here,⁵ but el-Hamed's repeated emphasis on "leather," combined with his lack of urgency about what to do with the scrolls, not to mention his use of the term "scrawling" when referring to the writings themselves, implies an overwhelming attitude of

---

2. The Bedouin's birth name was Muhammed Ahmed el-Hamed, but he is better known by his Arabic nickname Muhammed edh-Dhib, or Muhammed "the Wolf."

3. William Brownlee, "Muhammad ed-Deeb's Own Story of His Scroll Discovery," *JNES* 16, no. 4 (1957): 236–9; See also, John Trever, *The Dead Sea Scrolls: A Personal Account*, rev. edn (Grand Rapids: Eerdmans, 1977), 96–111, 191–4.

4. In contrast to the story recounted by John Trever, who indicates that it was el-Hamed's cousin Jum'a Muhammed Khalil who was responsible for finding Cave I, el-Hamed states that he was alone when he stumbled across the entrance to the cave. Brownlee, "Muhammad ed-Deeb's Own Story of His Scroll Discovery," 236–7; Trever, *The Dead Sea Scrolls: A Personal Account*, 98–9.

5. Ismael abu Saad, "Towards an Understanding of Minority Education in Israel: The Case of the Bedouin Arabs of the Negev," *Comparative Education* 27, no. 2 (1991): 235–42; Mar'i Sami Khalil, *Arab Education in Israel* (New York: Syracuse University Press, 1978).

disinterest towards the scrolls as texts.[6] If we add to this the fact that the interviewer signs the transcript using el-Hamed's nickname, as opposed to the Bedouin's given name, or having the Arab sign the document himself, one is left with the distinct impression that el-Hamed was illiterate.[7] As opposed to being a negative judgement on the Bedouin, or a way to get a cheap laugh from an audience, it may be possible to use this observation to understand the world of the scrolls—an era in which upwards of 95–98 percent of the populace was illiterate.

If Muhammed Ahmed el-Hamed's attitudes are anything to go by, not to mention the mindset of those highly literate audience members struggling to understand the thoughts of an illiterate, semi-nomadic shepherd who placed more value on the leather of the scrolls than the contents of the documents themselves, we may come closer to understanding the larger world behind the Dead Sea Scrolls and the attitudes that shape our understanding of the Second Temple period. In the following discussion, I would like to offer some observations about the relationship between literacy, orality, textual pluriformity, and thing theory. In so doing, I hope to show that the challenge of understanding and explaining textual pluriformity within the Dead Sea Scrolls is a problem of our own making.

Frankie Says "Relax"

It has often been said that the scribes of the Qumran community appear to have had a "liberal attitude" when it comes to the form of the texts that would eventually become canonized as the Hebrew Bible.[8] Not only do the "biblical" manuscripts from Qumran display a high degree of textual pluriformity, but so too do the manuscripts of the *Community Rule*

---

6. As Brownless notes, "The scrolls were to Muhammad only rolled leather covered with unintelligible scrawls—an authentic note." Brownlee, "Muhammad ed-Deeb's Own Story of His Scroll Discovery," 238.

7. The illiteracy of the Bedouin has been verified by several scholars, including John Trever. See John Trever, "When Was Cave I Discovered?" *RevQ* 3, no. 1 (1961): 135.

8. Charlotte Hempel, *The Qumran Rule Texts in Context* (Tubingen: Mohr Siebeck, 2013), 279–82; Paul Heger, *Cult as a Catalyst for Division: Cult Disputes as the Motive for Schism in the Pre-70 Pluralistic Environment*, STDJ 65 (Leiden: Brill, 2007), 104ff.; Florentino Garcia Martinez and Julio Trebolle Barrera, *People of the Dead Sea Scrolls: Their Writings, Beliefs, and Practices* (Leiden: Brill, 1995), 123; Shemaryahu Talmon, "The Old Testament Text," in *The Cambridge History of the Bible*, Volume I, ed. P. R. Ackroyd and C. F. Evans (Cambridge: Cambridge University Press, 1970), 185.

and *Damascus Document*. Numerous explanations have been forwarded concerning this phenomenon, but many of these hypotheses have been driven by a postcanonical mindset that fetishizes the Hebrew Bible and/or awards pride of place to manuscripts that are the most intact.[9] The simple fact that we now put quotation marks around such words as "Bible," "biblical," and "Scripture" when talking about the textual witness from Qumran indicates a growing awareness of our own postcanonical biases, but we can go further. As Charlotte Hempel rightly notes: "Much of the scholarship in recent decades has demolished the notion of a Bible at this time,"[10] but our continued and often casual use of the terms "non-biblical" and "biblical"[11]—categories that would not have occurred to the scribes of Qumran—indicates that more demolition work is needed.[12]

To say that a group has a "relaxed" or "liberal attitude" towards the literature in their collection implies that there is another mindset at work—a worldview that includes alternative attitudes, such as rigidity. While I have no doubt that there were a variety of thoughts about the literary patrimony of Jews during the Second Temple period, the suggestion that the presence of textual pluriformity at Qumran is indicative of a "relaxed"

---

9. "The fetish," observes William Pietz, "is always a meaningful fixation of a singular event; it is above all a 'historical' object, the enduring material form and force of an unrepeatable event. This object is 'territorialized' in material space (an earthly matrix), whether in the form of a geographical locality, a marked site on the surface of the human body, or a medium of inscription or configuration defined by some portable or wearable thing. The historical object is territorialized in the form of a 'reification': some thing (meuble) or shape whose status is that of a self-contained entity identifiable within the territory. It is recognizable as a discrete thing (a *res*) because of its status as a significant object within the value codes proper to the productive and ideological systems of a given society. This reified, territorialized historical object is also 'personalized' in the sense that beyond its status as a collective social object it evokes an intensely personal response from individuals." William Pietz, "The Problem of the Fetish, I," *RES: Anthropology and Aesthetics* 9 (1985): 12.

10. Hempel, *The Qumran Rule Texts in Context*, 279.

11. In his volume on Qumran scribal practices, Tov notes: "Throughout, the term 'biblical' refers to canonical books of Hebrew/Aramaic Scripture. Even though this usage is anachronistic for the Judaean Desert texts, it is made for the sake of convenience." Emanuel Tov, *Scribal Practices and Approaches in the Texts Found in the Judean Desert* (Atlanta: SBL Press, 2004), 6.

12. Several scholars have been sounding this warning bell. See Eva Mroczek, *The Literary Imagination in Jewish Antiquity* (Oxford: Oxford University Press, 2016), 22–4; and Robert Kraft, "Para-mania: Beside, Before and Beyond Biblical Studies," *JBL* 126 (2007): 5–27; See also, Michael Stone, "The Book of Enoch and Judaism in the Third Century BCE," *CBQ* 40 (1978): 479–92.

attitude presupposes that other Jewish communities embraced a narrow or conservative attitude—a presumption for which we have no evidence. "It seems possible, maybe even probable," claims Hempel, "that the liberal attitude to non-standardized texts was shared widely by Jews at this period...surprising and unexpected as that may seem to us."[13] Although I share the belief that a similar attitude was likely held by most Jews, the notion that a plurality of text forms for individual texts is "surprising" or "unexpected" has nothing whatsoever to do with the attitudes of the Second Temple period. Rather, these perspectives are being driven, in their entirety, by those of us who live in the postcanonical world—a world that has been shaped and defined by fixed-texts and *Endtexts*.

It is important to note that the presence of textual diversity and plurality in a collection of documents is not limited to the Dead Sea Scrolls or the pre-canonical era. Religious libraries the world over have, throughout their long histories, contained countless examples of textual pluriformity and writings that are in outright disagreement with one another. Even the Hebrew Bible, which is itself a library, contains numerous examples of incongruity and a variety of text forms, such as those found in the books of Kings and Chronicles. Similarly, the cache of texts from the genizah of the Ben Ezra synagogue in Old Cairo has yielded numerous examples of *halakhic* disagreement and books that would likely have been considered anathema to the architects of rabbinic Judaism, such as the *Damascus Document* and the *Book of Commandments* by Anan ben David. Many theories have been forwarded to explain the presence of these and other texts in the genizah of the Ben Ezra synagogue, from their intentional removal from circulation by Rabbanite Jews who wanted to prevent their faith community from being contaminated by heretical writings, to the hypothesis that some of these documents came from other Cairo synagogues and were accidentally joined with the Ben Ezra material during their retrieval and relocation to England during the late nineteenth century. Perhaps the most interesting theory, however, brings us back to the notion of leniency. As Adina Hoffman and Peter Cole have suggested, it may be possible that "the Fustat Jewish community [in Old Cairo] was

---

13. Similarly, Hempel notes: "Given that the notion of a Bible is anachronistic for this period, it may well be that Jewish attitudes to texts were rather relaxed and laid back in the late Second Temple period... This clearly also applies to cherished and authoritative texts. No text could have been more revered and cherished than the emerging Bible in a movement such as the one behind the Qumran library whose members were steeped in the scriptures... The fluidity of these ancient texts appears to cross the boundaries created by customary categories such as biblical and non-biblical Dead Sea Scrolls." Hempel, *The Qumran Rule Texts in Context*, 281, 284.

simply more flexible (and perhaps fickle) than we'd realized, and that there may have been serious interest in [certain] 'sectarian' works even within this mainstream Rabbanite context."[14] Similar arguments have been forwarded with regard to the multiple copies of the *Community Rule*, the *Damascus Document*, and 4QMMT at Qumran, some of which may have come to Qumran from other sectarian communities[15] and/or been used as educational devices for new initiates to the community.[16] But regardless of the strength of these hypotheses, the notion of having to be "flexible" with regard to textual diversity and/or pluriformity within a collection of literature would appear to be more at home in a tenth-century CE Rabbinic context than in the pre-canonical world of Second Temple Judaism where textual authority was a far more fluid concept and the standardization of various text forms had yet to be realized in full.

Eyes to See; Ears to Hear

It goes without saying that high degrees of literacy and complete illiteracy exist at opposite ends of a continuum with numerous levels of ability lying between. Given the constraints of time, however, I would like to focus on the two ends of this spectrum—adult Jewish males in the Second Temple period who were able to read, write and, interpret Hebrew, Aramaic, and/or Greek texts, on the one hand, and illiterate Jews, on the other. As Christopher Rollston has observed:

> For the southern Levant during antiquity, I would propose as a working description of literacy the possession of substantial facility in a writing system, that is, the ability to write and read, using and understanding a standard script, a terminology, and with minimal errors of composition or comprehension. Moreover, I would affirm that the capacity to scrawl one's name on a contract, but without the ability to write and read anything else is not literacy, not even some sort of "functional literacy."[17]

---

14. Adina Hoffman and Peter Cole, *Sacred Trash: The Lost and Found World of the Cairo Genizah* (New York: Schocken, 2011), 162.

15. John J. Collins, *Beyond the Qumran Community: The Sectarian Movement of the Dead Sea Scrolls* (Grand Rapids: Eerdmans, 2009); Allison Schofield, *From Qumran to Yahad: A New Paradigm of Textual Development for the Community Rule*, STDJ 77 (Leiden: Brill, 2009).

16. Maxine L. Grossman, *Reading for History in the Damascus Document: A Methodological Study*, STDJ 45 (Leiden: Brill, 2011); idem, "Reading 4QMMT: Genre and History," *RevQ* 20, no. 1 (2001): 3–22.

17. Christopher Rollston, *Writing and Literacy in the World of Ancient Israel* (Atlanta: SBL Press, 2010), 127.

Although Rollston's definition of literacy fails to take into account those individuals who may have been fluent in two or more languages—a position that an incredibly small number of individuals would have occupied in the Greco-Roman world—his interpretation is compelling and would appear to be in line with the epigraphic and archaeological evidence from ancient Palestine.[18] In particular, the texts from Qumran indicate that those individuals who were responsible for writing and copying the Dead Sea Scrolls were literate in precisely the way that Rollston has proposed—the ability to read and write through the use of a standard script (or scripts) that exhibits minimal compositional and comprehension errors. Furthermore, it must be stated that this observation applies to the scrolls regardless of whether they were written and edited at Qumran or if they were composed and redacted elsewhere. But who exactly were these individuals and what percentage of the populace did they represent?

By most estimates, literacy rates in the Second Temple period were incredibly low. Within the larger Greco-Roman world, from the conquest of ancient Palestine by Alexander the Great in 332 BCE to the fall of the Roman Empire in 474 CE, scholars such as William Harris,[19] Harry Gamble,[20] Alan Millard,[21] and Richard Horsley[22] have theorized that no more than ten to fifteen percent of the total populace was literate, with the urban centers exhibiting higher rates of literacy than rural areas. Moreover, literacy tended to be restricted to men who were in the upper end of the socio-economic spectrum—individuals who had the time, money, and status to devote themselves to the kinds of educational pursuits and leisurely activities that the average person did not. As Horsley has observed: "Writing was used mainly by the political and

---

18. By comparison, a 2006 report by UNESCO defines literacy as: "the ability to read and write with understanding a simple statement related to one's daily life... It involves a continuum of reading and writing skills, and often includes also basic arithmetic skills (numeracy)." Nicholas Burnett, "Literacy for Life: Education for All Global Monitoring Report—2006" (Paris: Unesco, 2005), 158 [cited 26 November 2017]. Online: http://unesdoc.unesco.org/images/0014/001416/141639e.pdf.

19. William Harris, *Ancient Literacy* (Cambridge, MA: Harvard University Press, 1991), 13, 328–30.

20. Harry Gamble, *Books and Readers in the Early Church* (New Haven: Yale University Press, 1995), 4–10.

21. Alan Millard, *Reading and Writing in the Time of Jesus* (Sheffield: Sheffield Academic Press, 2001), 154–6.

22. Richard Horsley, *Text and Tradition in Performance and Writing* (Eugene, OR: Cascade Books, 2013).

cultural elite, often as an instrument of power. While they knew that it was used by the elite, the vast majority of the people had no use for writing."[23] This perspective has been echoed by numerous scholars, such as Werner Kelber,[24] Ian Young,[25] and Martin Jaffee; the latter providing one of the more eloquent distillations of thought on the subject:

> [T]he group of people who could actually compose, transcribe and communicate the content of written compositions [in the Second Temple period]—whether brief letters or lengthy literary works—was quite small in relation to the society as a whole. Such skills were regarded as esoteric professional acquisition rather than a general cultural patrimony. Persons possessing them were, for the most part, members of elite scribal guilds associated with official institutions of palace, law court, and temple. Outside such groups, the ability to write was routinely limited to elementary forms of record-keeping... Except for those trained in technical scribal schools, individuals did not usually have equal facility in writing, composition, and reading."[26]

The upshot of Jaffee's thoughts, and similarly minded interpretations, is that the literary productivity of the Second Temple period was generated, read, and edited in its entirety by an elite group of well-healed men—highly trained individuals who represented an educated and wealthy minority. If we add to this Michael Wise's contention that no more than 2–5 percent of Roman Judea was literate up to and through the Bar Kokhba period,[27] it becomes clear that the overwhelming majority of Jews in the Second Temple period and beyond, including nearly 100 percent of women,[28] were either completely illiterate or had only the most basic

---

23. Horsley, *Text and Tradition*, 2.

24. Werner Kelber, *The Oral and the Written Gospel: The Hermeneutics of Speaking and Writing in the Synoptic Tradition, Mark, Paul, and Q* (Bloomington: Indiana University Press, 1997), 6.

25. Ian Young, "Israelite Literacy: Interpreting the Evidence: Part II," *Vetus Testamentum* 48 (1998): 408–22.

26. Martin Jaffee, *Torah in the Mouth: Writing and Oral Tradition in Palestinian Judaism, 200 BCE–400 CE* (Oxford: Oxford University Press, 2001), 15.

27. According to Wise: "...the data we have argue that a reasonably high percentage of the Judaean male elite could read a book; about 30 percent... For the full adult population, the same data suggest, the figure was far, far lower—probably on the low side of the range between 2.5 and 5 percent." Michael Wise, *Language and Literacy in Ancient Judaea: A Study of the Bar Kokhba Documents* (New Haven: Yale University Press, 2015), 350.

28. Heather D. D. Parker and Erin E. Fleming, "Education," in *The Oxford Encyclopedia of Gender and Bible Studies*, Vol. I, *ASI-MUJ*, ed. J. M. O'Brian (Oxford: Oxford University Press, 2014), 152–9; Wise, *Language and Literacy*, 350.

of skills when it came to reading and writing.[29] Stated another way, if Jaffee, Wise, and others are correct, then upwards of 95–98 percent of the population in the Second Temple period had no direct role in writing, reading, or redacting texts.[30] In short, the illiterate masses were the silent majority. Or were they?

Form critics of classical literature and the Hebrew Bible have long recognized the importance of the oral tradition and the ways in which orality has affected the written word. In particular, public performance, which was the only way for the vast majority of individuals throughout history to experience Scripture, had a profound impact on the form and structure of the Hebrew Bible. As Jaffee has noted: "Precisely because texts were composed under the assumption that they would be read in the setting of oral performance, their compositional styles drew deeply upon habits of speech and rhetorical traditions that had their living matrix in oral communication."[31] Although it is impossible for us to recover the actual words and phrasings of the oral world that resided behind, and alongside of, these ancient texts, "it is possible," as Jaffee notes, "to retrieve the oral-literary registers—reflected in stylized diction, speech patterns, and rhetorical conventions—that nourished the writings that emerge from cultures of the manuscript."[32] Given the rarified air that the educated elite of the Second Temple period breathed, it may come as somewhat of a surprise to recognize that the oral tradition served as both the inspiration behind, and the intended method of delivery for, the writings of ancient Judaism—documents that could only be accessed by a mere fraction of the Jewish population. But this revelation is only surprising if we continue to approach it from the mindset of a postcanonical world where the written word is king.

---

29. Wise describes the situation in ancient Palestine thusly: "A literate society filled with illiterates—especially women: that was Roman Judaea in a nutshell." Wise, *Language and Literacy*, 351.

30. Even the Qumran community, which is often romanticized as having been an educated and highly literate scribal fraternity, would have counted numerous illiterate and semi-literate individuals among their ranks. See Charlotte Hempel, "Reflections on Literacy, Textuality, and Community in the Qumran Dead Sea Scrolls," in *Is There a Text in this Cave? Studies in the Textuality of the Dead Sea Scrolls in Honour of George J. Brooke*, ed. A. Feldman, M. Cioata, and C. Hempel (Leiden: Brill, 2017), 69–82.

31. Jaffee, *Torah in the Mouth*, 18.

32. Ibid.

As scholars of the Bible, we have been indoctrinated into a field of research that emphasizes the primacy and the importance of *Urtexts* and *Endtexts* above all else. "I was taught as a graduate student," remarks Susan Niditch, "to choose the shortest reading, the best reading, the implicitly 'original' reading that has been corrupted."[33] And it is precisely this goal—the desire to identify "original" readings through the witness of a text's final form—that has preoccupied the imagination of scholars of the Bible for centuries.[34] The oral tradition, by contrast, has all too often been downgraded in importance or met with skepticism by those who claim it impossible to recover the contours of its discourse. And while there are difficulties inherent in discussing the shape and likely effects of the oral tradition, we must also recognize that the pre-canonical world of Second Temple Judaism was overwhelmingly populated by illiterate individuals and that the literary activities of the scribes were heavily influenced by oral and aural concerns. "Attention to oral traditional considerations," argues Niditch, "leads one instead to respect textual variation as evidence of the way in which qualities of the oral continue in written traditions. Various communities heard the text differently and indeed some like the Qumran community preserved written variants, longer and shorter, right within the same library."[35] Similarly, Jaffee notes: "The oral/aural setting of the Second Temple literary culture contributed to one other aspect of the book that needs to be considered here: a given book normally circulated in a variety of textual forms, some longer and some shorter, one copy distinct in a variety of ways from any other."[36] And herein lies a possible answer to the question of textual pluriformity at Qumran: It is not that the Qumran community was

---

33. Susan Niditch, "Oral Tradition and Biblical Scholarship," *Oral Tradition* 18, no. 1 (2003): 44.

34. "Qumran has shown," notes Hempel, "that the search for uncovering an *Urtext* in its pristine purity is obsolete at this period of Jewish history." Hempel, *The Qumran Rule Texts in Context*, 283.

35. Susan Niditch, "Oral Tradition and Biblical Scholarship," 44; See also, William Schniedewind, *How the Bible Became a Book: The Textualization of Ancient Israel* (New York: Cambridge University Press, 2004); Susan Niditch, *Oral World and Written Word: Ancient Israelite Literature* (Louisville: Westminster John Knox Press, 1996).

36. Jaffee, *Torah in the Mouth*, 18. Although I agree with Jaffee on this point, it is worth noting that he continues to embrace the notion that the scrolls reflect a certain amount of pliability when it comes to Scripture: "The Qumran scrolls, in which multiple copies of specific works are preserved, have been crucial in demonstrating the *flexible boundaries* of even the most authoritative books" (ibid., 166, my emphasis).

"flexible" or had a "liberal attitude" to the literature in their collection. Rather, it was the overwhelmingly oral/aural character of the world the authors lived in, combined with high levels of illiteracy among their audiences, which resulted in a body of literature that is far more reflective of the trends of oral transmission and performance than the textual standardization and rigidity of the post-canonical world.[37]

This is not to say, however, that the future books of the Hebrew Bible were completely bereft of standardization during the Second Temple period. As we now know, the Masoretic Text was well on its way to becoming a fixed text-type by the turn of the millennium and there is no denying that the MT's gradual ascent towards canonical authority was tied to an increasing concern on the part of the literati to enhance the authority of the written word and consolidate their ability to define what it meant to be a Jew.[38] This process was accelerated, of course, with the destruction of the Temple and the exile of Jews after the failure of the Bar Kochbah revolt, which led to a sharp decline in the number and variety of priestly sects and forced a literate remnant to reimagine Judaism with an eye towards accessibility, portability, and uniformity. It is at this juncture that Judaism moves in the direction of normativity through the lessening of ritual restrictions on lay Jews and by canonization of its literary patrimony—strategies that were designed to standardize and concretize

---

37. As Jaffee notes: "We find reading practices linked closely to public ceremony and instruction in which oral communication was the primary medium of textual knowledge... Torah was orally delivered and aurally received, communicated from mouth to ear in syllables laid forth in written words." Ibid., 61.

38. According to Timothy Lim: "Unlike the traditional Hebrew Bible that holds up one text, the Masoretic Text, as authoritative, the biblical scrolls found at Qumran attest to a plurality of text-types. Emanuel Tov has formulated a theory of multiple texts to account for this diversity of text-forms... Tov assigned various percentages to each one of these groups, with the proto-MT group having the largest share at 40 per cent..." Timothy Lim, "Authoritative Scriptures and the Dead Sea Scrolls," in *The Oxford Handbook of The Dead Sea Scrolls*, ed. T. H. Lim and J. J. Collins (Oxford: Oxford University Press, 2010), 318. See also Shemaryahu Talmon, "The Crystallization of the 'Canon of Hebrew Scriptures' in the Light of the Biblical Scrolls from Qumran," in *Bible as Book: The Hebrew Bible and the Judaean Desert Discoveries*, ed. E. D. Herbert and E. Tov (London: The British Library, 2002), 5–20; Emanuel Tov, *Textual Criticism of the Hebrew Bible* (Minneapolis: Fortress Press, 2001); and Eugene Ulrich, "Qumran and the Canon of the Old Testament," in *The Biblical Canons*, ed. J.-M. Auwers and H. J. De Jonge (Leuven: Leuven University Press, 2003), 57–80.

the religious tradition in the hopes of making it more manageable for all and resistant to change no matter the time or place.[39]

And yet, in spite of the dramatic reforms of the second century CE, and the myriad ways in which the aforementioned events shaped our understanding of canon and textual authority within the Jewish tradition, we cannot ignore the witness of the Dead Sea Scrolls and the presence of pluriformity within the sectarian and "biblical" manuscripts. Nor can we turn a blind eye to the large number of pseudepigraphic texts in this collection, which occasionally rival the "biblical" books in terms of their frequency of attestation and unmistakable influence on other literary compositions.[40] The witness of the Dead Sea Scrolls argues against a simplistic, linear development of Judaism's literary patrimony from oral to written. Rather, it is now clear that the overwhelmingly oral/aural character of Second Temple Judaism was just as potent, if not more so, as the written culture—with the former affecting the latter, and vice versa, in both a linear and non-linear fashion.[41] This was a world in which the stories of Abraham and the patriarchs were not limited to those now familiar passages from Genesis, but were supplemented by additional tales, such as those found in the book of *Jubilees* and the *Genesis Apocryphon*; stories that would have been received and transmitted by the illiterate and literate alike as being meaningful and authoritative.

---

39. For more on normative Judaism, see: E. P. Sanders, *Paul and Palestinian Judaism* (Philadelphia: Fortress Press, 1977); Sanders, *Judaism: Practice and Belief 63 BCE–66 AD* (London: SCM Press; Philadelphia: Trinity Press International, 1992).

40. As I have argued elsewhere, fifteen copies of *Jubilees* were found among the Dead Sea Scrolls and this book has been recovered in five of the eleven caves from Qumran putting *Jubilees* on a par with Genesis (20 copies), Exodus (16), and Leviticus (12) in terms of its frequency of attestation. Moreover, several texts from Qumran contain both explicit and implicit quotations from *Jubilees* suggesting that this text had a relatively high degree of authority for Jews during the Second Temple period. See Ian Werrett, "Salvation through Emulation: Facets of Jubilean Soteriology at Qumran," in *This World and the World to Come: Soteriology in Early Judaism*, ed. D. Gurtner (Sheffield: T&T Clark, 2011), 211–28.

41. As Lawrence Schiffman has argued: "Indeed it has been correctly observed that the Qumran sectarians saw themselves as living in the biblical age itself, and compilation and editing of biblical materials continued to some extent in Qumran and related sectarian circles up to the turn of the era." Lawrence Schiffman, "Light from the Qumran Scrolls on Rabbinic Literature," in *The Qumran Legal Texts between the Hebrew Bible and Its Interpretation*, ed. K. De Troyer and A. Lange (Leuven: Peeters, 2001), 114.

Textual pluriformity in the pre-canonical era, therefore, was not a liberal or flexible attitude to a canonical mindset that had yet to be established; it was the norm.

Object-ness and Thing-ness

As Muhammed Ahmed el-Hamed scrambled over the rocky scree of the Judaean desert searching for a missing goat, he claims to have come across a "cave with its entrance open at the top like a cistern."[42] Thinking that the animal might have fallen into the cavity, he began tossing stones into the opening. As he did so, he told his interviewer, he heard something like "the breaking of pottery." "I wanted to know what was in the cave," noted el-Hamed, "so I went down into the cave and found pottery jars. I began to break the jars with my staff, thinking I would find *treasure* [italics mine]." Much to his dismay, however, nine of the ten jars were either empty or contained reddish seeds. The Bedouin continues: "When I broke the tenth jar, which was the smallest of the jars, I found in it some rolled leather with scrawling on it." Unsure of what to do, the shepherd returned to his companions, cursing his "lack of good fortune" for having lost one of his flock.[43]

After the publication of el-Hamed's interview in 1957, the contents and details of his recollections came under intense scrutiny.[44] Concerns about the Bedouin's account ranged from a reluctance to accept his memories of the past, to denying his assertion that he had found the scrolls in 1945, and rejecting the notion that he had contemplated using the leather of the scrolls to repair his sandals.[45] Even a cursory reading of what has been said in print during the intervening years suggests that there is a high degree of uncertainty and skepticism when it comes to the accuracy of el-Hamed's story. And while John Trever's version of the discovery is

---

42. This description of the cave would appear to be more in keeping with the shape of Cave 4 than Cave 1—an observation first made by Brownlee. Brownlee, "Muhammad ed-Deeb's Own Story of His Scroll Discovery," 237.

43. Brownlee, "Muhammad ed-Deeb's Own Story of His Scroll Discovery," 237.

44. John C. Trever, "When Was Qumran Cave I Discovered?" *RevQ* 3, no. 1 (1961): 135–41; Roland de Vaux, *Archaeology and the Dead Sea Scrolls* (Oxford: Oxford University Press, 1973), vii.

45. According to John Trever, "Adh-Dhib's claim that he planned to use the scrolls for sandal straps is not very convincing. He surely would have noted at once how brittle the leather was and abandoned such a thought, even if it occurred to him." Trever, "When Was Qumran Cave I Discovered?" 140–1.

often cited as being one of the most authoritative,[46] Harmut Stegemann's synopsis of this remarkable find is one of the most honest: "The Bedouin recounted how one of their shepherd boys, Muhammad ed-Dhib, 'the Wolf,' had discovered the cave by accident when he had climbed up into the rocks after a runaway goat. What else happened just then can no longer be sorted out very well."[47]

Putting aside, for the moment, the details and accuracy of el-Hamed's story, it is worth contemplating the ways in which the Bedouin has been characterized in scholarly and popular publications on the Dead Sea Scrolls. To begin with, the vast majority of scholars and authors have opted to refer to the Bedouin by his nickname edh-Dhib, or "the Wolf," which simultaneously dehumanizes el-Hamed and conveys a sense of aggression and/or cunning without providing the actual context for the nickname.[48] By contrast, only the rarest of publications invoke Muhammad's proper name, Ahmed el-Hamed, the components of which are variations of the Arabic root Ḥ-M-D meaning "to praise" or "praiseworthy." Then there is the issue of the intelligence, age, and occupation of el-Hamed, who has been variously described as "uneducated," "illiterate," "ignorant," "simple," "rough-looking," "semi-nomadic," "young," a "boy," a "teen," a "shepherd," a "tribesman," a "herdsman," a "goat-herder," an "Arab," and a "fugitive." With the exception of el-Hamed's status as a youthful shepherd, which can be read in either a positive or negative light, the remaining descriptions tend to portray the man to whom we owe so much (i.e., a man whose discovery is truly "worthy of praise") in a less than edifying manner. And it is here, in the place where the history of the scrolls as books intersects with their value as artifacts and their importance as literary compositions, that we must begin to cultivate greater sensitivity and awareness. By resisting the historicist fetishisms of a bygone era "where possessing a thing comes to feel like possessing history itself," we may be able to "interrupt the habit of granting material

---

46. John Trever, *The Untold Story of Qumran* (Westwood, NJ: Fleming H. Revell Co., 1965).

47. In concert with Stegemann, Trever notes: "…it is apparent that the memories of those who were involved in the pre-1948 events surrounding the Qumran scrolls are very hazy." Hartmut Stegemann, *The Library of Qumran: On the Essenes, Qumran, John the Baptist, and Jesus* (Grand Rapids: Eerdmans, 1998), 2; Trever, "When Was Qumran Cave I Discovered?" 138–9.

48. As far as I am aware, John Trever is the only scholar to have explained the nickname edh-Dhib, which purportedly comes from el-Hamed's father who was "fierce like a wolf." See Trever, *The Untold Story of Qumran*, 103.

objects a value and power of their own,"[49] and come to see the Bedouin's role in history of the scrolls, and the scrolls themselves, in ways that we had not previously considered.

What is clear from Muhammed Ahmed el-Hamed's account of the discovery of Cave I is that the scrolls were little more than *things* to him; they were not *objects* in a Heidiggerian sense. And unlike things, "we look through objects," argues Bill Brown, "because there are codes by which our interpretive attention makes them meaningful, because there is a discourse of objectivity that allows us to use them as facts."[50] These systems of meaning allow us to see what an object "disclose[s] about history, society, nature, or culture—above all, what they disclose[s] about us."[51] Objects, therefore, are encoded by societies with a specific value or worth. "We begin to confront the thingness of objects," Brown continues, "when they stop working for us: when the drill breaks, when the car stalls, when the windows get filthy, when their flow within the circuits of production and distribution, consumption and exhibition, has been arrested however momentarily."[52] And this was precisely what el-Hamed experienced upon finding the scrolls on that fateful day in 1945. The meanings and value that had been ascribed to the scrolls by the authors of the Second Temple period were lost on el-Hamed and his Bedouin companions. This fact is verified through el-Hamed's own words, when he admits that he was "puzzled as to what [he] should do, whether to take the rolled leather or to leave it where it was."[53]

49. The recent controversy over the acquisition and authenticity of the Museum of the Bible's Dead Sea Scroll fragments is a testament to the perpetuation of such historicist fetishisms—the very attitudes that are responsible for creating and sustaining the merchants and forgers of the black and grey markets. Bill Brown, *A Sense of Things: The Object Matter of American Literature* (Chicago: University of Chicago Press, 2003), 8, 118. See also Kipp Davis, "Caves of Dispute: Patterns of Correspondence and Suspicion in the Post-2002 'Dead Sea Scrolls' Fragments," *DSD* 24, no. 2 (2017): 229–70; Michael Greshko, "Forgeries May Hide in the Museum of the Bible's Dead Sea Scrolls," n.p. [cited 6 December 2017]. Online: https://news.nationalgeographic.com/2017/11/museum-of-the-bible-dead-sea-scrolls-forgeries-history-archaeology/.

50. Bill Brown, "Thing Theory," *Critical Inquiry* 28, no. 1 (2001): 4.

51. Ibid.

52. Ibid. Elsewhere, Brown notes: "The difference between the apperceptive constitution of a thing, in what we might call its objecthood, and the experience of the thing, in what we might call its thinghood, emerges in the moment (and no doubt only as a moment) of re-objectification that results from a kind of misuse – turning the picture bottom up, standing on one's head." Brown, *A Sense of Things*, 76.

53. Brownlee, "Muhammad ed-Deeb's Own Story of His Scroll Discovery," 237.

While Brown's effort to distinguish between "things" and "objects" is insightful and provides us with a helpful way to understand the dilemma faced by el-Hamed, other scholars, such as John Frow, have argued that things and objects alike "are characterized by the possibility that their 'propriety', their 'proper' or inscribed or intended function, can be re-appropriated, [and] turned to a different use."[54] And yet, in spite of the inherent logic of Frow's observation, scholars continue to impose their own sense of what is proper onto the scrolls, either knowingly or unknowingly, and criticize those who have attempted to use the texts in ways that deviate from what the scholarly guild has deemed to be their intended function.[55] As Leah Price has observed:

> ...as twenty-first-century critics have moved from the abstract to the concrete, from the "history" represented or refracted within the text's verbal content to the "history" of the book itself, their own investment in interpretation has tended to obscure the simple fact that reading is only one among many uses to which printed matter can be put.[56]

Simply put, books can be handled, valued, and employed in ways that go far beyond the intentions of an author or the wishes of a subsequent community. Not only can they be "sold, exchanged, transported, displayed, defaced, stored, ignored, collected, neglected, dispersed, discarded," notes Price, "books can be enlisted (to state the obvious) in a range of transactions and rituals that stretch far beyond the literary or even the linguistic."[57] And while some of these uses may be deemed to be more legitimate than

---

54. John Frow, "A Pebble, a Camera, a Man Who Turns into a Telegraph Pole," *Critical Inquiry* 28, no. 1 (2001): 282.

55. Timothy Lim's comments are particularly insightful in this respect: "On 20-25 July 1997, scholars from around the world were invited to Jerusalem to mark the Jubilee celebration of the discovery [of the Dead Sea Scrolls]... The political capital made out of the Dead Sea Scrolls by Israel's leading politicians was not lost on us, but a dignified silence was maintained. It was only when it was mentioned that the Dead Sea Scrolls were vital for Jerusalem did a disapproving titter ripple through the audience. This was amusing to the assembled, since most experts believe that the Dead Sea Scrolls belong to a pious Jewish group of Essenes who, among other things, held that the Jerusalem priesthood was corrupt and as a result separated themselves from the majority of the people and went into a self-imposed exile in the Judaean Desert!" Timothy Lim, *The Dead Sea Scrolls: A Very Short Introduction* (Oxford: Oxford University Press, 2005), 9–10.

56. Leah Price, "The History of a Book to a 'History of the Book'," *Representations* 108, no. 1 (2009): 120, 123.

57. Ibid., 120.

others, it is often up to the individual to determine the value and most appropriate use of a book.

Although el-Hamed was unable to identify with the scrolls as literary objects, criticizing his financial motivations and lack of education, or holding him to a level of understanding that would have been at odds with his existence as a Bedouin shepherd, is simply a reflection of our own biases and our unwillingness to allow for the malleability of things and objects.[58] "Things in any minimally complex system" argues Frow, "carry an indefinite number of actual or potential overlapping uses, significations, and values."[59] From this perspective, even the scholarly use of the scrolls, which focuses on issues that go well beyond the original intentions of their authors, are simply the "effects of recognitions and uses performed within frames of understanding."[60] And although we may privilege our frames of understanding over others, the fact remains that we are taking advantage of the same functional and cultural hybridity inherent in the scrolls that allowed el-Hamed to see them as a source of leather and the basis for financial gain.[61]

58. In 1955, the State of Israel and pulp-paper magnate David Solomon Gottesman paid $250,000 for four scrolls from Cave I, which is roughly $2,260,000 in today's economy. Although el-Hamed and his cousins received only a fraction of this payment, the amount of money being offered for the scrolls in the 1950s was far greater than the collective earning power of several generations of Bedouin combined. Had I been in el-Hamed's position, and was offered millions of dollars for found objects that I had no emotional or intellectual attachment to, there is no doubt in my mind that I would have acted exactly as el-Hamed did. Concerning Israel's efforts to purchase the scrolls, see Teddy Kollek, "Correspondence to Dr. Martin Rosenblueth" (Jerusalem, February 25, 1957), 2.

59. Frow, "A Pebble, a Camera, a Man Who Turns into a Telegraph Pole," 284.

60. "No single game exhausts [a thing's] function; no single description exhausts the uses to which their properties might appropriately or inappropriately lend themselves, and they are always shadowed by the traces of virtual uses and the complicated circuits of knowledge, need, and desire that map those virtualities." Ibid.

61. "Cultural and functional hybridity is an ordinary condition of objects, and the most mundane thing, a teacup for example, must be readable in a number of different ways—as an aesthetic object, as a useful object, as the material product of certain highly evolved technologies, and so on. The teacup is inherently complex; it 'can only be known, used, recognized, and so on, because it can be so in relation to the confluence of more than a single system'. Conversely, if such things 'were ever given as hypothetically pure and simple productions and recognitions from within a single system, they wouldn't be knowable, usable or recognizable for us at all. (If there were such things, they would be noumenal, natural in the purest sense, and no art or science could know them)'." Ibid., 282–3.

Mirror, Mirror

Unlike the politicians of the Israeli nation-state, who have used the Dead Sea Scrolls to bolster their claims to the land,[62] or Muhammed Ahmed el-Hamed, whose material needs and illiteracy obfuscated his ability to see the texts as windows onto the Second Temple period, the academic worldview is one where linguistic and literary considerations rule the day; a "logic that privileges use above display, reading above collecting."[63] As members of the scholarly guild, we are unabashedly partial to the latter perspective, but the existence of a specialized academic community does not preclude others from offering their own interpretations or using the scrolls in ways that run counter to the scholarly world's inclinations or wishes. The rights of the nation-state and questions of legal ownership notwithstanding, the material culture and literary productions of previous generations belong to us all and the onus is on the scholarly community to serve the guild, and the general public, by providing rigorous and compelling hypotheses that are free from the subjectivity, fetishes, and post-canonical biases enumerated above.[64]

---

62. In Levi Eshkol's dedication speech at the Israel Museum in 1965, the former Prime Minister stated that the Shrine of the Book represented a "vividly inscribed sign of the rejuvenation of our covenant with the generations who lived in this land since ancient times" [translation mine]. Similarly, during President Donald Trump's recent visit to Israel, Benjamin Netanyahu remarked that the Dead Sea Scrolls represent "not simply the story of the past…[but] of a nation reborn, of a barren land brought back to life, of an ancient language revived, of an exiled people who returned, of Jewish sovereignty restored." Levi Eshkol, "פתיחת מוסיאין ישראל" (11 May 1965), 1; Benjamin Netanyahu, "PM Netanyahu's Remarks at the Israel Museum" (23 May 2017), 1.

63. Price, "The History of a Book to a 'History of the Book'," 120.

64. The question of the ownership of the Dead Sea Scrolls has come to the fore, yet again, with the cancelation of an exhibition at the Frankfurt Bible Museum, which was schedule to open in the fall of 2019. In response to the German government's refusal to issue an "immunity from seizure" agreement, Israel has elected not to loan scrolls to the Frankfurt museum in fear that the Jordanian and/or Palestinian governments may attempt to contest Israel's claims of ownership. As Liel Leibovitz has noted: "Palestinian activists argue that as the scrolls were discovered in the West Bank, they are Palestinian property, even as they are clearly a historical relic of an ancient Jewish sect and even if the scrolls were originally discovered in 1946, when Qumran, like the rest of mandatory Palestine, was under British control. Similarly, Jordanian activists are arguing that many of the scrolls were housed in the Rockefeller Museum in east Jerusalem, which Israel captured in the 1967 Six Day War, which, they say, makes the scrolls Jordan's purloined

In truth, the study of the Dead Sea Scrolls is as much about their history as books as it is about their literary contents. And yet, when it comes to Muhammad Ahmed el-Hamed's role in the story of the scrolls, we have tended to portray him as a "Wolf" with baser motivations, such as profit or greed, or as an illiterate youth whose inability to see the "true value" of the scrolls serves as a punchline to elevate and solidify our own level of authority. Rather than acknowledging that el-Hamed had more in common with the impoverished, illiterate, and bucolic masses of the Second Temple period than we do—a fact that has been almost universally ignored—we have privileged the witness of the scrolls and the literate minority who collected, copied, and edited these ancient texts.[65] Moreover, we have used the actions of the Bedouins, who kept the location of Cave I a secret after learning of the scrolls' potential value, to present el-Hamed and his brethren in a negative light.[66] But if things and objects are malleable, and

property. Boris Rhein, the culture minister from the German state of Hesse, told the German press last week that Germany's Foreign Ministry and federal commissioner for cultural affairs believe that the ownership of the Dead Sea Scrolls is unclear." Liel Leibovitz, "Germany: Dead Sea Scrolls Don't Belong to Israel," *Tablet* n.p. [cited 4 December 2017]. Online: http://www.tabletmag.com/scroll/250877/germany-dead-sea-scrolls-dont-belong-to-israel.

65. The account of el-Hamed's discovery, which Brownlee describes as being "almost Biblical in its directness and beauty...[suggesting] that his story had achieved precision and finesse through frequent telling," provides us with a possible analog for understanding the relationship between orality, literacy, and textual pluriformity in the Second Temple period. As Brownlee notes, the Bedouin's story "may be of interest to form critics as illustrating the oral form told by a simple Oriental might take." And while Brownlee's observations are reflective of the very biases I have been talking about, his comments about the relationship between the Bedouin's story and form criticism afford us with an interesting opportunity to understand the complex interplay between oral performance and the written word; particularly in light of el-Hamed's limited education and pastoral lifestyle, which parallels the experience of many in the Second Temple period. As Price has noted: "Outside of the object narrative's covers, no book speaks for itself. But the speech produced in (and by) its pages may provide one model for the stories that get told *about* books—and maybe even about their users." Brownlee, "Muhammad ed-Deeb's Own Story of His Scroll Discovery," 239; Price, "The History of a Book to a 'History of the Book'," 136.

66. An example of this attitude can be found in Frank Moore Cross' *The Ancient Library of Qumran*: "In the year between the Bedouin discovery and the first press releases announcing the discovery to the world...several clandestine excavations ravaged the cave site; additional materials came to light; there is evidence that a considerable amount of precious material was destroyed in the process... The

can be interpreted in ways that go beyond their intended use, then people can be understood similarly, for they too can be understood as things.[67] And herein lies what Frow has dubbed "the real strangeness"—the recognition that "persons and things are kin; the world is many, not double."[68]

Whether the central character in the discovery of the Dead Sea Scrolls is a naïve shepherd boy searching for a lost goat, an illiterate Bedouin eking out an impoverished existence in Bethlehem, or a calculating Arab looking for artifacts to sell on the black market, the manifold contours of Muhammed Ahmed el-Hamed's story, and the variations in its presentation and performance, bear witness to the complex interplay between the oral-literary registers; the very same registers that "nourished the writings that emerge from cultures of the manuscript."[69] In this instance, however, it is we, the scholars of the twentieth and twenty-first centuries, not the scribes of the Second Temple period, who have committed el-Hamed's story to memory in the form of the written word.

Like our precanonical forebears, we accept the pluriform versions of the Bedouin's discovery as encapsulating varying degrees of authority and truth. Our willingness to embrace this situation however, does not make us lenient or flexible. Rather, it is simply the reality of living in a time when a textually standardized version of the events has, for one reason or another, failed to materialize—an era where performance, memory, and biases (old and new) have been used to shape and reshape the contours of Muhammad Ahmed el-Hamed's narrative for the sake of entertaining audiences, educating the uninformed, and enhancing one's authority. The time has come, however, for us to move beyond those versions of the account that dehumanize el-Hamed and portray him as a "simple Oriental" or an unwitting rube.[70] Not only because it is the right thing to do; but because the act of dislocating oneself from a specific worldview has the effect of temporarily interrupting our ability to see the world and the objects within it.[71]

Ta'amireh clansmen, however, having made a successful debut in the archaeological field, were inclined to make a vocation of it… Their range lands were rich only in caves and they proposed to exploit them." Frank Moore Cross, *The Ancient Library of Qumran*, 3rd edn (Sheffield: Sheffield Academic Press, 1995), 22, 25.

67. Karl Marx, *Capital*, Vol. I (New York: Penguin, 1990), 209, 1054.
68. Frow, "A Pebble, a Camera, a Man Who Turns into a Telegraph Pole," 285.
69. Jaffee, *Torah in the Mouth*, 18.
70. Brownlee, "Muhammad ed-Deeb's Own Story of His Scroll Discovery," 239.
71. "Part of the point of such dislocations (which can be coded as misappropriations) is to interrupt the habits with which we view the world, the habits that prevent us from seeing the world—to call us to a particular and particularizing attention." Brown, *A Sense of Things*, 78.

And it is during this brief, yet necessary, interruption of habit that we become aware of an object's thingness and are forced to re-objectify the things under our consideration, and ourselves, anew.[72]

72. We would do well, argues Alec McHoul, to prioritize "empirical descriptions of the ordinary, everyday heterodoxies over theologies and critical orthodoxies." Given that moral evaluations are merely "one variety of cultural technology making up the necessarily multi-technological constitution of cultural objects," McHoul rightly suggests that "we, as cultural studies professionals, need to guard against... the uptake of positions along the traditional moral lines generated by cultural objects themselves in the first place. That tendency to be in the thrall of cultural technologies' 'natural' moral sub-technologies may be holding us back from achieving an adequate descriptive or analytic grasp of our chosen subject." Alec McHoul, "Ordinary Heterodoxies: Towards a Theory of Cultural Objects," *The UTS Review* 3, no. 2 (1997): 20, 14–15.

Part II

WRITING, READING, AND ABBREVIATING
CHRISTIAN SCRIPTURE

7

Signed with an "X":
Σταυρός and the Staurogram Among the
*Nomina Sacra**

Benjamin R. Overcash

The contracted form of the Greek word for "cross," σταυρός, is not usually included among the so-called "primary" group of *nomina sacra*, which includes the contracted forms of the four words θεός, κύριος, Ἰησοῦς (which also appears in suspended form), and Χριστός.[1] In the 65 New Testament manuscripts assigned dates in the Gregory-Aland registry between the second and third/fourth centuries (up to and including P.Oxy. 72.4934 or 𝔓[125]),[2] these four divine epithets are treated as *nomina sacra* virtually one

---

* This essay derives from a paper presented to the Papyrology and Early Chrisstian Backgrounds section at the annual meeting of the SBL, San Antonio, TX, 22 November 2016. I am grateful for the insights and critiques of session members and attendees. I am also especially grateful to Stephen Llewelyn and Brent Nongbri, both of whom provided feedback on this paper in its various earlier forms. All remaining shortcomings are, of course, mine alone.

1. The classification of *nomina sacra* into three groups on the basis of frequency of contraction was first suggested by C. H. Roberts in *Manuscript, Society and Belief in Early Christian Egypt: The Schweich Lectures 1977* (London: Oxford University Press, 1979), 27, and was later taken up by Larry Hurtado in his article "The Origin of the *Nomina Sacra*: A Proposal," *JBL* 117 (1998): 655–73. The primary group, according to Hurtado, is comprised of "the four earliest and most consistently rendered words": θεός, κύριος, Ἰησοῦς, and Χριστός; the secondary group consists of "three additional terms, which appear to be slightly later and less uniformly treated": πνεῦμα, σταυρός, and ἄνθρωπος; and the tertiary group consists of the remaining eight, "which are abbreviated less consistently and appear to have joined the list of sacred terms latest": πατήρ, υἱός, σωτήρ, μήτηρ, οὐρανός, Ἰσραήλ, Δαυειδ, and Ἰερουσαλήμ (Hurtado, "Origin of the *Nomina Sacra*," 655–6).

2. Based on the most recent online edition of the *Kurzgefasste Liste* (http://ntvmr.uni-meunster.de/liste), as of 3 January 2018. This count includes the majuscules

hundred percent of the time.³ Yet σταυρός and πνεῦμα, which constitute two-thirds of the so-called "secondary" group, follow surprisingly closely behind: πνεῦμα is rendered as a *nomen sacrum* in a total of 210 out of 232 occurrences, or 90.5 percent of the time, while σταυρός is contracted in eighteen out of nineteen occurrences, a rate of 94.7 percent.⁴ By way of comparison, these are followed by πατήρ at a rate of 54.4 percent, and ἄνθρωπος at a mere 44.9 percent.⁵

P.Oxy. 6.847 (0162), P.Berl. inv. 11765 (0189), P.Dura 10 (0212), and P.Schøyen 1.20 (0220). Papyri currently in the *Liste* with designations between 𝔓¹²⁶ and 𝔓¹³⁶ are excluded from this analysis as no transcriptions or quality photographs are yet available.

3. When uncontracted occurrences which are plural or otherwise decidedly non-sacral are omitted, the following rates of contraction result: θεός is contracted 991 times out of 991 total occurrences (= 100 percent); κύριος is contracted 499 times out of five hundred total occurrences (= 99.8 percent); Ἰησοῦς is contracted 805 times out of 805 total occurrences (= 100 percent); and Χριστός is contracted 463 times out of 463 total occurrences (= 100 percent). Note that these numbers include hits that occur within conjectural reconstructions, since in this case the bearing of conjectures on the resulting statistics is negligible or null. However, figures reported for all other *nomina sacra* in the following analysis omit hits that occur entirely within lacunae or for which the remaining traces are inconclusive.

4. This datum does not include the verb σταυρόω since its treatment is inconsistent in comparison to the noun σταυρός. The verb σταυρόω is contracted in 23 out of 30 occurrences (or 76.7 percent) in P.Beatty 1 (𝔓⁴⁵), P.Beatty 2 + P.Mich. 222 (𝔓⁴⁶), P.Beatty 3 (𝔓⁴⁷), P.Bodm. 2 (𝔓⁶⁶), P.Bodm. 14-15 (𝔓⁷⁵), P.Oxy. 71.4805 (𝔓¹²¹), and P.Dura 10 (0212). This inconsistency likely results from the volatility of verb forms, compared to the relative stability of noun forms, making a standardized formation for verbal *nomina sacra* difficult. For example, in P.Beatty 2 + P.Mich. 222 (𝔓⁴⁶), the verb συνεσταύρωμαι ("crucified together with") in Gal 2:19 and the participle ἀνασταυροῦντας ("crucifying again") in Heb. 6:6 are contracted as σuνε͞στραι and ανα͞στρες [*sic*], and in Gal. 5:25, the aorist ἐσταύρωσαν is contracted as ε͞σταν, omitting the rho.

5. The foregoing data were derived by conducting a lemmatized search for these words using the Accordance electronic edition of Philip W. Comfort and David P. Barrett (eds.), *The Text of the Earliest New Testament Manuscripts*, 2nd edn (Wheaton: Tyndale House, 2001), which includes papyri through P.Oxy. 71.4806 (𝔓¹²³) and all majuscules dated up to the third/fourth century, with the exception of P.Dura 10 (0212). In some cases, errors in the transcription of the electronic edition were identified and taken into account. Photographs and transcriptions were then examined for the remaining manuscripts dated in the Gregory-Aland registry up to the third/fourth century—namely, P.Oxy. 72.4934 (𝔓¹²⁵, 3rd/4th cent.), and P.Dura 10 (0212, 3rd cent.). Totals were then collated, against which the number of occurrences treated as *nomina sacra* were finally calculated. A comparable method was applied

Complicating the picture somewhat are nouns which frequently occur with non-sacral referents. While every instance of the noun σταυρός has a rather clear sacral significance, πνεῦμα, ἄνθρωπος, and πατήρ all appear a number of times in decidedly non-sacral contexts. For instance, in P.Berl. inv. 11765 (0189), ἀκαθάρτων πνευμάτων ("unclean spirits") is rendered in *scriptio plena* at Acts 5:16. Likewise, ἄνθρωπος in John 5:5—referring to a sick man healed by Jesus—appears in full spelling in P.Bodm. 2 ($\mathfrak{P}^{66}$). Hence, removing uncontracted forms which are either plural or which have decidedly non-sacral referents, the contraction rate for πνεῦμα is raised as high as 95.9 percent, σταυρός remains at 94.7 percent, ἄνθρωπος is raised significantly to 83.6 percent, and πατήρ is raised to 68.3 percent. Notwithstanding these adjustments, the divide remains remarkably persistent: while only about 5 percent of potential sacral occurrences of σταυρός and πνεῦμα are left uncontracted, with ἄνθρωπος the percentage of *plene* occurrences more than triples, and the contraction rate continues to decrease almost exponentially down the list.[6]

A chi-square analysis indicates that these figures have a high statistical significance at a level of 99 percent confidence (0.01 alpha level); that is, the distribution of contraction rates among the *nomina sacra* presented here has significantly less than a 1 percent chance of occurring randomly (p-value < 0.00001; see Table 1). The test also revealed that all of the *nomina sacra* in the primary group as well as πνεῦμα and σταυρός are contracted at a greater frequency than would have been expected proportional to the overall contraction rate, while all of the remaining *nomina sacra* are contracted at a lower frequency than expected (Table 1 and Figure 1). This draws an interesting statistical line between the two groups of *nomina sacra* in this set of New Testament manuscripts and further bears out the observations made in the preceding paragraphs.

As for dating, it is broadly recognized that the four primary *nomina sacra* must have come into use quite early.[7] The earliest New Testament

---

by Tomas Bokedal in "Notes on the *Nomina Sacra* and Biblical Interpretation," in *Beyond Biblical Theologies*, ed. Heinrich Assel, Stefan Beyerle, and Christfried Bötterich, WUNT 295 (Tübingen: Mohr Siebeck, 2012), 263–95. Although Bokedal includes manuscripts dated through the fourth century, the similarity of our results seems to be mutually corroborating.

6. Of the other seven *nomina sacra* not mentioned, two (Δαυίδ and σωτήρ) are never rendered as *nomina sacra* in these manuscripts. The other five are contracted at the following rates: υἱός (54.4 percent), Ἰερουσαλήμ (37.8 percent), Ἰσραήλ (35.1 percent), οὐρανός (5.2 percent), and μήτηρ (4.5 percent).

7. So A. H. R. E. Paap, *Nomina Sacra in the Greek Papyri of the First Five Centuries A.D.: The Sources and Some Deduction*, Pap.Lugd.Bat. 8 (Leiden: Brill, 1959),

papyri containing extant *nomina sacra* are assigned dates in the Gregory-Aland registry to the second and third centuries, although a number of papyrologists have recently expressed reservations about the narrow dating spectra applied to New Testament manuscripts solely on the basis of palaeography.[8] Be that as it may, the appearance of some of these *nomina sacra* in letters dated securely in the third century would seem to corroborate their existence in Christian literary manuscripts at least by this time, and almost certainly earlier.[9]

Once again, however, σταυρός and πνεῦμα are placed on near-equal footing with the primary four *nomina sacra*, appearing contracted in the

---

124; Schuyler Brown, "Concerning the Origin of the *Nomina Sacra*," *SPap* 9 (1970): 7–19; Roberts, *Manuscript, Society and Belief*, 28; Harry Y. Gamble, *Books and Readers in the Early Church: A History of Early Christian Texts* (New Haven: Yale University Press, 1995), 77; Hurtado, "Origin of the *Nomina Sacra*," 655 and passim.

8. Brent Nongbri, "Reconsidering the Place of Papyrus Bodmer XIV-XV ($\mathfrak{P}^{75}$) in the Textual Criticism of the New Testament," *JBL* 135 (2016): 405–37; idem, "The Limits of Palaeographic Dating of Literary Papyri: Some Observations on the Date and Provenance of P.Bodmer II (P66)," *MH* 71 (2014): 1–35; Pasquale Orsini and Willy Clarysse, "Early New Testament Manuscripts and Their Dates: A Critique of Theological Palaeography," *ETL* 88 (2012): 443–74; Don Barker, "The Dating of New Testament Papyri," *NTS* 57 (2011): 571–82; Roger S. Bagnall, *Early Christian Books in Egypt* (Princeton: Princeton University Press, 2009), 1–24. Also important, although it focuses on a manuscript that does not contain extant *nomina sacra*, is Brent Nongbri, "The Use and Abuse of $\mathfrak{P}^{52}$: Papyrological Pitfalls in the Dating of the Fourth Gospel," *HTR* 98 (2005): 23–48.

9. P.Bas. 16 (3rd cent. CE), almost certainly the earliest letter from an unambiguously Christian setting, contains a *nomen sacrum* in the closing farewell "in the Lord" (ἐν κ̄ω̄). *Nomina sacra* forms for "Lord" and "God" are also attested in letters belonging to the dossier of Sotas, which can be fairly securely placed in the latter part of the third century when he was bishop of Oxyrhynchus. See AnneMarie Luijendijk, *Greetings in the Lord: Early Christians and the Oxyrhynchus Papyri*, HTS 60 [Cambridge, MA: Harvard University Press, 2008], 88–102, whose argument is now confirmed by Alessandro Bausi and Alberto Camplani, "New Ethiopic Documents for the History of Christian Egypt," *ZAC* 17 (2013): 215–47 (247). See also Lincoln H. Blumell, *Lettered Christians: Christians, Letters, and Late Antique Oxyrhynchus*, NTTSD 39 (Leiden: Brill, 2012), 114–15. In a recently published study, Willy Clarysse and Pasquale Orsini identify 28 manuscripts that "may belong to the second century AD from a palaeographical point of view," among which sixteen contain extant *nomina sacra*: PSI XI 1200 bis, P.Ant. I 7, P.Oxy. L 3523 ($\mathfrak{P}^{90}$), P.Iand. I 4, P.Oxy. L 3528, P.Monts.Roca IV 41, P.Beatty VII (Isaiah), P.Oxy. I 1 (Gospel of Thomas), P.Egerton 2 + P.Köln VI 255 (unknown gospel), P.Beatty VI (Numbers/Deuteronomy), P.Schøyen II 26 (Leviticus), P.Schøyen I 23 (Joshua), P.Monts.Roca IV 48 ($\mathfrak{P}^{67}$, formerly P.Barc. inv. 1, which is presumably intended to include P.Magd.Gr. 17 = $\mathfrak{P}^{64}$), PSI I 2 (0171),

earliest manuscripts in which the words are attested, all assigned to the third century.¹⁰ As it happens, the single instance of σταυρός written in *plene* in this group of manuscripts occurs in P.Oxy. 4.657 + PSI 12.1292 (𝔓¹³), a copy of the letter to the Hebrews written on the back of a patched roll¹¹ containing a Latin epitome of Livy (= P.Oxy. IV 668 + PSI XII 1291) that gives the impression of a "non-professional" production.¹² The inferior quality of the copy and writing surface for this scriptural text suggests a copy produced in an uncontrolled setting, and perhaps intended for informal, private use.¹³ Additionally, the third/fourth century date assigned to this opisthograph is slightly later than the other manuscripts from this group in which σταυρός is attested (keeping in mind, of course, the provisional nature of these dates). If we allow for a tentative disqualification of P.Oxy. IV 657 + PSI XII 1292 (𝔓¹³) on these bases,

P.Oxy. XIII 1598 (𝔓30), and P.Dura 10 (0212) ("Christian Manuscripts from Egypt to the Times of Constantine," in *Das Neue Testament und sein Text im 2. Jahrhundert*, ed. J. Heilmann and M. Klinghardt, Texte und Arbeiten zum neuetestamentlicher Zeitalter 61 [Tübingen: Francke, 2018], 107–14 [112]).

10. Namely, P.Bodm. 1 (𝔓⁴⁵), P.Beatty 2 + P.Mich. 222 (𝔓⁴⁶), P.Bodm. 2 (𝔓⁶⁶), and P.Bodm. 14-15 (𝔓⁷⁵). In addition to these four manuscripts, πνεῦμα is rendered as a *nomen sacrum* in Suppl.Gr. 1120 (𝔓⁴), P.Oxy. 2.208 + 15.1781 (𝔓⁵), P.Oxy. 9.1171 (𝔓²⁰), and P.Oxy. 10.1335 (𝔓²⁷), which are also assigned dates in the third century. It also bears mentioning that the verb σταυρόω is treated as a *nomen sacrum* in all of the manuscripts mentioned above, as well as in the third-century manuscripts P.Beatty 3 (𝔓⁴⁷) and P.Oxy. 71.4805 (𝔓¹²¹), which do not preserve the cognate noun.

11. According to Grenfell and Hunt, "strips of cursive documents…were used to patch and strengthen the papyrus before the verso was used" (P.Oxy. IV, 37).

12. In a study on the re-inking habits of this scribe, Peter M. Head and M. Warren judge that "various lines of evidence suggest that the scribe responsible for this manuscript should be classified as 'non-professional'" on account of variations in column width and lines per column, the deterioration in the quality of the hand through the course of the manuscript, and errors in copying introduced when the scribe paused to re-ink his pen ("Re-Inking the Pen: Evidence from P.Oxy. 657 (𝔓¹³) Concerning Unintentional Scribal Errors," *NTS* 43 [1997]: 466–73 [469]).

13. In his recent study of P.Beatty III, Peter Malik rightly cautions that "we ought to be wary of taking the manuscript's physical details as straightforward evidence for its social setting" (*P.Beatty III (𝔓⁴⁷): The Codex, Its Scribe, and Its Text*, NTTSD 52 [Leiden: Brill, 2017], 222). This caution is noted; however, in this case I would suggest that the reuse of an old, patched literary roll amplifies the impression of "informality" and tips the balance of probability somewhat more in favor of private use. Luijendijk indicates that the roll, which was recovered from the rubbish heap at Oxyrhynchus, had been discarded as a whole rather than as leftover fragments from a repair, which may also hint at such a setting (AnneMarie Luijendijk, "Sacred Scriptures as Trash: Biblical Papyri from Oxyrhynchus," *VC* 64 [2010]: 217–54 [251–52]).

the contraction rate for σταυρός is raised to one hundred percent in third century manuscripts, along with "God," "Lord," Jesus," and "Christ."

One must surmise that such a high consistency of treatment as *nomina sacra* in what may be the earliest manuscripts preserving these words would suggest an already well-established convention. We are therefore left with a strikingly narrow dividing line between σταυρός and πνεῦμα on the one hand and the primary four *nomina sacra* on the other, both in terms of the frequency of their sacral treatment in this group of manuscripts, and in terms of the approximate dates at which their firm establishment as *nomina sacra* is attested in the material record. Even if the vagaries of palaeographical dating ultimately require an extended *terminus ante quem* for some of these manuscripts,[14] the overriding point still stands: the strikingly high degree of consistency with which σταυρός is treated as a *nomen sacrum* in this group of early New Testament manuscripts requires an explanation.

Problematizing "Cross" as a Nomen Sacrum

The foregoing analysis suggests that the scribal treatment of σταυρός and πνεῦμα as *nomina sacra* is more akin to the treatment of the primary group, styled by Schuyler Brown as *nomina divina*,[15] than it is to other later and/or less frequently attested forms. If these primary four—God, Lord, Jesus, and Christ—represent the earliest firmly established *nomina sacra*, then it is easy to see how "Spirit," another sacred appellative, might have easily found its place among them. Σταυρός, on the other hand, is unique in that it is the only *nomen sacrum* that is not actually a *nomen* at all; thus, how it came to be included among this core group with such sweeping consensus is much more puzzling. In addition, some contractions of σταυρός and its verbal cognate σταυρόω also employ the staurogram—a combination of the Greek letters tau and rho, formed on a single stem to resemble a cross—uniquely adding an iconic element to the contracted form (e.g. σ⳨ος).[16] This is a point to which we shall return below.

---

14. Of particular relevance here is Nongbri's recent contention that the range of possible dates assigned to P.Bodm. 2 ($\mathfrak{P}^{66}$) should be broadened to include the fourth century ("Limits of Palaeographic Dating"). Nongbri concludes his argument with a brief appeal to the use of the staurogram in this manuscript as part of the *nomen sacrum* form for the words σταυρός and σταυρόω, which, he argues, is "less out of place in the fourth century than in the late second or early third century" (ibid., 34).

15. Brown, "Concerning the Origin of the *Nomina Sacra*," 19.

16. No modern scholar has contributed more to the discussion of the staurogram than Larry Hurtado. See in particular Larry W. Hurtado, "The Earliest Evidence of an

The common assumption has been that the cross was contextually associated with Jesus, which resulted in the treatment of σταυρός as a *nomen sacrum* by extension.¹⁷ Some early evidence for such an association may be inferred from the widely cited passage from *Barn.* 9:7-9 (dated sometime between 70 and 135 CE¹⁸), in which the author interprets the number of the servants with Abraham when he rescued Lot—318, represented by the letters τιη—as a representation of the suspended *nomen sacrum* for Ἰησοῦς (ιη̅) plus the cross:

> Learn about the matter fully, then, children of love. For Abraham, the first to perform circumcision, was looking ahead in spirit to Jesus when he circumcised, receiving the doctrines of the three letters [τριῶν γραμμάτων δίγματα]. For it says, "Abraham circumcised eighteen and three hundred men from his household." What knowledge, then, was given to him? Observe that it mentions the eighteen first, and then, after a pause, the three hundred. As for the eighteen, the ι is ten and the η is eight; thus you have "Jesus" [τὸ δεκαοκτὼ ἰῶτα δέκα, ἦτα ὀκτώ· ἔχεις Ἰησοῦν]. And because the cross was about to have grace in the letter tau, it mentions also the three hundred [ὅτι δὲ ὁ σταυρὸς ἐν τῷ ταῦ ἤμελλεν ἔχειν τὴν χάριν, λέγει καὶ τοὺς τριακοσίους]. (*Barn.* 9:8-9)

Yet, with all other *nomina sacra* in this set of early New Testament manuscripts referring either to a personal name, a title, or a place name

---

Emerging Christian Material and Visual Culture: The Codex, the *Nomina Sacra* and the Staurogram," in *Text and Artifact in the Religions of Mediterranean Antiquity: Essays in Honour of Peter Richardson*, ed. Stephen G. Wilson and Michel Desjardins, SCJ 9 (Waterloo: Wilfrid Laurier University Press, 2000), 271–88; idem, "The Staurogram," in *New Testament Manuscripts: Their Texts and Their World*, ed. Thomas J. Kraus and Tobias Nicklas, TENTS 2 (Leiden: Brill, 2006), 207–26; idem, *The Earliest Christian Artifacts: Manuscripts and Christian Origins* (Grand Rapids: Eerdmans, 2006), 135–54; and recently, idem, "Earliest Christian Chraphic Symbols: Examples and References from the Second/Third Centuries," in *Graphic Signs of Identity, Faith, and Power in Late Antiquity and the Early Middle Ages*, ed. Ildar Garipzanov, Caroline Goodson, and Henry Maguire (Turnhout: Brepols, 2017), 29–32.

17. See, for example, Scott D. Charlesworth, "Consensus Standardization in the Systematic Approach to *Nomina Sacra* in Second- and Third-century Gospel Manuscripts," *Aegyptus* 86 (2006): 37–68 (51); Kurt Aland, "Bemerkungen zum Alter und zur Entstehung des Christogrammes anhand von Beobachtungen bei 𝔓⁶⁶ und 𝔓⁷⁵," in *Studien zur Überlieferung des Neuen Testaments und seines Texts*, ANTF 2 (Berlin: de Gruyter, 1967), 178.

18. Reidar Hvalvik, *The Struggle for Scripture and Covenant: The Purpose of the Epistle of Barnabas and Jewish-Christian Competition in the Second Century*, WUNT 82 (Tübingen: Mohr, 1996), 17–34.

(barring two possible anomalies[19]), surely a simple contextual explanation cannot be accepted as fully satisfactory. Indeed, if objects and concepts could be included among the *nomina sacra* simply on the basis of their association with Jesus, then there are a number of other words whose omission demands an explanation. As Roberts pondered, "Why should λόγος or even σοφία be excluded? More striking still is the omission of the eucharistic words αἷμα, ἄρτος, οἶνος, σάρξ, σῶμα."[20]

Surely the most economical explanation for the inclusion of "cross" among the most firmly established *nomina sacra* in these manuscripts is that, like the other words in the core group, σταυρός was somehow understood as a representation of a sacred name. In what follows, I propose what I believe is a plausible solution to this perceived incongruity—namely, that the treatment of "cross" and "crucify" as *nomina sacra* in early Christian literary manuscripts may derive from pre-Christian traditions associated with the paleo-Hebrew letter *tav*, an oblique (×) or upright (+) cross-shaped mark that is known to have been associated with the cross of Jesus by ancient Christians. While the material and general conclusions presented in the following synopsis are neither new nor controversial, I suggest that its explanatory potential in this regard has been overlooked and merits exploration.[21]

---

19. To my knowledge, the only potential exceptions are κ̄μ̄οῡ for κόσμου at 1 Cor 7:31 and 7:33 in P.Oxy. VII 1008 (𝔓15), δ̄ῡμ̄ι for δυνάμει at 1 Pet 1:5 in P.Bodm. VII–VIII (𝔓72). It should be noted that α̅ι̅μ̅α̅ appears at Heb 9:14 in P.Beatty II + P.Mich 222 (𝔓46), but this is the result of a corrected reading involving an original π̄ν̄ᾱ which was overwritten with αἷμα, and the corrector did not erase the supralinear line; thus this instance cannot be considered a true exception (see James R. Royse, *Scribal Habits in Early Greek New Testament Papyri*, NTTSD 36 (Leiden: Brill, 2008], 236 n. 181).

20. Roberts, *Manuscript, Society and Belief*, 40.

21. The literature on this subject is abundant. The most recent general treatment, although problematic in places, is Bruce W. Longenecker, *The Cross Before Constantine: The Early Life of a Christian Symbol* (Minneapolis: Fortress Press, 2015). Also especially important to this subject is the work of Erich Dinkler, in particular, *Signum Crucis: Aufsätze zum Neuen Testament und zur Christlichen Archäologie* (Tübingen: Mohr Siebeck, 1967). See also S. Heid, "Kreuz," *RAC* 21:1099–148; Erika Dinkler-von Schubert, "ΣΤΑΥΡΟΣ: Vom 'Wort vom Kreuz' (1 Cor. 1,18) zum Kreuz-Symbol," in *Byzantine East, Latin West: Art-Historical Studies in Honor of Kurt Weitzmann*, ed. Doula Mouriki, Christopher Moss, and Katherine Kiefer (Princeton: Department of Art and Archaeology, 1995), 29–39; Jack Finegan, *The Archeology of the New Testament: The Life of Jesus and the Beginning of the Early Church* (Princeton: Princeton University Press, 1992), 339–89; Everett Ferguson, *Baptism in the Early Church: History, Theology, and Liturgy in the First Five Centuries* (Grand Rapids: Eerdmans,

Signing with an "X":
The Cross and the Investiture of the Name

Before the *tav* was appropriated by Christians as a symbol for the cross, it was already a part of a robust tradition within Judaism that invested it with apotropaic power, eschatological significance, and of particular importance for our purposes here, the divine name.[22] The tradition of the *tav* seems to derive from Ezek. 9:4-6, where Yahweh sends an angel to place his mark on the foreheads of the faithful in Jerusalem; all those without the mark would be subject to destructive judgment. Since the underlying Hebrew word for this mark, *tav* (תו), is also the last letter of the Hebrew alphabet, there is some evidence that it could function as shorthand for the divine name, and thus as a mark of Yahweh's ownership.[23] A similar substitutive function for one's name may also be suggested elsewhere in the Hebrew Bible, such as in Job's exclamation, "Here is my signature!"—literally, "Here is my *tav* [הן־תוי]!" (Job 31:35).

Although the Hebrew script had changed, the memory of Ezekiel's *tav* was very much alive in Second Temple Jewish and early Christian thinking. According to the Damascus Document, the Jewish sectarians at Qumran believed that the scene from Ezekiel would be repeated in messianic times: only the so-called "poor of the flock" who bore the *tav* on their foreheads—that is, apparently, the Qumran community—would be saved (CD 19:10-14). This also appears to be the idea behind the "seal" (σφραγίς) placed on the foreheads of the faithful in Revelation:

2009), 196 and passim; Jean Daniélou, *Primitive Christian Symbols*, trans. Donald Attwater (Baltimore: Helicon Press, 1964), 136–45; Geoffrey W. H. Lampe, *The Seal of the Spirit: A Study in the Doctrine of Baptism and Confirmation in the New Testament and The Fathers* (London: SPCK, 1967), 261–96.

22. On the latter, see in particular Charles A. Gieschen, "The Divine Name in Ante-Nicene Christology," *VC* 57 (2003): 115–58, esp. 133–4; and idem, "Baptismal Praxis and Mystical Experience in the Book of Revelation," in *Paradise Now: Essays on Early Jewish and Christian Mysticism*, ed. April D. DeConick (Atlanta: Society of Biblical Literature, 2006), 341–54. See also Lampe, *Seal of the Spirit*, 284–96.

23. In *m. Gen. Rab.* 81:2, the seal of God is said to consist of the first, middle, and last letters of the Hebrew alphabet, forming the word אמת ("truth"). In *b. Šabb.* 55a, special importance is given to the letter *tav*: "And what is different about the letter *tav*, that it was inscribed on the foreheads of the righteous?... And Reish Lakish said: The letter *tav* is the last letter of the seal of the Holy One, blessed be he, as Rabbi Ḥanina said: The seal of the Holy One, blessed be he, is 'truth' [אֱמֶת], which ends with the letter *tav*." Cf. the designation "alpha and omega," which corresponds to the Hebrew letters *aleph* and *tav*, applied to Jesus in Rev. 1:8, 21:6, and 22:13. Other examples are given in Finegan, *Archaeology of the New Testament*, 345–6.

> And I saw another angel ascending from the east, having the seal of the living God [ἔχοντα σφραγῖδα θεοῦ ζῶντος]. And he cried out in a loud voice to the four angels to whom the destroying of the earth and the sea was appointed, saying "Do not destroy the earth or the sea or the trees until we seal the servants of our God on their foreheads [ἄχρι σφραγίσωμεν τοὺς δούλους τοῦ θεοῦ ἡμῶν ἐπὶ τῶν μετώπων αὐτῶν]." And I heard the number of those who were sealed [τῶν ἐσφραγισμένων]: one hundred and forty-four thousand from all the tribes of Israel. (Rev. 7:2-4)

The author is obviously drawing on the tradition of Ezekiel 9, but here the mark is called the "seal of God" (7:2; 9:4) and, significantly, is later explicitly identified with the names of God (22:4) and the Lamb (14:1).[24]

As it happens, a recently published amulet from Oxyrhynchus, P.Oxy. LXXXII 5306, contains a patchwork of incantations that seems to incorporate part of a pre-baptismal exorcism liturgy which alludes to Revelation 7:2: "Each of them [i.e. the apostles] has the seal of the living God [σφραγίδα τοῦ θ(εο)ῦ τοῦ ζῶντος], and, sealed on top (of the head) by the sign [ἐσφραγισμένοι ἐπάνω σημίου (sic)], they have remedies so that [the demons] do not draw near" (lines 20-22).[25] The "sign" (Syr. ʾāṯā) worn by the faithful in Odes of Solomon also appears to function both as an apotropaion and as a designation for the name of God:

> Raging rivers (are like) the power of the Lord, that turn head downward those who despise him and entangle their steps and destroy their fords and seize their bodies and ruin their souls, for they are more sudden than lightnings and faster. But those who traverse [ʿbar] them in faith shall not be disturbed, and those who walk in them without blemish will not be perturbed. For the sign [ʾāṯā] on them is the Lord, and the sign [ʾāṯā] is the way for those who traverse in the name of the Lord [ba-šmeh d-māryā]. Put on, therefore, the name [šmā] of the Most High and know him; then you shall traverse without danger, because rivers will be obedient to you. (Odes Sol. 39:1-9)[26]

---

24. Likewise, the corresponding "mark" (χάραγμα) placed on the forehead of the unfaithful in Rev. 13:17 is said to be "the name of the beast or the number of his name" (τὸ ὄνομα τοῦ θηρίου ἢ τὸν ἀριθμὸν τοῦ ὀνόματος αὐτοῦ).

25. This amulet and the two others known to have originated from the same scribe (P.Oxy. VI 924 and P.Oxy. LXXXII 5607) also end with an acclamation that consists of the expression δύναμις Χ(ριστο)ῦ Ἰ(ησο)ῦ, "Power of Jesus Christ," and the designations "Father," "Son," "Mother," "Holy Spirit," "ΑΩ," and "Abrasax," symmetrically arranged around a large cross. See P.Oxy. LXXXII, 76-91, and P.Oxy. VI, 289-90.

26. Translation modified from Michael Lattke, *Odes of Solomon: A Commentary*, Hermeneia (Minneapolis: Fortress Press, 2009), 539.

The use of the term "seal" (σφραγίς) in Revelation—as opposed to "mark" (σημεῖον), which designates the Hebrew term *tav* in the LXX—may suggest a further important connection to the divine name. According to Exod. 28:36, the golden plate worn on the forehead of the high priest bore the inscription "holy to Yahweh"; however, according to Philo (*Mos.* 2.114) and Josephus (*Ant.* 3.178), the inscription only consisted of the four letters of the Tetragram. In any case, Exod. 28:36 says that the inscription is to be "like the inscription of a seal" (MT: ופתחת עליו פתוחי חתם; LXX: ἐκτυπώσεις ἐν αὐτῷ ἐκτύπωμα σφραγῖδος). It is therefore plausible to interpret the "seal" placed on the foreheads of the faithful in Revelation, which is said to be invested with the names of God and the Lamb, as an allusion to the inscription of the sacred name worn on the priestly headplate in the Jerusalem temple.[27]

Another Christian apocalypse, the second-century Shepherd of Hermas, contains a lengthy discussion of baptism in the Similitudes and indicates that at the time of baptism, the baptizand received a "seal" (σφραγίς) which was identified with "the name of God" (τὸ ὄνομα τοῦ θεοῦ):

> "It was necessary," he said, "for them to rise up through the water in order to be made alive, for otherwise they could not enter into the kingdom of God, unless they laid aside the deadness of their former life. Therefore, even those who have fallen asleep received the seal of the Son of God [τὴν σφραγῖδα τοῦ υἱοῦ τοῦ θεοῦ] and entered into the kingdom of God. For before a person," he said, "bears the name of God [φορέσαι τὸν ἄνθρωπον τὸ ὄνομα τοῦ θεοῦ], he is dead. But whenever he receives the seal, he lays aside his deadness and receives life." (Herm. *Sim.* 9.16.2-3)

This procedure of applying the divine name through the baptismal seal is also preserved in the Latin version of the second-century *Acts of Peter*, where upon baptizing Theon, Peter prays: "God Jesus Christ, in your name he was just baptized and sealed with your holy sign [*deus iesu christe, in tuo nomine mox lautus et signatus est sancto tuo signo*]" (5). The third-century *Acts of Thomas* also confirms this practice and clarifies that the seal of the name applied at baptism is done so with oil poured over the head: "And the apostle, taking the oil and pouring it over their heads and anointing and chrisming [χρίσας] them, began to say: '...And seal them in the name of the Father and Son and Holy Spirit [καὶ ἐπισφράγισον αὐτοὺς εἰς ὄνομα πατρὸς καὶ υἱοῦ καὶ ἁγίου πνεύματος]'" (27).

---

27. Revelation is famously permeated by allusions to Exodus and the Jerusalem temple cult. For a survey of the scholarship on temple themes in Revelation, see Gregory Stevenson, *Power and Place: Temple and Identity in the Book of Revelation* (Berlin: de Gruyter, 2001), 28–32.

The rabbis mention a very similar practice in which the priests were anointed with oil in the shape of the Greek letter *chi* (*b. Hor.* 12a)—a likely misidentification of the angled paleo-Hebrew *tav*, which in rabbinic times may have been more readily identifiable as the letter *chi*. Charles Gieschen, among others, has demonstrated persuasively that many of the features of early Christian baptism are rooted in the priestly traditions of the Jerusalem temple.[28] If this is the case, then the Christian seal of Revelation, Shepherd of Hermas, *Acts of Peter*, and *Acts of Thomas* seems to refer to this practice of anointing in the shape of the angled, cross-shaped *tav*.

The cross shape of the seal is further supported by *Sib. Or.* 8:244-250, an acrostic poem in which the first letter of each line spells out the word σταυρός. In the first line of the poem, the σταυρός is called a "mark [σῆμα] for all mortals" and an "inscribed seal [σφρηγὶς ἐπίσημος]"—language which again seems to allude to the inscribed priestly headplate. Tertullian and Origen also confirm the shape of the seal, remarking on the resemblance of Ezekiel's *tav* to the cross that Christians trace on their foreheads. Tertullian says that Christ signed the apostles with "the very seal of which Ezekiel spoke" and that it is in "the form of the cross [*species crucis*], which he predicted would be on our foreheads in the true and catholic Jerusalem" (*Adversus Marcionem* 3.22.5-6). Origen offers a similar explanation, which he claims to have received from a Jewish Christian: "The *tav* in the ancient script resembles the cross [τῷ τοῦ σταυροῦ χαρακτῆρι] and predicts the mark [σημεῖον] that is placed on the foreheads of Christians" (*Selecta in Ezechielem* 9).

The *tav*, then, seems to have suited the purposes for Christian appropriation as the sign of the cross both in form and in function. Furthermore, as the baptismal texts reveal, ancient Christians connected this tradition with the investiture of the divine name at baptism. It is within the context of this tradition, I suggest, that we may begin to locate the motivation for the widespread early treatment of σταυρός as a *nomen sacrum*.

The Staurogram and Multimodal Discourse

As we briefly observed above, several of the New Testament manuscripts that attest σταυρός as a *nomen sacrum* incorporate a cross-like compendium of the letters tau and rho (⳨), called a staurogram, into the abbreviation.

---

28. Gieschen, "Baptismal Praxis and Mystical Experience," 341–54. See also Lampe, *Seal of the Spirit*; Margaret Barker, *The Great High Priest: Temple Roots of Christian Liturgy* (London: T&T Clark, 2003).

Larry Hurtado's important work on the staurogram and the *nomina sacra* has framed these scribal phenomena as material instantiations of an emerging "visual culture" within ancient Christianity.[29] He has plausibly argued, furthermore, that the staurogram represents the first Christian depiction of the crucifixion.[30] Given the web of associations traced above, however, it also seems possible that the staurogram served as a visual metonym within the *nomina sacra* forms of "cross" and "crucify," pointing intertextually and intersemiotically to the traditions surrounding the sacred name that was applied to the forehead of Christian initiates at baptism in the form of a cross.[31]

Multimodal semiotic theory recognizes that verbal modes of communication (speech and writing) are always accompanied, contextualized, and enhanced by visual and other modes (e.g. script or typography, layout, gesture, facial expression, inflection or tone of voice).[32] Thus, for example, Christian literary manuscripts combine writing with other visual signs—supralineation, spatial configuration, style of hand, or image (e.g. staurograms)—which creates an integrated whole that is rich with meaning potential beyond the semantic content of language alone. From this perspective, the staurogram, the *nomina sacra* in which it functions, and the linguistic content they conjointly encode are viewed as a dialectic that is both mutually constitutive and mutually informative, and thus must be "read" as a whole in order for the full communicative intent to be realized.

A useful concept in this regard is that of "provenance," which refers to the importation of existing signs, together with their histories and associations and condensations of meaning from prior use, from one discourse

---

29. Hurtado, "The Staurogram," 207–26; idem, *Earliest Christian Artifacts*, 135–54; idem, "The Earliest Evidence," 271–88.

30. Ibid.

31. Many years ago, Matthew Black suggested that the designs of the staurogram and christogram might have been influenced by the traditions associated with the *tav*, but failed to connect this possibility with the earliest attested use of the staurogram within *nomina sacra* forms ("The Chi-Rho Sign—Christogram and/or Staurogram?" in *Apostolic History and the Gospels: Biblical and Historical Essays Presented to F. F. Bruce on His 60th Birthday*, ed. W. W. Gasque and R. P. Martin [Grand Rapids: Eerdmans, 1970], 319–27).

32. Gunther Kress and Theo van Leeuwen, *Multimodal Discourse: The Modes and Media of Contemporary Communication* (London: Arnold, 2001), 1–23; Gunther Kress, *Multimodality: A Social Semiotic Approach to Contemporary Communication* (London: Routledge, 2010), 1–5.

into another. Kress and van Leeuwen describe the concept of provenance in this way:

> The idea here is that we constantly "import" signs from other contexts (another era, social group, culture) into the context in which we are now making a new sign, in order to signify ideas and values which are associated with that other context by those who import the sign.[33]

In the case of the staurogram, cruciform imagery is imported from ritual discourses, where it functions as a representation of the divine name, into the discourses of Christian literary and scribal practices, where sacred appellatives are treated in a particular way. Hence, the embedded staurogram both necessitates and validates the designation of the terms "cross" and "crucify" as *nomina sacra*. In addition, the visual and conceptual potency afforded by the multimodal constitution of the staurogram and the *nomina sacra* allow them to be visually dislocated from surrounding text and "read" as texts in their own right, making the dissemination and reception of meaning possible independently from the use of language.[34]

This suggestion is given additional weight when one considers the evolution of the staurogram from a ligature within the *nomina sacra* forms of σταυρός and σταυρόω in third-century manuscripts to a freestanding symbol in manuscripts,[35] documents,[36] letters,[37] and amulets from the

33. Kress and van Leeuwen, *Multimodal Discourse*, 10.
34. Ibid., 56–63.
35. A freestanding staurogram appears as a terminus marker on both sides of P.Monts.Roca 4.51 ($\mathfrak{P}^{80}$, formerly P.Barc. inv. 83), a papyrus fragment containing a Johannine ἑρμηνεία, which is assigned to the third century in the Gregory-Aland catalogue, but was assigned to the third/fourth century by the *editio princeps*, and has recently been assigned to the sixth century by Orsini and Clarysse ("Early NT Manuscripts and Their Dates," 459–60; *ed. pr.* Ramon Roca-Puig, "Papiro del evangelio de San Juan con 'Hermeneia': P.Barc. inv. 83—Jo. 3,34," in *Atti dell' XI Congresso Internazionale di Papirologia, Milano 2-8 Settembre 1965* [Milan: Instituto Lombardo Di Scienze E'Lettere, 1966], 225–36). The sixth-century date proposed by Orsini and Clarysse accords best with its identification as a Johannine ἑρμηνεία, all the rest of which are dated between the sixth and eighth centuries, and with its use of the freestanding staurogram, which is less out of place after the third century.
36. For a list of documents containing a staurogram or a simple cross, see Malcolm Choat, *Belief and Cult in Fourth-Century Papyri*, StAA 1 (Turnhout: Brepols, 2006), 117 n. 529.
37. For staurograms in letters, see ibid., 117 n. 530; and Blumell, *Lettered Christians*, 310.

fourth century on.³⁸ This evolution happens to coincide with a regression in the treatment of "cross" and "crucify" as *nomina sacra* in Christian literary manuscripts beginning in the fourth century,³⁹ which suggests that the trend towards independent use of the staurogram and away from its function as an element within these *nomina sacra* made their connection to the divine name less readily apparent.

While the association of σταυρός and σταυρόω with the divine name seems to have diminished once the staurogram began to function as a freestanding symbol, there is evidence to suggest that the interdiscursivities and intertextualities that engendered the metonymic relationship between the staurogram and sacred names were retained. A number of amulets, which tend to give special emphasis to the combination of visual devices and mystical names,⁴⁰ employ the freestanding staurogram in juxtaposition with *nomina sacra* or other powerful or esoteric names. For instance, a fourth-century amulet against an ill-tempered man named Theodosius (P.Ross.Georg. 1.23) ends with a fourfold repetition of "amen," followed by ⳨ ⳨ ⳨ | κύριε κύριε κύριε, centered near the bottom of the page and set off from the main text of the incantation.⁴¹ Similarly, a sixth-century amulet against fever (P.Batav. 20) opens with a series of seven creedal statements, each set on a separate line beginning with a staurogram followed by the *nomen sacrum* for "Christ" (⳨ χ̄ς̄ ...).⁴² In

---

38. On the staurogram in amulets, see Theodore de Bruyn, *Making Amulets Christian: Artefacts, Scribes, and Contexts* (Oxford: Oxford University Press, 2017), 62–4 and passim.

39. See the tables (which now need updating) in Paap, *Nomina Sacra in the Greek Papyri*, 6–75. In his discussion of the evidence, Paap notes: "It is noteworthy that in 254 [i.e. Codex Washingtonensis (W)] (4ᵗʰ–beg. 5ᵗʰ c. CE) neither the noun nor the verb is contracted, although the former occurs 14 times and the latter 29 times" (ibid., 113). It merits mentioning that in the five occasions when σταυρός or σταυρόω is contracted in manuscripts from the fourth century on, according to Paap's tables, four employ the staurogram (but three of the four without a supralinear line; see ibid., 98)

40. On which, see de Bruyn, *Making Amulets Christian*, 55–67.

41. Image available at http://papyri.info/apis/hermitage.apis.21. The bottom of the papyrus has broken away, but traces of further text are visible beneath the staurogram/κύριε repetition.

42. Image available at http://ullet.net/papyrology/LPI0514.jpg. For other amulets containing staurograms and/or *nomina sacra*, see the tables in Theodore S. de Bruyn and Jitse H. F. Dijkstra, "Greek Amulets and Formularies from Egypt Containing Christian Elements: A Checklist of Papyri, Parchments, Ostraka, and Tablets," *BASP* 48 (2011): 163–216.

these examples, the staurograms and sacred names are afforded a sense of visual coherence through their proximity, layout, and visual salience,[43] which in turn links them conceptually.[44]

The significance of freestanding staurograms in letters, where they frequently precede the salutation or address, is more difficult to detect. However, during the period where their presence in letters overlaps with that of *nomina sacra*,[45] they are often clustered near the beginning of the letter—where recipients are greeted "in the Lord" (ἐν κ̅ω̅) or "in the Lord God" (ἐν κ̅ω̅ θ̅ω̅)—thus creating a similar cohesion and coherence when the two items are co-present.[46]

Conclusion

The remarkable consistency with which σταυρός was treated as a *nomen sacrum* in the earliest manuscripts of the New Testament, and the otherwise unprecedented inclusion of a pictographic element in its abbreviated form, is as puzzling as it is fascinating. This essay has attempted to find a plausible solution to this puzzle. In the first section, we discovered

---

43. I use "salience" here to mean "the degree to which an element draws attention to itself, due to its size, its place in the foreground or its overlapping of other elements, its colour, its tonal values, its sharpness or definition, and other features" (Gunther Kress and Theo van Leeuwen, *Reading Images: The Grammar of Visual Design*, 2nd edn [London: Routledge, 2006], 210). The visual salience of the *nomina sacra* is rightly recognized by Theodore de Bruyn in his recent study on papyrus amulets that incorporate Christian elements. De Bruyn includes *nomina sacra* within the category of "visual elements," noting that the supralinear line "had the effect of distinguishing the abbreviation visually," thus making it "part of the visual appearance of the text, which is why we treat it as a visual element in incantations and amulets" (*Making Amulets Christian*, 60).

44. Theo van Leeuwen, *Introducing Social Semiotics* (London: Routledge, 2005), 219–30; Kress, *Multimodality*, 119–20.

45. At Oxyrhynchus, Blumell observed that the staurogram does not appear in any letter before the mid-fourth century; however, the use of *nomina sacra* in letters begins to decrease already in the fifth century and virtually disappears by the sixth and seventh century (*Lettered Christians*, 45, 51).

46. Staurograms also sometimes appear before the address of letters, but the use of *nomina sacra* in addresses is rare. A particularly interesting example of the clustering of the two devices in an address is P.Oxy. 56.3862, where a staurogram appears in the middle of the address marking where the letter had been sealed. The letter is addressed "in the Lord God" (ἐν κ̅ω̅ θ̅ω̅), using *nomina sacra*. A staurogram also appears together with *nomina sacra* in the address of P.Stras. 7.680 (⳨ ἐπίδ(ος) σὺν θ̅ω̅ τῷ [...], "⳨ Deliver, with God's help, to [...]").

that σταυρός is situated more closely in terms of date and consistency of sacral treatment to the primary four so-called *nomina divina*—God, Lord, Jesus, and Christ—than other later and/or less consistently rendered *nomina sacra* which follow it. Next, it was suggested that this peculiar phenomenon may derive from traditions connected to the of the *tav* of Ezek. 9:4-6, which ancient Christians associated with the divine name that was applied to baptismal initiands at baptism in the form of the sign of the cross. Finally, we briefly explored how the staurogram embedded in the *nomina sacra* for "cross" and "crucify" creates a potent visual metonym that points intersemiotically to this baptismal ritual, thus necessitating and validating the treatment of these words as *nomina sacra*. While the question is by no means resolved, it has at least now been raised, and I hope that this brief probing will prompt future investigation. Future research could expand the scope of this study to include a more comprehensive treatment of non-literary materials, such as letters and amulets, in which the staurogram is employed.

Table 1. Frequency of Contraction in Second- through Third/Fourth-Century New Testament Manuscripts

	Contracted		*Uncontracted*	
	Observed	Expected	Observed	Expected
θεός	991	891	0	100
κύριος	499	450	1	50
Ἰησοῦς	805	724	0	81
Χριστός	463	416	0	50
πνεῦμα	210	197	9	22
σταυρός	18	17	1	2
ἄνθρωπος	148	159	29	18
πατήρ	196	258	91	29
υἱός	92	152	77	17
Ἰερουσαλήμ	14	33	23	4
Ἰσραήλ	13	33	24	4
οὐρανός	6	104	110	11
μήτηρ	1	20	21	2

confidence level: 99% ($\alpha = 0.01$) χ^2 critical value: 26.217
p-value: < 0.00001 χ^2 observed value = 2044.50

Note. Δαυίδ and σωτήρ are omitted from this analysis as they never appear rendered as *nomina sacra* in this set of New Testament manuscripts.

Figure 1. Percent Difference from Expected Contraction Rate

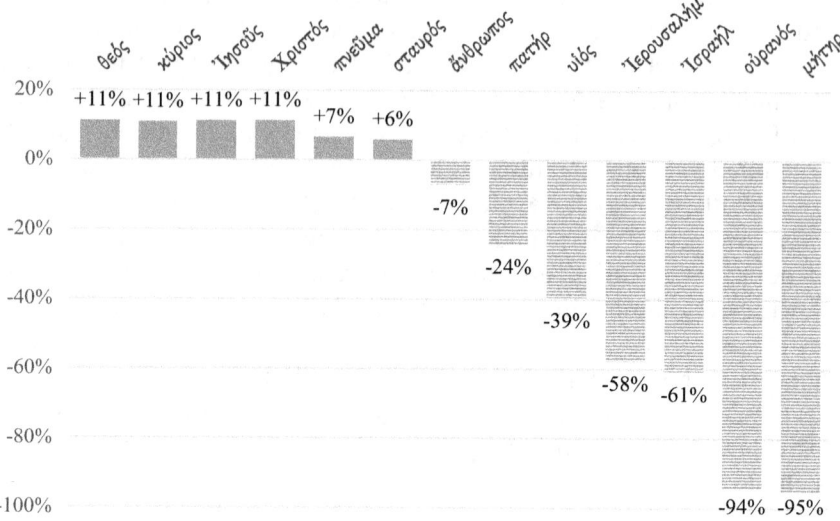

8

New Light from the Papyri:
The Sacred Background of βίβλος
in Matthew 1:1

Michael P. Theophilos

1. *Introduction*

The fifth-century anonymous Latin commentary on Matthew's Gospel known to us as the *Opus Imperfectum in Matthaeum* had, up until the sixteenth century, been attributed to John Chrysostom,[1] but is now considered to be a spurious work.[2] In its opening lines regarding the Matthean genealogy the text asks, "Why is it that Matthew says, 'The book of the genealogy of Jesus Christ, descendant of David, descendant of Abraham,' while the prophet Isaiah exclaims, 'And who will tell of his lineage?' [Isa. 53:8]. Matthew is setting forth his fleshly line, while Isaiah proclaims that his divine lineage is an unfathomable mystery."[3] Modern commentators have characteristically understood the phrase βίβλος γενέσεως (Matt. 1:1) as a deliberate "allusion to the formulaic title used in the LXX,"[4] specifically in regard to the Hebrew expression

---

1. John Chrysostom, *Opus Imperfectum in Matthaeum* (PG 56:611-946).
2. James A. Kellerman and Thomas C. Oden, *Incomplete Commentary on Matthew (Opus Imperfectum)* (Downers Grove: InterVarsity Press, 2010), xx. Possible authors include Timothy, an Arian priest of Constantinople, and Anianus of Celeda. See further J. Banning, "The Critical Edition of the *Opus Imperfectum in Matthaeum*: An Arian Source," in *Studia Patristica 17* (Oxford: Oxford University Press, 1982), 382–7; R. Étaix, "Fragments Indits de l'Opus Imperfectum in Matthaei," *Revue bénédictine* 84 (1974): 271–300.
3. John Chrysostom, *Opus Imperfectum in Matthaeum* (PG 56:612).
4. D. A. Hagner, *Matthew 1–13*, WBC 33a (Dallas: Word Books, 1993), 8.

תּוֹלְדוֹת (*tôlĕdôt*) in Gen. 2:4a, "These are the *generations* of the heavens and the earth when they were created," and Gen. 5:1, "This is the *list of the descendants* of Adam. When God created humankind, he made them in the likeness of God." Commentators regularly appeal to the frequent and notable Greek parallels of βίβλος attested in the Septuagint,[5] and conclude that the phrase may be reminiscent of Hellenistic Jewish use.

To what, however, does the phrase βίβλος γενέσεως refer in Matt. 1:1? There have been at least four positions held by commentators. First, A. H. McNeile,[6] M. J. Lagrange,[7] E. Lohmeyer,[8] J. Schmid,[9] W. Trilling,[10] J. H. Moulton and G. Milligan,[11] R. Gundry,[12] and D. Hagner,[13] et al. argue that the introductory phrase refers only to verses 2-17, that is, the genealogy proper. Indeed G. Schrenk boldly states that βίβλος γενέσεως, "is taken from Gn. 5:1 (for סֵפֶר תּוֹלְדֹת). As in Gn., it relates only to the succeeding genealogy and not to the whole Gospel or even to the infancy stories up to Mt. 2:23. Otherwise we do violence to the traditional formula."[14] Whether or not this identification does or does not do violence to the formula remains to be seen.

Second, U. Luz[15] and A. Vögtle[16] maintain that the reference is to the first chapter in its entirety on the basis that "βίβλος would lead one to think of the entire book, γένεσις only of the genealogy or only of the birth

---

5. Exod. 32:32-33; Josh. 1:8; 2 Chron. 17:9; 1 Esd. 1:33, 42; 5:49; 7:6, 9; Tob. 1:1; 2 Macc. 6:12; 8:23; Ps. 68:28; Job 37:20; 42:17b; Sir. 1:30; 24:23; Jer. 36:1; Bar. 1:3; 4:1; Dan. 7:10; 9:2.

6. A. H. McNeile, *The Gospel according to St. Matthew* (London: Macmillan, 1915), 1.

7. M. J. Lagrange, *Évangile selon saint Matthieu*, 7th edn (Paris: J. Gabalda, 1948), 3.

8. E. Lohmeyer, *Das Evangelium des Matthäus* (Göttingen: Vandenhoeck & Ruprecht, 1951), 4.

9. J. Schmid, *Das Evangelium nach Matthäus* (Regensburg: Pustet, 1965), 35.

10. W. Trilling, *Das wahre Israel*, 3rd edn (Munich: Kosel, 1964), 93.

11. James Hope Moulton and George Milligan, *The Vocabulary of the Greek Testament* (London: Hodder & Stoughton, 1930), 111.

12. R. H. Gundry, *Matthew: Commentary on His Handbook for a Mixed Church Under Persecution*, 2nd edn (Grand Rapids: Eerdmans, 1994), 13.

13. Hagner, *Matthew 1–13*, 9.

14. Gerhard Kittel, Geoffrey W. Bromiley, and Gerhard Friedrich (eds.), *Theological Dictionary of the New Testament* (Grand Rapids, MI: Eerdmans, 1964–), 616.

15. Ulrich Luz, *Matthew 1–7*, Hermeneia (Minneapolis: Fortress Press, 2007), 69.

16. A. Vögtle, "Die Genealogie Mt 1:2-16 und die matthäische Kindheitsgeschichte," *Evangetium* (1971): 73.

stories."¹⁷ Luz says that this dilemma is resolved when "βίβλος is understood…in a more narrow sense and refers only to a particular section of the book. Γένεσις, on the other hand, designates not only a genealogy but in a broader sense also a story of origin,"¹⁸ hence Luz's delineation to the conclusion of chapter 1.

Third, A. Plummer¹⁹ and W. C. Allen argue that βίβλος γενέσεως refers to the first two chapters of the Gospel, in that it is a "biblical phrase which might be used to describe a narrative containing, as in the case of Noah, a list of descendants, and some account of the life of the person named."²⁰ Allen concludes that "[i]t seems probable that the title should be taken as covering not the whole Gospel, but only that portion of it which gives Christ's ancestry and the circumstances of His birth and childhood."²¹

Fourth, E. Krentz²² and J. D. Kingsbury²³ contend the reference to βίβλος γενέσεως in 1:1 includes 1:1–4:16 on the basis of the editorial "from that time on, Jesus began to preach" in Matt. 4:17. Both of these analyses are nested within arguments for the structure of the Gospel as a whole as is evident from Krentz's comment that the phrase βίβλος γενέσεως "thus mark[s] off the first section of the gospel,"²⁴ and that it "must be understood in the sense of Gen 5.1…[which] covers the patriarchal period from Adam to Noah. It concludes with the statement in 6.8 that Noah found favor before the Lord God…[and] gives the genealogy of Noah and his personal history down to the point where he is to serve as the agent for the salvation of humankind from the flood. The parallelism with Matt 1.1–4.16 is clear."²⁵

---

17. Luz, *Matthew 1–7*, 69–70.
18. Ibid.
19. A. Plummer, *An Exegetical Commentary on the Gospel according to St. Matthew* (London: Scribner, 1909), 1.
20. Willoughby C. Allen, *A Critical and Exegetical Commentary on the Gospel according to St. Matthew*, ICC (New York: C. Scribner's Sons, 1907), 1.
21. Ibid., 1–2.
22. E. Krentz, "The Extent of Matthew's Prologue: Toward the Structure of the First Gospel," *JBL* 83 (1964): 411.
23. J. D. Kingsbury, *Matthew* (Philadelphia: Fortress Press, 1977), 2.
24. Krentz, "Extent," 411.
25. Ibid., 414.

Finally, H. C. Waetjen,[26] W. D. Davies and D. C. Allison Jr.,[27] E. Klostermann,[28] P. Bonnard,[29] and T. Zahn[30] expand the purview of βίβλος γενέσεως to the entirety of Matthew's Gospel, so that the phrase becomes a title for the Gospel as a whole. We will return to explore the important implications which emerge from our own analysis that might contribute to this particular question.

2. *Context of Argument and Methodology*

This paper is part of the larger *Papyrologische Kommentare zum Neuen Testament* project,[31] for which I am currently writing the monograph entitled, *The Matthean and Lukan Sondergut*.[32] The commentary series examines all published papyri, ostraca, and tablets (of which there are approximately 60,000), and evaluates their contribution to the contemporary historical, social, and linguistic contextualization of the New Testament documents.

One important methodological question which needs to be addressed is whether the assumption that the papyri and related documents, predominantly preserved in Egypt, are representative of a broader Mediterranean phenomenon can be maintained, or whether the Egyptian papyri are merely idiosyncratic for a handful of nomes in Egypt. In response, we can note four points which support a representative view of the papyri for the broader Mediterranean context. First, one can note the general probability argument. Approximately 120 documents from the Roman era were discovered at Wadi Murabbaʻât (18 km south of Qumran; cf. P. Murabbaʻât), and a substantial cache of papyri from the so-called Cave of Letters at Nahal Hever.[33] Several of the latter, as is well known, include

26. H. C. Waetjen. "The Genealogy as the Key to the Gospel according to Matthew," *JBL* 95 (1976): 215.

27. W. D. Davies and Dale C. Allison Jr., *A Critical and Exegetical Commentary on the Gospel according to Saint Matthew: Introduction and Commentary on Matthew I–VII* (London: T&T Clark International, 2004), 150–4.

28. E. Klostermann, *Das Matthäusevangelium* (Tübingen: Mohr Siebeck, 1927), 1–2.

29. P. Bonnard, *L'Évangile selon saint Matthieu* (Neuchâtel: Delachaux & Niestle, 1970), 16.

30. T. Zahn, *Das Evangelium des Matthäus* (Leipzig: Deichert, 1922), 39–44.

31. Online: https://www.uni-salzburg.at/bwkg/pknt.

32. Michael P. Theophilos, *The Matthean and Lukan Sondergut* (Göttingen: Vandenhoeck & Ruprecht, forthcoming).

33. P.Yadin refer, to the documents from the Bar Kochba period in the Cave of Letters. Thus far three volumes have been published in the Judean Desert Studies

letters signed by Simon Bar Kochba. Most, however, illuminate the decades leading up to the Bar Kochba revolt. In addition to the biblical fragmentary texts of Genesis, Deuteronomy, Isaiah, and the Minor Prophets scroll, most of the documents are legal documents pertaining to deeds of land sale, marriage contracts, debt acknowledgements, one is a and a divorce certificate. An analysis of the morphology and structure of the Judean loan contracts, for instance, and their Egyptian counterparts reveals a high degree of similarity. Second, Mishnaic discussion regarding loans, together with practices of crop sharing and leasing arrangements, reflect the same reality that we find documented in the Egyptian papyri.[34] Third, there is also the argument of probability through historical derivation. When Jerusalem and environs were under Ptolemaic (i.e. Egyptian) control, their administrative system is known to have been efficient and workable. When the Seleucids gain control after the Battle of Panium (part of the Fifth Syrian War) in which Antiochus III the Great defeated the Ptolemies in 198 BCE, the Seleucids seemed to have maintained a similar if not identical administrative structure.[35] Fourth, there is also an absence of contrary evidence, and although it is an argument from silence, it should be noted that there is no extant material (be it papyrological, epigraphic, or numismatic) to suggest the sort of discontinuity in Egypt that would overturn the responsible use of papyri to illustrate textual phenomena more broadly in the Mediterranean world.[36]

series: Yigael Yadin, *The Finds from the Bar Kokhba Period in the Cave of Letters* (Jerusalem: Israel Exploration Society, 1963), P.Yadin 1 and 2. See further Yigael Yadin, *Bar-Kokhba: The Rediscovery of the Legendary Hero of the Second Jewish Revolt Against Rome* (New York: Random House, 1971); Richard A. Freund, *Secrets of the Cave of Letters: Rediscovering a Dead Sea Mystery* (Amherst: Humanity Books, 2004); Yigael Yadin, *Bar-Kokhba: The Rediscovery of the Legendary Hero of the Second Jewish Revolt Against Rome* (New York: Random House, 1971).

34. See, for example, J. J. Rabinowitz, "A Legal Formula in Egyptian, Egyptian-Aramaic and Murabba'at Documents," *BASOR* 145 (1957): 33–4.

35. Csaba A. La'da, *Foreign Ethnics in Hellenistic Egypt* (Louvain: Peeters, 2002), 106–14; Livia Capponi, *Il tempio di Leontopoli in Egitto: Identità politica e religiosa dei Giudei di Onia (c. 150 a.C.–73 d.C.)* (Pisa: ETS, 2007).

36. In a related but tangential discussion on the question of how representative the New Testament papyri from Egypt are of broader traditions, Eldon Epp argues that they are more than merely witnesses to a local Egyptian textual tradition. Epp first posed the question in 1980; see Eldon J. Epp, "A Continuing Interlude in New Testament Textual Criticism," *HTR* 73 (1980): 131–51, and has addressed it in two subsequent studies supporting a broader representation. See Eldon J. Epp, "The Significance of the Papyri for Determining the Nature of the New Testament Text in the Second Century: A Dynamic View of Textual Transmission," in *Perspectives on*

Taken together, these four points, at the present moment, can allay any serious methodological fears about the use of Egyptian papyri for non-Egyptian Roman texts. Cumulatively, it is thus evident that the same administrative practices and struggles existed throughout the broader context of the Mediterranean, with the allowances of some minor variation.

3. *Papyrological Comparanda*

Let us return to Matt. 1:1, and in particular to the word βίβλος in the opening phrase. Irrespective of the solution to the synoptic problem one adopts, be it one that assumes the priority of Mark (Two-Source hypothesis, Farrer theory) or not (Griesbach hypothesis, Augustinian hypothesis), Matt. 1:1 is the work of the evangelist.[37] That is, Matthew has intentionally selected the word βίβλος from a relatively large pool of related lexical possibilities including: (i) χάρτης, a sheet of papyrus used for writing (cf. 2 John 12), (ii) μεμβράνα, a sheet of specially prepared animal skin on which one could write with pen and ink (2 Tim. 4:13), (iii) πινακίδιον, a small writing tablet, normally made of wood (Luke 1:63), (iv) πλάξ, a flat stone on which inscriptions could be made (Heb. 9:4), (v) ἐπιστολή / γράμμα, an object containing writing addressed to one or more persons, a letter normally written on papyrus (Acts 23:33; 28:21), (vi) βιβλίον / βίβλος, a document consisting of a scroll or book, implying a literary work (Luke 4:17; Acts 19:19), (vii) βιβλαρίδιον, a diminutive derivative of βίβλος (Rev. 10:10), (viii) κεφαλίς, section of a scroll or of a long composition (Heb. 10:7).

At the most basic level, the term βίβλος can refer to the physical papyrus stalks themselves, as is evident in P.Tebt. 2.308.7 (174 CE) where Ammonios and Theon acknowledge receipt of the price (not stated) for papyrus from Petesouchos, son of Petesouchos and priest of Tebtunis.

ἔτους ιε Αὐρηλίου Ἀντωνίνου	The 15th year of Aurelius Antoninus
Καίσαρος τοῦ κυρίου Ἀθὺρ ιγ.	Caesar the Lord, Hathyr 13.
διέγρα(ψεν) Ἀμμωνίῳ καὶ Θέωνι	has paid to Ammonios and Theon,

---

New Testament Textual Criticism, ed. Eldon J. Epp (Leiden: Brill, 2005), 345–81, and Eldon J. Epp, "New Testament Papyrus Manuscripts and Letter Carrying in Greco-Roman Times," in *The Future of Early Christianity*, ed. B. A. Pearson (Minneapolis: Fortress Press, 1991), 35–56.

37. Even if it did belong to an earlier source, Matthew has opted to retain the word in his gospel.

μισθωτα[ῖ]ς δρυμῶν καὶ ἐρήμου	lessees of marshes and desert
αἰγιαλοῦ Πολέμωνος μερίδος	shore in the division of Polemon
Πετεσοῦχος Πετεσούχου ἱερεὺς	Petesouchos son of Petesouchos, priest
Τεπτύνεως τιμὴν **βίβλου**	of Tebtunis, the price of **papyrus stalks**
μυριάδων δύο ἐν Ἰβίωνι	20,000 at Ibion
Ἀργαίου εἰς Τεπτῦνιν ἄρας	Argaiou, which he has transported to Tebtunis
διὰ Ἡρακλείδ(ου) ἀδελφοῦ Ἀμμωνίου	by Herakleides, the brother of Ammonios.

Identification of βίβλος as the physical papyrus plant is not only attested in the documentary receipts on antiquity but also in philosophical literary traditions such as Plotinus' *Enneads*:

Τοῦτο δὲ αὐτὸ ἐφ' ἑαυτοῦ ζητητέον, τί συμβαίνει, ὅταν ὅσπερ ἦν ὄγκος ὕδατος ἀὴρ γίγνηται, πῶς τὸ μεῖζον ἐν τῷ γενομένῳ· νῦν δὲ τὰ μὲν εἰρήσθω πολλῶν καὶ ἄλλων παρ' ἑκατέρων λεγομένων. Ἡμεῖς δὲ ἐφ' ἑαυτῶν σκοπῶμεν τί χρὴ λέγειν περὶ τούτου, τίς δόξα σύμφωνος τοῖς λεγομένοις ἢ καὶ τίς ἄλλη παρὰ τὰς νῦν λεγομένας φανεῖται. Ὅταν τοίνυν διὰ τοῦ ἐρίου ῥέῃ τὸ ὕδωρ ἢ **βίβλος** ἐκστάζῃ τὸ ἐν αὐτῇ ὕδωρ, πῶς οὐ τὸ πᾶν ὑδάτινον σῶμα δίεισι δι' αὐτῆς; Ἢ καὶ ὅταν μὴ ῥέῃ, πῶς συνάψομεν τὴν ὕλην τῇ ὕλῃ καὶ τὸν ὄγκον τῷ ὄγκῳ, τὰς δὲ ποιότητας μόνας ἐν συγκράσει ποιησόμεθα; Οὐ γὰρ δὴ ἔξω τῆς **βίβλου** ἡ τοῦ ὕδατος ὕλη παρακείσεται οὐδ' αὖ ἔν τισι διαστήμασιν αὐτῆς· πᾶσα γὰρ ὑγρά ἐστι καὶ οὐδαμοῦ ὕλη κενὴ ποιότητος. Εἰ δὲ πανταχοῦ ἡ ὕλη μετὰ τῆς ποιότητος, πανταχοῦ τῆς **βίβλου** τὸ ὕδωρ. Ἢ οὐ τὸ ὕδωρ, ἀλλ' ἡ τοῦ ὕδατος ποιότης. Ἀλλὰ ποῦ ὄντος τοῦ ὕδατος; Πῶς οὖν οὐχ ὁ αὐτὸς ὄγκος; Ἢ ἐξέτεινε τὴν **βίβλον** τὸ προστεθέν· ἔλαβε γὰρ μέγεθος παρὰ τοῦ εἰσελθόντος. Ἀλλ' εἰ ἔλαβε, προσετέθη τις ὄγκος· εἰ δὲ προσετέθη, οὐ κατεπόθη ἐν τῷ ἑτέρῳ, δεῖ οὖν ἐν ἄλλῳ καὶ ἄλλῳ τὴν ὕλην εἶναι.

But this is a subject which requires separate investigation, what happens when what was a mass of water becomes air, and how the increase of volume in the air which has come into being is to be explained. Now, however, let us content ourselves with what has been said, although there is a great deal else which is said on both sides. But let us consider independently what we ought to say about this problem, what view will be in accordance with the arguments stated, or what new one will appear going beyond the present arguments. Well, then, when water runs through a fleece, or **papyrus** exudes the water which is in it, how can we deny that the whole body of the water goes right through the papyrus? Or even when it does not run through, how can we put matter in contact with matter and mass with mass and make the qualities alone coalesce? For surely the matter of the water will not lie outside the **papyrus**, nor, again, in any interstices of it; for the whole papyrus is wet and its matter is nowhere destitute of the quality [of wetness]. But if the matter is everywhere accompanied by the quality of wetness, the water is everywhere in the **papyrus**. But perhaps it is not the water but the quality of the water. But where is the water? Why, then, does the mass not remain the same? What was added to the **papyrus** has extended it: for it took size from the water which entered into it. But if it took size, a mass was added to it; but if it was added, it was not absorbed in the other, and so the matter of the water and the matter of the papyrus must be in two different places.[38]

However, the semantic domain of βίβλος extends beyond purely the physical representation of papyrus reeds. As early as 1904, Theodor Nägeli referred to the sacred nature of βίβλος in reference to the Greek rhetorician Lucian of Samosata.[39] Further to this, in P.Par. 19.1 (p. 237; 138 CE), the author of an elaborate astrological horoscope relating to Anoubion son of Psansos refers to the "old, wise, that is Chaldaean books" (σκεψάμενος ἀπὸ πολλῶν βίβλων ὡς παρεδόθη ἡμεῖν ἀπὸ σοφῶν ἀρχαίων, τουτέστι Χαλδαϊκῶν).

P.Oxy. 3.470, a third-century papyrus containing descriptions of astronomical instruments replete with technical phraseology, contains a reference to the book of Hermes introduced by the phase βίβλος λέγει (line 24). Grenfell and Hunt, authors of the *editio princeps*, suggest that a book of Hermes could be the "authority upon which…[P.Oxy. 3.470] is based."[40]

P.Oxy. 6.886, currently housed in the Cairo, Egyptian Museum (JdE 47411) is a 25-line formula for obtaining an omen. The text claims to be copied from a sacred book, which is a regular feature of Hermetic writings.[41]

	Μεγάλη Ἶσις ἡ κυρία.	Great is the Lady Isis.
	ἀντίγραφον ἱερᾶς **βίβλου**	Copy of a **sacred book**
	τῆς εὑρεθείσης ἐν	found in
	τοῖς τοῦ Ἑρμοῦ ταμίοις.	the archives of Hermes.
5.	ὁ δὲ τρόπος ἐστὶν τὰ περὶ	The method is concerned
	τὰ γράμματα κθ,	with the 29 letters
	δι' ὧν ὁ Ἑρμῆς καὶ ἡ Ἶσις	used by Hermes and Isis
	ζητοῦσα ἑαυτῆς τὸν ἀ-	when searching for her brother
	δελφὸν καὶ ἄνδρα Ὀ-	and husband Osiris.

38. Plotinus, *Enneads*, trans. A. H. Armstrong, LCL 441: 200–203.
39. Theodor Nägeli, *Der Wortschatz des Apostels Paulus* (Göttingen: Basel, 1904), 19.
40. B. P. Grenfell and A. S. Hunt in P.Oxy. 3, p. 142, 144–5.
41. P.Leid. is a similar magical text which introduces the entire work (W, pag. 6.19, pag. 8.22; 2nd/3rd cent. CE) with the phrase βίβλος ἱερά and supports the general picture sketched thus far.

10	σιριν. ἐπικαλοῦ μὲ<ν>	Invoke
	τὸν ("Ηλιον)⁴² καὶ τοὺς ἐν βυ-	the sun and all the gods
	θῷ θεοὺς πάντας, πε-	in the deep concerning
	ρὶ ὧν θέλεις κληδονις-	those things about which
	θῆναι, <καὶ> λαβὼν φοίνι-	you wish to receive an omen. Take
15	κος ἄρσενος φύλλα κθ'	29 leaves of a male palm,
	ἐπίγραψον ἐν ἑκάστῳ τῶν	and inscribe on each of the
	φύλλων τὰ τῶν θεῶν	leaves the names of the gods;
	ὀνόματα καὶ ἐπευξά-	then after a prayer
	μενος αἶρε κατὰ δύο	lift them up two by
20	δύο. τὸ δὲ ὑπολιπόμε-	two, and read that which
	νον ἔσχατον ἀνάγνω-	is left at the last,
	θι, καὶ εὑρήσεις σου τὴν κλη-	and you will find wherein
	δόνα, ἐν οἷς μέτεστιν,	your omen consists, and you will
	καὶ χρηματισθήσῃ τη-	obtain an illuminating
25	λαυγῶς.	answer.

In a report of judicial examinations P.Tebt. 2.291.43 (162 CE) records that a candidate for the priesthood gave proof of his knowledge of hieratic and Egyptian writing by reading from a hieratic book produced by the sacred scribes,⁴³ τοῦ ἐπίστασθαι [ἱε]ρατικὰ [καὶ] Αἰγύπτια γράμ[ματ]α ἐξ ἧς οἱ ἱερογραμματεῖς προήνεγκαν βίβλου ἱερατικῆς. The full text is as follows:

[ρσι]σοῦχ[ο]ς Μαρ[. . . .]ς μητρὸς Θ[εν]κή[β]κιος
[ἀπ]όδειξιν δοὺς τοῦ ἐπίστασθαι [ἱε]ρατικὰ
[καὶ] Αἰγύπτια γράμ[ματ]α ἐξ ἧς οἱ ἱερογραμματεῖς
προήνεγκαν **βίβλου** ἱερατικῆς [ἀκο]λούθως
τῷ γενομένῳ ὑπομνήματι τῇ ιβ τοῦ
Τῦβι μηνὸς τοῦ [ἐ]νεστῶτος β (ἔτους) καὶ Παχῆβκις
ὁ καὶ Ζώσιμος Παχήβκιος μητρὸς Θαισᾶτος
ἐξ ὧν παρέθεντο τοῦ γένους ἀσφαλειῶν
ἐφάνησαν εἶναι γένους ἱερατικ[ο]ῦ.
ἐρρῶσθ(αι) ὑμᾶς εὔχομ(αι).
50(ἔτους) β Αὐτοκράτορος Καίσαρος Μάρκου Αὐρηλίου
Ἀντωνίνου Σεβαστοῦ καὶ Αὐτοκράτορος Καίσαρος
Λουκίου Αὐρηλίου Οὐήρου Σεβαστοῦ
Μεχεὶρ ιβ

Marsisouchos son of Mar[ ] and Thenkebkis, having given proof of a knowledge of hieratic and Egyptian writing from a hieratic **book** produced by the sacred scribes in accordance with the memorandum of the 12th of

---

42. Pictographic abbreviation in the text, expanded by the editor.
43. James Hope Moulton and George Milligan, *The Vocabulary of the Greek Testament* (London: Hodder & Stoughton, 1930), 111.

the month Tybi of the present 2nd year, and Pakebkis also called Zosimus, son of Pakebkis and Thaisas, on the strength of proofs produced concerning parentage, were respectively shown to be of priestly family. I pray for your health. The 2nd year of Imperator Caesar Lucius Aurelius Verus Augustus, Mecheir 12.

Albeit a later papyrus from the fourth century, SB 14.11858 provides evidence of further specificity in relation to the application of the term. In a short five-line receipt acknowledging a book to be illustrated, the term βίβλος is almost certainly used in reference to Christian religious material:

ἐγὼ Ἡράκλειος πρ(εσβύτερος) ὁμολογῶ ἐσχη- κέναι παρά σου τὴν **βίβλον** εἰς κόσμησιν ἐπ{ε}ὶ τῷ με πάλιν εἴσω μηνὸς ἀποκαταστῆσαί σοι ἄνευ εὑρεσιλογίας.	I, Herakeios the presbyter, acknowledge that I have received from you the **book** for adornment on condition that I again within a month restore (it) to you without argument.

The editor of the *editio princeps* suggested that Aurelius Herakleios may have been "a member of a monasterial scriptorium."[44] Peculiar, however, is the brevity of the text: "the name of the customer, the title of the book, the date, or a reference to any arrangement with regard to payment are lacking."[45] The absence of the customer's name can be explained because the receipt was issued for the customer. The absence of the title of the book and that it was being adorned point to the probability of the βίβλος being a Bible.

Ostrakon SB 26.16373 (O. Narm. 1.49) is a list of cultic payments from the second century in the Arsinoite nome, including 24 drachmae "for books" (line 6, βίβλοις (δραχμαὶ) κδ). The full text reads:

Γονιέος (δραχμαὶ) ρκ
Κολλαῦθις (δραχμαὶ) ρη
Ἅρπαλος (δραχμαὶ) υξ
ἀρταβίας (δραχμαὶ) ρο
Ἀρθωοῦνις (δραχμαὶ) η
βίβλοις (δραχμαὶ) κδ

---

44. George M. Parássoglou, "A Book Illuminator in Byzantine Egypt," *Byzantion* 44 (1974): 362 n. 1.

45. Ibid., 364–5.

Ἀκῆς (δραχμαὶ) μ
γερδιακοῦ (δραχμαὶ) ρ
(γίνονται) (τάλαντον) α (δραχμαὶ) Α (δραχμαὶ) Ασδ
ἐνοικία (δραχμαὶ) ρ
θεῶν ξενίας (δραχμαὶ) κ
προφηδίας (δραχμαὶ) υμ
ἱματισμῶν (δραχμαὶ) τ
χρυσώματα (δραχμαὶ) τ
. . . . . .αιτην (δραχμαὶ) φ
ὁμοίως Ανου. . .(δραχμαὶ) β

The word βίβλος, however, can be used in reference to a request for a grant and/or the physical papyrus within the same document, as P.Mil. 1.6 is dated to 18 June 26 CE (Tiberius, year 12, Pauni 24) from Theadelphia (Arsinoites) outlines:

	Ἀφροδισίωι Ζωίλου ἐγλήμπτορι **βίβλου** Ἰουλίας Σεβαστῆς καὶ τέκνω(ν) Γερμανικοῦ Καίσαρος παρὰ Ἀρθώιτου τοῦ Μαρρείους.	To Aphrodisius son of Zoilus, contractor of the **papyrus** of Julia Augusta and the children of Germanicus Caesar, from Herthoites son of Marres.
5	ἐπιχωρηθέντος μοι **βίβλου**	If the concession is granted to me to gather **papyrus**
	φέρειν ἀπὸ συνορίας Θεοξενίδ(ος) μέχρι ὁρίων Φιλωτερίδος καὶ φλοῦν ἐκ τοῦ δρυμοῦ καὶ **βίβλου** καὶ πλέκειν ψιάθους	from the borders of Theoxenis to those of Philoteris and reeds from the marsh as well as **papyrus**, and to weave mats
10	καὶ πωλεῖν ἐν αἷς ἐὰν αἱρῶ-μαι τοῦ νομοῦ κώμαις εἰς τὸ ιβ (ἔτος) Τιβερίου Καίσαρος Σεβαστοῦ, ὑφίσταμαι τε-λέσειν ἀργυρίου δραχμὰς	and sell them in whatever villages of the nome I choose for the 12th year of Tiberius Caesar Augustus, I undertake to pay
15	τέσσαρες καὶ ὀβολοὺς δέκα πέντε σὺν καθήκουσι καὶ προσδιαγραφομένοις καὶ συμβολικοῖς, ἃς καὶ ἀποδώισωι ἐν ἀναφοραῖς	4 silver dr. 15 obols with the charges pertaining thereto, both supplementary fees and receipts. These I shall pay in three instalments
20	τρσὶ Ἐπεὶφ Μεσορὴι καὶ ἐξενίαυτ(α) μηνὶ Σεβαστῶι, ἐὰν φαίνητ(αι) ἐπιχωρῆσαί μοι ἐπὶ τοῖς προκειμ(ένοις).	in Epiph, Mesore, and in the following year in the month Augustus, if it seems good to give the concession on the terms stated.

εὐτ[ύχει].	Farewell.[46]
(ἔτους) ιβ Τιβερίου Καίσαρος	Year 12 Tiberius, Caesar Augustus
25 Σεβαστοῦ	
Παῦ[ν]ι κδ	Pauni 24

Although additional papyrological data (e.g. P.Fay. 331; P.Mil.Vogl. 2.66; P.Ryl. 4.627, 628, 638) could be brought into our discussion to further illustrate the above-delineated semantic domains, there is sufficient evidence to include, among other aspects, the connotation of sacredness as a distinct dimension of the semantic domain of βίβλος.

4. *Other Attestations of* βίβλος *in the New Testament*

The "sacred/holy" semantic trajectory evidenced in the papyri is also corroborated in the New Testament where the term can refer to Scripture (Mark 12:26, "And as for the dead being raised, have you not read in the βίβλῳ of Moses…"; Luke 3:4, "as it is written in the βίβλῳ of the words of the prophet Isaiah…"; Luke 20:42, "For David himself says in the βίβλῳ of Psalms…"; Acts 1:20, "For it is written in the βίβλῳ of Psalms…"; Acts 7:42, "But God turned away from them and handed them over to worship the host of heaven, as it is written in the βίβλῳ of the prophets…"), the "Book of Life" (Phil. 4:3, "Yes, and I ask you also, my loyal companion, help these women, for they have struggled beside me in the work of the gospel, together with Clement and the rest of my co-workers, whose names are in the βίβλῳ of life"; Rev. 3:5, "If you conquer, you will be clothed like them in white robes, and I will not blot your name out of the βίβλου of life…"; Rev. 20:15, "and anyone whose name was not found written in the βίβλῳ of life was thrown into the lake of fire"), or even magical writings (Acts 19:19, "A number of those who practiced magic collected their βίβλους and burned them publicly; when the value of these books was calculated, it was found to come to fifty thousand silver coins").

5. *Literary Evidence*

A revealing additional dimension of the word βίβλος is apparent when the broader classical literary tradition is taken into consideration. Very frequently the term βίβλος within literary evidence is used to denote

---

46. Allan Chester Johnson, *Roman Egypt to the Reign of Diocletian* (Baltimore: Johns Hopkins University Press, 1936), 360.

history in general, or more specifically *sacred history*, a sample of which is provided below.

MANETHO, *The Sacred Book*, trans. W. G. Waddell, LCL 350: 188–9.
Η ΙΕΡΑ ΒΙΒΛΟΣ Fr 76. Eusebius, *Praeparatio Evangelica* II Prooem., p. 44 C (Gifford).
Πᾶσαν μὲν οὖν τὴν Αἰγυπτιακὴν ἱστορίαν εἰς πλάτος τῇ Ἑλλήνων μετείληφε φωνῇ ἰδίως τε τὰ περὶ τῆς κατ' αὐτοὺς θεολογίας Μανεθὼς ὁ Αἰγύπτιος, ἔν τε ᾗ ἔγραψεν Ἱερᾷ **βίβλῳ** καὶ ἐν ἑτέροις αὐτοῦ συγγράμμασι.

Now the whole history of Egypt and especially the details of Egyptian religion are expounded at length in Greek by Manetho the Egyptian, both in his Sacred **Book** and in other writings of his.

DIODORUS SICULUS, *The Library of History*, trans. C. H. Oldfather. LCL 279: 4–5
ΒΙΒΛΟΣ ΠΡΩΤΗ
Τοῖς τὰς κοινὰς ἱστορίας πραγματευσαμένοις μεγάλας χάριτας ἀπονέμειν δίκαιον πάντας ἀνθρώπους, ὅτι τοῖς ἰδίοις πόνοις ὠφελῆσαι τὸν κοινὸν βίον ἐφιλοτιμήθησαν· ἀκίνδυνον γὰρ διδασκαλίαν τοῦ συμφέροντος εἰσηγησάμενοι καλλίστην ἐμπειρίαν διὰ τῆς πραγματείας ταύτης περιποιοῦσι τοῖς ἀναγινώσκουσιν. ἡ μὲν γὰρ ἐκ τῆς πείρας ἑκάστου μάθησις μετὰ πολλῶν πόνων καὶ κινδύνων ποιεῖ τῶν χρησίμων ἕκαστα διαγινώσκειν, καὶ διὰ τοῦτο τῶν ἡρώων ὁ πολυπειρότατος μετὰ μεγάλων ἀτυχημάτων, πολλῶν ἀνθρώπων ἴδεν ἄστεα καὶ νόον ἔγνω· ἡ δὲ διὰ τῆς ἱστορίας περιγινομένη σύνεσις τῶν ἀλλοτρίων ἀποτευγμάτων τε καὶ κατορθωμάτων ἀπείρατον κακῶν ἔχει τὴν διδασκαλίαν.

BOOK I
It is fitting that all men should ever accord great gratitude to those writers who have composed universal histories, since they have aspired to help by their individual labours human society as a whole; for by offering a schooling, which entails no danger, in what is advantageous they provide their readers, through such a presentation of events, with a most excellent kind of experience. For although the learning which is acquired by experience in each separate case, with all the attendant toils and dangers, does indeed enable a man to discern in each instance where utility lies—and this is the reason why the most widely experienced of our heroes suffered great misfortunes before he, Of many men the cities saw and learned Their thoughts; yet the understanding of the failures and successes of other men, which is acquired by the study of history, affords a schooling that is free from actual experience of ills.

DIODORUS SICULUS, *The Library of History*, trans. C. H. Oldfather. LCL 279: 348–9

ΒΙΒΛΟΣ ΔΕΥΤΕΡΑ

Ἡ μὲν πρὸ ταύτης **βίβλος** τῆς ὅλης συντάξεως οὖσα πρώτη περιέχει τὰς κατ' Αἴγυπτον πράξεις· ἐν αἷς ὑπάρχει τά τε περὶ τῶν θεῶν παρ' Αἰγυπτίοις μυθολογούμενα καὶ περὶ τῆς τοῦ Νείλου φύσεως καὶ τἄλλα τὰ περὶ τοῦ ποταμοῦ τούτου παραδοξολογούμενα, πρὸς δὲ τούτοις περί τε τῆς κατ' Αἴγυπτον χώρας καὶ τῶν ἀρχαίων βασιλέων τὰ ὑφ' ἑκάστου πραχθέντα.

Book 2

The preceding **Book**, being the first of the whole work, embraces the facts which concern Egypt, among which are included both the myths related by the Egyptians about their gods and about the nature of the Nile, and the other marvels which are told about this river, as well as a description of the land of Egypt and the acts of each of their ancient kings.

DIODORUS SICULUS, *The Library of History*, trans. C. H. Oldfather. LCL 375: 120–1

ΒΙΒΛΟΣ ΕΝΔΕΚΑΤΗ

Ἡ μὲν οὖν πρὸ ταύτης **βίβλος**, τῆς ὅλης συντάξεως οὖσα δεκάτη, τὸ τέλος ἔσχε τῶν πράξεων εἰς τὸν προηγούμενον ἐνιαυτὸν τῆς Ξέρξου διαβάσεως εἰς τὴν Εὐρώπην καὶ εἰς τὰς γενομένας δημηγορίας ἐν τῇ κοινῇ συνόδῳ τῶν Ἑλλήνων ἐν Κορίνθῳ περὶ τῆς Γέλωνος συμμαχίας τοῖς Ἕλλησιν· ἐν ταύτῃ δὲ τὸ συνεχὲς τῆς ἱστορίας ἀναπληροῦντες ἀρξόμεθα μὲν ἀπὸ τῆς Ξέρξου στρατείας ἐπὶ τοὺς Ἕλληνας, καταλήξομεν δὲ ἐπὶ τὸν προηγούμενον ἐνιαυτὸν τῆς Ἀθηναίων στρατείας ἐπὶ Κύπρον ἡγουμένου Κίμωνος.

Book 11

The preceding **Book**, which is the tenth of our narrative, closed with the events of the year just before the crossing of Xerxes into Europe and the formal deliberations which the general assembly of the Greeks held in Corinth on the alliance between Gelon and the Greeks; and in this Book we shall supply the further course of the history, beginning with the campaign of Xerxes against the Greeks, and we shall stop with the year which precedes the campaign of the Athenians against Cyprus under the leadership of Cimon.

DIODORUS SICULUS, *The Library of History*, trans. Russel M. Geer. LCL 390: 8–9.

ΒΙΒΛΟΣ ΠΕΝΤΕΚΑΙΔΕΚΑΤΗ

Ἐπ' ἄρχοντος δ' Ἀθήνησιν Εὐάνδρου¹ Ῥωμαῖοι κατέστησαν ἀντὶ τῶν ὑπάτων χιλιάρχους ἕξ, Κόιντον Σολπίκιον, Γάιον Φάβιον, Κόιντον Σερουίλιον, Πόπλιον Κορνήλιον. ἐπὶ δὲ τούτων Λακεδαιμόνιοι κατελάβοντο τὴν Καδμείαν ἐν ταῖς Θήβαις διά τινας τοιαύτας αἰτίας.

Book 15
When Evander was archon at Athens, the Romans elected six military tribunes with consular power, Quintus Sulpicius, Gaius Fabius, Quintus Servilius, Publius Cornelius. During their term of office, the Lacedaemonians took possession of the Cadmeia in Thebes for the following reasons.

DIODORUS SICULUS, *The Library of History*, trans. Charles L. Sherman, LCL 389: 2–3.

ΒΙΒΛΟΣ ΕΝΝΕΑΚΑΙΔΕΚΑΤΗ
Τοῦ δ' ἔτους τούτου διελθόντος Ἀθήνησι μὲν ἦρχε Νικόδωρος, ἐν Ῥώμῃ δ' ἦσαν ὕπατοι Λεύκιος Παπείριος τὸ τέταρτον καὶ Κόιντος Πόπλιος τὸ δεύτερον.

Book 19
After this year had passed, Nicodorus was archon at Athens, and at Rome Lucius Papirius was consul for the fourth time and Quintus Publius for the second.

DIODORUS SICULUS, *The Library of History*, trans. Russel M. Geer, LCL 390: 144–7.

ΒΙΒΛΟΣ ΕΙΚΟΣΤΗ
Τοῖς εἰς τὰς ἱστορίας ὑπερμήκεις δημηγορίας παρεμβάλλουσιν ἢ πυκναῖς χρωμένοις ῥητορείαις δικαίως ἄν τις ἐπιτιμήσειεν· οὐ μόνον γὰρ τὸ συνεχὲς τῆς διηγήσεως διὰ τὴν ἀκαιρίαν τῶν ἐπεισαγομένων λόγων διασπῶσιν, ἀλλὰ καὶ τῶν φιλοτίμως ἐχόντων πρὸς τὴν τῶν πράξεων ἐπίγνωσιν μεσολαβοῦσι τὴν ἐπιθυμίαν. καίτοι γε τοὺς ἐπιδείκνυσθαι βουλομένους λόγου δύναμιν ἔξεστι κατ' ἰδίαν δημηγορίας καὶ πρεσβευτικοὺς λόγους, ἔτι δὲ ἐγκώμια καὶ ψόγους καὶ τἆλλα τὰ τοιαῦτα συντάττεσθαι· τῇ γὰρ οἰκονομίᾳ τῶν λόγων χρησάμενοι καὶ τὰς ὑποθέσεις χωρὶς ἑκατέρας ἐξεργασάμενοι κατὰ λόγον ἂν ἐν ἀμφοτέραις ταῖς πραγματείαις εὐδοκιμοῖεν. νῦν δ' ἔνιοι πλεονάσαντες ἐν τοῖς ῥητορικοῖς λόγοις προσθήκην ἐποιήσαντο τὴν ὅλην ἱστορίαν τῆς δημηγορίας. λυπεῖ δ' οὐ μόνον τὸ κακῶς γραφέν, ἀλλὰ καὶ τὸ δοκοῦν ἐν τοῖς ἄλλοις ἐπιτετεῦχθαι, τόπων καὶ καιρῶν τῆς οἰκείας τάξεως 4διημαρτηκός. διὸ καὶ τῶν ἀναγινωσκόντων τὰς τοιαύτας πραγματείας οἱ μὲν ὑπερβαίνουσι τὰς ῥητορείας, κἂν ὅλως ἐπιτετεῦχθαι δόξωσιν, οἱ δὲ διὰ τὸ μῆκος καὶ τὴν ἀκαιρίαν τοῦ συγγραφέως ἐκλυθέντες τὰς ψυχὰς τὸ παράπαν ἀφίστανται τῆς ἀναγνώσεως, οὐκ ἀλόγως τοῦτο πάσχοντες· τὸ γὰρ τῆς ἱστορίας γένος ἁπλοῦν ἐστι καὶ συμφυὲς αὑτῷ καὶ τὸ σύνολον ἐμψύχῳ σώματι παραπλήσιον, οὗ τὸ μὲν ἐσπαραγμένον ἐστέρηται τῆς ψυχικῆς χάριτος, τὸ δὲ τὴν ἀναγκαίαν σύνθεσιν ἔχον εὐκαίρως τετήρηται καὶ τῷ συμφυεῖ τῆς ὅλης περιγραφῆς ἐπιτερπῆ καὶ σαφῆ παρίστησι τὴν ἀνάγνωσιν.

Book 20
One might justly censure those who in their histories insert over-long orations or employ frequent speeches; for not only do they rend asunder the continuity of the narrative by the ill-timed insertion of speeches, but also

they interrupt the interest of those who are eagerly pressing on toward a full knowledge of the events. Yet surely there is opportunity for those who wish to display rhetorical prowess to compose by themselves public discourses and speeches for ambassadors, likewise orations of praise and blame and the like; for by recognizing the classification of literary types and by elaborating each of the two by itself, they might reasonably expect to gain a reputation in both fields of activity. But as it is, some writers by excessive use of rhetorical passages have made the whole art of history into an appendage of oratory. Not only does that which is poorly composed give offence, but also that which seems to have hit the mark in other respects yet has gone far astray from the themes and occasions that belong to its peculiar type. Therefore, even of those who read such works, some skip over the orations although they appear to be entirely successful, and others, wearied in spirit by the historian's wordiness and lack of taste, abandon the reading entirely; and this attitude is not without reason, for the genius of history is simple and self-consistent and as a whole is like a living organism. If it is mangled, it is stripped of its living charm; but if it retains its necessary unity, it is duly preserved and, by the harmony of the whole composition, renders the reading pleasant and clear.

APPIAN, *Roman History* 6. *The Wars in Spain*, trans. Brian McGing, LCL 2: 160–1.

τούτοιν ὁ μὲν Πόπλιος παρὰ Μασσαλιωτῶν ἐμπόρων πυθόμενος Ἀννίβαν διὰ τῶν Ἀλπείων ὀρῶν ἐς τὴν Ἰταλίαν ὑπερβάντα, δείσας μὴ ἀδοκήτως τοῖς Ἰταλιώταις ἐπιπέσοι, παραδοὺς Γναίῳ τῷ ἀδελφῷ τὴν ἐν Ἰβηρίᾳ στρατιὰν διέπλευσεν ἐπὶ πεντήρους ἐς Τυρρηνίαν. καὶ ὅσα ἔπραξεν ἐν τῇ Ἰταλίᾳ οὗτός τε καὶ ὅσοι μετ' αὐτὸν ἄλλοι στρατηγοὶ τοῦδε τοῦ πολέμου ἐγένοντο, ἕως Ἀννίβαν ἑκκαιδεκάτῳ μόλις ἔτει τῆς Ἰταλίας ἐξήλασαν, ἡ ἑξῆς **βίβλος** ὑποδείκνυσιν, ἣ τὰ ἔργα Ἀννίβου τὰ ἐν Ἰταλίᾳ πάντα περιλαμβάνει, καὶ παρ' αὐτὸ λέγεται Ῥωμαϊκῶν Ἀννιβαϊκή.

The former (Publius), learning from Massilian merchants that Hannibal had crossed the Alps and entered Italy, and fearing lest he should fall upon the Italians unawares, handed over to his brother the command in Spain and sailed with his quinqueremes to Etruria. What he and the other Roman generals after him did in Italy, until, at the end of fifteen years and with exceeding difficulty, they drove Hannibal out of the country, is set forth in the following **book**, which contains all the exploits of Hannibal in Italy, and is therefore called the Hannibalic book of Roman history.

LIBANIUS, *Oration 1, The Autobiography*, trans. A. F. Norman, LCL 478: 60–1

ἓν ἕδρων μόνον, μνήμῃ τὰ τῶν παλαιῶν ἐκτώμην συνὼν ἀνδρὶ μνημονικωτάτῳ τε καὶ οἵῳ τῶν παρ' ἐκείνοις καλῶν ἐμπείρους ἀπεργάζεσθαι νέους. καὶ οὕτω δή τι αὐτῷ προσεκείμην ἀκριβῶς, ὥστ' οὐδ' ἀπαλλαττομένου τῶν νέων ἀπηλλαττόμην, ἀλλὰ καὶ δι' ἀγορᾶς ἐν χεροῖν τε ἡ **βίβλος**, καὶ ἔδει τι τὸν ἄνδρα καὶ πρὸς ἀνάγκην λέγειν, ἣν ἐν τῷ παραχρῆμα μὲν δῆλος ἦν δυσχεραίνων, χρόνοις

I concentrated upon one thing only—the memorization of the works of classical authors—and studied under a man of prodigious memory who was capable of instilling into his pupils an appreciation of the excellence of the classics. I attached myself to him so wholeheartedly that I would not leave him even after class had been dismissed, but would trail after him, **book** in hand, even through the city square, and he had to give me some instruction, whether he liked it or not. At the time he was obviously annoyed at this importunity

POLYBIUS, *The Histories*, trans. S. Douglas Olson, W. R. Paton, F. W. Walbank, and C. Habicht. LCL 161: 434–5

Ὅτι ἡ λη' **βίβλος** περιέχει τὴν συντέλειαν τῆς τῶν Ἑλλήνων ἀτυχίας.

The thirty-eighth **book** contains the completion of the disaster of Greece.

6. *Implications and Conclusions*

We conclude with highlighting three main implications of our analysis. First, in light of our survey above, it is evident that the term βίβλος has a broad semantic domain including, (i) papyrus stalks (P.Tebt. 2.308.7), (ii) astrological texts and horoscopes (P.Paris 19.1; P.Oxy. 3.470; P.Oxy. 6.886), (iii) magical texts (P.Leid. 2.W, pag. 6.19, pag. 8.32), (iv) a report of judicial examinations (P. Tebt. 2.291.43), (v) a Christian religious book (SB 14.11858), (vi) a list of payments to a cultic entity (Ostrakon SB 26.16373), or (vii) a request for a grant (P.Mil. 1.6). By far the most common meaning and use of βίβλος in the papyri is within the context of the sacred, that is, in reference to and in relation to religiously orientated materials. In light of this, LSJ surely is far too vague when it states that βίβλος is "the inner bark of the papyrus...[or] a book, of which the leaves were made of this bark."[47] We therefore would caution Nolland's estimation that "βίβλος is the normal word for 'book'"[48] The second

---

47. H. G. Liddell, *A Lexicon: Abridged from Liddell and Scott's Greek–English Lexicon* (Oak Harbor, WA: Logos Research Systems, 1996), 150.

48. J. Nolland, "Preface," in *The Gospel of Matthew: A Commentary on the Greek Text*, New International Greek Testament Commentary (Grand Rapids, MI: Eerdmans; Carlisle: Paternoster Press, 2005), 71.

most common use of the term in antiquity was in reference to historiography. As briefly illustrated through reference to Polybius' *The Histories*, Appian's *Roman History*, and Diodorus Siculus' *The Library of History*, the term can relate to the summative historical enterprise. The combination of these two elements, i.e. the sacred and the historical, seems to be precisely how the author of Matthew is casting his gospel, namely as sacred history. R. Walker[49] is generally credited with underscoring the importance of Matthew's *Heilsgeschichte*,[50] and that Matthew was to be envisioned as sacred history by which he identifies as a "symbolic presentation of salvation history."[51] This then lends support to the argument by Davies and Allison, Klostermann, Lindblom, and Zahn that βίβλος γενέσεως refers to the entirety of Matthew's Gospel, so that the phrase becomes a title for the Gospel as a whole. Additional weight for this view is evident in the lack of a definite article in Matt. 1:1 yet its presence in Gen. 2:4 and 5:1 where the term has a more limited scope.

Second, the definition of the term βίβλος has implications for how we understand the development of the codex and the early Christian preference for it. Roberts and Skeat argue in their Markan hypothesis that it is derivative of Peter's notebook, yet one could legitimately ask why notebook contents affects format. The Antioch hypothesis correlates *nomina sacra* and the codex at Antioch, yet this ultimately rests on the faulty assumption that the Hebrew *apiporin* from *m. Kelim* 24:7 is a transliteration of πάπυρος rather than an unworked wooden tablet. Other proposals have been offered, including the socioeconomic hypothesis which holds that the codex was adopted for lower-status notebooks rather than rolls, but this too is unconvincing; even if most members of the community were "lower class," it does not follow that they would have then decided on the format of the scriptures, since it is likely that higher status members would also have had the opportunity not only to have a say but also to finance the production of the manuscripts. Finally, there is also the *Roman hypothesis* which sees the gospels as a notebook manual of sorts, but one could legitimately ask whether there were new works being written on rolls at this time. The earliest attestations suggest that the codex was a Roman innovation but there are still many questions

---

49. R. Walker, *Die Heilsgeschichte im ersten Evangelium* (Göttingen: Vandenhoeck & Ruprecht, 1967).

50. J. P. Meier, "Salvation-History in Matthew: In Search of a Starting Point," *CBQ* 37 (1975): 203.

51. D. Senior, *What Are They Saying about Matthew?* (New York: Paulist Press, 1983), 30.

pertaining to the reasons which led to the change of format (economics, compactness, comprehensiveness, convenience of use, ease of reference, length).

Finally, it is hoped that this study contributes to the emerging consensus that consultation of the documentary papyri and related material culture can help temper the reductionistic and compressed semantic ranges provided in the glosses of contemporary ancient Greek dictionaries, which are often guilty of regurgitating older lexical definitions rather than providing fresh analyses on the basis of material evidence.

9

THE EARLY PAPYRI, "GOSPEL-PARALLEL" VARIANTS, AND THE TEXT OF THE NEW TESTAMENT IN THE SECOND CENTURY

Roy D. Kotansky

Introduction

One of the governing mandates of textual criticism in New Testament scholarship today is to ascertain, as much as it is possible, the character of the text in the second century, the prospect of ever recovering an "original" or "autograph" being beyond the pale of reasonable likelihood.[1] The eventuality of such an initiative has been hampered for many years, of course, by the limitations of our papyrological record, in that the number of early papyri was relatively few, compared to the wealth of the larger codices of the fourth and fifth centuries (Sinaiticus, Alexandrinus, Vaticanus, and Codex Bezae), and they often proved rather fragmentary, as well. With each new discovery of a papyrus from the second (or third) century CE, great expectations hung upon the degree to which its readings might support those represented by the larger and more fulsome codices, and to see, as a consequence, to which of the broader

---

1. It is practically a given dictum in textual criticism today that "the magnitude of Greek and versional manuscripts and patristic citations...as well as the enormous quantity of textual variants," to borrow the sobering words of Eldon Jay Epp, "militates against a single, simplistic original" in respect of identifying the New Testament autographs (or even an "earliest attainable text"); see, Epp 2007: 294, who continues in noting the "greater diversity among the texts in the first few centuries of Christianity than in the later periods," and of "the fact, long affirmed among New Testament textual critics, that the bulk of textual variants arose prior to 200 C.E." (Epp 2007: 295); see, further, Parker 1997: 188; and esp. Koester 1989: 37. On the issue of "originality," see, e.g., Epp 1999.

text-families—Alexandrian, Western, "Caesarean," or even Byzantine—they might belong.[2]

With the watershed acquisition from 1930–1931 of the famous Chester Beatty Papyri ($\mathfrak{P}^{45}$, $\mathfrak{P}^{46}$, $\mathfrak{P}^{47}$), which included considerably new texts of the Gospels, Paul, and the book of Revelation, matters were not, unfortunately, as easily resolved as one might have expected, even though $\mathfrak{P}^{46}$ (Pauline epistles) dated, palaeographically, to as early as c. 200 CE, and $\mathfrak{P}^{45}$ (Gospels and Acts) and $\mathfrak{P}^{47}$, as early as the first quarter of the third century CE—that is, as much as two centuries earlier than the big codices.[3] Although the text of the Pauline Epistles ($\mathfrak{P}^{46}$) showed close affinities with the Alexandrian text-type—the erstwhile basis for Westcott

---

2. The difficulty in acquiring any certitude in respect of the New Testament text in the second century is also hindered by the fact that our two major text-types, that of the "Alexandrian" (exemplified by B) and that of the "Western" (exemplified by D) had their origins in the second century (cf. Epp 1997: 70f.; 2007: 306). A duality (or even multiplicity) of text-types—no matter one's bias towards either family—already existing in the second century points to textual diversity, not unity, at an early stage. The early Church Fathers, who often show a marked proclivity towards the Western-type texts (Epp 1993 [1974]: 89), are also (in)famous for their often-divergent variants, which, though representing citations of biblical verse and not manuscript copying of text (Hurtado 2006), often preserve manuscript readings, nonetheless, that reflect a text-tradition different from what we possess in our present manuscripts. They noted, for instance, that certain manuscripts—unavailable to us, of course—not only contained variant readings, but also that in at least one instance—that of the Freer Logion (Mark 19:14 in Codex W)—Jerome mentions multiple mss. preserving a wild variant that was not known until the twentieth century (Metzger 1992: 153; 57); hence, it is quite conceivable that the Fathers may have possessed additional manuscripts with readings not presently known to us; see Metzger 1992: 151–4, with particular reference to Origen (Metzger 1963), St. Jerome (Hulley 1944), and St. Augustine. There are also the multiple issues associated with Tatian's *Diatessaron* and other early "harmonies" (such as that of his teacher's, Justin) that preserve early witnesses to texts not supported by our present manuscript traditions (see further the discussion, to follow), as well as texts of the so-called "Apocryphal Gospels." The version of Marcion's gospel, as well, proves especially troublesome in respect of recovering the original form of Luke's gospel; see, e.g., Tyson 2006: esp. 79–120; Roth 2015. The important issue of Marcion's gospel as a possible precursor to our canonical gospels is boldly addressed in a series of new studies; cf. Klinghardt, et al. 2017.

3. $\mathfrak{P}^{45}$ is comprised of six leaves of Mark, seven of Luke, and thirteen of Acts (but only two fragmentary leaves of Matthew and John); $\mathfrak{P}^{46}$ contains much of the Pauline Corpus; and $\mathfrak{P}^{47}$ preserved approximately chapters 9:10–17:2 of the book of Revelation. As far as dates are concerned, the latest assessment, places the papyri

and Hort's "Neutral Text," the best hopes for attaining an early if not "original" New Testament text—the verdict of the Gospels ($\mathfrak{P}^{45}$) was not as promising; the text of Mark that it contained, as the former "docent" of New Testament papyrology, Bruce Metzger, once noted, "is nearer to the Caesarean family than to either the Alexandrian or the Western text-types"; moreover, "In the other Gospels (where the Caesarean text has not yet been fully established)," he continues, "it is also intermediate between Alexandrian and Western" (Metzger [1964, 1992]: 37). But for the problematic issue of the text of Acts, only minor affinities with the Western tradition showed up.

As every student of the New Testament today knows, the publication in 1935 of the famous John Rylands fragment (= Gospel of John 18:31-33, 37-38) proved to be one of the most exciting and significant events in the history of biblical textual criticism, for its presented the scholarly world with the "oldest copy of any portion of the New Testament known to be in existence" (Metzger [1992]: 38), being initially dated to the remarkably early date of c. 125–150 CE, that is, very close to the putative "original" of the Gospel of John. Unfortunately, for all its significance, the text was entirely too fragmentary to ascertain its textual affinity; furthermore, it preserved a portion of John for which there were relatively few variant readings extant among our manuscript witnesses, even though a troubling loss of the second <εις τουτο> could be detected in the lacuna of verse 37, an important variant reading that we address in greater detail, below.

In the 1960s with the publication of the Bodmer Papyrus (= $\mathfrak{P}^{75}$), all that potentially changed, for at long last we encountered the highly significant discovery of an early papyrus preserving huge portions of Luke (3:18–24:53) and extensive sections of John, chapters 1–15, that allied closely with the "Alexandrian" text of the fourth-century Codex Vaticanus (B), arguably the most important of all Greek New Testament manuscripts. Its original assignation of date, based on palaeographical factors, placed it in the surprisingly early period of c. 175–225 CE (Martin-Kasser), although this has been recently called into question.[4]

---

more generally to the period c. 200–225 CE and c. 200–250 CE (Orsini-Clarysse); see below. For a detailed analysis of the papyri, their history, and scribal variants, see Royse 2007: esp. 103–398. On $\mathfrak{P}^{45}$, further, Elliott 2004.

4. E.g., Nongbri (2016), who suggests, but does not insist upon, a possible date in the mid-fourth century CE based on new palaeographical and codicological considerations, presents arguments that are at times informative, at times circular. Understandably, he may not have been aware of the reliable and highly exacting assessment of Orsini-Clarysse (2012), who maintain the date of c. 200–250 CE for $\mathfrak{P}^{75}$ (and who do, justifiably, cite Nongri [2011], favorably). They are the most expert

From the time of the publication of the 27th edition of Nestle-Aland in 1993 to that of the 28th in 2012, the number of papyri has fortunately increased measurably from 𝔓⁹⁸ to 𝔓¹²⁷—following the standard superscript enumeration of Caspar René Gregory—with papyri numbering up to 𝔓¹³⁶ waiting in the wings.⁵ But not all of these, of course, represent papyri of the Gospels—the primary focus of our initial enquiry here— but the number of new and early papyri of the four gospels remains impressive for the almost twenty years intervening before the publication of the latest edition of Nestle-Aland. Approximately half-way from the time of the appearance of the two latest editions of this storied edition of the New Testament, Eldon J. Epp noted the following in respect of the evidence of the papyri, especially those of the second and early third centuries: "very early and extensive papyri, such as 𝔓⁴⁵, 𝔓⁴⁶, 𝔓⁶⁶, and 𝔓⁷⁵ (where they overlap), show numerous differences from one another and from the grand parchments ℵ and B,"⁶ while other early papyri (e.g., 𝔓²⁹, 𝔓³⁸, 𝔓⁴⁸, and 𝔓⁶⁹) align with the Western text-type, or with the "abortive"

---

papyrologists to date who have examined anew the whole corpus of early papyri of the New Testament and tend to uphold, with remarkably few exceptions, the dating reflected in Nestle-Aland (see their Table 1, pp. 469–72). The dating of the original editors of volumes like the Oxyrhynchus papyri, and elsewhere, rests in the hands of experienced papyrologists of the likes of Lobel, Parsons (and many others), who have handled thousands, if not tens-of-thousands, of documentary and literary papyri and have good reasons for proffering their dates. Their skills prove far less "subjective" than some younger scholars might think nowadays. Thus, certain attempts to assign implausibly earlier dates (as well as late dates) for the New Testament papyri (i.e., the "theological palaeography" of O'Callaghan, Thiede, Jaroš, Comfort-Barrett, and others, that Orsini-Clarysse [2012: esp. 447–51] rightly call to task) need also to be put to permanent rest; the article by Orsini-Clarysse, in a word, should remain the standard for the foreseeable future; see also Bagnall 2009.

5. See https://en.m.wikipedia.org/wiki/List_of_New_Testament_papyri, clearly written and regularly updated by a knowledgeable New Testament text-critic. See also *The New Testament Virtual Manuscript Room* (https://ntvmr.uni-muenster.de), *The Center for the Study of New Testament Manuscripts* (https://csntm.org/manuscript/View/GA_P103?filter=1), and related sites.

6. Epp 2007: 294–5, noting, of course, the evidence of 𝔓⁷⁵'s association with the text-type of Vaticanus (B) (see further, below); see also his earlier studies (1989, 1995), and especially his remarks already in 1974: "…my major concern is with the *dynamic* situation of the text in those first centuries, as it can be observed by looking at the papyri, not in isolation, but in their broader historical context… In other words, the tracing of textual streams or trajectories shows us that something was happening between 200 and 300…" (Epp 1993 [1974]: 95).

Caesarean text-type ($\mathfrak{P}^{45}$).[7] What kind of new evidence has emerged in the last decade, or so, to challenge, if at all, this current state of affairs? Does a kind of impasse, or "interlude," still exist in the discipline of New Testament textual criticism as regards to the effort to recover the "earliest retainable" text, much less the "original"?[8] In order to answer vexing questions such as these, even if they prove at times intractable, it seems obligatory to initiate a closer examination of the corpus of these early papyri, especially the more recently published ones.

Notes on the Early Gospel Papyri

In a now well-known reworking of his 1981 Graduate Theological Union (Berkeley) ThD thesis, James R. Royse has commandingly analyzed in well over a thousand pages of published material, the texts and variants of a handful of the most important early New Testament Papyri: $\mathfrak{P}^{45}$, $\mathfrak{P}^{46}$, $\mathfrak{P}^{47}$, $\mathfrak{P}^{66}$, $\mathfrak{P}^{72}$, and $\mathfrak{P}^{75}$, of which only three deal with the Gospels ($\mathfrak{P}^{45}$, $\mathfrak{P}^{66}$, and $\mathfrak{P}^{75}$), our immediate focus here. After examining in exacting detail the scribal habits of each, and taking particular note of their singular readings, corrections, and orthographic peculiarities (note, for example, his Appendices A–C), Royse, following the older works of E. C. Colwell, and others, drives home the unequivocal conclusion that, contrary to current textual *praxis* nowadays, the dictum that the shorter reading is to be preferred (the well-worked *lectio brevior potior* rule) is, as a matter of fact, without concrete merit. In terms of examining the theoretical text of the second century, Royse's work will remain important for some time to come, for it turns on its head the age-old notion that a scribe's tendency has always been to expand a text, rather than to shorten it, the re-evaluation of which now carries great implications for the whole copying process of the Western tradition of textual history, especially in respect of Codex Bezae (D), the Latin witnesses, and the other supporting

---

7. See, e.g., Epp (2005 [1997]: 70–1; and earlier (Epp 1989: esp. 282; 1993 [1974]: 89–91, 92f.; 1993 [1989]; 1995: esp. 17; Hurtado 1981); see also, e.g. Colwell 1969; Royse 1979; Head 1990; Royse 1995: 244–49 (for additional studies). See, further, below.

8. Epp (1993 [1974]). As Epp cogently observed as recently as a decade ago (2007: 295), "If—as a traditional view has it—there were a single original that was carefully copied as its sacred contents became an authoritative, canonical text, should not the quantity of variants have been fewer in the early period, followed over a long time by increasing numbers of variants in later copies of copies of copies?" In point of fact, the opposite has occurred, and little in the intervening years has challenged this perspective.

versions. But each manuscript reading must be looked at, of course, on a case-by-case basis, and our purpose here is to show from the character of the texts of many of the early papyri that it is not always easy to classify them according to preconceived notions of what text-family they might belong to, nor to establish, a fortiori, whether the reading of a papyrus manuscript might align prejudicially with one's "favored" textual family (such as the "Alexandrian," for example, vis-à-vis the too often dismissed "Western"). The evidence of the early papyri, it would seem, especially the more recently published ones, might well demonstrate a continued diversity of texts in an inceptive period such as that of the early second century.

By first examining some of the early papyri we hope to ascertain, whenever possible, the character of their texts before turning to the less appreciated subject of the "gospel-parallel" variants, about which relatively little work has been carried out. For those who have examined the original editions of these published papyri, a lot of the assessments below will not appear new, at least not in respect of the older numbered papyri; however, the issue with the newer papyrus fragments might prove another matter altogether. The problem is that we have relied too often upon the published determinations in the apparatuses of the critical editions of Nestle-Aland, particularly the most recent, the 28th, for resolving whether or not a given variant reading of a new papyrus is properly represented, much less recorded. Our judgments about the reliability or stability of the texts of the papyri, especially in respect of our understanding of the early transmissional history of the gospels depends upon an examination of the texts of the original papyri themselves, whenever possible, and not upon a reliance on the sometimes random occurrences of papyrological citations in the critical apparatuses of our published New Testament editions, which in themselves may provide less than an accurate representations of the whole character of the papyrus text in question.

In the following, we present a brief description of the text and character of most of the important Gospel papyri of the second and third centuries CE, in order to ascertain what sort of variants they might preserve and to settle, whenever possible, the identity of the text-type to which they might belong. We also make notes, when relevant, on the dating of some of the papyri (above, n. 4), by adopting the most recent assessment of Orsini-Clarysse (2012).[9]

---

9. In 1989 Epp (1993 [1989]) examined all of the papyri, not just the earliest ones, and sought to categorize their texts according to the major text-types, Groups

𝔓¹ = Matt. 1:1-9, 12-13, 14-20, 23. P.Oxy. 1.2. C. 200–300 (Orsini-Clarysse). The text-type has been judged most recently to be close to Codex Vaticanus (Comfort-Barrett 2001: 39), although this was not the initial judgment of Herman C. Hoskier (1914), who lists many disagreements with the Alexandrian text-type.

𝔓⁴ (see 𝔓⁶⁴, below).

𝔓⁵ = John 1:23-31, 33-40; 16:14-22, 22-30; 20:19-20, 22-25. P.Oxy. 2.208; 15.1781. C. 200-300 (Orsini-Clarysse). Although prematurely judged as being Alexandrian, its text has affinities with Western readings, not noted in N-A²⁸, who are known to remain unfavorably predisposed against Codex Bezae (D): although they record, e.g., the omission at 1:35 of the article ὁ in 𝔓⁵ᵛⁱᵈ,⁷⁵, they fail to mention the Western reading in 1:34 of ο εκλεκτος for ο υιος in this papyrus, citing only ℵ* b e ff²* sy^s.c (cf. Metzger 1971: 200, who correctly place 𝔓⁵ᵛⁱᵈ before the other witnesses). This recent omission in Nestle-Aland²⁸ seems intentional, since earlier editions contained it (cf., e.g., Nestle-Aland²⁶ [1979]); it was apparently first removed in Nestle-Aland²⁷ (1993), perhaps due to the fact that most of the word is in a lacuna; but υιος is too short for the required space; εκλεκτος is not. Similarly, in 1:38, ερ]μηνευομενον must be read for μεθερμηνευομενον, with all other mss. The Western reading is also supported by 𝔓¹⁰⁶, another early papyrus, which Nestle-Aland²⁸ also fails to record here. More remarkable, perhaps, according to Comfort-Barrett (2001: 74–8), the reading of 16:17 includes the following singular addition before εκ των μαθητων αυτου, an addition that clearly improves the reading of John according to all known mss.: the pronoun τινες: sc., **17** εἶπαν οὖν <u>τινες</u> ἐκ τῶν μαθητῶν αὐτοῦ πρὸς ἀλλήλους, "Therefore <u>some</u> of his disciples said to one-another…" The sentence without it otherwise presents something of a solecism. The papyrus preserves an original reading not found in any of the previously known manuscripts. Another interesting reading occurs at 1:25, where the redundancy of the first phrase, και ηρωτησαν αυτον + και ειπαν αυτω, "and they asked him" + "and said to him" has caused, e.g., ℵ a e sy^c, to omit the first phrase. Clearly, there were once two variants on a common phrase of speaking, and most manuscripts included both, by mistake. Here, though, in 𝔓⁵ it is the second phrase that is missing. The

---

A (Koine); B (Alexandrian); C ("Caesarean"); and D (Western), and came to the justifiable conclusion that already in the second century, as reflected in the papyri, these text-types were in existence (see esp. 294f., with chart); see also, above, n. 7, and Elliott (2003, 2010).

bigger problem is with the lacuna of 20:16, which, as already noted by the Grenfell and Hunt, does not have the required space to fit the usual reading ο λεγεται διδασκαλε. Peter Head (2004: 405), supporting an earlier view of Elliott and Park (cf. 1995: 34), suggests the reading should be ο λεγεται κ(υρι)ε, which follows in part the reading of D (it).

𝔓²² = John 15:25–16:2, 21-32. P.Oxy. 10.1228. C. 250–300 (Orsini-Clarysse). Shows no remarkable divergences from our known mss. and follows Alexandrian readings.

𝔓²⁸ = John 6:8-12, 17-22. P.Oxy. 13.1596. C. 250–350 (Orsini-Clarysse). Formerly recognized as an Alexandrian text-type closer to Vaticanus than Sinaiticus, with numerous spelling inconcinnities, especially marked by the usual itacisms. Nestle-Aland²⁷, ²⁸ note, however, the reading ευχαριστησας εδωκεν in verse 11, which is supported by the sometimes wayward 𝔓⁶⁶ and by Ν Γ 69 579—manuscripts with the exception of 579 that are hardly Alexandrian. Much the same can be said for the reading ωσει πεντακισχιλιοι in verse 10. In verse 22, the papyrus's reading ειδεν is supported more meagerly by א (!) D lat, showing a strong Western proclivity. With so few verses preserved, and with a rather high percentage of variant readings, it is best to see this papyrus as a mixed-type. It may date, however, to as late as the mid-fourth century CE.

𝔓³⁷ = Matt. 26:19-37; 26:37-52. P.Mich. 3.137. C. 250–350 (Nestle-Aland). Although the text of this papyrus is mixed, it shows a lot of Western affinities, and has been dated most recently by Orsini-Clarysse (2012) to c. 250–300, and hence it is still third century CE.

𝔓³⁹ = John 8:14-18; 8:18-21. P.Oxy. 15.1780. C. 275–300 (Orsini-Clarysse). Although the *ed. pr.* dated it to the fourth-century Alexandrian text-type, there is little here to go on: the variant word order of verse 14 is clearly Alexandrian, over-and-against D's singular word order; however, the only other variant, the absence of ο Ιησους in verse 21, is a reading shared by Alexandrian as well as Western text-types.

𝔓⁴⁵ = Gospels and Acts. P.Beatty 1. C. 200–250 CE (Orsini-Clarysse). This well-known Chester Beatty Papyrus 1, which originally contained all of the Gospels and Acts, has long been recognized and studied for its textual importance, and the fact that it displays a sometimes bewildering mixture of text-types (cf. Metzger 1992: 37; Royse 2007: 103–98), especially "Caesarean" (with Codex Washingtonianus [W]), although this text-type is referred to as "an abortive…textual complexion midway between the Alexandrian and 'Western'" (Epp 1997: 71f.), as noted above (n. 7). Unfortunately, the preservation of Matthew and John is rather scanty, whereas these gospels are the most common among our earliest papyrus mss. This, along with 𝔓⁴⁶ (most of the Pauline Epistles), P.Beatty 3, c. 175–225 CE (Orsini-Clarysse, date it to c. 200–225), is one of the most important papyrus manuscripts, because of its preservation of much gospel material. We also note a tendency to see early harmonized readings in 𝔓⁴⁵, which seems remarkable in so early a papyrus (see below, e.g., at Luke 9:27). For the singular readings in this papyrus, see esp. Elliott 2006, 2010).

𝔓⁵² = John 18:31-33, 37-38. P.Ryl. 3.457. C. 125–175 CE (Orsini-Clarysse). The famous John Rylands fragment, sometimes dated to as early as c. 100–125 CE. Our oldest New Testament papyrus, as short as it is, already gives a variant, the omission of a second <εις τουτο> in John, in a lacuna, whose space is not large enough to accommodate the phrase, hence the editorial emendation in all published versions of the text.[10] How are we to understand this "omission"? Is it simply a "scribal error"? Regardless of the cause, our concern is that arguably the most important New Testament papyrus ms. appears to show an error—or variant—in so small a fragment at such an early period, that is, one not chronologically far removed from a putative "autograph." Percentage wise, this represents a potentially huge omission, among the so few letters preserved on the fragment. How many more could there have been in the whole of the original text of 𝔓⁵²'s copy of the Gospel of John? That might prove troubling enough, were this the sizable scribal error that it appears to be, but that is not the view that we choose to espouse here. Rather, we believe that 𝔓⁵²'s omission does *not* represent a scribal error but preserves the more original reading against all extant mss. of John. In the "canonical" version of John, the second εἰς τοῦτο is altogether superfluous, sc., "*For this reason* (εἰς τοῦτο) I was born and *for this reason* (εἰς τοῦτο) I came into the world." It is a text that is hardly to be preferred to 𝔓⁵²'s reading,

---

10. The papyrus preserves portions of approximately thirty words. Because of the spacing of the letters, it is known that the fragment did not read the second εις τουτο in 18:37. The fragment is also marred by notable itacisms: ημε[ιν for ημ[ιν] in recto, line 1 (John 18:31) and ισ[ηλθεν for εισ[ελθεν in recto, line 4 (John 18:33), which is particularly flagrant. There is also an improper use of the diaeresis in the ϊνα of verso, line 2. The misspellings were evidently already in the writer's model, and who knows how far back they extend? Nevertheless, the overall error-rate is rather high for so early, and sparse, a papyrus.

sc. "For this reason (εἰς τοῦτο) I was born and I came into the world."[11] In any event, Nestle-Aland[28] (and earlier editions) should have at least noted the variant reading in their apparatus.

𝔓[64 [+67+4]] = Matt. 3:9, 15; 5:20-22, 25-28; 26:7-8, 10, 14, 15, 22-23, 32-33. Oxford, Magdalen College Gr. 17 + P.Monts.Roca 4.48, etc. C. 175–200 CE (Orsini-Clarysse). The main concern with the "Magdalene" papyri, of Alexandrian text-type, is the recent abortive attempts to date this earlier than the late second–third century CE. Textually, there is a somewhat anomalous reading in Matt. 5:28, where the pronoun αυτης is missing, with ℵ*, Tert Cl, corrected in ℵ¹ and f¹ only, whereas all other mss. read αυτην. This must represent a very early second-century reading. Further, some form of the phrase εἷς ἕκαστος in 26:22 is also missing (with ms. 1424).

𝔓[66]. This outstanding papyrus preserving large portions of the Gospel of John (P.Bodm. 2) and dating to around c. 200–250 CE (Orsini-Clarysse, et al.), has a remarkable number of corrections through the manuscript, numbering some 450 in all (Metzger 1981; 1991: 66), as well as many idiosyncrasies, including numerous itacisms. Its text type is mixed, with a large number of Western readings in chapters 6–7 and 11–12, as well as readings reflecting the Byzantine text-type. Most remarkably, though, is the number of singular readings in this early gospel fragment.[12] The addition, too, in the middle of John 21:6 of the long verse from Luke 5:5—about labouring all night at the nets—is also not only supported (with variants) by 𝔓[66], but also by ℵ¹ Ψ vg[mss] sa, that is, a mixture of Byzantine, Alexandrian, and Western text-types.

𝔓[70]. Now dated to c. 300–350 CE (Orsini-Clarysse), so outside the range of our present study.

---

11. Jack Finegan, some 45 years ago, suggested that the reading without the second <εις τουτο> was the more original, as well: "On the other hand, our papyrus is a very early witness, and it is possible that the repetition of the two words as found in the other manuscripts is the result of a later alteration. Without the two words in Line 2, the text would read: 'For this I have been born and have come into the world…' " (Finegan 1974: 90). The second εις τουτο could have originated in a scribe's marginal note meant to mark and identify a missing phrase in the body of the text that got omitted, whereas the marginal note itself was not intended to be copied into the body of the text. The phenomenon is sometimes loosely referred to as "Brinkmann's Rule"; see Daniel 1991, with Appendix (= Brinkmann 1902); Kotansky 2015: esp. 131 n. 6.

12. See, e.g., most recently Schrader 2017; cf. Royse 2007: 399–594.

𝔓⁷⁵. This other very famous Bodmer Papyrus (P.Bodm. 14–15), considered close to Vaticanus (B), and even the somewhat wayward 𝔓⁶⁶, has recently come under closer scrutiny, as to its date (Nongbri 2016). C. 175–225 (*ed. pr.*); 200–250 (Orsini-Clarysse). Palaeographically speaking, the papyrus is certainly not a fourth-century manuscript. The document is of great papyrological significance, to be sure, but it is not without its faults and oddities, including a remarkable number of itacisms for so neat and accurate a copy.[13] Although the scribe is often referred to as being careful and accurate, the issue here is not the scribe's tendency, but the character of the text that he copied.[14] Especially troublesome for the "stability" of a second-century text is the unusual reading of ονοματι Νευης, following the phrase ending with πλουσιος—the spelling of the name itself being a scribal error (*leg.* N<ιν>ευης)! This identity of the Rich Man at Luke 16:19, a reading supported by the Sahidic Coptic (sa) and a few minuscules, has forced Metzger to admit that "This reading perhaps was formerly more widespread than we are able to ascertain today" (Metzger 1977: 136; cf. Metzger 1971: 165f.]). He goes on to note that the two minuscules (36 and 37) preserve the following scholium: εὗρον δέ τινες καὶ τοῦ πλουσίου ἔν τισιν ἀντιγράφοις τοὔνομα Νινεύης λεγόμενον. The Sahidic text, which combines elements of both Alexandrian and Western types, does not therefore necessarily support 𝔓⁷⁵'s direct association with a text-type close to that of Vaticanus (B) alone, although it does show that in Egypt as early as the second half of the second century CE, an Alexandrian text-type must have been in circulation; but much the same can be said of other text-types, as well. Another unusual reading of 𝔓⁷⁵ is that found in John 10:7, where Jesus' pronouncement, "I am the door of the sheep" (ἡ θύρα τῶν προβάτων) becomes "I am the shepherd of the sheep" (ὁ ποιμήν, + sa ac cw).[15]

---

13. In just the single page published by Metzger 1991 [1981]: 68, pl. 9, one notes, e. g., μεισησει for μισησει at Luke 16:12; γεινωσκει for γινωσκει at 16:15; and the particularly bad κερεαν for κεραιαν at 16:17. For a more thorough analysis, see the daunting treatment in Royse (2007: 615–704, esp. 656–9, 704), on the many orthographic errors, nonsense readings, and slip-ups of 1-2 letters, although the text is judged to be highly reliable overall.

14. Royse (2007: esp. 356–9, 630–1, 656, 704, 902), softening Colwell's (1969) position somewhat, not only points out the omission of texts and harmonizations, but also a number of "significant" singular readings (166 in Luke and John) and corrections (116) in 𝔓⁷⁵, but also a scarcity of additions and low rate of error; see also Royse 1995: 345–6; Head 1990.

15. Royse 2007: 694–5; elsewhere, there might be other evidence of theologically motivated changes (cf. Parsons 1986: 474–5).

$\mathfrak{P}^{77}$ = Matt. 23:30-39. P.Oxy. 34.2683 + 64.4405. Originally dated to c. 175–200, it is perhaps later, c. 250–300 (Orsini-Clarysse). Although often considered "Alexandrian," the competing word order of verse 30, which is split between $\mathfrak{P}^{77}$'s reading with ℵ C K L W Γ Δ, etc. and that of B D $f^{1.13}$ 700 (only) suggests otherwise: the preferred reading here is the second, with relatively few witnesses that nevertheless shows an ancestor common to the two major text-families represented by Vaticanus and Codex Bezae. It is a reading that is quite old and probably original against that of $\mathfrak{P}^{77}$ and the welter of other mss. A different kind of split, however, is found in verse 39, where ερημος is absent (with B L ff² sy^s sa bo^{pt}), over-and-against its presence in a host of other mss., this time ones that combine ℵ, not Vaticanus (B), with D. Early Committee members (see Metzger 1971: 61) thought to explain ερημος's absence as due to copyists who felt it was superfluous after the verb αφιεται—hardly a convincing argument at all! There is also a variant spelling ορνιξ (for ορνις) in verse 37, not noted in Nestle-Aland²⁸.

$\mathfrak{P}^{90}$ = John 18:36–19:1; 19:1-7. P.Oxy. 50.3523. C. 150–200 CE (Orsini-Clarysse). Fragmentary as it is, the text does not appear to follow the unique word order of Sinaiticus (ℵ), η εμη βασιλεια that occurs three times in verses 36-37. Not noted in Nestle-Aland²⁸ is the divergent word order συ ει in 18:37 of $\mathfrak{P}^{90}$, a reading unique to this papyrus. Furthermore, in verse 39, the papyrus appears to read ουν ινα απολυσω, a reading also not noted in Nestle-Aland, even though it is attested in ℵ K U W Π (and 700; cf. Swanson 1995: 4:252). The rare reading with λαβων in 19:1 is also supported only by ℵ W (L 33 579)—hardly the Alexandrian "preferred" reading of Nestle-Aland²⁸. The variant reading at παλιν in 18:40 is also not noted by Nestle-Aland²⁸. At the beginning of 19:3 the presence of the initial phrase is supported by Alexandrian, with some Western, readings. The reading in verse 4 of εξηλθεν for και εξηλθεν, less favored in Nestle-Aland, is supported by $\mathfrak{P}^{90}$ along with ℵ D^s Γ f^{13} 33 565 lat sy^h—that is, a mixture of Alexandrian and Western readings—but a reference to $\mathfrak{P}^{90}$ is missing here in Nestle-Aland. One wonders if this is again due to a bias against Western readings, for $\mathfrak{P}^{90}$ here would show support from an early papyrus for a reading consigned to their apparatus. Remarkable—but this time recorded in Nestle-Aland—is the reading ο Πειλατος for the usual εξω ο Πιλατος, a variant attested elsewhere only in 579 and e. The εξω is entirely superfluous and may not have been original. Also the variant word order and wording (no ουδεμιαν!) in 19:4 finds support only in $\mathfrak{P}^{66}$ W (f^{13}) against all other witnesses and is probably more Western oriented (or "stratified") than anything else. Very peculiar, indeed, is the omission in Nestle-Aland²⁸ of the variant εκραζαν in $\mathfrak{P}^{90}$ (for εκραυγασαν), which is also supported by the original reading of Sinaiticus (ℵ*): εκραξαν (Swanson 1995: 4:254). Are Nestle-Aland intentionally skewing readings that do not support a strong Alexandrian bias? In any event, the reading of 𝔓⁹⁰ (ℵ*) may be more original, if one sees that the reading εκραυγασαν arose from an unintentional assimilation to the vowel-sequence of the words σταυρωσον, σταυρωσον that immediately follow, even though the second σταυρωσον does not occur in the papyrus itself, an omission supported only by 𝔓⁶⁶ and a e r¹—hardly an Alexandrian reading! Also non-Alexandrian, but widely supported by a mixture of texts, including Western (and hence rejected in Nestle-Aland's text) is the inclusion of αυτον in the same verse. Later in 19:6, the wording υμεις αυτον και is strongly Western (D^s L W Ψ *l* 844 e q r¹), as is the omission of αυτω in verse 7. There are also a number of itacistic spellings (Πειλατης, ημειν) throughout the papyrus.

𝔓⁹⁵ = John 5:26-29, 36-38. P.Laur. inv. PL II 31. C. 200–225 (Orsini-Clarysse); 250 CE, or early third century CE (Comfort 2002: 627; 2005: 75). There is a significant variant, it appears, at verse 26, where all mss. read εν εαυτω ουτως, followed by the phrase και τω υιω εδωκεν ζωην, which itself has a handful of variants as to word order. The problem with 𝔓⁹⁵ is that its **26** reads [ε]αυτω κα[ι + c. 14-15 letters], followed by **27** και εξουσιαν εδ[ωκεν, κτλ. Nestle-Aland²⁸ gives the text of 5:26 as follows: **26** ... εν εαυτω <u>ουτως</u> και τω υιω εδωκεν ζωην εχειν εν εαυτω. **27** και εξουσιαν εδωκεν, κτλ., sc. **26** "(For just as the Father has life in) himself, <u>thus</u> also to the Son he gave life to have in himself. **27** And he gave authority to him, etc." But 𝔓⁹⁵ has omitted altogether the word ουτως (underlined, above), a significant variant not noted in Nestle-Aland²⁸. Can we assume that it is a scribal error? If so, we are confronted once again, as with the text of 𝔓⁵², with a significant variant, in the form of an omitted word, showing up in a papyrus scrap that preserves so little—here, an error percentage rate of approximately 8.2 percent. The problem is compounded by what comes next: no matter the word order of **26**, beginning with και, whatever 𝔓⁹⁵ had does not match up in any way to any of the text, or variants, of Nestle-Aland²⁸. The number of missing letters in these lines of the papyrus is approximately 14, give or take one or two, at most. The Greek text as we have it at the end of **26**, is made up of more than 30 letters, twice as many that can fit into the lacuna of the papyrus after the κα[ι of **26**! The text of 𝔓⁹⁵ must have had something very different.¹⁶

---

16. We proffer the thesis, rather, that neither the text of 𝔓⁹⁵, nor its exemplar, ever had the word ουτως to begin with, and that the text of the second part of **26** had

𝔓⁹⁸ = Rev. 1:13-20. Although 𝔓⁹⁸ (= P.IFAO inv. 237b [+a]) is not a Gospel papyrus, it is relevant because of its possible early age, dating as early as the mid-second century CE, or even earlier, according to the *ed. pr.*, although Orsini-Clarysse now assign it to c. 200–250. Besides a simple spelling error in 1:13 (περ]ιζωσμμεν[ον, the text has a significant variant in omitting και ο ζων with the Vulgate and the Codex Gigas. The importance of this agreement with Codex Gigas (*g*., *gg*.) is that its text of Acts and Revelation preserves an Old Latin version, itself of the 13th century, which agrees with the fourth-century scriptural citations of Lucifer of Cagliari in Sardinia (Metzger 1977: 314; 1992: 75). The omission of this phrase, then, in this short fragment again pushes back a decidedly Western reading to as early as the second century CE, something not really in doubt, except among a limited few.

𝔓¹⁰¹ = Matt. 3:1-12; 3:16–4:3. P.Oxy. 64.4401. C. 250 CE. C. 200–300 CE (Orsini-Clarysse). At 3:11 the papyrus omits, amazingly, οπισω μου, an omission supported only by a couple of Latin mss. and the Sahidic (a d sa^mss; Cyp), a distinctly Western omission. The reading of 3:16]ως περιστ[εραν also points to the Western reading of καταβαινοντα εκ του ουρανου ως (D it vg^mss (sy^h)), which Nestle-Aland²⁸ disingenuously omit (again, probably because of their inherent bias against Codex Bezae). The edition also fails to note the absence of the [και], also supported by ℵ* B lat; Ir^lat, that is, a kind of pre-text type reading that must be original (hence, the bracketed word). The word order of 4:1 follows that of B C D L P W Γ Δ, *f* ^1,13, etc., that is, a rather mixed group of text-types, rather than the reading of ℵ K 892 1424, etc. A mixture is also supported by the word order of 4:2, και τεσσερακοντα νυκτας (ℵ D 892). What is remarkable about this sequence, however, is its dual attestation by Sinaiticus and Codex Bezae, against Vaticanus and the majority of witnesses. A rare, shared reading such as this with both a Western and Alexandrian witness in an early papyrus should give this reading the highest priority. It is neither "Western" nor Alexandrian, therefore, but older than both, sharing a common and, hence, very old, ancestor. The support of 892 which contains "many remarkable readings of an early type" (Metzger 1992: 64) also points to an

something very different than that preserved in our extant mss. Taking the whole context of vv. 26-27, we propose that 𝔓⁹⁵ must read something like the following: **26** [ὥσπερ γὰρ ὁ πατὴρ ἔχει ζωὴν ἐν] ἑαυτῷ, κα[ὶ τῷ υἱῷ ζωὴν **27** καὶ ἐξ]ουσίαν ἔδ[ωκεν, καὶ κρίσιν π]οιεῖν ὅτι υἱ[ὸς ἀνθρώπου ἔστι]ν., sc. ["Just as the Father has life in] himself, [to the Son] he also g[ave life and au]thority [even to e]xecute [judgment], because [he is the Son of Man]."

early reading that is pre-Alexandrian, despite the known affinities of this ms. with the Alexandrian text-type. In the reading at 4:1, above, on the other hand, 𝔓¹⁰¹ goes against ℵ and 892! At the end of 3:17, the papyrus also plainly reads ηυδοκ[ησα] for the usual ευδοκησα. This Atticistic reading is supported by ℵᶜ K 157 1424 (Swanson 1995: 1:25), mss. not followed in the reading at 4:1, again pointing to a mixed text-type for 𝔓¹⁰¹. There is also a clearly singular and remarkable reading at 3:10 which has και προς πυρ βαλλεται against all mss. readings with εις πυρ. (The papyrus reads [πρ]ος πυρ βα[λλεται.) Did the scribe miscopy the προς of προς την ριζαν, from the beginning of the line? At 3:17, the papyrus does not follow the Western "harmonized" gospel parallel συ ει. What it does do, however, is show the reading λυσαι at 3:11, in lieu of βαστασαι, a singular reading ignored by Nestle-Aland²⁸. It is clear, it would seem, that this reading, if present, is an assimilated reading of the text of Mark 1:7, for the papyrus has the apparent space for the Markan variant κυψας above the line, as well.

𝔓¹⁰² = Matt. 4:11-12, 22-23. P.Oxy. 64.4402. C. 300 CE. 300–400 (Orsini-Clarysse). The text is too short to identify any variants or assign a text-type and lies outside our chronological range.

𝔓¹⁰³ = Matt. 13:55-56; 14:3-5. P.Oxy. 64.4403. C. 175–225 CE (*ed. pr.*); third century (Orsini-Clarysse). Although thought to be Alexandrian, or Proto-Alexandrian (cf. Comfort 2005: 73), this seems premature, or perhaps even inaccurate. Based on our limited evidence, it is at best a mixed type ("Caesarean" and largely Byzantine): In verse 55, the name of Jesus' second brother can only be restored [Ιωσ]ης (K L W Δ 0106 *f*¹³ 565 1241 *pm* k qᶜ sa boᵐˢˢ), over-and-against [Ιωανν]ης, for which there is not enough space in the lacuna (c. 10 letters), as rightly noted in the *apparatus criticus* of N-A²⁸. This reading goes against ℵ, or its corrector, for example. But in 14:4, the lacuna (12-13 letters, max.) only allows the reading [γαρ Ιωαννης αυτω], found in ℵ² alone, that is, the name without the article—and not the reading with the shorter names.

𝔓¹⁰⁴ (see below).

𝔓¹⁰⁶ = John 1:29-35, 40-46. P.Oxy. 65.4445. C. 200–250 CE (*ed. pr.*); 200–300 CE (Orsini-Clarysse). Seemingly Alexandrian, or Proto-Alexandrian, but D (06) is missing this portion of John. Although 𝔓¹⁰⁶ sides with other early papyri (𝔓⁵, 𝔓⁶⁶, and 𝔓⁷⁵) in reading υπερ for περι in 1:30, it omits λεγων (with ℵ*) in 1:32 (a variant not noted in

Nestle-Aland²⁸). Also not noted is the word order εγω ελθον in 1:31 (shared with C*) nor the use of ως (with 𝔓⁵⁵, 𝔓⁷⁵ A B C) instead of ωσει in 1:32 (𝔓⁶⁶, et al.). These omissions in variants unnecessarily skew the text-type of 𝔓¹⁰⁶ towards Alexandrian. Particularly interesting are a handful of readings whereby 𝔓¹⁰⁶ sides with either the other early papyri or the Majority, but goes against readings of the beloved Sinaiticus (א), a number of which are singular readings, e.g., εκ του (in 1:32); μενον (1:32); ην Φιλιππος (1:44); the omission of the article before Jesus' name (1:43); and the omission of και (1:46), of which most represent uncorrected readings. Since Sinaiticus does share readings with the "Western" type frequently enough, these may belong to that text-type; cf. the omission of και at 1:46 (א a b e sy^{s.p}). The reading of εκλεκτος in א* (for υιος, at 1:34), supported by other "Western" readings (b e ff²* sy^{s.c}; codex Bezae is defective here), is also shared by 𝔓¹⁰⁶ (and 𝔓¹, see above) and, again, surprisingly omitted by Nestle-Aland²⁸. 𝔓¹⁰⁶ also omits ουτος at 1:41 and the article τον before Jesus' name in 1:42; singular readings (again, neither of which are recorded in Nestle-Aland²⁸). These might be scribal omissions, or true variant readings; in 1:44, however, the presence of του before Ανδρεου represents a singular reading that cannot be a scribal error. The reading εμβλεψας in 1:42, supported by א A B and 𝔓⁶⁶*, is also not found in the apparatus of Nestle-Aland²⁸. In 1:42, ηγαγεν follows the early papyri, א and B, but is again overlooked by Nestle-Aland²⁸.

𝔓¹⁰⁷ = John 17:1-2, 11. P.Oxy. 65.4446. C. 200–300 CE (Orsini-Clarysse). Of an irregular text-type, closest to the mixed type of Codex Washingtonianus (W), dated to the late fourth–early fifth century CE. If so, then we have an early example of a papyrus' text-type matching up with a later codex in a manner comparable to that seen 𝔓⁷⁵ in relationship to Codex Sinaiticus and Vaticanus (= Alexandrian text-types).

𝔓¹⁰⁸ = John 17:23-24; 18:1-5. P.Oxy. 65.4447. C. 200–300 CE (Orsini-Clarysse). In verse 24 the papyrus reads εδωκας (B K N Γ Θ 209; Cl; but cf. Swanson 1995: 4:236) for δεδωκας, a mixture of texts, including Byzantine (which may preserve early readings). One might consider it the preferred reading here; cf. also its reading κακεινοι in verse 24, as well (Swanson 1995: 4:236). Most of the other readings follow texts that are a mixture of Sinaiticus with Western support (e.g., the δε at the beginning of verse 4) or a mixture of Sinaiticus with Byzantine and Western readings, but not readings strongly supported by Vaticanus (e.g., 18:4's εξελθων ειπεν vis-à-vis εξηλθεν και λεγει).

𝔓¹⁰⁹ = John 21:18-20, 23-25. P.Oxy. 65.4448. C. 200–300 CE (Orsini-Clarysse). The variants at 21:18 are fairly widespread in the mss. tradition. The papyrus here preserves in lieu of the Majority reading αλλος σε ζωσει the following: αλλοι [αποισ]ουσιν σε, [οπου ου θελεις, κτλ.], which though not recorded in Nestle-Aland²⁸, provides a variant reading nowhere else attested. It appears to represent a simpler version of the mss. tradition by having others carry the elderly John where he does not want to go, with no reference to his being girded. In this, the reading complies somewhat with the second half of the verse, where א¹ D W 1 33 565 sy^hmg have αποισουσιν (απαγουσιν D) σε οπου, κτλ. Also in verse 24, the lacuna requires a και with B C W; Or *only*, another apparently early reading, not noted in Nestle-Aland²⁸. It also appears to support the reading και ο in verse 24 (found only in B D!), a reading that has been adopted by Nestle-Aland²⁸ (sans reference to the papyrus). The papyrus thus supports a very ancient pre-Vaticanus/pre-Western variant here. The papyrus, too, supports the widely witnessed bracketed reading [τι προς σε] in verse 23, which, surprisingly, is also not noted in Nestle-Aland²⁸.

𝔓¹¹⁰ = Matt. 10:13-15, 25-27. P.Oxy. 66.4494. C. 300–400 (Orsini-Clarysse). Others: C. 300 CE, or earlier (Comfort 2005: 76: c. 250–300 CE). This papyrus, whose singular readings are largely ignored by Nestle-Aland²⁸ (who correctly date it to the fourth century anyway) severely challenges our assumptions that the early papyrus readings will support the later witnesses of the great majuscules like Sinaiticus and Vaticanus. At Matt. 10:14, where all extant mss. read εξερχομενοι εξω, 𝔓¹¹⁰ gives the remarkable genitive absolute εξερχομενων υμων ("as you [pl.] are leaving…"). Further, where all mss. give εκτιναξατε our papyrus reads εκμαξατε, another singular reading not recorded in Nestle-Aland²⁸. In addition to these singular readings, the use of απο in lieu of εκ in a reading otherwise supported only by א C 0281 22 892 lat (whereas all other mss. have no preposition at all), suggests that a preposition must have been original to the text here, supported by so weighty a ms. as Sinaiticus and now 𝔓¹¹⁰. The papyrus also adds, moreover, the addition of η κωμης following πολεως, a reading though that is consigned to the apparatus in Nestle-Aland²⁸. As far as verses 25-27 go, we find further surprises: the unique word order of βεελζεβουλ επεκαλεσαν, a reading found only here (all other mss. have the words switched, a variant not noted except as a "minor variant," in Nestle-Aland²⁸, p. 820); and the reading τοις οικιοις (corrected to οικιους)—again not noted in Nestle-Aland²⁸—over-and-against τους οικιακους (τοις οικιακοις: B!). Further, although the Majority reading of Βεελζεβουλ is noted by the new edition, whereas both א and

B have Βεεζεβουλ, we do not read in their apparatus that Βεελζεβουλ is a corrected reading of Βεελσεβουλ. To the welter of variants on επεκαλεσαν at verse 25, the scribe of 𝔓¹¹⁰ has also written an original επεκαλεσεν in error, which was subsequently corrected to επεκαλεσαν. For so small a preserved fragment, this papyrus shows a remarkably high percentage of variant readings.

𝔓¹¹¹ = Luke 17:11-13, 22-23. P.Oxy. 66.4495. C. 200–300 CE (Orsini-Clarysse). The papyrus is very fragmentary, preserving only a handful of verses, but indicating noteworthy variants, nonetheless. At 17:12 it supports απηντησαν with 𝔓⁷⁵ A B K W Γ Δ Ψ 565 700 1424 𝔐 against υπηντησαν, with the weight of Sinaiticus and other witnesses (א $f^{1.13}$, etc.) behind it. At 17:12, again, it reads πορωθεν against all other mss., including 𝔓⁷⁵, a clear misspelling. It also gives the Western reading, supported by the Farrar Group, of του επιθυμησαι (D, 157, f^{13}) against 𝔓⁷⁵ and the Majority's οτε επιθυμησητε (with other minor variants). Remarkably, this variant is not even noted in Nestle-Aland[28] (again, perhaps, due to their bias against Western readings). It is surprising to see an early fragmentary New Testament papyrus preserving just a handful of extant letters that contains variant readings of a mixed nature and an anomalous spelling.

𝔓¹¹⁹ = John 1:21-28, 38-44. P.Oxy. 71.4803. C. 250 CE. This papyrus, preserved only in a long narrow strip, is too exiguous to offer any text-critical insights.

𝔓¹²¹ = John 19:17-18, 25-26. P.Oxy. 71.4805. C. 250 CE. The fragment contains only approx. 38 letters (recto/verso), so its text-type cannot be determined. However, it is significant to note that of these few letters one error is detected: a καί written κä, without the *iota* and with a diaeresis written above the *alpha*. That is an error-rate of 5.26 percent (counting two errors). Although, tenuous to judge on so short a fragment, it remains significant that an error occurs at all on even the shortest of papyrus fragments.

𝔓¹³⁴ = John 1:49–2:1. The Willoughby Papyrus. Third century CE. The otherwise relatively insignificant variant και τη τριτη [ημερα] in 2:1, in lieu of the wider tradition of reading καὶ τῇ ἡμέρᾳ τῇ τρίτη is supported only by B (03), Θ (038), and f^{13}. The fact that these witnesses belong to somewhat divergent groups ("proto-Alexandrian," "pre-Caesarean," or even Byzantine, despite the limitations of this nomenclature) points to variant reading that has its origins considerably earlier; hence, the papyrus' reading should not be overlooked: The Bodmer Papyrus 𝔓⁷⁵ here diverges from B, and the Alexandrian witness with which it has been duly compared, by siding with the majority of witnesses, including 𝔓⁶⁶. (𝔓⁷⁵ also contains the singular reading of the article τῇ before Κανά in the words that follow.) One wonders how many other variant readings a text such as the copy of the Gospel of John reflected by 𝔓¹³⁴ might have contained. As with the short, super early, Johannine text of 𝔓⁵², which already preserves an apparent singular reading, here so short a relatively early papyrus of only eighteen fragmentary words preserves an important variant. The percentage of variant readings found in the exiguous remains of an early papyrus text such as this remains astoundingly high: a putatively 5.55 percent variant ratio. We do not know, moreover, because of a gap at the end of the line, whether 𝔓¹³⁴ read μειζω with the Majority reading, or μειζων with 𝔓⁶⁶ (and a few other mss.). Nor do we know, because of the inopportune lacuna right before the fragment's πιστευεις μειζω [---/] (line 3 = John 1:50), whether 𝔓¹³⁴ sided with 𝔓⁶⁶'s singular reading υπο την συκην (for all other mss. reading υποκατω της συκης). What we do know, however, is that 𝔓¹³⁴ did not read απ αρτι before the verb ὄψεσθε (1:51), a reading based on a widely attested harmonization (with the text of Matt. 26:64) about which we shall have more to say in the discussion to follow.[17]

𝔓¹³⁷ = Mark 1:7-9, 16-18. P. Oxy. 5345. Late second/early third century CE. This recently published Oxyrhynchus papyrus offers a fragmentary, but important, remnant from Mark, a gospel which is under-represented among the early papyri. Remarkable is the reading in v. 17, where αυτοις is read in lieu of the usual αυτοις ο Ιησους (sc. και ειπεν αυτοις), for which Nestle-Aland²⁸ (nor Swanson 1995: vol. 2) cite no variants, but whose shorter reading here is, in fact, supported by Φ 1194, and some minuscules, according to von Soden (see *ed. pr., ad loc.*, p. 7). Whether this is an intentional variant or a scribal error (parablepsy due to an abbreviation of the *nomina sacra*, yielding a supposed sequence αυτοιςο͞ι͞ς), the fact remains that we are presented with yet another example of an early papyrus of very few lines offering an alternative reading. Also, in v. 8, both υδατι (with ℵ B Δ, 33 892*, etc. = Alexandrian) and πν(ευματ)ι (with B L bt vg, etc. = Alexandrian + "Western") occur without the preposition εν. In v. 16 αλε[εις may also be read instead of αλι[εις.

---

17. The text is based on Brice J. Jones' reading of the text in the *New York Times*, as reported by Tommy Wasserman, "A New Papyrus of the Gospel of John," in the blog: Evangelical Textual Criticism (Saturday, November 21, 2015).

𝔓¹⁰⁴ = Matt. 21:34-37, 43-45? P.Oxy. 64.4404. C. 175–200 CE (*ed. pr.*). second century (Orsini-Clarysse). The text of verses 34-37 offers little for comparison except to say that it supports the Majority reading of πάλιν at the beginning of line 36, against the καὶ πάλιν of ℵ* and sy^p. The text of the verso is so fragmentary as to admit the reading of only a few letters + minor traces. The issue is whether the text ever contained the famous "interpolation" of verse 44, presumptively from Luke 20:18. Most manuscripts contain the verse, but surprisingly here, it is omitted by D 33 it sy^s; Eus—that is the Western witnesses omit the verse, thus presenting an important "Western non-interpolation" against the majority of witnesses. Gregory R. Lanier (2016), in an important article, has recently firmly established the reading of the very difficult and scantly preserved verso to prove that 𝔓¹⁰⁴ follows the Western witnesses in omitting verse 44 against the welter of Alexandrian and other text-types.[18] His interpretation of the letters following verse 43 thus confirms the absence of verse 44 in an early copy of Matthew that is in congruence with the Western witnesses against the Majority; thus, 𝔓¹⁰⁴ (c. 150 CE) notably supports a primitive Western non-interpolation. We have left discussion of this papyrus to the end of this section because it offers a nice segue into the second half of our essay on the "Gospel-parallel" variants. On the one hand, we appear to have an interpolation in Luke 20:18 into the text of Matthew, following his verse 21:43. But the text of "Luke 20:18" that has been inserted into the welter of manuscripts of Matt. 21:44 is slightly different than all mss. readings of Luke 20:18! Here, then, is a comparison of the two texts:

Matt. 21:[44]: <u>καὶ</u> ὁ πεσὼν ἐπὶ τὸν λίθον <u>τοῦτον</u> συνθλασθήσεται· ἐφ' ὃν δ'ἂν πέσῃ λικμήσει αὐτόν (= Luke 20:18).

Luke 20:18: <u>πᾶς</u> ὁ πεσὼν ἐπ' <u>ἐκεῖνον</u> τὸν λίθον συνθλασθήσεται· ἐφ' ὃν δ'ἂν πέσῃ λικμήσει αὐτόν.

On this interpolation Metzger (1971: 58) briefly writes, "On the other hand the words are not the same, and a more appropriate place for its insertion would have been after ver. 42." The operative phrase here is "the words are not the same"—that is, we appear to have a "version" of Luke

---

18. One can read at least four portions of v. 43, the letters C KA for τ[ο]ὺς καρ[πού]ς, with all pointed letters practically non-existent, from a visual perspective. But what comes next in line 7 of the papyrus is problematic. Lanier, who examined the papyrus under magnification, was able to confirm the following reading (similarly as Comfort-Barrett and the INTF): [ΑΥΤΗC ΚΑΙ ΑΚΟΥ]ϹΑ[Ν]ΤΕϹΟ[Ι, for the end of v. 43 and the beginning of v. 45, sc. [αὐτῆς. Καὶ ἀκού]σα[ν]τες ο[ἱ, κτλ.

20:18 at Matt. 21:[44] that does not represent an exact copy of the text of Luke that we possess in all of our manuscripts of Luke 20:18! It must represent, rather, an important textual variant that seems to have been somewhat cavalierly ignored. If it is an assimilated text of Luke 20:18, as it clearly appears to be, one must account for the diversity of its reading and see in what manner it belongs to a body of important variant readings recorded in rather unexpected places. As an important "gospel-parallel" variant we will see in greater detail in the section to follow how such readings provide a valuable window into a seemingly overlooked source of variant readings that appear to stem from the early second century CE.

Summary of the Early Papyri

Already in 1995, Royse rightly observed the following in respect of the early papyri: "Despite these difference in exactness, the case of P^{75} shows clearly that at least some scribes were capable of care. Nonetheless, the other substantial early papyri show just as clearly that as a rule early scribes did not exercise the care evidenced in later transcriptions" (Royce 1995: 248). These words echo, as well, the sentiments, discussed earlier, of Eldon Jay Epp, a veritable giant among New Testament textual critics, who identified much diversity in the texts of the early papyri obtainable to him. With the availability of ever more early New Testament papyri, especially those in respect of the Gospels, we can see that $\mathfrak{P}^{75}$, as far as care of writing and affinity to important later codices like Vaticanus (B) are concerned, may represent something of a wistful exception to our hope that the early papyri would automatically reflect the readings of our often-favored and highly championed "Alexandrian" text-type—the "Neutral" original of Westcott and Hort's that formed the basis for all our subsequent New Testament critical editions. Westcott and Hort were not as ill-disposed towards Codex Bezae (B)—and the supporting Western readings, early versions, and Church Fathers—as some of their modern inheritors appear to be nowadays; nevertheless, the existence of a highly fascinating text-type, still ignominiously referred to as if some unwanted step-child, remains with us as a valuable, and beloved, family member. With all of its inherent difficulties and problems of text-variant interpretation, the Western tradition of manuscripts like Codex Bezae represents somewhat of a "prodigal" text whose presence can no longer be ignored for its viable witness to an early second-century tradition of text-history.

In the foregoing, we have begun by looking at the text-types and variant readings of a number of the early New Testament Gospel papyri to learn that diversity and even anomaly often characterize their readings and the kinds of texts they maintain. Of the early papyrological texts examined, a surprisingly sizeable representation of them offer readings not supported by the larger codices or other mss. (e.g., 𝔓⁵, 𝔓⁴⁵, 𝔓⁶⁶, 𝔓⁷⁵, 𝔓⁹⁰, 𝔓⁹⁵, 𝔓¹⁰¹, 𝔓¹⁰⁶, 𝔓¹¹⁰, and even 𝔓⁵², etc.), and an equal number of them show a proclivity towards "Western," or at least mixed, readings (e.g., 𝔓²⁸, 𝔓³⁷, 𝔓³⁹, 𝔓⁶⁶, 𝔓⁷⁷, 𝔓⁹⁰, 𝔓¹⁰¹, 𝔓¹⁰⁶, 𝔓¹⁰³, 𝔓¹⁰⁴, 𝔓¹⁰⁶, 𝔓¹⁰⁷, 𝔓¹⁰⁸, 𝔓¹¹¹, 𝔓¹³⁴, etc.). Although often claimed initially to be representative of Alexandrian text-types, closer examination shows that many of these papyri betray a strong inclination towards other families of manuscripts. At an early stage, as well, there seems to be a preponderance of singular readings and new variants not always recorded in Nestle-Aland²⁸. Some of the readings we have presented come as a result of fresh examinations of the papyri and their texts from edited editions and photographs available online; others are the result of new and challenging research by young scholars in the field. In the main, however, it has been our requisite aim to look at the individual papyri as whole and integral texts, to the extent that this is possible with fragmentary papyri, rather than to envision them as scattered readings individualized across the critical apparatuses of our New Testament textual editions.

The "Gospel-Parallel" Variants

In the Gospels, there occurs a number of variants that are based on readings from other gospel passages, usually the Synoptics, that have evidently served as the source for the variant reading. Most of these, which are fairly numerous and innocuous, give only single-word variants, or short phrases, of little immediate textual consequence; for example, in Mark 3:4 the widely attested reading αποκτειναι (א A B C D K Γ 1241 *l* 3311 𝔐 syʰ saᵐˢˢ bo) is apparently replaced by the equally widely read απολεσαι (L W Δ Θ *f* ¹·¹³ 28 565 579 700 892 1424 2542 latt syˢ·ᵖ saᵐˢ), a reading that, although of broad support, is rightly relegated to the *apparatus criticus*, since it is clearly based upon the parallel passage of Luke 6:9: απολεσαι. In other words, what has occurred is that a scribe at an early stage has *assimilated* the standard reading of Mark's αποκτειναι to Luke's απολεσαι in 6:9. Similarly, at Mark 3:3, the reading εγειρε εις το μεσον, in D c (e f) sa, shows the interpolated phrase και στηθι from the parallel passage at Luke 6:8, which reads εγειρε <u>και στηθι</u> εις το μεσον. In this case, a scribe at some early stage has not so much as assimilated the text to Luke, as *harmonized* it to the Lukan reading.

Hundreds of such "parallel-gospel" readings occur as variants in the textual apparatus of our Greek New Testament and have been identified by the editors of Nestle-Aland, for easy reference, by the siglum *p)*: "If a reading is derived from a parallel passage (especially in the Gospels), the sign *p)* is added," after which follows a brief description of various details of its use in the apparatus (p. 46*). In the 27th edition of Nestle-Aland (followed by the 28th) this has been simplified to read: "*p)* refers to parallel passages in the Gospels, which are listed in the margin at the beginning of the pericopes" (p. 57*).[19]

The profusion of these examples, although they remain largely unstudied, prove interesting for the textual critic in that they betray an early attempt at assimilating gospel parallels to one another, and ultimately of creating a harmonized gospel among at least the three principal Evangelists, but especially between Matthew and Luke.[20] Although seemingly of little textual importance, as far as the variants themselves are concerned in that they merely reproduce, at least in the shorter cases, known parallel texts from other gospels, there is much to be seen in these gospel-parallel variants for the mere fact of their existence. In the example above, for instance, the weight of the witnesses that reproduce the Lukan απολεσαι at Mark 3:4 shows such a wide range of text-familial support that the reading must go back to the second century; and even if it is an assimilated text, it must be rather ancient. For example, the reading is supported by ms. L (Codex Regius), which frequently agrees with Codex Vaticanus (B), albeit apparently not here; whereas W, in the portion that contains Mark 3:4, is distinctly Western, as is possibly the

---

19. Here, though, the final phrase is somewhat confusing: it is the parallel passages themselves (e.g., "Mt 12,9-14; L,6-11; 14, 1-6," sc., for Mark 3:1-6) that are provided in the margins at the beginning of each and every pericope, regardless of whether there is actually a parallel passage itself in the critical apparatus of that pericope or not. What should have been stated is that the siglum *p)* occurs in the apparatus, followed by the "parallel" reading and the supporting witnesses, in the verse in which it occurs, along with all the other variant readings. For the parallel, if present, one can then consult the corresponding (Synoptic) parallel provided in the marginal reference.

20. Vogels (1910) studied in detail the phenomenon of harmonized readings in Codex Bezae in an attempt to show the use of Tatian's *Diatessaron*, but his aim was not to examine the parallel-gospel readings in other mss., overall, nor to show how these readings might have differed from their source-gospels. Briefly, too, Fee (1993 [1978]) looked at the relationship of harmonized readings in respect of the Synoptic Problem. Koester (below) has examined in much greater detail the phenomenon of early harmonized texts among the early Patristic writers.

Sahidic (otherwise, Alexandrian); Δ is Alexandrian (in Mark), as is Ms. 892[21]; and Codex Koridethi (Θ) in Mark "is akin to the type of text which Origen and Eusebius used in the third and fourth century at Caesarea," as is also the text-family f^1 (Metzger 1992: 58, 61), as well as mss. 28, 565, 1424. Thus, the fact that this reading is represented among all three of the largest—and earliest—text-families, demonstrates that the reading extends rather far up the theoretical ancestral tree of text-familial relations. Such readings as this, whether assimilations or harmonies, must be at least as old as the common ancestor to the Alexandrian and Western (and "Caesarean") families, since the reading is attested in both (or in all) groups. It is a reading even represented by the Old Syra, which alone dates in origin to possibly the second century. All of this proves how very early assimilated texts and harmonies came to characterize the Synoptic Gospels. Helmut Koester (1957, 1989, 1990) demonstrated the use of harmonies in gospel texts already quoted by Justin Martyr (c. 150–160 CE) and even as early as the *Second Epistle of Clement* (c. 95–140 CE), that is, prior to the publication of Tatian's *Diatessaron*. The harmonies of the "gospel-parallels" by virtue of their attestation across all groups of text-families, themselves of second-century origin, all but proves that the harmonies themselves derive from copied texts that must originate at least in the earlier second century. The scribes who found them imbedded in the manuscripts that they copied presuppose even older manuscripts whose common ancestors had to be more enduring than the large text-families that preserved them. In certain scribal circles, it would seem, the harmonization and assimilation of gospel texts must have originated very soon after the circulation of the gospels in separate forms (cf. Hurtado 2006).

But the focus of this study is not on the numerous short "gospel-parallel" texts that proliferate among the three Synoptic Gospels (and with John, to a lesser extent). Rather, we aim to examine a special category of "gospel-parallel" texts: those longer examples whose readings actually provide heretofore unexplained variants that differ to some degree—sometimes remarkably so—from the source gospel from which they are said to derive. In the critical apparatus of Nestle-Aland (and other Greek New Testaments, for that matter), the parallel-gospel variants are duly noted, for the most part, but what has not been carried out systematically is an examination of the actual gospel-parallel against the canonical form of the verse from which it derives. Most students and scholars,

---

21. "It contains many remarkable readings of an early type, belonging chiefly to the Alexandrian text" (Metzger 1992: 64).

we presume, will take for granted that the gospel-parallel, whether an interpolation or a variant reading, will match the parallel text from which it comes. This, as we shall see, is far from the case, and what an examination of a handful of the most important of these will show is that the parallel texts go back to a *Vorlage* which, in point of fact, must be ancestral to the actual canonical versions of their source gospels: they provide readings, in other words, that do not match the exact wording or text of the parallel gospel from which they have been copied. Since these parallel texts are drawn from the same source from which all readings of the New Testament stem, namely, handwritten, copied manuscripts, they must represent faithfully copied texts that lie right before the scribes in some manuscript form or another, rather than, say, texts somehow cited from memory from a parallel passage.[22] In other words, these parallel readings prove to be invaluable witnesses to versions older than the extant manuscripts we possess of the source gospels from which they come. The "parallel-gospel" citations do not always agree with our canonical texts, nor any of their variant mss. readings, but preserve readings in manuscripts older than the ones that we now possess. They therefore offer a unique window into the text of the New Testament in the (early) second century, much in the same way that some of the texts of our early papyri, discussed above, have provided new readings that differ from the received texts of our abundant manuscript pool.

"Gospel-Parallel" Variants in Mark

In the Gospel of Mark there are relatively few important "gospel-parallel" variants, and here we are confronted with the enduring problem of the representation of Mark's text among the early papyri; one should note, however, that a handful of these in which an expanded, or variant, text is produced, based on the parallel texts of Matthew or Luke, occurs in $\mathfrak{P}^{45}$, which although early (c. 250 CE) is known for its singular readings and early harmonizing tendencies (see, e.g., Elliott 2004), which clearly go

---

22. Fee (1993 [1978]: 175), who notes briefly on these in a short article, is incorrect, then, in assuming that "Harmonization is far more likely to have occurred in the sayings of Jesus than in the Evangelists' narratives." The examples we present below show the opposite to be true. Harmonies do appear regularly in the sayings of Jesus in 2 Clement and Justin Martyr (Koester 1990: 360–402, for example), but that is because the passages that they do cite are mostly from a source containing Jesus' sayings, due to the possible "lectionary" provenance of the harmonies that may serve as their sources. Justin, however, does quote from narrative materials.

back to an earlier prototype, although its mixed text-type remains difficult to access, as it shows different tendencies in different parts of the Gospels and Acts (cf. Hurtado 1981).

Mark 6:7 (= Matt. 10:1)
The variant in D (565 ff² sy³) at Mark 6:7 which reads as follows, και προσκαλεσαμενος τους δωδεκα μαθητας (- 565) απεστειλεν αυτους ανα (+ δυο 565), stands in lieu of the Majority reading, και προσκαλειται τους δωδεκα μαθητας και ηρξατο αυτους αποστελλειν δυο δυο. (*f*¹ reads ηρξατο αποστελλειν ... δυο; cf. 892^mg). This looks like a harmonization of Matt. 10:1's και προσκαλεσαμενος τους δωδεκα μαθητας αυτου, a text, however, that does not have the *sending by two's*, but rather a phrase *granting them authority*. Does at least the absence of αυτου in the D (etc.) variant in Mark point to an older text in Matthew without it? No surviving ms. of Matthew shows its absence. This is perhaps too little to go on, but more significant would be the variant found at the end of 6:11. (The readings of *f*¹ and 892^mg appear to show harmonizations between the Majority reading of Mark 6:7 and D's, etc., version.)

Mark 6:11 (= Matt. 10:15)
The variant appended to the end of Mark 6:11 reads as follows:

αμην λεγω υμιν ανεκτοτερον εσται Σοδομοις η Γομορροις εν ημερα κρισεως ἤ τη πολει εκεινη (A 0133 *f* ¹·¹³ 𝔐 [Swanson (1995: 2:84 adds: K M N U Π *f* ¹·¹³ 2 157 700, etc., Ω]).

But, surprisingly, the mss. tradition of Matthew here reads something somewhat different:

αμην λεγω υμιν ανεκτοτερον εσται γη Σοδομων και Γομορρων εν ημερα κρισεως ἤ τη πολει εκεινη

The only notable variant in the extant manuscript tradition of Matthew here is the reading Γομορας (D L N P Θ *f* ¹). But curiously the noun γῆ is also absent in the single ms. L, but here the genitive plural of the city names is retained, as required for the dative noun γῆ ("...*for* the *land of* Sodom and Gomorrah," rather than the Mark parallel "...*for* Sodom and Gomorrah" [dat.]). Thus, it is difficult to say whether this supports the Markan "parallel" addendum, or represents a scribal omission; it is possible, however, that L preserves a remnant of the older Markan "parallel" reading not otherwise attested in the manuscript tradition of Matthew. This possibility is enhanced by the fact that a marginal reading of ms. 28 reads γη Σοδομοις η Γομοροις, that is, a reading that has seemingly conflated the variant readings of the Markan "parallel" reading with the γῆ (Swanson 1995: 2:84). In any event, the distinctive reading at Mark 6:11 of the text of Matt. 10:15 attested in Codex Alexandrinus and the Majority witnesses, shows (especially with the distinctive character of the families 1 and 13), a variant reading covering a fairly wide spectrum, even if much of it is Byzantine.

Mark 6:43
The text of this verse, which reads as follows, is characterized by a bewildering number of variants:

Και ηραν κλασμα__τα__ δωδεκα κοφιν__ων__ πληρ__ωματα__, κτλ. ($\mathfrak{P}^{45}$ B [L Δ] 892 2542 sy^{s,p})

And they picked up (enough) broken pieces (of bread) for the fullness(es) of twelve baskets.

Here, there are several variants, seemingly based on parallel readings (here simplified, somewhat):

a)
Και ηραν κλασματ__ων__ (κλασματα 28 *l*2211) δωδεκα κοφιν__ους__ πληρ__εις__, κτλ. (A D K N Γ, etc.)

And they picked up twelve baskets full of broken pieces (of bread), etc.

b)
Και ηραν __περισσευματα__ κλασματ__ων__ δωδεκα κοφιν__ους__ __πληρεις__, κτλ. (33^{vid} 700 1241, etc.)

And they picked up an abundance of broken pieces (of bread), twelve baskets full, etc.

c)
Και ηραν κλασματ__ων__ (-*f*^{1}) δωδεκα κοφινων πληρωματα, κτλ. (ℵ W *f*$^{1.13}$)

And they picked up the fullness(es) of twelve baskets of broken pieces, etc.

The variant of b) seems to follow the reading of Matt. 14:20, και ηραν __το__ __περισσευον__ __των__ κλασματων δωδεκα κοφινους πληρεις (*"And they picked up an abundance of __the__ broken pieces—twelve baskets full"*), itself paralleled by Luke 9:17, whose standard text reads και ηρθη __το περισσευσαν__ αυτοις κλασματων κοφινοι δωδεκα ("*And what was left over [in abundance] was twelve baskets of broken pieces taken up for them*"), but a major variant of which reads ηρθη περισσευμα αυτοις κλασματων κοφινοι δωδεκα ("*And an abundance was taken up for them—twelve baskets of broken pieces*"). The two texts of Matthew and Luke, of course, represent good examples of the conundrum of Minor Agreements against Mark; we suffice it to say that both το περισσευον and το περισσευσαν are matched by the Markan variant reading περισσευματα. The reading, attested by only a few minuscules and Latin mss., seems to preserve a variant reading of the more difficult Lukan and Matthean forms.

Mark 6:53, etc.
In respect of the omission of και προσωρμισθησαν based on parallels in D W Θ *f* [1, 13] 28. 265. 700. 2542 it sy[s.p], this shows a kind of Western non-interpolation based on a Minor Agreement. Also, the nearby parallel at Mark 7:8, whether at the beginning of the verse, or the end, is difficult to assess, but does not present any unusual internal variant readings. The addition, as well, at Mark 8:20 of the noun αρτους, from Matt. 16:10, though not presenting a variant reading, is interesting in itself in being preserved by 𝔓[45] ℵ, C, W, etc.; whereas in Mark 8:34, the presence of ελθειν (ℵ A B C², et al.), for ακολουθειν (𝔓[45] C* D W Θ, etc.)—the former presumably assimilated to the verb in Matt. 16:24—shows a change from N-A[25]; it sides with 𝔓[45] and many Western traditions against Sinaiticus. Similarly, in 8:36, the wording of the saying on "gaining the world" is assimilated to the text of Matt. 16:26 in 𝔓[45] and A, etc.—again—over-and-against the reading of ℵ B, etc. These variants that "split" among early families of manuscripts clearly demonstrate an early second-century tendency towards assimilation, if not out-right harmonization. The ninth-century bilingual ms. Δ (with the sa[mss]), which in Mark is representative of an Alexandrian text-type (Metzger 1992: 58) is remarkable in presenting the remnants of a harmonization in reading ελθειν και ακολουθειν.

Mark 9:2
In Mark 9:2 the addition of εν τω προσευχεσθαι <u>αυτους</u> ("and while <u>they</u> were praying") in 𝔓[45] W *f* [13] (traditionally, "Caesarean" in respect of the latter two) shows a distinctive harmonization with the text of Luke 9:29, which has, however, in all mss., the reading: εν τω προσευχεσθαι <u>αυτον</u> ("and while <u>he</u> was praying"). Since the presence of the disciples is required in both Gospels, there was no need for the shared tradition behind the reading αυτους to have intentionally changed a Lukan reading that was in the singular; the reading with αυτους, in other words, must

represent a possible "pre-canonical" reading of Luke not attested in any ms. tradition of Luke. It must be quite old; indeed, it should be the preferred reading, being both more "difficult," and representing a reading that cannot be so easily explained as deriving from αυτον (it is more easy to explain αυτους > αυτον, than vice versa); Jesus praying alone, at a slight remove from the disciples, can be more readily accommodated to being the object of a transfiguration vision, rather than having a group of three disciples praying together *with* Jesus, while he is being transfigured. The variant reading in Mark among 𝔓⁴⁵, W, etc., must then represent the more original reading of Luke's Gospel. This same group of mss. (𝔓⁴⁵ W *f*¹³) is also responsible for the harmonization of και διεστραμμενη at Mark 9:19 (from both Matthew and Luke). An early assimilation of Mark 9:31 (μετα τρεις ημερας) to Matt. 17:23 (τη τριτη ημερα) is also preserved in a wide range of good mss. (cf. Mark 10:34).

Mark 10:27
The variant in D (it) about the saying that "all things are possible with God" (εστιν, παρα δε τω θεω δυνατον = Luke 18:27) vs. all other mss. (αλλ' ου παρα θεω· παντα γαρ δυνατα παρα τω θεω) begins in Mark a group of distinctly Western Gospel parallel "assimilations" that are much more common among the variants in the Gospel of Luke (see below). The whole word order of this *logion* in both here and in Luke is disturbed, and one wonders if the differences result from a very early circulation of the saying in oral form. (Witness, for example, the relative ease with which the word order becomes indistinguishable in English: "With God all things are possible" vs. "All things are possible with God.")

Mark 11:8
Instead of αλλοι δε στιβαδας κοψαντες ἐκ των αγρων (ℵ B [εκοπτον C] L Δ Ψ 892* [sy^hmg sa]; Or), (*"and others, having cut leafy branches from the fields"*), another group of mss. reads the following:

αλλοι δε στιβαδας ἐκοπτον ἐκ τῶν (-28) δένδρων (αγρων 579) και εστρωννυον εἰς (- D) τὴν ὁδὸν (A Δ Γ *f* ¹·¹³ 28, 1241, 1424, etc.), (*"and others were cutting leafy branches from the trees and spreading them on the road"*).

The reading derives from the gospel-parallel at Matt. 21:8:

αλλοι δε εκοπτον κλαδους ἀπὸ των δενδρων και εστρωννυον ἐν τῇ ὁδῷ.

But here the text that those mss. use at Mark 11:8 must have all differed slightly from the received text that was borrowed from Matt. 21:8. The κλαδους, of course, was dropped, because of the assimilation to the initial group of mss.'s στιβαδας; but in other minor details where exactness might not only be expected, but required, we find surprising differences: εκ for Matthew's απο, and εις την οδον for Matthew's εν τη οδη (cf. the assimilated readings of K N Θ 565, 579, 700, 2542, *1844*, at Mark 11:8). Admittedly, Matthew's απο could have been "back"-assimilated to the Markan text, but there should not have been a change in the final phrase: the reading of εις την οδον must reflect an older reading of Matt. 21:8 not attested in all extant mss. of Matthew. What is also notable is that the reading of D at Mark 11:8 that has been assimilated to the text of Matt. 21:8, has at Matt. 21:8 itself εστρωσαν (ℵ* D it; Or) for εστρωννυον. In other words, D's assimilated reading of εστρωννυον is not the verb actually found at D's own reading of Matt. 21:8, which has εστρωσαν. This suggests that εστρωννυον is considerably older than the text of D itself.

Mark 13:2

The end of Mark 13:2 has a verse added in some Western mss. that derives from a reading found elsewhere in Mark, not from a parallel in another Gospel. The reading is evidently from 14:58. Let us compare the two readings:

13:2 + και δια τριων ημερων αλλος <u>αναστησεται</u> <u>ανευ</u> <u>χειρων</u> (D W it)

14:58 και δια τριων ημερων αλλον αχειροποιητον οικοδομησω (maj. mss.)
και δια τριων ημερων αλλον <u>αναστησω</u> <u>αχειροποιητον</u> (D it)!

The variant attached to 13:2 (D W it), interestingly, has its closest parallel to the text of D it, where the readings, again, differ. Since the D's (etc.) text of 13:2 is not the same as that of the text of D itself at 14:58, its apparent source, it must be older than the second-century tradition behind D. If the scribe of D (etc.) is borrowing at 13:2 from a text of Mark 14:58, he is clearly not flipping through his own ms. to find his reading of Mark 14:58, but is copying from a text that already has this borrowed reading from 14:58 inserted into his text at 13:2; the reading of that verse comes from his exemplar, which, for all we know, has to be at least several generations older than D—again, clearly a reading more ancestral than that of D's own text of 14:58. In other words, the reading must be even older than the common ancestor of W and D (+ it)—it is important to note that the reading of W here is in a so-called "Caesarean" section of the ms., not a Western part (Metzger 1992: 56f.). Therefore, the reading certainly is more ancient than, and therefore preferable to, the reading of Nestle-Aland[28] at 14:58, which, of course, does not place the reading of 13:2 at 14:58.

Mark 15:3

Following a number of assimilations of little text-variant consequence in chapter 14 of Mark (14:9, 21, 24, 25, 27, 38, 40, 41, 47, 62, 65),[23] the end of 15:3, καὶ κατηγόρουν αὐτοῦ οἱ ἀρχιερεῖς πολλά, adds the following harmonized reading of widespread attestation, apparently from Luke 23:9 (cf. Matt. 27:12):

> αυτος δε ουδεν απεκρινατο (N W Δ Θ Ψ f[13] 33 565 1424 2542[s] a c vg[mss] sy[s.h] sa[ms]).

But Luke's own text at 23:9 reads as follows:

> αυτος δε ουδεν απεκρινατο αυτω (with Matt. 27:12 reading only ουδεν απεκρινατο).

No single manuscript of Luke includes the phrase without αυτω, but here it is Pilate who is not answered and not the chief priests, so there is good reason for the αυτω to be dropped by scribes in the harmonization process. Judging from the wide swath of mss. in Mark's reading here (Alexandrian, Western, Caesarean), for which two in particular, Koridethi (Θ) and Athous Laurae (Ψ), preserve texts of Mark that are judged particularly early, we must have here an especially early harmonization.

Mark 15:15b (20), 17

The reading και παρεδωκεν τον Ιησουν φραγελλωσας of nearly all mss. of Mark 15:15 (repeated in 15:20), has a (mostly) word order variant, from Matt. 27:26, that preserves it more or less verbatim: (+ και 700) τον δε (− 700) Ιησουν φραγελλωσας παρεδωκεν in D 565 700 2542[s] (k); however, Vaticanus (B) presents it slightly differently as παρεδωκεν δε τον Ιησουν φραγελλωσας, as if the Matthean "parallel" that the ancestor to the scribe

---

23. In v. 62, the συ ειπας οτι (of Θ f[13] 565 700 pc; Or) adds a οτι not found in the mss. of Matt. 26:54; and in v. 65 (D Θ 565 700 (a) f sy[p]) αυτου τω προσωπω differs from Matt. 26:67's εις το προσωπον αυτου. An additional variant in Mark 14:65, deriving from Matt. 26:68, follows the source text closely, with the exception of Δ's singular reading of πεμψας for παισας.

of B had before him preserved the Markan word order + the Matthean δε, as either an assimilation or a harmonized reading. In 15:17, the words χλαμυδα κοκκινην και (from Matt. 27:28) in Θ f^{13} 565, 700, etc., form an early, if not somewhat peculiar, "harmonized" reading: *"...a scarlet robe and purple (garment)."*

"Gospel-Parallel" Variants in Matthew

Matthew 8:13
Near the end of the pericope on the Centurion of Capernaum (a Q-like passage), a handful of mss. (ℵ*.2b C Θ f^1 g^1 sy^h) add, from the gospel-parallel in Luke 7:10 (και υποστρεψαντες εις τον οικον οι πεμφθεντες ευρον τον δουλον υγιαινοντα), the following verse: και υποστρεψας ο εκατοναρχος εις τον οικον αυτου εν αυτη τη ωρα ευρεν τον παιδα (+ αυτου sy^h) υγιαινοντα (αυτον *loco* τον παιδα N 33. 1241). This clearly represents a harmonized reading that has been adapted to the Matthean narrative (e.g., the παῖς instead of Luke's δοῦλος, and so on), so that it is difficult to assess its value, if any, for text-critical purposes. The nature of Matthew's different text requires more than the usual amount of editing on the adapter's part.

Matthew 9:20
In the story of the haemorrhagic woman, a single ms. L, interpolates a phrase apparently adapted from John 5:5 (εχουσα εν τη ασθενεια), with a necessary change in the gender of the participle (εχων). Manuscript L (Codex Regius, eighth century), though badly copied, is a faithful representative of a B-type text (Codex Vaticanus [cf. Metzger 1992: 54]), so this reading is a bit surprising if it indeed represents some kind of harmonization from a text that is not, in fact, a parallel.

Matthew 13:13
The Matthean adaption in verse 13 of the quote from Isa. 6:9f. has several variants, of which one represented by 1424 ff¹ sa mae, is an *assimilation*, for the most part of Luke 8:10b's text. The other, found in D Θ $f^{1.13}$ it; (Eus), is a *harmonization* of Luke 8:10b's text with that of Mark, in that it adds to the end of Luke's saying the phrase μηποτε επιστρεψωσιν from Mark 4:12.

Matthew 17:[21] (cf. Matthew 18:[11])
This passage, as noted by Metzger (1971: 43) represents an assimilated text from the parallel at Mark 9:29. However, the two passages differ in several key places:

[21] τουτο δε το γενος <u>ουκ εκπορευεται</u> (εκβαλλεται ℵ²; <u>εξερχεται</u> 118. 209. *l* 2211) ει μη εν προσευχη και νηστεια (ℵ² C D K L W Γ Δ *f*¹·¹³ 565. 700. 892ᶜ. 1241. 1424. *l* 2211 𝔐 lat sy⁽ᵖ⁾·ʰ (mae) boᵖᵗ).

Mark 9:29: τουτο το γενος <u>εν ουδενι δυναται</u> εξελθειν ει μη εν προσευχη (και νηστεια, var.).

In addition to the extra δε, the verbs of expulsion, except in the variant of the third example which gives another form of the original Marcan verb, are remarkably different. First, though, it should be noted that this assimilated variant has a very broad support from witnesses across a wide spectrum of family text-types; therefore, it must be quite old even if it is an assimilation. The three variant readings of "casting out," then, must be seen as old Marcan variants that never made it into the majority of manuscript readings of Mark itself; they are readings that each independently derive from mss. that the copyists of the numerous scribes who recorded them must have possessed in some form in the exemplars at their disposal. No current manuscript of Mark has the δε of [21], but, amazingly, at least two important later mss., 579 and 33 (frag.), give the variant <u>ουκ εκπορευεται</u>, a particularly good Markan verb, by the way! These important readings, even though they are contained as singular readings in important mss., are not recorded in Nestle-Aland²⁸, but are found in Swanson (1995: 2:146). The fact that ουκ πορευεται is attested in mss. 33 (the "Queen of the Cursives") and 579—both important representatives of Alexandrian text-types—as well as being imbedded as a variant reading in a wide swath of mss. of Matt. 17:[21] points to an old reading of Mark that must precede all other present mss. readings of the second gospel. It powerfully vouches, as well, for the importance of the eclectic approach to textual criticism. Even the reading of εξερχεται in the second corrector of Sinaiticus should be given precedence over the Markan reading that stands in the printed Greek edition of Nestle-Aland²⁸.

We add here, as well, that at Matt. 18:[11], we find a similar verse added between verses 10 and 12, a verse that derives from Luke 19:10. The reading here, except for the mss. that include just σωσαι, as opposed to ζητησαι και σωσαι in all mss. of Luke 19:10, does not show an appreciable difference with the text of Luke; nonetheless, the very wide attestation of the variant of Matt. 18:[11] with σωσαι alone (D K Lᵐᵍ N W Γ Δ Θᶜ 028ᵛⁱᵈ 565 579 700 892ᶜ 1241 1424 𝔐 lat syᶜ·ᵖ·ʰ boᵖᵗ) suggests a variant reading older than any of the extant mss. of Luke 19:10.

Matthew 19:9
At the end of the verse yet again, a handful of gospel-parallel variants have been added from apparent parallels from Mark 10:12 and Luke 16:18, each of which has its own variants, as well:

Matt. 19:9 (a): και ο απολελυμενην (απολυμενην Θ 565, + απο ανδρος 579) γαμων (γαμησας B K Z Γ 700 892 𝔐) μοιχαται (B C* K N W Z Γ Δ Θ 078 ƒ^{1.13} 33 565 579 700 892 1424 𝔐 lat sy^{p.h} bo)

Matt. 19:9 (b): ωσαυτως και ο γαμων απολελυμενην μοιχαται (𝔓^{25} mae)

Mark 10:12: και εαν αυτη απολυσασα τον ανδρα αυτης γαμηση αλλον μοιχαται (+ var.)

Luke 16:18: ο απολελυμενην απο ανδρος γαμων μοιχευει

The added reading at **Matt. 19:9 (a)** certainly looks like a harmonization of Luke and Mark: the καί and the μοιχᾶται (and possibly the variant γαμησας) come from Mark, whereas the ο απολελυμενην (+ the απο ανδρος of 579) γαμων comes from Luke. The fact that the phrase απο ανδρος in Luke 16:18 is omitted by the Western D sy^{s.c.p} bo^{ms} and is also absent, with the exception of 579, in the witnesses of the harmonized reading at Matt. 19:9, proves that the text without the phrase (in D, et al., at Luke 16:18), must be the more original reading: it is absent in "gospel-parallel" reading at Matt. 19:9, supported by a wide spectrum of manuscript families. This parallel reading, insofar as it is attested in all the major manuscript families, has to stem from a *Vorlage* that is ancestral to all of these "families," which themselves originate in the second century CE, including the "Western" group. The reading without απο ανδρος is thus probably pre-mid-second century, and ultimately derives from a harmonizer whose text of Luke 16:18 did not include the phrase about the husband. We add, in passing, here that at the beginning of Matt. 9:19, we find some minor variants based on parallel readings (assimilations) to the text of Matt. 5:32.

Matthew 19:16-17
In the pericope about The Rich Young Man, there are a couple of gospel-parallel readings, in verses 16 and 17. In 19:16, the query about, "What (good) shall I do to have eternal life?" (ποιήσω ἵνα σχῶ ζωὴν αἰώνιον;) contains a variant assimilated to Luke 18:19 (ποιήσας ζωὴν αἰώνιον κληρονομήσω;), with no appreciable differences with the Lukan

"canonical" reading. However, in the next verse, the rhetorical question, τι με ερωτας περι του αγαθου; εις εστιν ο αγαθος, has a variant culled from parallel passages in Mark 10:18 = Luke 18:19, sc. τι με <u>λεγεις αγαθον; ουδεις</u> αγαθος <u>ει μη εις ο θεος</u>, with a couple of minor differences in several mss. What is noteworthy here, however, is the new variant in the apparatus of Nestle-Aland[28], according to a Marcosian reading found in Irenaeus. It reads as follows: τι με λεγεις αγαθον εις εστιν ο αγαθος, sc. "Why do you call me good? There is One (who is good): The Good (One)!" Here the saying of Marcus, from the early second century CE, is close to the Markan/Lukan parallel reading for the first half of the verse (τι με λεγεις αγαθον;), but identical to the Matthaean in the second part (εις εστιν ο αγαθος), that is, without the addition of ο θεος / ο πατηρ, as in some variants. It looks as if we have here a very primitive harmonization of texts.

Matthew 20:22, 23
The pair of variants και το βαπτισμα ο εγω βαπτιζομαι βαπτισθηναι appended to each of the verses 22 and 23, from Mark 10:38, 39, respectively, do not offer any significant variants. Here we suggest that the consulted mss. show readings that are the same as our present mss. of Mark.

Matthew 20:28
A significant variant appended to the end of verse 28 in D Φ (it vg[mss] sy[c. hmg]) has been compared to the logion in Luke 14:8-10 about places of honor while being seated at a banquet. The account in Luke has no other parallel. Metzger (1971: 53) is no doubt correct in stating, "This interpolation is a piece of floating tradition," but errs in calling it "an expanded but inferior version of Lk 14:8-10." The similarities between it and Luke 14:8-10 have wholly to do with subject matter only; there are absolutely no verbal similarities whatsoever between the Greek texts of either passage, so that it is impossible to say that the writer of the Matthean logion could have been influenced by, or even familiar with, the Lukan parallel. Nor can the logion be dismissed, out of hand, as an insignificant "Western" interpolation, seeing that a version of it occurs, as well, in Φ (Codex Beratinus), a deluxe purple vellum written in silver ink, that is not otherwise Western, but Koine and Caesarean (see, further, on Matt. 27:16, below). It seems, rather, that the logion appended to Matt. 20:18 is rather a Q-like passage, whose parallel to Luke 14:8-10 is absent in Matthew; it occurs in a context of Matthew/Luke that is heavily populated with Q-pericopae. The logion is certainly a pre-Western text and hence quite early.

Matthew 23:[14]
On the interpolation of this passage at the end of 23:13 from Mark 12:40 or Luke 20:47, Metzger (1971: 60) rightly observes that it is absent from the best and earliest witnesses of all three major text-families. The differences in the text of Matt. 23:14 from the source-gospels' readings (Matthew's κατεσθίετε vs. κατέσθοντες / κατεσθίουσιν; and Matthew's διὰ τοῦτο λήμψεσθαι vs. οὗτοι λήψονται) are not textually significant, since they can be explained as scribal adaptations of the syntax to Matthean style and context: in Matthew, the Scribes and Pharisees are being addressed directly, in the second person plural.

Matthew 24:31
At the end of verse 31, a long phrase from the Gospel of Luke (21:28) has been added in D 1093 it, sc., "Now when these things begin to take place, *look up* (ἀνακύψατε) and raise your heads, because your redemption is drawing near." The "D" text in Matthew, in all instances, is the same as that in Luke, except for Luke's verb for "looking up" (ἀνακύψατε), which literally means "to lift up the head" (LSJ, s.v.), a verb that, in being redundant with Luke's own verbal phrase that follows, ἐπάρατε ("raise [your heads]"), has occasioned the remarkable variant ἀνακαλύψατε, sc. "*unveil* and raise your heads" in the Lukan mss. of W Ψ f^1. The variant in the Matthean interpolation, on the other hand, has neither verb, but instead reads ἀναβλέψατε, sc. "*look up* and raise your heads," sc. αρχομενων δε τουτων γινεσθαι αναβλεψατε και επαρατε τας κεφαλας υμων διοτι εγγιζει η απολυτρωσις υμων. Whatever the original verb, something in the mss. of Luke must have occasioned the variants, because none of the extant readings makes good sense. Even the interpolated verse's ἀναβλέψατε, the most meaningful of all the variants, should be viewed as an improvement on Luke's ἀνακύψατε. But here we proffer the view that Luke originally had only a single verb, ἀνακύψατε, which, in being somewhat uncommon and of limited classical usage was glossed with the phrase ἐπάρατε τὰς κεφαλάς, that is, ἀνακύψατε = ἐπάρατε τὰς κεφαλάς, sc. "to raise up" = "to lift up the heads." Thus two verbs were introduced, creating, first, a redundancy, and then the additional variants. Even the Matthean interpolation's ἀναβλέψατε, although a second-century variant, must be seen as an attempt to ameliorate a difficult Lukan text; the fact that Matthew's gospel-parallel variant cannot be original finds support, too, in the fact that its presence creates an incorrect word order: one cannot look up and see *before* one raises the head! The word order should have been ἐπάρατε τὰς κεφαλὰς ὑμῶν καὶ ἀναβλέψατε, sc., "raise your heads *and look up*!"

That the phrase ἐπάρατε τὰς κεφαλάς is a gloss is also supported by D's absence of the pronoun ὑμῶν after the phrase, "lift up the heads" (a variant not noted in Nestle-Aland[28]). The original gloss, reflected more closely in D's reading here, would not, of course, have had a pronoun. That the D-reading of Matt. 24:31—and hence all of the readings of these "gospel-parallel" variants—are considerably older than the text of D itself is not only proved by the fact that it records readings in variance with the canonical text of Luke—and its variants *ad loc.*—but also by virtue of the fact that D's *own* text *at* Luke 21:28 is different from this "imbedded" version of Luke 21:28 in Matt. 24:31! For not only does D's reading at Luke 21:28 preserve the standard ανακυψατε και επαρατε (not αναβλεψατε και επαρατε), it contains a peculiar, additional variant there in ερχομενων (D 13) in lieu of αρχομενων. D's version of Luke 21:28 at the end of Matt. 24:31 must be older, of course, than a text that has subsequently introduced ερχομενων for αρχομενων.[24]

Matthew 27:16
At Matt. 27:16 the manuscript Φ, as well as *pc* (*f*[13], vg[mss] [sy[s,h]] mae), offers a remarkably different "gospel-parallel" reading than that found in the Nestle-Aland[28] text of Mark 15:7.[25] Ms. Φ (043), a sixth-century manuscript in Tirana (Staatsarchiv, Nr. 1), is supported by the "Ferrar Group" of minuscules, the Vulgate, the Sinaitic Syriac (Old Syra), and by the *versio mediae Aegypti* (mae = Middle Egyptian Coptic). Apart from Φ

---

24. We add, in passing, that the minor gospel-parallel variants at, e.g., 25:27 (sg. for pl.) and in ch. 26 (26:7 [πολυτιμου for βαρυτιμου], 26 [ευχαριστησας for ευλογησας], 28 [added καινης], 36 [αυτοις for τοις μαθηταις], and 70 [added ουδε επισταμαι D Δ *f*[1] it sy[s] = a harmonization with Mark 14:68] show assimilations (and a harmonization) that often bridge large, competing text-families, and hence show a process of assimilation earlier than the individual text-families to which they belong, and hence they must be quite old. Further, at the end of 26:39, verses interpolated from Luke 22:43-44 occur in C[mg] *f*[13]. On the antiquity of these added verses from Luke (where they appear in double brackets [[*a,b,c*]] in N-A) "from an early source, oral or written, of extra-canonical traditions concerning the life and passion of Jesus," see Metzger 1971: 177. The Matthew version offers no variants with the mss. of Luke.

25. Although all previous editions of Nestle-Aland cite Φ here, it has since been removed by the 28th edition. It also has removed the word στασιν from the reading. Swanson (1995: 1:279) has only *f*[13] and 1071 with this reading (plus another reading, based on Luke 23:19, in ms. 124, where it is exactly verbatim). Further, ms. 1346 gives the same reading as above but with ην coming after the participle βεβλημενος. There is also a long reading in ms. S not found elsewhere.

and family 13, usually assigned to the sometimes dismissed "Caesarean" text-type, all of these have a "Western" textual orientation, even if these designations are often misleading and inaccurate.

The text of Matt. 27:16 begins as follows: εἶχον δὲ τότε δέσμιον ἐπίσημον λεγόμενον °[Ἰησοῦν] Βαραββᾶν. To this our manuscripts have appended the "Markan" parallel from 15:7b: ὃς διὰ φόνον καὶ στάσιν ἦν βεβλημένος εἰς φυλάκην: sc., "Now they had then a notorious prisoner called [Jesus] Barabbas, *who because of murder and sedition was thrown into prison*" (the "Markan" addition in italics). It looks as if, of course, the Matthean addition again represents a manuscript tradition of harmonization of gospel-parallel readings. The beginning of either verse—that of Matt. 27:16(a) vs. that of Mark 15:7a—differs, as shown below.

The text of Mark 15:7, to which Nestle-Aland[28] compares this reading, is rather different, than the Matthean addendum, however. Placed side-by-side, with the similarities underlined, one can see the general lack of specific correspondence:

Mark 15:7b:
μετὰ τῶν στασιατῶν δεδεμένος οἵτινες ἐν τῇ <u>στάσει</u> <u>φόνον</u> πεποιήκεισαν.

Ms. Φ (et al.) ad Matt. 27:26:
ὃς διὰ <u>φόνον</u> καὶ <u>στάσιν</u> ἦν βεβλημένος εἰς φυλάκην (N-A[27]).

Little in canonical Mark's reading really made it into the Matthean addition; besides the mention of φόνον and στάσις—the latter, in a different case, besides—nothing of canonical Mark is reflected in the neo-Matthean reading. There is no correlation whatsoever with the insurrectionists (μετὰ τῶν στασιατῶν), with Barabbas' "being bound" (δεδεμένος), and with the verb of "committing" (πεποιήκεισαν) murder. Mark also seems to refer to a *specific* insurrection (<u>ἐν τῇ στάσει</u>) not noted in the parallel gospels.

Was Nestle-Aland[28] incorrect in naming the "parallel" at Mark 15:7b as the "source" of the appended text of Matt. 27:16b? We think not. However, it might have been more useful to have cited the text of Luke, as a parallel as well (here, again, the Markan parallels are underlined).

Luke 23:19:
ὅστις <u>ἦν</u> <u>διὰ</u> <u>στάσιν</u> τινὰ γενομένην ἐν τῇ πόλει <u>καὶ</u> <u>φόνον</u> <u>βεβλημένος</u> ἐν τῇ φυλακῇ.

In the mss. tradition Luke's βεβλημένος (ℵ[1] A D W Θ Ψ 063 $f^{1.13}$ 𝔐) is very well supported against the reading βληθείς (𝔓[75] B L T 0124 892 *pc*), although Nestle-Aland[28] chooses the latter. There is a major problem here, however. If Luke used Mark as his source, as is inevitable, why is it that there is so little correspondence between Luke and canonical Mark? And for that matter between Matthew and Mark, as well? Luke's reading, rather, is closer to the Matthean addendum of Φ, etc., than it is to our "canonical" version of Mark! The text of Mark 15:7 belongs to the infamous Minor Agreements of Matthew and Luke against Mark that are not part of the Q-tradition. It is a conundrum of the Synoptic Problem that has never been satisfactorily solved. I follow Koester here in suggesting that Matthew and Luke had a version of Mark before them that differed somewhat from the Mark that we possess (see below)—a "pre-canonical" version of Mark, as it were. That version of Mark that Luke (and Matthew) had before them, we argue, is rather the "gospel-parallel" text of Mark found in the ms. of Matt. 27:16 in Φ, etc. In other words, the "pre-canonical" version of Mark 15:7 that Luke used, but was preserved more-or-less wholesale in only a few mss. of Matthew, must have looked something like the following (showing the context of verse 6):

6 Κατὰ δὲ ἑορτὴν ἀπέλυεν αὐτοῖς ἕνα δέσμιον ὃν παρῃτοῦντο. **7** ἦν δὲ ὁ λεγόμενος Βαραββᾶς, <u>ὃς διὰ φόνον καὶ στάσιν ἦν βεβλημένος εἰς φυλάκην</u>.

6 *Now at the festival he would release for them a single prisoner, whom they would request.* **7** *Now, there was one called Barabbas, <u>who because of murder and sedition, was cast into prison</u>.*

Here we would appear to have a text from a gospel-parallel variant that gives an altogether unattested and new reading of Mark, reflected in the reading of Mark 15:7 imbedded in Φ (?) f^{13} 1071 (1346), as an interpolated reading of Matt. 27:16! Here is one of those rare cases where a gospel-parallel variant, preserved here in Matthew, must reflect a pre-Markan version of a text not reflected in any of our known Markan mss. at Mark 15:7, the apparent source-gospel of the variant. It provides a remarkable glimpse into a possible pre-canonical version of Mark 15:7 nowhere else attested that must be quite primitive, if not original.

"Gospel-Parallel" Variants in Luke

Luke 1:63-64
In the pericope of the Birth of John the Baptist, a curious pair of variants occurs in the episode where Zechariah regains his speech after being struck speechless by the angel of the Lord for his disbelief (cf. 1:20):

a) **63** και εθαυμασαν παντες **64** ανεωχθη δε το στομα αυτου παραχρημα και η γλωσσα αυτου (Maj)

b) **63** και εθαυμασαν παντες **64** ανεωχθη δε το στομα αυτου παραχρημα <u>και ελυθη ο δεσμος της γλωσσης αυτου</u> (*f*¹)

c) **63** και παραχρημα <u>ελυθη</u> **64** η γλωσσα αυτου και εθαυμασαν παντες· ανεωχθη δε το στομα (D a b vg^ms [sy^s])

The peculiarity of this "gospel-parallel" is that it has been seemingly imported from an entirely different context—a verse from the pericope of the healing of a deaf and mute person at Mark 7:35, where the phrase καὶ ἐλύθη ὁ δέσμος τῆς γλώσσης αὐτοῦ occurs. What are we to make of this? It seems that we do not have a case of a harmonized reading, for the text in Luke is unique, and it is difficult to imagine a copyist having a version of Mark 7:35 ready at hand, alongside Luke's, but nor is it likely that the text was recalled from memory, seeing that there are no viable variants other than those of word order. But there are other peculiarities in the received Lukan text as well: the phrase, "and all were amazed," seems out of place, with the version of c) representing a more natural word order. It hardly seems correct that the story's amazement would have attended Zechariah's asking for a tablet and indicating his son's name rather than amazement at miraculous restoration of Zechariah's speech![26] Secondly, the "received" version in Matthew lacks a verb with the phrase ἡ γλώσσα αὐτοῦ—hardly a "zeugma with στόμα ἀνεῴχθη," as Creed (1950: 25), again, once noted, for tongues are "loosed" not "opened," a verb wholly reserved for mouths! What we have in our variants, b) and c), is something closer to the original, with b)'s reading representing an early, half-way point between the two antipodes of a) and c): sc. b)'s version retains the loosening of the tongue (with the Markan δεσμός-phrase) and the required verb, while c) contains the more proper word order, although its redundancy must be removed. In other words, the original of Luke must have read something like the following:

καὶ παραχρῆμα <ἐλύθη> ἡ γλῶσσα αὐτοῦ καὶ ἐθαύμασαν πάντες

---

26. Note, e.g., among older commentaries, the rather forced explanation that the amazement was "at the miraculous agreement between what Elizabeth had said and what the deaf mute Zacharias had written" (Creed 1950: 25)!

A harmonized version of this reflected in the group of mss. of f^1 resulted in the following:

καὶ παραχρῆμα καὶ ἐλύθη ὁ δεσμὸς τῆς γλώσσης αὐτοῦ

That Luke's ἀνεῴχθη δὲ τὸ στόμα αὐτοῦ is a redundancy that in part contributed to the awkward syntax of a following παραχρῆμα καὶ ἡ γλῶσσα αὐτοῦ is also suggested heavily by the Markan gospel-parallel reading that has the deaf-mute's *hearing* "opened": καὶ <u>ἠνοίγησαν</u> [var. <u>διηνοίχθησαν, ἠνοίχθησαν</u>! L] αὐτοῦ αἱ ἀκοαί. Having one's *mouth* opened alongside a tongue loosed (not *opened*, as Luke's present text has it), condemns the verse as badly jumbled in the Lukan transmission.

Luke 2:9
The occurrence of σφοδρα (from Matt. 17:6—again, not a direct "parallel" text) in lieu of the mss.'s φοβον μεγαν in B(!) is answered by a "harmonized" version carrying both expressions, sc. φοβον μεγαν σφοδρα in W bo. These two ms., where W in the first part of Luke, as here, is Alexandrian, and the Bohairic, also Alexandrian, shows an early *Vorlage* up the "Alexandrian" stem that inclined towards harmonized readings.

Additional Parallel Passages in Codex Bezae (D):

Luke 2:39: <u>καθως ερρεθη</u> δια τ<u>ου</u> προφητ<u>ου</u> οτι Ναζωραιος κληθησεται (D a) =

Matt. 2:23: <u>οπως πληρωθη το ρηθεν</u> δια των προφητων οτι Ναζωραιος κληθησεται

(The text of Luke 3:23, we note in passing, is particularly difficult and deserves an independent treatment elsewhere.)

Luke 4:31
Following the notice of Jesus' arrival in Capernaum, a city of Galilee, D adds an additional phrase from gospel-parallels:

την παραθαλασσιον εν οριοις Ζαβουλων και Νεφθαλιμ

The reading, from Matt. 4:13, differs only slightly in reading τὴν παραθαλασσί<u>αν</u>.

Luke 5:10/11
The long-variant in D (e) of this peculiar version of the call of the disciples in Luke (with its famous parallels to John 21) has some clear assimilations with the parallels in Mark 1:16-20 and Matt. 4:18:22 (e.g., the wording <u>ο</u> δε <u>ειπεν αυτοις· δεῦτε</u> και μη <u>γινεσθε αλιεις</u> ιχθυων, <u>ποιησω</u> γαρ <u>αλιεις ανθρωπων</u>), but there are also whole phrases not accounted for. The problem with assessing the parallel as a whole is that it stems from a context in Luke that already has a number of source-critical problems inherently associated with the origin of Luke's own version of the story. The odd Western variant on this verse only compounds and exacerbates an already difficult text-critical problem.

Luke 5:14
At the end of verse 14, D adds a verse drawn directly from a parallel at Mark 1:45–2:1a:

D: ο δε εξελθων ηρξατο κηρυσσειν και διαφημιζειν τον λογον ωστε μηκετι δυνασθαι <u>αυτον</u> φανερως εις πολιν εισελθειν, αλλ<u>α</u> εξω <u>ην</u> εν ερημοις τοποις και <u>συνηρχοντο</u> προς αυτον και <u>ηλθεν</u> παλιν εις Καφαρναμουμ

Mark: ο δε εξελθων ηρξατο κηρυσσειν και διαφημιζειν τον λογον ωστε <u>αυτον</u> μηκετι δυνασθαι φανερως εις πολιν εισελθειν, αλλ<u>᾽</u> εξω <u>επ᾽</u> ερημοις τοποις <u>ην</u> και ηρχοντο προς αυτον <u>παντοθεν</u> και <u>εισελθων</u> παλιν εις Καφαρναμουμ

The interpolated D-version of Mark has seven variants not attested in the mss. of the text of Mark itself, according to Nestle-Aland[28]:

1. The pronoun αυτον comes after the phrase μηκετι δυνασθαι, whereas in canonical Mark it comes before the phrase;
2. The αλλα is not elided before the vowel, as in Mark;
3. The verb ην in D is placed before the preposition εν, whereas in Mark in comes after the whole phrase;
4. D has εν ερημοις for επ᾽ ερημοις;
5. D has the anomalous <u>συνηρχοντο</u>;
6. D does not have the adverb παντοθεν;
7. D has ηλθεν for εισελθων.

But of these variants, Swanson (1995: 2:23), shows some mss. support for items 1), 2), 4), and 7), whereas items 3), 5), and 6) are not attested heretofore in the manuscript evidence. Insofar as the readings of D itself at Mark 1:45–2:1a do not follow the imbedded text of Mark at D's position at Luke 5:14, it must obviously represent a reading of Mark that is older than D's and possibly the others as well.

Luke 5:19

The healing of the paralytic by lowering him through the roof in verse 19 of Luke is paralleled by Mark 2:4 (but not by Matthew):

Mark 2:4: απεστεγασαν την στεγην οπου ην, και εξορυξαντες χαλωσα τον κραβατον οπου ο παραλυτικος κατεκειτο

They removed the roof where he was, and having made an opening, they lowered the pallet on which the paralytic lay.

Luke 5:19: αναβαντες επι το δωμα δια των κεραμων καθηκαν αυτον συν τω κλινιδιω

They went up on the roof and through the tiles, they let him down with his bed.

The essence of the account, *but not a single word* of Luke's, derives from his Marcan source.

The version of D, here, of Luke 5:19 comes somewhat closer to what Mark has, but also included Luke's reading, an early attempt at harmonizing a text of Luke's that is remarkably different than that of Mark's:

ανεβησαν επι το δωμα και απεστεγασαντες **τους κεραμους** οπου ην **καθηκαν** τον κραβαττον **συν τω παραλυτικω**

Here the underlined portion mirrors <u>Mark</u>, and the bold + underlined reflects **Luke**.

Throughout this chapter there are also a number of minor assimilations in D of texts with parallel gospels (e.g., at 5:21, 22, and 25).

A similar, but less thorough-going harmonization occurs, as well, in D, at Luke 5:33, where the phrase "disciples of the Pharisees" in addition to those of John are made to fast and pray as well (cf. also Luke 6:2).

Luke 5:27

The beginning of the pericope of the Call of Levi that derives from Mark 2:13-14a reads as follows:

και <u>ελθων</u> παλιν παρα την θαλασσαν <u>τον επακολουθουντα αυτω</u> οχλος εδιδασκεν και παραγων ειδεν Λευι τον του Αλφαιου

The big difference here, besides the presence of ελθων for εξηλθεν, is the fact that the version in D seems to present a somewhat smoother version than that actually found in Mark, in writing <u>τον επακολουθουντα αυτω οχλος εδιδασκεν</u> instead of Mark's και πας ο οχλος ηρχετο προς αυτον, και εδιδασκεν αυτους. What are we to make of this difference?

What is additionally odd is that in the version of Mark 2:14 that D (and Θ f^{13} 565 it) preserve, it is not Λευι himself who is "called," but Ιακωβος, a name that itself is an assimilation of Mark 3:18!

Luke 6:6
Again, the reading of D in Luke here gives a harmonized version of Mark 3:1 + Luke 6:6 (cf., e.g., Vogels 1910: 15ff.):

Και εισελθοντος αυτου εις την συναγωγην σαββατω, εν η ην ανθρωπος ξηραν εχων την χειρα

See also Luke 6:11.

Luke 6:42
The phrase αυτος την εν τω οφθαλμω σου δοκον ου βλεπων is replaced in D it sy^s by a version taken from Matt. 7:4:

και ιδου η δοκος εν τω οφθαλμω σου υποκριτα

However, the canonical version of Matthews's own text differs somewhat:

και ιδου η δοκος εν τω σω οφθαλμω υποκειται

Apparently, the imbedded "Western" reading of ὑποκεῖται at Luke 6:42 offers an interesting variant on ὑποκριτά, showing differences in only a few letters. The D-version of Matt. 7:4, although probably not original, preserves an early variant, perhaps a copyist's error (?), not attested in any later mss. versions of Matt. 7:4. The pronoun, as well, gives an independent reading.

Luke 8:45
In lieu of the simple και ειπεν ο Ιησους, D a presents a version of Mark 5:30 that differs somewhat from the received versions of Mark:

8:45 (D a): ο δε Ιησους γνους την εξελθουσαν εξ αυτου δυναμιν επηρωτα

Mark 5:30: και ευθυς ο Ιησους επιγνους εν εαυτω την εξελθουσαν δυναμιν εξελθουσαν ... ελεγεν

In the same verse, at the end, D, along with some other verses, interpolates the following phrase from the end of Mark 5:31: και λεγεις τις μου ηψατο;

What is noteworthy here, though, is that this interpolation from Mark is found in a host of other witnesses that are *not* Western, and with a difference:

και λεγεις τις <u>ο αψαμενος μου</u> (A C K P W Γ Δ Θ Ξ ƒ¹³ 33 565, etc.).

The participial form is not attested in a single ms. of Mark, but here we find, across a wide spectrum of witnesses, a form of a text of Mark interpolated at an early stage into the text of Luke. Another non-Western interpolation at Luke 8:54, εκβαλων <u>εξω</u> (- C) παντας και (A K W Γ Δ, etc.), of Mark 5:40, has an additional <u>εξω</u> that is attested only by ƒ¹³ among the actual mss. of Mark.

Luke 9:27
Jesus' predictive reference to seeing the "kingdom of God" (την βασιλειαν του θεου) before his Transfiguration is written differently in D; (Or), sc., τον υιον του ανθρωπου ερχομενον εν τη <u>δοξη</u> αυτου. The closest parallel, in Matt. 16:28, has τον υιον του ανθρωπου ερχομενον <u>εν τη βασιλεια αυτου</u>, which is nearer to the original Lukan text. But an early Patristic variant, not noted in Nestle-Aland²⁸ (but cf. Nestle-Aland²⁵ [1963], etc.), reads in lieu of Matthew's εν τη βασιλεια αυτου the simple noun δόξη (Cl^pt), whereas other mss. include variants also with δόξη: τη <u>δοξη</u> αυτου (1279 a; sa Cl^pt Epiph); τη <u>δοξη</u> του πατρος αυτου (ℵ³ *pc* bo); and the harmonized version of sy^c (τη βασιλεια αυτου και τη <u>δοξη</u> αυτου). This shows that the Western reading of D, supported by a number of other Western patristic readings, is probably older than the Majority readings of Luke 9:27 in having a reference to the Son of Man coming *in glory*, not coming into his kingdom. We further note that there are also a number of additional minor "gospel-variant" readings throughout Luke, chapter 9 (e.g., at vv. 10, 12, 13, 14, 16, 19, 22, 23, 25, 29, 33, 34, 35, 45, 49, 50), including some early harmonizations in 𝔓⁴⁵ (e. g., απαρνησασθω at v. 23; συνλαλουντες at v. 30; επεσκιασεν at v. 34; cf. v. 29; 12:24).

Luke 9:6
Instead of Luke's phrase ανακαμψει here, D has επιστρεψει η ειρηνη υμων, presumably taken from the text of Matt. 10:13, which reads rather differently, however: η ειρηνη υμων <u>προς υμας επιστραφητω</u>. Does the text of D derive from a copy of Matthew that has a somewhat different reading of the received mss.? It would appear so.

Luke 11:2

An interpolation in D, borrowed from a harmonized reading of Matt. 6:7, reads here as follows:

μη βαττολογειτε ως οι λοιποι· δοκουσιν γαρ <u>τινες</u> οτι εν τη πολυλογια αυτων εισακουσθησονται· αλλα προσευχομενοι

The text of Matt. 6:7, itself, however, is as follows:

μη βατ<u>ταλογησατε</u> ωσ<u>περ οι εθνικοι</u> (var. υποκριται)· δοκουσιν γαρ οτι εν τη πολυλογια αυτων εισακουσθησονται.

Its text of Matthew derives from a manuscript that offers readings not attested in any of the extant mss. of Matt. 6:7. At least six other, relatively short, parallel-variants here in the Lord's Prayer do not offer any variant readings at all (vv. 2 [bis], 4 [tris]).

Luke 11:14

On the Beelzebul Controversy, D (c f) provides an incipit that differs both from the received Lukan text, and from the Matthean parallel (12:22) from which it draws:

Luke: Και ην εκβαλλων δαιμονιον, και αυτο ην κωφον· εγενετο δε του δαιμονιου εξελθοντος ελαλησεν ο κωφος· και εθαυμασαν (παντες) οι οχλοι

Matt.: Τοτε προσηνεχθη αυτω δαιμονιζομενος τυφλος και κωφος· και εθεραπευσεν αυτον ωστε τον κωφον λαλειν και βλεπειν. και εξισταντο παντες οι οχλοι, κτλ.

Luke (D): ταυτα δε ειποντος αυτου <u>προσφερεται</u> αυτω δαιμονιζομενος κωφος και εκβαλοντος αυτου παντες εθαυμαζον

The version from Codex D is remarkable. Its ending seems reminiscent enough of Luke's "canonical" ending, but the beginning is Matthean, but without, *inter alia*, the typical Matthean "doublet" of blindness and deaf-muteness. The Beelzebul Controversy is quite an old gospel account. Is it possible that the *Vorlage* of D is borrowing from a pre-Matthean text of Matthew? More likely, in an attempt at a very primitive harmonization, the copy of the account in D's manuscript derives from a harmony that removed the τυφλος reference and kept whatever else harmonized with Luke and Matthew. Do note that for canonical Luke's εξελθοντος, C A φ *al* lat reads εκβληθεντος, which agrees rather with Luke (D)'s εκβαλοντος.

Luke 11:30
At the end of verse 30, D (it) interpolates from Matt. 12:40 the verse about Jonah being in the belly of the whale and Jesus being in the earth. The differences are that D's version reads και καθως...εγενετο for Matthew's ωσπερ γαρ, and D has εν τη γη for Matthew's εν τη καρδια της γης.

In a series of parallels in Luke verses 35/36, 43, 44, and 51 that are somewhat longer than the usual shorter examples, we find parallels with no distinguishing variant readings; several of these, however, are gospel parallels that are not exclusive to D, or Western texts, but are shared by other manuscript families. It is worth noting that the fact that these represent longer "parallel" variants, yet at the same time reproduce verbatim the readings (from the "source" gospels) in our majority manuscripts makes all the more acute the readings in D, and elsewhere, of the gospel-parallels that happen to differ from the readings of their "source"-gospels. In the lengthy example at Luke 11:51 about the murder of Zechariah, son of Barachiah, between the sanctuary and the altar, the Western versions have μεταξυ instead of the Matthean-Lukan αναμεσον and the words for altar and sanctuary are reversed. Otherwise, the verses are the same.

Luke 12:2
This Q passage, with Matthew's additional phrase about killing the soul (10:28), has in D been turned into a harmonized text of which the Lukan phrase, μη...περισσοτερον appears slightly differently in D as μηδε...περισσον.

Luke 12:10
The version of the logion about blaspheming against the Holy Spirit in D, conforms to the version in Matt. 12:32, but retains the form εις δε το πνευμα, κτλ., as found in Luke.

Luke 12:59
The version of this verse in D it vg[mss] gives αποδοις in lieu of Matt. 5:26's αποδως.

Luke 17:6
The interpolation in D (sy[c]) of the parallel from Matt. 17:20 gives a slightly different variant in reading, e.g., μετεβαινεν for μεταβησεται.

Luke 17:[36]
This verse was either omitted by homoeoteleuton or assimilated from the text at Matt. 24:40 (see Metzger 1971: 168).

Luke 18
A cluster of minor gospel parallels in verses 20, 21, 22, 25, 28, 29, 30, 35, and 37 are of little textual consequence.

Luke 19:27
The long interpolation at the end of verse 27 in D matches verbatim its source in Matt. 25:30. This identicality of text again demonstrates that when D, elsewhere, does preserve gospel-parallels that differ somewhat from the mss. of their source-gospel, they derive from copies that are not supported by other mss. of the gospel from which they come.

Luke 19:45
The long interpolation in D it sy^h** at the end of verse 45 agrees, for the most part, with the texts of Matt. 21:12 and Mark 11:15, except that it takes from John 2:15 the verb εξεχεεν, thus showing an early harmonizing tendency.

Luke 23:53
At the end of verse 53 we find two different interpolations, one a Western version, the other a non-Western version:

a) και προσεκυλισεν λιθον μεγαν επι την θυραν του μνημειου (f^{13} 700 bo).

b) και θεντος αυτου επεθηκεν (επεθηκαν 070) τω μνημειω λιθον (+ μεγαν 070) ον μογις εικοσι (+ ανδρας 070) εκυλιον (D 070 c [sa]).

The reading of a) is based directly upon the parallel at Mark 15:2, word-for-word. The reading of b), whatever its age or veracity, must be based on an apocryphal logion, or oral tradition, of some kind.

Some "Non-D" Gospel-Parallels in Luke:

Luke 20:30
The long variant replacing και ο δευτερος in A W Γ Δ Θ (λ φ) *pm*, etc. is probably not a parallel-gospel variant (note, e.g., *app. crit.* in Aland 1964: 247) since it is not at all close to any of the known Synoptic parallels. It must represent an old, independent variant from an unknown tradition.

Luke 22:64
The gospel-parallel reading αυτον ετυπτον αυτου το προσωπον και (and variants) in A (D) N W Γ Δ Θ Ψ, etc., gives a widely attested variant based

on gospel-parallels such as that found at Matt. 26:67 (τοτε ενεπτυσαν εις το προσωπον). The wording, however, of the saying is so different to suggest, again, an unknown source.

Luke 23:[17]

The glossed verse [17], apparently based on the text of Matt. 27:15 and Mark 15:6 is clearly secondary, as rightly noted by Metzger (1971: 179f.). But the texts are too different to suggest a variant reading based on gospel-parallels:

> Luke 23:[17]: αναγκην δε ειχεν απολυειν αυτοις κατα εορτην ενα ℵ (D sy[s.c] *add. p.* 19) W (Θ Ψ), etc.
>
> Matt.: Κατα δε εορτην ειωθει ο ηγεμων απολυειν ενα τω οχλω δεσμιον ον ηθελον
>
> Mark: Κατα δε εορτην απελυεν αυτοις ενα δεσμιον ον παρητουντο

The presence of αυτοις in the Lukan gloss might suggest a harmonized reading. But the whole verse takes us full circle to the earlier reading, discussed above, in respect of the peculiar gospel-parallel Barabbas reading suggesting a remarkable pre-canonical source.

"Gospel-Parallel" Variants in John

Because the Gospel of John is not a "Synoptic" Gospel, it has relatively fewer parallel-gospel variants. But here are a few of note.

John 1:27

The end of verse 27 is glossed in N (according to Nestle-Aland[28]):

> αυτος υμας βαπτισει εν πνευματι αγιω και πυρι

The source-verse, Matt. 3:11, apparently reads the same:

> αυτος υμας βαπτισει εν πνευματι αγιω και πυρι (although βαπτιζει in N-A[26] appears to be an error).

The text of Nestle-Aland[26] had previously printed this differently: εκεινος υμας βαπτιζει εν πνευματι αγιω και πυρι (N *pc*). Swanson (1995: 4:11), however, gives for mss. E F G H 2* εκεινος for αυτος, and has αυτος for N, as well (with all readings showing βαπτισει). Thus, the reading with εκεινος—not found in any mss. of Matt. 3:11—represents a pre-canonical version of Matt. 3:11.

John 8:58
In the remarkable pericope of Jesus "becoming hidden" (ἐκρύβη), and thus escaping a stoning at the Temple, a large body of mss. borrows from Luke 4:30 very similar phrasing, as follows: και διελθων δια μεσου επορευετο και παρηγεν ουτως (C L N Ψ 0124 33 892, etc.). The wording is nearly identical to that of Luke, which reads instead αυτος δε at the beginning and does not include the added phrase (underlined), above. Και may very well reflect a different mss. reading than Luke's own αυτος δε, but the end-phrase in the Johannine gloss may rather be an early scribe's independent gloss, describing the manner in which Jesus was said to pass by. The Syriac Diatessaronic tradition gives a very different account of this miraculous escape of Jesus, in Luke, who is led to the brow of the hill to be cast down. In this account, which may reflect an earlier pre-canonical version of the story that can only be discussed more thoroughly in a different context, T. Baarda (1986) convincingly demonstrated, based on the Syriac Diatessaron and other witnesses, that the extant version of Luke 4:29-30 that served as the basis for the Syriac text contained a series of verses that not only presented Jesus actually being cast off the cliff, but had him "pass through their midst" by flying down safely, quite literally, unharmed, to Capernaum (καὶ κατῆλθεν εἰς Καφαρναούμ, 4:31). Baarda can only claim that Tatian probably had a corrupted version of Luke at 4:29-30 before him and that this factored into his own "creation of the new version of the episode at the hill near Nazareth" (Baarda 1986: 336).[27]

Conclusions

In this study we have looked at two, among several, possible sources for recovering the text of the New Testament in the second century. One of these, the early papyri of the second (and third) centuries CE, whose texts have been examined to various degrees by previous scholars, has upon closer scrutiny betrayed an unusually large amount of singular and variant readings, some of them unique, that do not always correspond closely with the known textual makeup of the later New Testament codices. The texts of many of these papyri also show a surprisingly early process of harmonization, a mixture of early text-types, and a sometimes unexpectedly high rate of scribal anomalies and copying errors, even in

---

27. Baarda (1986: 335f.) suggests a possible *vario lectio* at Luke 4:30, where a verb of flying (ἐπέτο, ἐπέτατο, περιεπέτετο, or περιπέτατο) stood in lieu of ἐπορεύετο. Could the interpolator's phrase καὶ παρῆγεν οὕτως at John 8:58 (a verse not acknowledged by Baarda) also be an original phrase from this older tradition?

respect of the famous John Rylands fragment ($\mathfrak{P}^{52}$), our earliest published gospel papyrus to date. An examination of many of these early papyri also shows an alarming number of overlooked or omitted readings in the critical apparatus of Nestle-Aland[28], especially those of the most recently published ones.

A second area of enquiry addressed in this article, which has not received the scholarly attention it deserves, is that related to the so-called "gospel-parallel" variants, alternative readings from a surprisingly neglected source; these are the long-time documented readings found in the critical apparatuses of the pages of our *Novum Testamentum Graece* that record variants culled from parallel readings from other gospels, particularly the Synoptics. But these variants, in copying texts from parallel passages in the Gospels, do not always preserve readings that match exactly those of the "source"-gospels from which they derive. Like the readings of the early papyri, they give us new readings, some of greater significance than others, that are not testified to in the whole body of the manuscript texts of the parallel gospel passages from which they come.

In one case, that of Matt. 27:16, we have identified a text whose "gospel-parallel" from Mark 15:7 differs so remarkably from the canonical version we possess of all extant mss. of Mark that we are forced to wonder whether the new reconstruction we have proffered might represent the true "pre-Markan" reading of this second gospel. Here we may have recovered an earlier version of a Markan verse that is not attested in any of the extant manuscripts of Mark; for this, we have had to look in a gospel-parallel reading found only in a handful of manuscripts of an unexpected source: the Gospel of Matthew. Elsewhere among our gospel-parallel variants we have presented we have also found similar "new" readings, though not as variant as that attested in Mark 15:7.

Such re-examinations of possible second-century precursors to canonical texts from the advantage of a closer reading of early papyri, like that of $\mathfrak{P}^{66}$—and the utilization of lesser known manuscript sources—has been carried out recently with remarkable attention to scribal detail in respect of the text of John 11–12. There, Elizabeth Schrader has convincingly argued that Martha of Bethany was not part of the auctorial version of the Gospel of John but was later added to the Fourth Gospel in the second century.[28]

---

28. Schrader (2017), who demonstrates that "the figure of Martha of Bethany shows significant instability in the Greek and Vetus Latina text transmission of the Fourth Gospel" (2017: 385), further writes, "I believe we can still see a literary prehistory reflected in P[66], giving us a window into a predecessor circulating text form

In a less recent assessment of the origins of the Gospel of Mark, a gospel for which our early papyrological record is rather limited, Helmut Koester has maintained that the second Gospel, the source for our two other main Synoptic Gospels, has only come down to us in revised form. Matthew and Luke did not possess the exact "canonical" form of Mark that we have. In other words, "With respect to Mark, one can be fairly certain that only its revised text has achieved canonical status, while the original text (attested only by Matthew and Luke) has not survived" (Koester 1989: 37). His observations have ingeniously unraveled the age-old conundrum of the "Minor Agreements" in a way that manages to successfully preserve the priority of Mark, while at the same time maintaining the standard model of the Four-Document Hypothesis.[29] He has also demonstrated Justin Martyr's utilization of a single gospel, in the mid-second century, that harmonized the text of Matthew and Luke with a great deal of liberty in respect of the original text; but this textual liberty was not witness to a free use of gospel material, but rather the adaptation of an already existing collection. The nature of his source(s) suggests a reliance upon gospel texts that were more original, at times, than the canonical versions preserved in our own manuscript tradition. Although it has been suggested in more recent counter-arguments that the second century was perhaps *not* a period of free textual transmission, Helmut Koester reminds us that, whatever the consequences, the first one hundred years, from the time of writing of the gospel autographs to the appearance of their initial papyrological record in the period of c. 200 CE, represented a span when substantial revisions were not only possible but highly likely (Koester 1989).

---

with only Mary and Lazarus present, now overlaid with secondary interpolations of the figure of Martha" (2017: 391). The changes were caused, in part, remarkably, by "an early harmonization of the Johannine Lazarus story to the Lukan story of Mary and Martha" (2017: 391).

29. By making comparisons with the formerly—and incorrectly—discredited *Secret Gospel of Mark*, he has suggested that Matthew and Luke used an earlier, "pre-canonical" version of the Gospel of Mark. This would certainly explain such gaps in the text of Mark 10:46 a + b: *"And they came to Jericho... And when he was leaving Jericho and his disciples..."*! Cf. Mark 3:20 + 21, where the whole middle part of the narrative seems to have similarly gone missing: *"And he came into a house, and again the crowd came with him so that they were unable to eat bread"... "And when his family heard this, they went out to arrest him, for they were saying, 'He is crazy'."* We would need to see more early Markan papyri in order to determine the nature of texts such as these.

All this suggests that the period of the second century still remains an era of unusual freedom, liberality, or even "uncontrolled" recomposition, in respect of the transmitted text of the living Gospels. The bundles of extant textual variants found during the post-inaugural period of the second century points to an era when the gospel texts appeared, early on, to have grown rather freely. As Epp (2002: 57) noted in his forthright appraisal of D. C. Parker's (1997) "disarmingly small volume," one can persuasively argue that the earliest period of the gospel texts was not firmly fixed, but rather represented the product of much "interpretive rewriting of tradition," to slightly rephrase Parker's words (1997: 93). Does that mean we must despair of ever recovering anything close to an "original" gospel text or that our extant evangels do not reflect something close to an auctorial autograph? Of course not, for they surely do. But a number of competing texts, at times, among the welter of biblical manuscripts, will continue to challenge our assumptions about the integrity of a given reading, even if the bulk of what we have remains surprisingly accurate and stable. Perhaps we must accept in our academic praxis that a "variant-conscious approach" (Epp 2007) will remain the best way to address the vagaries of the text of our New Testament, a text that early on, seemed especially open to vibrancy and modification. Until the discovery of more light from the papyri, or further insights from the early Church Fathers, or fresh *comparanda* from the Apocryphal Gospels, or even new readings of the *Diatessaron*, our best hopes for attempting new inroads into an "original" text of the Gospels must be measured one papyrus at a time, and perhaps even one "gospel-parallel" at a time. With the caveat, of course, that it will always remain important to endeavor to champion one reading over-and-against another, or to envision how a particular text might have given rise to another, we must remain at the mercy of discovery and insight in order to achieve a closer appreciation of the original text of the New Testament. For the faith-minded, the Scriptures will always remain Holy Writ, and a good measure of credo may be required in reminding us that what we have inherited in the New Testament is surely the product of a remarkable, and unmistakably divine, legacy of scribal endeavor.

References

Baarda, T. (1986), "'The Flying Jesus': Luke 4:29-30 in the Syriac Diatessaron," *VC* 40: 313–41.

Bagnall, Roger S. (2009), *Early Christian Books in Egypt*, Princeton/Oxford: Princeton University Press.

Bellinzoni, Arthur J. (1967), *The Sayings of Jesus in the Writings of Justin Martyr*, NovTSup 17, Leiden: Brill..

Black, David Alan, and Jacob Creole, eds. (2016), *The Pericope of the Adulteress in Contemporary Research*, LNTS 551, London: Bloomsbury T&T Clark.

Brinkmann, A. (1902), "Ein Schreibgebrauch und seine Bedeutung für die Textkritik," *Rheinisches Museum für Philologie* 57: 481–97.

Colwell, Ernest C. (1969), "Method in Evaluating Scribal Habits: A Study of P^{45}, P^{66}, P^{75}," in *Studies in Methodology in Textual Criticism of the New Testament*, 106–24, NTTSD 9, Leiden: Brill/Grand Rapids: Eerdmans.

Colwell, E. C., and Ernst W. Tune (1969), "Method in Classifying and Evaluating Variant Readings," in *Studies in Methodology in Textual Criticism of the New Testament*, 96–104, NTTSD 9, Leiden: Brill; Grand Rapids: Eerdmans.

Comfort, Philip W., and David P. Barrett (2001), *The Text of the Earliest New Testament Greek Manuscripts*, Wheaton, IL: Tyndale House.

Comfort, Philip W. (2005), *Encountering the Manuscripts: An Introduction to New Testament Palaeography and Textual Criticism*, Nashville: Broadman & Holman.

Daniel, Robert W. (1991), *Two Magical Papyri in the National Museum of Antiquities in Leiden. A Photographic Edition of J 384 and J 395 (= PGM XII and XIII)*, Papyrologia Coloniensia 19, Oplanden: Westdeutscher Verlag.

Ehrman, Bart D. (1993), *The Orthodox Corruption of Scripture: The Effect of the Early Christological Controversies on the Text of the New Testament*, Oxford: Oxford University Press.

Ehrman, Bart D., and Michael W. Holmes (1995), *The Text of the New Testament in Contemporary Research. Essays on the* Status Quaestionis, Studies & Documents 46, Grand Rapids, MI: Eerdmans.

Elliott, J. K. (1994), "Codex Bezae and the Earliest Greek Papyri," in D. C. Parker and C.-B. Amphoux (eds.), *Studies from the Lunel Colloquium, June 1994*, 162–82, NTTSD 22, Leiden: Brill. Repr. in *New Testament Textual Criticism: The Application of Thoroughgoing Principles: Essays on Manuscripts and Textual Variation*, 79–102, SNT 137, Leiden: Brill, 2010.

Elliott, J. K. (2003), "The Nature of the Evidence Available for Reconstructing the Text of the New Testament in the Second Century," in Christian-B. Amphoux and J. Keith Elliott (eds.), *The New Testament Text in Early Christianity. Le Texte du Nouveau Testament au début du christianisme. Proceedings of the Lille Colloquium, July 2000. Actes du colloque de Lille, juillet 2000*, 9–18 Lausanne: Editions du Zèbre. Repr. in *New Testament Textual Criticism: The Application of Thoroughgoing Principles: Essays on Manuscripts and Textual Variation*, 29–39, SNT 137, Leiden: Brill, 2010.

Elliott, J. K. (2004), "Singular Readings in the Gospel Text of P^{45}," in Charles Horton (ed.), *The Origins and Transmission of the Earliest Christian Gospel: The Contribution of the Chester Beatty Gospel Codex P^{45}*, 122–31, JSNTSup 258, London and New York: T&T Clark, 2004. Repr. in *New Testament Textual Criticism: The Application of Thoroughgoing Principles: Essays on Manuscripts and Textual Variation*, 53–64, SNT 137, Leiden: Brill, 2010.

Elliott, J. K. (2010), *New Testament Textual Criticism: The Application of Thoroughgoing Principles*: *Essays on Manuscripts and Textual Variation*, SNT 137, Leiden/Boston: Brill.

Epp, Eldon Jay (1993 [1989], "The Significance of the Papyri for Determining the Nature of the New Testament Text in the Second Century: A Dynamic View of Textual Transmission," in Eldon Jay Epp and Gordon D. Fee (eds.), *Studies in the Theory and Method of New Testament Textual Criticism*, 274–97, Grand Rapids: Eerdmans, 1993.

Epp, Eldon Jay (1989), "The New Testament Papyrus Manuscripts in Historical Perspective," in Maurya P. Horgan and Paul J. Kobelski (eds.), *To Touch the Text: Biblical and Related Studies in Honor of Joseph A. Fitzmyer, S.J.*, 261–88, New York: Crossroad. Repr. in *Perspectives on New Testament Textual Criticism: Collected Essays, 1962–2004*, 309–42, NovTSup 116, Leiden: Brill.

Epp, Eldon J. (1993 [1974]), "The Twentieth-Century Interlude in NT Textual Criticism," in Eldon Jay Epp and Gordon D. Fee (eds.), *Studies in the Theory and Method of New Testament Textual Criticism*, 83–108, Grand Rapids: Eerdmans.

Epp, Eldon Jay (1995), "The Papyrus Manuscripts of the New Testament," in Bart D. Ehrman and Michael W. Holmes (eds.), *The Text of the New Testament in Contemporary Research: Essays on the* Status Quaestionis, 3–21, Studies & Documents 46, Grand Rapids, MI: Eerdmans. Repr. in *Perspectives on New Testament Textual Criticism: Collected Essays, 1962–2004*, 411–35, NovTSup 116, Leiden: Brill.

Epp, Eldon Jay (1997), "Textual Criticism in the Exegesis of the New Testament, with an Excursus on Canon," in Stanley E. Porter (ed.), *Handbook to Exegesis of the New Testament*, 45–97, Leiden: Brill. Repr. in *Perspectives on New Testament Textual Criticism: Collected Essays, 1962–2004*, 595–639, NovTSup 116, Leiden: Brill.

Epp, Eldon Jay (1999), "The Multivalence of the Term 'Original Text' in New Testament Textual Criticism," *HTR* 92: 245–81. Repr. in *Perspectives on New Testament Textual Criticism: Collected Essays, 1962–2004*, ch. 20, NovTSup 116, Leiden: Brill.

Epp, Eldon Jay (2002), "Issues in New Testament Textual Criticism. Moving from the Nineteenth Century to the Twenty-First Century," in *Rethinking New Testament Textual Criticism*, 17–76, ed. David Alan Black, Grand Rapids: Baker Academic. Repr. in *Perspectives on New Testament Textual Criticism: Collected Essays, 1962–2004*, 641–97, NovTSup 116, Leiden: Brill.

Epp, Eldon Jay (2005), *Perspectives on New Testament Textual Criticism: Collected Essays, 1962–2004*, NovTSup 116, Leiden: Brill.

Epp, Eldon Jay (2007), "It's All about Variants: A Variant-Conscious Approach to New Testament Textual Criticism," *HTR* 100: 275–308.

Fee, Gordon D. (1968), *Papyrus Bodmer II (P^{66}): Its Textual Relationships and Scribal Characteristics*, SD 34, Salt Lake City: University of Utah Press.

Fee, Gordon D. (1974), "P^{75}, P^{66}, and Origen: The Myth of Early Textual Recension in Alexandria," in Richard N. Longenecker and Merrill C. Tenney (eds.), *New Dimensions in New Testament Study*, 247–73, Grand Rapids: Zondervan.

Fee, Gordon D. (1993 [1978]), "Modern Textual Criticism and the Synoptic Problem: On the Problem of Harmonization in the Gospels," *Studies in the Theory and Method of New Testament Textual Criticism*, Studies & Documents 45, Grand Rapids: Eerdmans.

Fee, Gordon D. (1993), "The Use of Greek Patristic Citations in New Testament Textual Criticism: The State of the Question," *Studies in the Theory and Method of New Testament Textual Criticism*, 344–59, Studies & Documents 45, Grand Rapids: Eerdmans.

Finegan, Jack (1974), *Encountering New Testament Manuscripts. A Working Introduction to Textual Criticism*, Grand Rapids: Eerdmans.

Head, Peter M. (1990), "Observations on Early Papyri of the Synoptic Gospels, especially on the 'Scribal Habits'," *Bib* 71: 240–7.

Head, Peter M. (2004), "The Habits of New Testament Copyists Singular Readings in the Early Fragmentary Papyri of John," *Bib* 85: 404.

Head, Peter M. (2008), "Scribal Behaviour in P. Bodmer II (P^{66})," in H. A. G. Houghton and David C. Parker (eds.), *Textual Variation: Theological and Social Tendencies?*, 55–74, Piscataway, NJ: Gorgias.
Hill, Charles E., and Michael J. Kruger (2012), *The Early Text of the New Testament*, Oxford: Oxford University Press.
Holmes, Michael W. (2011), "Text and Transmission in the Second Century," in Robert W. Stewart (ed.), *The Reliability of the New Testament: Bart Ehrman and Daniel Wallace in Dialogue*, 47–65, Minneapolis: Fortress Press, 2011.
Hoskier, Herman (1914), *Codex B and its Allies: A Study and an Indictment*, London: Bernard Quaritch.
Hulley, K. K. (1944), "Principles of Textual Criticism Known to St. Jerome," *Harvard Studies in Classical Philology* 55: 87–109.
Hurtado, Larry (1981), *Text-Critical Methodology and the Pre-Caesarean Text: Codex W in the Gospel of Mark*, Studies & Documents 43, Grand Rapids: Eerdmans.
Hurtado, Larry (2006), "The New Testament in the Second Century: Text, Collections, and Canon," in J. W. Childers and D. C. Parker (eds.), *Transmission and Reception: New Testament Text-Critical and Exegetical Studies*, 3–27, Piscataway, NJ: Gorgias Press.
Klinghardt, Matthias, Jason Beduhn, and Judith Lieu (2017), "*Quaestiones disputatae:* Marcion's Gospel and the New Testament: Catalyst of Consequence," *NTS* 63: 318–34.
Koester, Helmut (1957), *Synoptische Überlieferung bei den apostolischen Vätern*, TU 65, Berlin: Akademie Verlag.
Koester, Helmut (1989), "The Text of the Synoptic Gospels in the Second Century," in William L. Petersen (ed.), *Gospel Traditions in the Second Century: Origins, Recensions, Text, and Transmission*, 19–37, Christianity and Judaism in Antiquity 3, Notre Dame: University of Notre Dame.
Koester, Helmut (1990), *Ancient Christian Gospels: Their History and Development*, London: SCM Press; Philadelphia: Trinity Press International.
Kotansky, Roy D. (2015), "The *Lex Sacra* from Selinous: Introduction, Translation, and Notes," in Alessandro Iannucci, Federicomaria Muccioli, and Matteo Zaccarini (eds.), *La Città Inquieta. Selinunte tra* Lex Sacra *e* Defixiones, 127–34, Milan/Udine: Mimesis Edizioni.
Kraeling, Carl H. (1935), *A Greek Fragment of Tatian's Diatessaron from Dura*, ed. Kirsopp Lake and Silva Lake, Studies and Documents 3, London: Christophers.
Lanier, Gregory R. (2016), "A Case for the Assimilation of Matthew 21:44 to the Lukan 'Crushing Stone' (20:18), with Special Reference to 𝔓^{104}," *TC: A Journal of Biblical Textual Criticism* 21: 1–21.
Metzger, Bruce M. (1963), "Explicit References in the Works of Origen to Variant Readings in the New Testament Manuscripts," in J. N. Birdsall and R. W. Thomson (eds.), *Biblical and Patristic Studies in Memory of Robert Pierce Casey*, 78–95, Freiburg.
Metzger, Bruce M. (1971), *A Textual Commentary on the Greek New Testament*, London/New York: The United Bible Societies.
Metzger, Bruce M. (1977), *The Early Versions of the New Testament. Their Origin, Transmission, and Limitations*, Oxford: Clarendon Press.
Metzger, Bruce M. (1992), *The Text of the New Testament. Its Transmission, Corruption, and Restoration*, 3rd edn, Oxford: Oxford University Press, 1963, 1968.
Nongbri, Brent (2011), "Grenfell and Hunt on the Dates of Early Christian Codices: Setting the Record Straight," *BASP* 48: 149–62.

Nongbri, Brent (2014), "The Limits of Palaeographic Dating of Literary Papyri: Some Observations on the Date and Provenance of P. Bodmer II (P^{66})," *MH* 71: 1–35.

Nongbri, Brent (2016), "Reconsidering the Place of Papyrus Bodmer XIV-XV ($\mathfrak{P}^{75}$) in the Textual Criticism of the New Testament," *JBL* 135: 405–37.

Orsini, Pasquale, and Willy Clarysse (2012), "Early New Testament Manuscripts and Their Dates. A Critique of Theological Palaeography," *ETL* 88: 443–74.

Parker, D. C. (1992), *Codex Bezae: An Early Christian Manuscript and its Text*, Cambridge: Cambridge University Press.

Parker, David C. (1997), *The Living Text of the Gospels*, Cambridge: Cambridge University Press.

Parsons, Mikeal C. (1875), "A Christological Tendency in P75," *JBL* 105: 463–79.

Petersen, William L. (1990), "Textual Evidence of Tatian's Dependence upon Justin's ΑΠΟΜΝΗΜΟΝΕΥΜΑΤΑ," *NTS* 36: 512–34.

Petersen, William L. (1995), "The Diatessaron of Tatian," in Bart D. Ehrman and Michael W. Holmes (eds.), *The Text of the New Testament in Contemporary Research. Essays on the* Status Quaestionis, 77–96, Studies & Documents 46, Grand Rapids, MI: Eerdmans.

Pott, August (1919), *Der Text des Neuen Testaments nach seiner geschichtlichen Entwicklung*, 2nd edn, Leipzig: E. G. Teubner.

Roth, Dieter T. (2015), *The Text of Marcion's Gospel*, Leiden/Boston: Brill.

Royse, James R. (1995), "Scribal Tendencies in the Transmission of the Text of the New Testament," in Bart D. Ehrman and Michael W. Holmes (eds.), *The Text of the New Testament in Temporary Research: Essays on the* Status Quaestionis, 239–52, Studies & Documents 46, Grand Rapids, MI: Eerdmans.

Royse, James R. (2007), *Scribal Habits in Early Greek New Testament Papyri*, NTTSD 36, Leiden: Brill.

Schmid, Ulrich (2003), "How Can We Access Second Century Gospel Texts? The Cases of Marcion and Tatian," in Christian-B. Amphoux and J. Keith Elliott (eds.), *The New Testament Text in Early Christianity: Proceedings of the Lille Colloquium, July 2000*, 139–50, HTB, Lausanne: Editions du Zebre.

Schrader, Elizabeth (2017), "Was Martha of Bethany Added to the Fourth Gospel in the Second Century?" *HTR* 110: 360–92.

Swanson, R. J. (1995), *New Testament Greek Manuscripts. Variant Readings Arranged in Horizontal Lines Against Codex Vaticanus*, 4 vols., Sheffield: Sheffield Academic Press.

Tyson, Joseph B. (2006), *Marcion and Luke-Acts: A Defining Struggle*, Columbia, SC: University of South Caroline Press.

Vaganay, Léon, Christian-Bernard Amphoux (1991), *An Introduction to New Testament Textual Criticism*, 2nd edn, Cambridge: Cambridge University Press.

Vogels, Heinrich Joseph (1910), *Die Harmonistik im Evangelientext des Codex Cantabrigiensis. Ein Beitrag zur Neutestamentlichen Textkritik*, Leipzig: J. C. Hinrichs.

10

Terms of Kinship from Usage in Everyday Language to Official Christian Life*

Eleonora Angela Conti

As part of a broader study on the use of terms of kinship in private letters and their evolution in Christian society, I have chosen to dwell on two rare nouns, *amma* and *appa*,[1] which are not terms of kinship in the strict sense, but terms of affection typical of childish language. In this connection, the definition by P. Chantraine, which insists on the almost onomatopoeic nature of these names with their use of the "a" vowel and doubling of the consonant, is fundamental.[2]

The aim of the present study is to investigate the papyrological evidence of *amma* and *appa*, in order to analyse the evolution of their usage within private letters on papyrus. Christian uses of *amma* and *appa* is well known:[3] they can be found referring to spiritual women and men, nuns and monks, and female or male saints.[4]

---

* This study is part of what I presented at the "Annual Meeting on Christian Origins" held at the University Residential Centre of Bertinoro, Italy, September 29–October 1, 2016.

1. The forms are written in different ways, especially in publications, which often display different accents: hence, I have chosen to deal generically with the transliterated forms, *amma* and *appa*.

2. See P. Chantraine, "Les noms du mari et de la femme, du père et de la mère en grec," *REG* 59–60 (1946): 241: "A côte de ce vocabulaire noble, il a existé un vocabulaire familier, caractérisé dans sa structure même par le vocalism *a*, la gémination de consonnes, le redoublement."

3. See S. Elm, *"Virgins of God": The Making of Asceticism in Late Antiquity* (Oxford: Clarendon Press, 1994), 245–6; T. Derda and E. Wipszycka, "L'emploi des titres abba, apa et papas dans l'Égypte byzantine," *JJP* 24 (1994): 23–56; M. A. Eissa, "The Use of the Title Apa for the Sender in an Opening Epistolary Formula," *JCS* 16 (2014): 115–24.

4. See F. Cabrol and H. Leclerque, *DACL*, I *s.v.*

In this study I will attempt to reconstruct diachronically the transformation that *amma* and *appa* underwent over the centuries, and, if possible, give some clarifications on their meaning, without going into a linguistic and etymological analysis, because these terms co-existed in Graeco-Roman Egypt alongside very similar Coptic and Semitic forms, in a linguistic melting pot that is often hard to reconstruct.[5] The forms dealt with in the present study are all seen in papyri and literary Greek, even though the examples are few in number.

The term ἀμμά, of which ἀμμάς is a redetermined form, is seen in ancient lexicons, Hesychius, Photius, and the *Etymologicum Magnum*, but in the whole of non-Christian literature it only appears once, in Herodas, where we find the diminuitive form ἀμμίη.[6] As Chantraine[7] and the aforesaid lexicons have it, ἀμμά and ἀμμάς are items of children's vocabulary referring to both the wet nurse and the mother; furthermore, ἀμμά is also a name for some specific divinities: the wet nurse of Artemis,[8] Rhea, and Demeter, the latter divine figures both known as mothers *par excellence*.[9]

The forms ἀμμά and ἀμμάς have been found in eight private letters dated between the second and fourth centuries.[10] In these examples, the

---

5. This study excludes the forms μάμμη and πάππος. These specific terms of kinship to indicate grandparents maintain this meaning/function in the papyri too, and are both used in abundance not just in the private context of letters, but also in official technical contexts (sales, divisions of assets, etc.). Also not included is the noun ἀββά, of Semitic derivation, which as specified by Derda and Wipszycka in "L'emploi des titres abba," 44, as of the fourth century, but above all the sixth, became the typical name for monks or former monks. Neither has the Homeric form ἄττα been taken into consideration because it has never been found in papyri. The forms αμα and απα, probably of Coptic origin, will not be dealt with either. These are not seen in the pre-Christian era, but begin to be found in papyri as honorific titles preceding the proper name απα in the fourth century and αμα in the fifth century.

6. See *Mim.* 1, 7.

7. See also Chantraine, *DEG s.v.*, p. 76: "Ce terme familier a donc peu désigner la mère, mais il se rapporte en général à la nourrice."

8. Cf. Hdt. 2.156.5, which hints at a myth according to which Artemis is the daughter of Isis and Dionysus and was entrusted to Latona, who became her wet nurse (τροφός).

9. Indeed Photius *s.v.*, reads: "ἡ τροφὸς καὶ ἡ μήτηρ. καὶ ἡ Ῥέα, καὶ ἡ Δημήτηρ, καὶ Ἀρτέμιδος τροφός"; in Hesychius similarly, *s.v.*: "ἡ τροφὸς Ἀρτέμιδος. καὶ ἡ μήτηρ. καὶ ἡ Ῥέα. καὶ ἡ Δημήτηρ," *RE s.v.*, p. 1843, also puts forward the possibility that the term derives from the Eastern minor divinity Ma, later identified as Rhea or Demeter.

10. For a systematic dissertation on the papyrological evidence of *amma* in non-Christian contexts, see E. A. Conti, "Lessico familiare nei papiri greci dell'Egitto romano e bizantino: alcune considerazioni su ἀμμά," *Aegyptus* 98 (2018): 147–59.

context does not reveal whether the term refers to a wet nurse.[11] However, in at least one case, SB 8.9882.5, ἀμμάς is definitely used with reference to the mother. In this letter it is unmistakably clear that ἀμμάς indicates the mother, as it is coupled with the male equivalent ἄππας, and then followed by other proper names accompanied by the respective terms of kinship; nevertheless, that their usage is distinguishing is evident, owing to the lack of article with ἀμμάς and ἄππας, which confirms that the terms are used as terms of affection, while actual terms of kinship, such as ἀδελφός and υἱός, are accompanied by the article.[12]

Of the other seven instances, the term only appears in the body of the letter on two occasions, while in the remaining cases it is used in the salutations section; in five instances it is accompanied by the possessive, which indicates the affectional bond, and also whose *amma* they are, and in four instances it is found together with the proper name of the person called *amma*.[13] From these papyrological findings it is clear that in the Greek in use in Egypt more or less between the second and fourth centuries, *amma* was felt to be a term of affection, rather than a noun indicating a precise function. A first piece of evidence of this is the fact that there are few instances of this term, and only in the strictly private context of letters within the family: they are people writing to their parents, or vice versa, or letters between siblings or people with close affective ties. Secondly, it is important to clarify the opposite discourse: in not strictly familiar contexts, and therefore in the great majority of letters, the usual terms for addressing or referring to a mother or wet nurse are μήτηρ and τροφός: these are functional terms that are found in many other types of document.

---

11. The possibility that the term may also refer to the wet nurse is backed by the lexicon by Preisigke (F. Preisigke and E. Kiessling [eds.], *Wörterbuch der griechischen Papyrusurkunden, mit Einschluss der griechischen Inschriften, Aufschriften, Ostraka, Mumienschilder usw. aus Ägypten*, I, *A-K* [Berlin: Selbstverlag der Erben, 1925], *s.v.*). Under the entry ἄμμα [sic] the dictionary proposes the only possible translation as "Amme," therefore "wet nurse." At times this has driven the publishers of papyri towards this translation, as a consequence bringing them to hypothesize imminent births in cases where, unfortunately, there can be absolutely no certainty (see in particular P.Mich. 8.488.19).

12. Owing to the lack of the possessive, it is not possible to establish whose parents Taubàrin and Dios were, whether of the sender or the addressee, or both. Elm, *"Virgins of God,"* 246, suggests that the use of ἀμμάς and ἄππας in SB 8.9882 could represent a step towards the use of these terms of affection as honorific titles for *pneumatikoi*.

13. See Table 1.

Furthermore, the most important thing that emerges from the papyrological sources, between the second and fourth centuries, is that *amma* in both of the forms is always found without an article, even when it is accompanied by a possessive pronoun or proper noun. This means that it is used as an epithet and, whoever this term was precisely aimed at, the purpose was not to indicate kinship or a function, but to underline an affectional bond.

Table 1

	Source	Date	Text	Position	Relationship	Proper noun
1	P.Bastianini 22.3	II^P	[γι]νωσκέτω ἀμμὰς Ταῦρις ὅτι	in the text	–	Ταῦρις
2	P.Mich. 3.208.8-9	II^P	ἀσπάζε|[τε ...] Ἡραίσκος καὶ ἀμμὰς αὐτοῦ	salutations	αὐτοῦ	–
3	P.Mich. 8.488.18-20	II^P	καὶ πότε θέ|[λεις] γένητ[αι] ἀμμὰς | [πρὸ]ς σέ;	in the text	–	–
4	P.Oslo 3.153.16-17	II^P	ἐπισκοπούμεθα | ἀμμάν μου Πτολέμαν	salutations	μου	Πτολέμαν
5	SB 14.12042.7-8	II^P ex.	ἀσπάζεται σε| ἀμμάς μου	salutations	μου	–
6	BGU 2.449.11-12	II-III^P	ἀσπ[ά]ζεται ὑμᾶς | κατ' ὄνομα Σωτηρὶς καὶ ἀμμὰς αὐτῆς	salutations	αὐτῆς	–
7	SB 8.9882.2.5	II-III^P	ἀσπάζετε σὲ ἀμμὰς Θαυβάριν	salutations	–	Θαυβάριν
8	BGU 3.948.15-16	IV^P	προσαγορεύει σε | ἄμμα σ[ου] καὶ ἐγὼ Κοφήνα	salutations	σ[ου]	Κοφήνα

The situation in Christian sources, in a monastic context, is different, both in literature and papyri, with *amma* having undergone a complete resemantization.[14]

---

14. It is difficult to say if in P.Oxy. 56.3862 (V-VI^P) ἀμμάς (line 16) is still referred to the mother, as M. Choat, *Belief and Cult in Fourth-Century Papyri* (Turnhout: Brepols 2006), 68–69, suggests, or if it should be understood in the Christian meaning of *spiritual mother*.

Despite the many gaps in the text by P.Köln 2.111 (V-VI^P), it is clear that the context in which the term ἀμμά is found has changed profoundly. Indeed, it is a letter addressed to an abbot, *apa Heraklammon* (as can be seen from the address preserved on the *verso* of the fragment), probably from a nun or nevertheless from a woman very close to religious backgrounds.[15] This woman had been punished (line 4) for a reason unknown to us by a certain ἀμμά, correctly interpreted by the publisher as the "abbess" (lines 4-5): thus, it is correct to insert the article, ἡ, essential for specifying the function that the term indicates in this context, into the gap.

P.Oxy. 16.1874 (VI-VII^P)[16] is a letter of condolence written by a religious person or someone familiar with the Holy Scriptures,[17] addressed to a woman who had probably lost her children. On line 12 the text says ἔπαθες ὁμοίως ἄμμα Εὔα ὁμοίως Μαρία, therefore comparing the suffering of the woman to whom the letter was addressed to that of Eve and Mary. In this case, ἀμμά is still used as a term of affection, but in reference to a "divine" woman, Eve, understood as the mother of all of the living.[18]

P.Paramone 14 (VI-VII^P) is a very interesting letter concerning the relics of Shenoute in a convent. The letter is written by a certain Peter on behalf of the mother of the convent, who is named on two occasions: on line 8 where we can see the periphrase ἡ μεγάλη τῶν αββα Σινούθου; and on line 14, where we read: ἐκ τῆς δεσπ(οίνης) ἡμῶν τῆς ἀμμάδος. Note how the presence of the determinate article makes it unmistakable that the noun has now taken on a technical meaning to indicate the function of abbess. In addition to this, it is noteworthy the presence of the noun, alone without the proper name, declined to the genitive case, thus far mainly seen in direct cases (nominative, accusative). With this text, ἀμμάς becomes a specific term to indicate the function of *mother superior of a convent*.

This transformation of the noun *amma*, which takes place in Christian papyri, is also found in Christian literature. Of particular significance is a section from Palladius, *Historia Lausiaca* XXXIV 6.8 where the term ἀμμᾶς [*sic*], referring to a nun, recurs with the meaning of "spiritual mother." In the same way, again in Palladius, *HL* LIX 1.2 we find ἀμμᾶ

---

15. See *ed. pr.* introd., 187 and R. S. Bagnall and R. Cribiore, *Women's Letters from Ancient Egypt: 300 BC–AD 800* (Ann Arbor: University of Michigan Press, 2006), 230.

16. See J. Chapa, *Letters of Condolence in Greek Papyri*, Papyrologica Florentina 29 (Florence: Gonnelli, 1998), no. 12, pp. 149–59.

17. Ibid., 150.

18. See ibid., 154–5.

referring to an ascetic at the head of a convent. Furthermore, it is clear that ἀμμά and ἀμμάς also act as honorific titles, and therefore are used without an article, addressed to women of a high degree of spirituality.

Afterwards the use of these terms changes. One particular example is a passage from *Apophthegmata Patrum* 420.25 entitled περὶ τῆς ἀμμᾶς Σάρρας, in reference to an ascetic. From an even later date, we find ἀμμάς in Theodore the Studite, *Ep.* 458.9-10, where it is used in reference to the Virgin Mary ἡ καλὴ ἀμμάς, ἡ χριστοφόρος γυνή. In these two instances, *amma* has at this point become a specialized noun indicating a function.

The situation for *appa* is slightly different, if only for the fact that there is an even smaller number of instances of the noun, not just in literature, but also in papyri.

In ancient lexicons we find the term in Hesychius, where it is said that ἄππα (*s.v.*) is a synonym of τροφεύς. Here we see once more the same confusion between "father" and "preceptor" that we saw for *amma*, as "mother" and "wet nurse." However, the Suda perfectly clarifies the meaning, saying that [Πάππα· ὅτι] πάππα καὶ τέττα καὶ ἄππα οὐχ ὁ τροφεύς, ἓν ἀνθ'ἑνός ἐστιν, ἀλλὰ προσφώνησις πρὸς τροφέα. καὶ τὸ πάππα καὶ ἄππα οὐ ψιλῶς ὁ πατήρ, ἀλλὰ πρὸς πατέρα σεπτικὴ φωνή· καὶ τὸ τέττα ἑταίρου. Hence, it confirms what was said about *amma*, that is, *appa* does not mean "preceptor" or "father," but is a form used to affectionately address one's preceptor or father.[19]

It is also significant that for *appa*, like for *amma*, we have only one non-Christian literary source: Callimachus, *Hymn.* III, 6. The term ἄππα is said by the child Artemis, as she sits on the lap of Zeus, her father, as she makes a series of requests of him. The aim of the scene is to create a domestic, intimate, familiar picture. This is therefore different to the case of the diminutive ἀμμίη which in Herodas can be interpreted as "mummy" but also as an endearing form of "wet nurse." In the passage from Callimachus it is clear that *appa* is said by a daughter affectionately addressing her father.

In a private family context, there are only three papyrological instances of *appa*:[20] among these are the already cited SB 8.9882, where *amma* and *appa* occur together (lines 5-6).

From these few sources, it seems possible to assert a similar use to what was established for *amma*.

---

19. See also the *Etymologicum Magnum*, where *appa* is found under the Homeric entry Ἄττα· Ἐπίφθεγμα τιμητικὸν νεωτέρου πρὸς παλαιότερον. Εἴρηται παρὰ τὸ ἀππὰ κατὰ Μακεδόνας, τροπῇ τοῦ π εἰς τ.

20. See Table 2.

Table 2

	Source	Date	Text	Position	Relationship	Proper noun
1	BGU 3.714.15-16	II^p	ἀσπάζεται ὑμᾶς | ἄππα Σατορνεῖλος	salutations	–	Σατορνεῖλος
2	SB 8.9882.2.5-6	II-III^p	ἀσπάζετε σὲ ἀμμὰς Θαυβάριν καὶ ἄπ|πας Δῖος	salutations	–	Δῖος
3	P.Mert. 1.28.8-9	ex. III^p	μετὰ δύο ἡμέρας ἔρχετέ μου | ἄππας ἐνθάδε	text	μου	–

BGU 3.714 is part of a group of five letters, all written by Tasoucharion to her brother Neilos.[21] This specific letter concerns the delivery of something, but most of what has been preserved consists of the large section of salutations. In this case, it is difficult to say exactly who ἄππα Σατορνεῖλος (line 16) is for two reasons. First of all, because Satorneilos is also named in another letter from the archive without the term ἄππα (BGU 2.601.27); and second, in this same letter, because the writer also asks the recipient to give his greetings to \τ/ὸν πατέρα ἡμῶν Ἥρωνα (line 13), who could be Tasoucharion and Neilos's father. These elements, which do not give much help in understanding the exact kinship with the person called ἄππα, in reality confirm something else, that is, once again, the very affectionate nature of the noun, which must have indicated the existence of a relationship that was more than a specific family tie.

Also in P.Mert. 1.28 if we consider ἄππας to be a synonym of father, we find ourselves faced with a conflict. The publisher, who indeed does take μου ἄππας (line 9) to mean "my father" in the translation, declares in a note that the Ἀμμωνᾶν τὸν πατέρα μου (line 14) mentioned in the salutations cannot be the same person previously indicated as ἄππας.[22]

21. See Bagnall and Cribiore, *Women's Letters from Ancient Egypt*, 179.
22. Indeed, again according to the publisher, the news that ἄππας would reach the sender in two days (lines 8-9) makes one think that it cannot be the same father, Amon, to whom the writer sends his greetings. However, if we are to follow E. Dickey, "Literal and Extended Use of Kinship Terms in Documentary Papyri," *Mnemosyne* 57 (2004): 145–8, terms of kinship in letters are not always used in a literal sense, especially if they are accompanied by a proper noun. The person known as ἄππας μου, instead, does not require any further specifications, hence, even if he was not the sender's father, it is clear that he was a figure held in the same affection.

The different way of using the two terms ἄππας and πατήρ nevertheless remains significant. The first is used to represent an affectionate relationship, the second to indicate a function: indeed ἄππας is dealt with as a term of affection and hence it occurs without an article with the sole indication of the possessive, while πατήρ is preceded by a proper noun, the determinate article, and followed by the possessive.

In the Christian religious context, there are without doubt more instances, but often it is not easy to distinguish whether we are dealing with the Greek or the Coptic form. It is definitely worth pointing out the letter P.Lond. 6.1926 (IV^p) which reads on lines 1-3 τῷ τιμιοτάτῳ [sic]... Ἄππα Πα|φνουθίῳ (corrected to Πα|φνουθις), addressee of the letter, and on the reverse τῷ τιμιοτάτῳ [sic] πατρὶ Ἄππα Παφνουτ[ίῳ] παρὰ τῆς θυγατρὸς Οὐαλερίας. The first most obvious change consists of the fact that the term ἄππα appears before the proper name of the addressee in the prescript of the letter.[23] Bagnall and Cribiore interpret "Appa" as the name of a priest or spiritual father.[24] On the *verso*, in the address, the addition of πατρὶ is a clear demonstration of the transformation of this noun, which went from an affectionate term to a specialized name for men of a specific religious stature, a sort of honorific title.

The numerous other instances of the term follow this same line. Amongst these, it is worth noting P.Oxy. 59.4006.3 (VI/VII), a letter which names a certain Ἄππα Κύρου τοῦ καθοσιωμενου [sic], where καθωσιωμένος is a title indicating that Appa Cyrus was a soldier or "civil servant" in the *militia officialis* (see *ed. pr.* in the note). The *ed. pr.* specifies that the title ἄπ(π)α is an integral part of the proper noun, common in papyri, with the aim of clarifying that the figure was called this in honour of a saint or martyr (Appa Cyrus),[25] rather than in reference to the Persian king.

The term *appa* occurs many times as a first name alongside proper names in the group of ostraca from Abu Mina, which contain receipts of various kinds and are dated to the beginning of the seventh century. In this period, Appa and the specifically Coptic form Apa, were wholly customary nouns which could be used as a mark of respect, not exclusively in reference to religious figures, but also lay persons.[26]

---

23. Therefore, the publisher's choice to transcribe the term with a capital letter is correct.

24. See Bagnall and Cribiore, *Women's Letters from Ancient Egypt*, 205. See also Derda and Wipszycka, "L'emploi des titres abba," 38–45.

25. See Derda and Wipszycka, "L'emploi des titres abba," 52.

26. See ibid., 41–2, and N. Gonis, "Abu and Apa. Arab Onomastics in Egyptian Context," *JJP* 31 (2001): 47–9.

In Christian literature, instead, unlike *amma*, *appa* is much rarer, probably because it was soon supplanted by the Coptic *apa*, which as of the fourth century completely replaced the Greek form. However, there are some illustrious examples: with different accents, ἀππᾶ is found in Ammon, *De sanctis Pachomio et Theodoro epistula Ammoni episcopi*, referring to the Antinoite monk Appà Pammon (e.g. 34.18), and in Joannes Moschus, *Fragmenta e Prato Spirituale*, VII 3 referring to Paul (ἀππᾶ Παῦλε). These instances demonstrate that the term *appa* underwent a different transformation to the noun *amma*: in the case of *appa*, the noun never loses its function as an epithet, while what does instead change is the field in which it is used. Indeed, we go from the private family context to the monastic context, before its extension as a title of respect to lay persons too. In some cases, it is clear that no degree of affection is present, nor is it always strictly religious, but rather a mark of respect, a bit like our "sir" or "mister."

To sum up, it can be said that in time and with the evolution of Christian society the two terms underwent at first a similar, and then a different change: while *amma* underwent a profound transformation, going from a term of affection to a term of function in the sources where it is found declined and with the determinate article (the *Amma* of the convent is the abbess), the term *appa* does not undergo this second transformation. Instead, after specializing as an honorific title used in reference to religious persons and men of a high spiritual stature,[27] at a later date *appa* also seems to extend to lay people worthy of respect.

Finally, looking at the matter the other way round, it can be said that more than the point of arrival, what appears truly significant is the point of departure, that is, what *amma* and *appa* meant in the private family context. Indeed, two terms that play such an important and distinct role in the Christian sphere, in reality had an intimate and private origin:[28] they were childish terms that in the Egyptian Greek maintained a very much affectionate, intimate, and familiar meaning.[29] From here it is possible to clarify the environment through which this resemantization took place: the private and family sphere. Indeed, it was precisely in this sphere that Christianity found its first and most solid roots, and then extended to other contexts of life.

27. See Derda and Wipszycka, "L'emploi des titres abba," 23–56.
28. Unfortunately it is not possible to say if the presence of *amma* and *appa* in the private letters quoted here (see Tables 1 and 2) could suggest, or confirm, a Christian milieu.
29. It is no coincidence that the literary instances of these terms are very rare and concern two "sophisticated" authors such as Herodas and Callimachus.

11

Early Christian Rolls

Marco Stroppa

1. *The Roll as the Format for Christian Books*

Until the third century CE, in Egypt and throughout the (primarily Mediterranean) area of Greek language and culture, the standard format of book was the roll, used horizontally. Only during the third to fourth centuries do we see the diffusion of the codex format: the direct documentation from this period on consists of an increasing number of fragments of codices compared to roll fragments. Hence, the most ancient codices have been subject to in-depth studies and the change of medium represents an epoch-making event.[1]

Two concrete pieces of data emerge from the general picture.

1. From the direct documentation, coming both from excavations and purchases, it appears that rolls were used for literary texts until the fourth century, and only on very rare occasions in the following centuries (there are some significant exceptions, which I will mention shortly).
2. Christianity spread in this period, and it is seen that Christians adopted the codex for texts of the holy scriptures. But what link is there between Christians and the roll format?

To answer this question it is useful to consider the direct evidence at our disposal of Christian rolls in general. As can be seen from the Leuven

---

[1]. The bibliography on the topic is endless: here I shall indicate just two texts as a starting point, J. Chapa, "Textual Transmission of 'Canonical' and 'Apocryphal' Writings within the Development of the New Testament Canon: Limits and Possibilities," *Early Christianity* 7 (2016): 113–33, and B. Harnett, "The Diffusion of the Codex," *Classical Antiquity* 36 (2017): 183–235.

Database of Ancient Books, they number around a hundred texts which are dated from a period between the second and eighth centuries.[2]

First of all, the Christian rolls can be divided roughly into three groups based on their contents: there are Old Testament texts, but in this case it is not always possible to establish with any certainty whether they are of Jewish or Christian origin. There are very few examples of the New Testament (see *infra*). The majority of the Christian rolls are Patristic texts, some of which are known from other sources different from papyri, and some not. An element emerging clearly in the recent studies by Larry Hurtado and Roger Bagnall[3] is the use of rolls for non-biblical texts. As of the second century, the documentation provides examples of treatises by the fathers of the Church as well as other material. It would seem that for books, written by human hands so to speak (such as treatises, homilies, apologetic discourses), the roll format would commonly be used, while codices were instead reserved for the "word of God." Works with a recognized "human author" (such as Irenaeus, Origen, Julius Africanus) are similar in format to the works of Greek authors from almost the same era (such as Favorinus, Plutarch, Aelius Aristides).

Worth pointing out, as indeed has been done, is the particular case of *The Shepherd of Hermas*: for this work we have a total of 23 sources, in both roll and codex form. In general, it can be said that the format onto which the text is copied varies depending on whether the work is deemed part of the canon of the Holy Scriptures.[4]

Second, it is interesting to attempt to classify the rolls with Christian texts on the basis of type, by noting whether the text has been written on the recto, the verso, or *transversa charta*.

---

2. The subject is dealt with in part by Nathan Carlig in his paper presented at the 28th International Congress of Papyrology, Barcelona, 1–6 August 2016, "Les rouleaux littéraires grecs de nature composite profane et chrétienne (début du IIIe–troisième quart du VIe siècle)."

3. L. W. Hurtado, *The Earliest Christian Artifacts: Manuscripts and Christian Origins* (Grand Rapids: Eerdmans, 2006), and R. S. Bagnall, *Early Christian Books in Egypt* (Princeton: Princeton University Press, 2009).

4. For the attribution of papyrus texts to a canon, see Chapa, "Textual Transmission of 'Canonical' and 'Apocryphal' Writings," 113–33. On *The Shepherd of Hermas*, in particular see M. Choat and R. Yuen-Collingridge, "The Egyptian Hermas: The Shepherd in Egypt before Constantine," in *Early Christian Manuscripts: Examples of Applied Method and Approach*, ed. T. J. Kraus and T. Nicklas (Leiden: Brill, 2010), 191–212, and also D. Batovici, "A New Hermas Papyrus Fragment in Paris," *APF* 62 (2016): 20–36 and idem, "Two Notes on the Papyri of the Shepherd of Hermas," *APF* 62 (2016): 384–95.

1) Rolls written on the recto, that is, on the internal part of the roll, the first part to be written on. The following are some examples:

   a. A uniform group (five specimens) of original festal letters: the oldest dates from the fifth century, while the most recent is from the eighth century. Another specific example can also be included in this group: P.Oxy. 76.5074, a fragment of the 28th festal letter by the Patriarch Cyril which is clearly not an original specimen but a copy made after Cyril's era, probably in the sixth–seventh centuries, as can be deduced from the type of writing used, a sloping pointed majuscule and not an Alexandrian majuscule.[5] P.Oxy. 13.1603, a fragment of the homily *In decollationem sancti Joannis* incorrectly attributed to John Chrysostom, from the fifth–sixth centuries, also presents similar characteristics.[6]
   b. A letter of an uncertain type, P.Ryl. 3.469 (see *infra*, section 2, point 2), from the end of the third century, attributed to the patriarch of Alexandria Theonas: in all likelihood, the papyrus is an actual letter of the type whose theological value meant that, after being written, it was put together with others to form a collection. It is a type of letter similar to festal letters.
   c. Two examples of *The Shepherd of Hermas*: BKT 6.2.1 (= P.Berol. inv. 5513) and P.Oxy. 69.4706.
   d. Some patristic texts: for example, P.Oxy. 3.405 by Irenaeus and 412 by Julius Africanus: in this second case, the author can be considered Christian, but the piece which the fragment comes from, the *Kestoi*, is not a religious work.[7]
   e. Furthermore, there are some "anomalous" cases which are worth further investigation: for example, the roll of Jena (P.Jena inv. 18 recto + 21 recto = LDAB 2460) with a portion of the *Adversus Haereses* by Irenaeus on the recto and notes on the myth of Horus and Osiris on the verso (see *infra* section 2, point 3).

---

5. For dating to the fifth/sixth centuries CE, see P. Orsini, "La maiuscola ogivale inclinata. Contributo preliminare," *Scripta* 9 (2016): 101.

6. Another two fragmentary examples of this homily, P.Bodl. 1.6 and BKT 9.175, could be from rolls; on the papyri relating to this work, see A. Papathomas, "'Keine Bestie auf der Welt gleicht der schlechten Frau.' Frauenfeindliche Polemik aus der ps.-chrysostomischen Homilie 'In decollationem Praecursoris' in einem Berliner literarischen Papyrus," *MH* 58 (2001): 49–50.

7. For Julius Africanus see M. Wallraff and L. Mecella, *Die Kestoi des Julius Africanus und ihre Überlieferung* (Berlin: de Gruyter, 2009).

2) Reused rolls, written on the verso, that is, the external side, the side always used second, after the recto. The practice adopted by Christians of using the material they found at their disposal is quite normal. The following are some examples:

   a. Two examples of *The Shepherd of Hermas*: P.Mich. 2.130, from the third century, written on the verso of a land register; P.Oxy. 69.4705, from the third century, written on the verso of an unidentified literary text.
   b. A list of names, a text perhaps linked to the *Onomasticon* by Origen, written on the verso of a land register (P.Oxy. 36.2745, from the third century).
   c. Four examples of the New Testament (P 13, P 18, P 22 and P 98, on the latter see *infra* section 2, point 4) written on recycled material.

3) Lastly, there is a third type of roll, namely rolls written on vertically, that is, *transversa charta*: in this case, the roll is rotated by 90°. The name often used is *rotuli*.

By comparing different *rotuli*, even those reduced to small fragments, it has been possible to hypothesize that they had a specific use, only documented from the sixth century on: the *rotuli* were used for community reading before an assembly. For example, we have examples of works by Basil of Caesarea, Basil of Seleucia, Didymus, and Abbot Isaiah.[8] This practice had not been seen (hitherto) in the earlier second and third centuries, when there were fewer Christians and the ecclesiastical structure was less complex. Therefore, in the centuries prior to the fourth century CE, it can be hypothesized that there was less differentiation between the various book products: until the third century, the basic purpose was simply to put the teachings in writing. Only thereafter did the production of copies increase, with specific formats used for specific requirements.

2. *The Early Christian Rolls: Examples from the Second to the Start of the Fourth Century*

We now come to the Christian rolls from the second to the fourth centuries.[9] We must remember that as of the end of the fourth century, the use

---

8. M. Stroppa, "L'uso di *rotuli* per testi cristiani di carattere letterario," *APF* 59 (2013): 347–58.

9. The data are deduced from the *conspectus* of the project "Papyri from the Rise of Christianity in Egypt" by Macquarie University, cross compared with the results of a search in the LDAB on Christian rolls in Greek from 100 to 400.

of rolls in any field or sphere had almost been abandoned: there were no more rolls for literary texts and, as of the fifth century, documentary texts, such as various types of registers, also began to be written on codices. As a consequence, from the fifth century on, it was a significant choice to use rolls, not just in the Christian sphere.

In terms of numbers, there are six fragments of the Old Testament dating from the second century on, some of which are certainly Jewish, one without doubt Christian, and others of an uncertain origin;[10] there are four fragments that contain the text of the New Testament; then there are twenty texts with theological contents, some by known authors, some not; lastly, there are also five examples of apocryphal texts.

Within this group, some texts can be considered emblematic, because they present material characteristics, in particular the appearance of the writing, which offer important information that can place them within the society and culture where they were made on one hand, and enable the principal features of the Christian rolls to be highlighted on the other:

1. PSI 11.1200 bis: patristic text (LDAB 4669)
2. P.Ryl. 3.469: letter by the patriarch Theonas (LDAB 4016)
3. P.Jena inv. 18 recto + 21 recto: Irenaeus, *Against Heresies* (LDAB 2460)
4. P.IFAO 2.31: *Revelation* (LDAB 2776)
5. P.Mich. inv. 4157a verso + 4170a verso, commentary to the Gospel of Matthew (LDAB 145321)

1) PSI 11.1200 bis is certainly a fragment from an elegant roll, a type of book product commonly seen for texts of Greek literature. Indeed, on the basis of the similar writing in the pieces, this fragment at first was classified among the fragments of PSI 11.1200, all coming from a roll of *Gorgias* by Plato, which can be dated to the second century CE. PSI 11.1200 bis, however, contains some *nomina sacra* and the contents display a similar formulation to the *Epistle* by Barnabas.[11] It is a *unicum*, which stands apart from other similar products due to the very elegant style of writing (it could easily be a Plato...), the early, second-century dating,[12] and the

---

10. See the considerations in PSI 16, p. 4.
11. See A. Carlini, "Amicus Plato...: a proposito di PSI XI 1200, Gorg. 447b ss.," in *Miscellanea Papyrologica*, ed. R. Pintaudi (Florence: Gonelli, 1980), 41–5.
12. On the dating see P.Oxy. 3.454 + PSI 2.119, another example of Plato's *Gorgias*, from the late second century (plate in E. G. Turner, *Greek Manuscripts of the Ancient World*, 2nd edn [London: Institute of Classical Studies, 1987], no. 62).

definitely Christian contents. The intriguing question—what text might it be?— is destined, for the moment, to remain unanswered. Recently, a parallel was pointed out with Clement of Alexandria[13] and the papyrus was included among a special category of texts, "Other fragments possibly from unidentified non-canonical gospels," but on the basis of these data, it would be surprising to find a gospel, even if it is not canonical and not known, transcribed on a roll of this kind.[14]

It is therefore quite problematic to say something new and definitive about this text. The possible alternatives are not very convincing. An attempt to shift the date to the fourth century could be made, purporting the use of an archaic style of writing which reflects elements from the second century: in this era, in the fourth century, rolls were abandoned, but remained in use only for festal letters, for example, by the Patriarch Athanasius (328–373 CE). Alternatively, it could be acceptable to date a work by Origen or some other leading figures in the Egyptian Church of the time to the third century, but, from a palaeographical point of view, I would firmly exclude dating it to this period.

For the moment, this fragment remains enigmatic.

2) The contents of P.Ryl. 3.469 (see *supra* section 1, point 1b), of which the final part remains, are from a letter against the Manichaeans; the author is probably the patriarch of Alexandria Theonas (282–300 CE). It is very unlikely that it is a festal letter, since the final part does not include references to the date of Easter.[15] The hypothesis that concrete indications of dates would follow in a subsequent column is not convincing either as the text displays the final salutations, similar to what is seen in P.Berol. inv. 10677.323-326, which preserves the whole final section of a festal letter.[16]

Even though the Rylands papyrus is not a festal letter, a comparison can be proposed by product type with PSI 16.1576, an original copy of the festal letter written by Patriarch Cyril for Easter in 421 CE. The palaeographical aspect is very interesting: in the fifth century, Patriarch Cyril's festal letter was written using the Alexandrian majuscule, a canonized

---

13. See L. H. Blummell and T. A. Wayment, *Christian Oxyrhynchus: Texts, Documents, and Sources* (Waco, TX: Word Books, 2015), 286 no. 79.

14. See S. Charlesworth, *Early Christian Gospels: Their Production and Transmission* (Florence: Gonelli, 2016), 135 and 140; the definition of the group betrays how hard it is to classify this and other similar papyri.

15. See the observations in P.Ryl. 4, p. 38–9.

16. See BKT 6, pp. 55–109 (= LDAB 194), from 713 or 719 CE.

and very elegant script that reflects the position of Cyril's church at the beginning of the fifth century, that is, much more rich and powerful than it was at the end of the third century.[17] In my opinion, the letter by Patriarch Theonas reflects the status of a simpler and less well-organized church: the writer, who could have been Theonas or someone on his behalf, used a current script, a beautiful chancery hand like others from the same period (later third–early fourth century).

Comparable pieces are P.Oxy. 58.3930, with official correspondence from 290 CE, and also P.Oxy. 24.2417, containing deeds of the Oxyrhynchus city senate, from 286 CE. These documents, dated to a specific year, are from the time when Theonas was in office as patriarch and reflect the custom of using professional scribes, accustomed to producing a large quantity of official documents.

With regard to the script, I would like to point out a curious detail: the text of the letter displays a variant at col. 1.16, where the word κρινει is written above μεισι (*lege* μισεῖ). The handwriting of the added word is totally different from that of the text of the letter and is more similar to a book script. In particular, the *kappa* is traced in a much slower and more careful manner than the *kappa* in the main text. Evidently, the person who made this intervention opted in favour of formality and solemnity, marking a change at a time when the need was felt to boost the aesthetic and graphic appearance of important documents.

3) The third papyrus is the famous Jena papyrus (P.Jena inv. 18 recto + 21 recto = LDAB 2460, see *supra* section 1, point 1e), a portion of the *Adversus Haereses* by Irenaeus: V 3, 2–12, 2 on the recto and V 12, 2–13 on the verso. Again another text appears on the verso concerning the myth of Horus and Osiris (P.Eirene 1.2 = LDAB 5522). Both texts are contemporary, probably written in later third–early fourth century.

Therefore, we have two different texts, written by different people, but which belong to the same item. The texts are probably linked, but the structure of the roll is not very clear and it is a complex product. One hypothesis is that the text by Irenaeus on the recto was written after a previous text had been washed off, therefore it should be a palimpsest. If this is the case, three different texts would have been found on the same medium at different times: the first, totally unknown, of which no traces remain; the second, mythographic text on the verso; and lastly the text

---

17. On the evolution of the festal letter genre and the organization of the Church, see *Le lettere festali di Atanasio di Alessandria*, ed. A. Camplani (Rome: CIM, 1989), 25–34.

by Irenaeus, again on the recto, written after the first had been "wiped off."[18] But there is no certainty as to this reconstruction.

However the situation is reconstructed, we have evidence of a roll that was repeatedly reused, a practice that was quite common. There is a good deal of evidence of rolls written and used on both sides: one of the most significant is P.Berol. inv. 9780: on the recto it displays Didymus' commentary on Demosthenes (LDAB 769) and on the verso the *Elements of Ethics* by Hierocles (LDAB 1286). In the case of the Jena roll, it might have been a product used by a person of quite a high level of culture, who was interested in theological subjects and compared Christian and pagan reflections on death and the resurrection of divinities.[19] In the case of the Berlin papyrus, it is also a book for specialists, for people who would read a commentary on the orator Demosthenes and a philosophy book by the Stoic Hierocles, by no means one of the most common authors (the papyrus is the only direct evidence of Hierocles' work).

4) And now let us come to one of the four papyri that display texts from the New Testament, P.IFAO 2.31 (= P 98, see *supra* section 1, point 2c), which contains a passage from the initial part of the book of Revelation and is written on the verso of a document, whose type cannot be reconstructed from the few surviving letters.[20] The remains of a column can be seen on the verso, and the top margin is also conserved: in all likelihood the text did not start from this column and therefore the space to the left-hand side should be the intercolumn, in turn preceded by another column.

The script is a not very carefully written book script, and has been dated to the end of the second or the beginning of the third century by Dieter Hagedorn and to the first half of the third century by Pasquale Orsini and

---

18. See the case of PSI 2.120, described in precise detail in F. Maltomini, "Use and Reuse of Papyrus Rolls and Scraps: Some Bibliological Matters," in *Proceedings of the 27th International Congress of Papyrology*, Warsaw 29 July–3 August 2013, ed. T. Derda, A. Lajtar, and J. Urbanik (Warsaw: Journal of Juristic Papyrology, 2016), 2:1105–9.

19. See M. S. Funghi and E. Giannarelli, "P. Jen. Irenaeus verso: una polemica sulla mortalità degli dèi pagani," *Eirene* 34 (1998): 9–30 (22–3).

20. See D. Hagedorn, "P. IFAO II 31: Johannesapokalypse 1,13-20," *ZPE* 92 (1992): 243–7, which contains a new edition of this papyrus and the identification of the text; another edition without any substantial new findings is in P. Malik, "Another Look at P.IFAO II 31 (𝔓⁹⁸)," *NovT* 58 (2016): 204–17.

Willy Clarysse.²¹ The ink is very damaged: hence it is particularly difficult to read and not easy to analyse from a palaeographical perspective.

In this case, too, it is not clear what type of artifact it was at the outset: the impression is that perhaps it was a short note, perhaps limited to the first verses of Revelation, rather than an actual roll with the whole work. The fact that a document is present on the other side also leads to the impression that it may have been a single sheet with a relatively short passage divided into a couple of columns.

5) A papyrus that could come from a roll or from a single sheet, is P.Mich. inv. 4157a + 4170a.²² The verso, the side which we are most interested in here, displays a commentary on the Gospel of Matthew, while the text on the recto contains a petition. The clear and rapid writing can be dated to the third–fourth centuries, also on the basis of the text on the recto.

The commentary is truly surprising because it displays many technical characteristics of the commentaries to works of Greek literature, such as Homeric poems or orations of Demosthenes, of which we have numerous examples on papyrus.²³ The structure of the text is marked by the distinction between lemmas and explanations, with the lemmas in *ekthesis*; dots are used to divide the sentences.

The aspect that is most striking is the use of abbreviations, with no fewer than three types:

1. The *nomina sacra*, characteristic of Christian texts: their presence here is by no means surprising; see, for example, θ̄ῡ= θεοῦ in ll. 3, 4 and 7.
2. Abbreviations of documentary origin, which involve the truncation of the word and writing the last letter high. This type of abbreviation was universally used by scribes in Egypt: any word could be abbreviated in this way. Here for example in l. 3: λεγ = λέγει.
3. Lastly, this definitely Christian text uses a well-codified and known system of abbreviations, that of the so-called "scholarly abbreviations," because this complex system was found precisely

---

21. See W. Clarysse and P. Orsini, "Early New Testament Manuscripts and Their Dates: A Critique of Theological Palaeography," *ETL* 88 (2012): 443–74 (471).

22. See R. Caldwell and N. Litinas, "P.Mich. invs. 4157a + 4170a Petition and Exegetical Text on Matthew," *ZPE* 183 (2012): 229–33, and M. Stroppa, "Esegesi al Vangelo di Matteo nella testimonianza di un papiro Michigan del III-IV d.C.," *Aegyptus* 98 (2018) 93–105.

23. See M. Del Fabbro, "Il commentario nella tradizione papiracea," *SPap* 18 (1979): 69–132.

in commentaries or examples of scholarly books. The system involved the use of non-alphabetic signs (oblique and horizontal strokes), placed above certain letters, representing prepositions (or preverbs) and particles.

Here are the details of the scholarly abbreviations definitely used in the Michigan papyrus: τ′ = τῶν; γ′ = γάρ; ο′ = οὖν; κ′ = καί; δ′ = δέ; δ` = διά.[24] These abbreviations are used both for single words and to express the same sequence of letters within a word: for example in l. 4 ποιότες = ποιο(ῦν)τες.

Other abbreviations that are used in the text are found in common practice: for example α) = απο; τ̄ = τους; μ̄ = μους.

Furthermore, use of the sign " ′ " to abbreviate any word ending in -ων in the papyrus: for example in l. 2 αφορ′ = ἀφορ(ῶν) and l. 5 ονειδιζ′ = ὀνειδίζ(ων).

It is a very interesting example—and the only one of its kind that I know—of the use of a practice current in the world of culture in general in a product that is certainly Christian.

Through the analysis of these five papyri, I have tried to highlight some characteristics of Christian books, which are totally comprehensible if their production is inserted among second- to fourth-century scriptoria practices and non-Christian book production. When the Christians could choose, they chose the codex for biblical texts; in the second and above all in the third century for texts on theological subjects at times they chose rolls and at times codices, as was also the case for non-Christian literary texts. It was a period of transition for book production in general, both Christian and non-Christian. As of the end of fourth century, the codex would become the format for all types of literary texts, and the roll would be relegated to specific and limited fields: in the religious sphere we have festal letters and texts to be read in public. I have presented various examples and different aspects, from the material production of the articles to the characteristics of the scripts. In some cases the papyri analysed give up evidence of unexpected elements, which as yet have not found a convincing explanation: I hope that the publication of new papyri and the further investigation of already published texts will enable a more precise outline of the value of these important testimonies of the production of early Christian rolls.

24. See the list in CPF I.1, pp. 277–81 and CLGP I.1.1, p. 20.

Index of References

Hebrew Bible/Old Testament

Genesis
1:26	157
2:4	206
5:1	206, 207
17:12	153

Exodus
1:15-16	152
8	112
8:12	112
12:13	134, 145
12:23	134
12:27	134
15:2	139
20:3	66
21:22	156
22:20	66
28:36	197
32:32-33	206
34:28	80

Leviticus
12:3	153

Numbers
16:33	133

Deuteronomy
13:9	133
25:4	79
28–30	112

Joshua
1:8	206
10:12	112

Judges
9:15	132

1 Samuel
25:20 LXX	132

2 Chronicles
5:8	133
17:9	206

Esther
3:13	142
4:14	132
8:11	142

Job
21:28	132
31:35	195
37:20	206
42:17	206

Psalms
4:5	81
16:8	132
35:8	132
60:5	132
62:8	132
68:28	206
70:6	139
73:19	152
156	29

Proverbs
2:14	132

Isaiah
5:21	80
16:14	132
30:2-3	132, 133
30:3	133
31:5	134
53:8	205

Jeremiah
14:9	152
36:1	206

Ezekiel
9:4-6	195, 203
14:14-20	80

Daniel
3:29	142
7:10	206
9:2	206

New Testament

Matthew
1:1–4:16	207
1:1	205–7, 210, 222
2:23	206, 264
3:1-12	237
3:9	233
3:10	238
3:11	238, 272
3:15	233
3:16–4:3	237
3:16	237
3:17	238
4:1	237, 238
4:2	237
4:11-12	238
4:13	264
4:17	207
4:18-22	265

4:22-23	238	19:17	257	27:26	254, 261		
5:20-22	233	20:1-16	46	27:28	255		
5:25-28	233	20:18	258				
5:26	270	20:22	258	*Mark*			
5:27-30	158	20:23	258	1:7-9	242		
5:32	257	20:28	258	1:7	238		
6:7	269	21:8	252, 253	1:8	242		
7:4	267	21:12	271	1:16-20	265		
8:13	255	21:34-37	243	1:16-18	242		
9:13	80	21:42	243	1:16	242		
9:19	257	21:43-45	243	1:17	242		
9:20	255	21:43	243	1:45–2:1	265		
10:1	249	21:44	243, 244	2:4	266		
10:10	79	21:45	243	2:13-14	266		
10:13-15	240	22:14	80	2:14	267		
10:13	268	23:13	259	2:17	80		
10:14	240	23:14	259	3:1-6	246		
10:15	249, 250	23:30-39	235	3:1	267		
10:25-27	240	24:31	259, 260	3:3	245		
10:25	241	24:40	270	3:4	245, 246		
10:28	270	25:27	260	3:18	267		
12:9-14	246	25:30	271	3:20	275		
12:22	269	26	260	3:21	275		
12:32	270	26:7-8	233	4:12	255		
13:13	255	26:7	260	5:30	267		
13:55-56	238	26:10	233	5:31	267		
13:55	238	26:14	233	5:40	268		
14:3-5	238	26:15	233	6:7	249		
14:4	238	26:19-37	231	6:11	249, 250		
14:20	250	26:22-23	233	6:43	250		
15:17	152	26:22	233	7:8	251		
16:10	251	26:26-29	159	7:35	263		
16:24	251	26:26	260	8:20	251		
16:26	251	26:28	260	8:36	251		
16:28	268	26:32-33	233	9:2	251		
17:6	264	26:36	260	9:19	252		
17:20	270	26:37-52	231	9:29	251, 255, 256		
17:21	255, 256	26:39	260				
17:23	252	26:54	254	9:31	252		
18:1-14	158	26:64	242	10:12	257		
18:10	256	26:67	254, 272	10:18	258		
18:11	255, 256	26:68	254	10:27	252		
18:12	256	27:12	254	10:34	252		
19:9	257	27:15	272	10:38	258		
19:16-17	257	27:16	258, 260–2, 274	10:39	258		
19:16	257			10:46	275		

Mark (cont.)		5:5	233	11:43	270
11:8	252, 253	5:10	265	11:44	270
11:15	271	5:11	265	11:51	270
12:8	152	5:14	265	12:2	270
12:26	216	5:19	266	12:10	270
12:40	259	5:21	266	12:24	268
13:2	253, 254	5:22	266	12:59	270
14	254	5:25	266	14:1-6	246
14:9	254	5:27	266	14:8-10	258
14:21	254	6:2	266	15:8	47
14:22-25	159	6:6-11	246	16:12	234
14:24	254	6:6	267	16:15	234
14:25	254	6:8	245	16:17	234
14:27	254	6:9	245	16:18	257
14:38	254	6:42	267	16:19	234
14:40	254	7:10	255	17:6	270
14:41	254	8:10	255	17:11-13	241
14:47	254	8:45	267	17:12	241
14:58	253, 254	8:54	268	17:22-23	241
14:62	254	9	268	17:36	270
14:65	254	9:6	268	18	271
15:2	271	9:10	268	18:19	257, 258
15:3	254	9:12	268	18:20	271
15:6	272	9:13	268	18:21	271
15:7	260–2, 274	9:14	268	18:22	271
15:15	254	9:16	268	18:25	271
15:17	254, 255	9:17	250	18:27	252
15:20	254	9:19	268	18:28	271
15:25	26	9:22	268	18:29	271
19:14	225	9:23	268	18:30	271
		9:25	268	18:35	271
Luke		9:27	232, 268	18:37	271
1:20	262	9:29	268	19:10	256
1:57-60	153	9:33	268	19:15	47
1:63-64	262	9:34	268	19:23	47
1:63	210	9:35	268	19:27	271
2:9	264	9:45	268	19:45	271
2:21	153	9:49	268	20:18	243, 244
2:39	264	9:50	268	20:30	271
3:4	216	10:7	79	20:42	216
3:14	151	11:2	269	20:47	259
3:18–24:53	226	11:4	269	21:2	47
4:17	210	11:14	269	21:28	259, 260
4:29-30	273	11:30	270	22:14-23	159
4:30	273	11:35	270	22:43-44	260
4:31	264, 273	11:36	270	22:64	271

23:9	254	8:58	273	*Acts*	
23:17	272	10:7	234	1:20	216
23:19	260, 261	11–12	233	5:16	189
23:53	271	15:7	274	7:16	47
		15:25–		7:42	216
John		16:2	231	15:23	150
1–15	226	16:14-22	230	16:20-21	61
1:3	115	16:17	230	19:11-17	47
1:21-28	241	16:21-32	231	19:19	47, 58, 210,
1:23-31	230	16:22-30	230		216
1:25	230	17:1-2	239	23:26	150
1:27	272	17:11	239	23:33	210
1:29-35	238	17:23-24	239	28:21	210
1:30	238	17:24	239		
1:31	239	18:1-5	239	*Romans*	
1:32	238, 239	18:4	239	6:23	151
1:33-40	230	18:31-33	226, 232	16:22	23
1:34	230	18:31	232		
1:35	230	18:33	232	*1 Corinthians*	
1:38-44	241	18:36–		7:31	194
1:38	230	19:1	235	7:33	194
1:40-46	238	18:36-37	235	9:7	151
1:41	239	18:37-38	226, 232	11:23-25	159
1:42	239	18:37	232, 235		
1:44	239	18:39	235	*Galatians*	
1:46	239	18:40	235	2:19	188
1:49–2:1	241	19:1-7	235	5:25	188
1:50	242	19:1	235	6:11	22
1:51	242	19:3	235		
2:1	241	19:4	235	*Ephesians*	
5:5	189, 255	19:6	236	4:26	81
5:26-29	236	19:7	236		
5:26-27	237	19:14	25	*Philippians*	
5:36-38	236	19:17-18	241	4:3	216
6–7	233	19:25-26	241		
6:8-12	231	20:16	231	*1 Timothy*	
6:10	231	20:19-20	230	5:18	79
6:11	231	20:22-25	230		
6:17-22	231	21	265	*2 Timothy*	
6:22	231	21:6	233	4:13	210
6:48-58	159	21:18-20	240		
6:54	159	21:18	240	*Philemon*	
8:14-18	231	21:23-25	240	19	22
8:14	231	21:23	240		
8:18-21	231	21:24	240		
8:21	231				

Hebrews
6:6	188
9:4	210
9:14	194
10:7	210

James
1:1	150

1 Peter
1:5	194

2 Peter
3:16	79

2 John
1	150
5	150
10	150
11	150
12	210

Revelation
1:8	195
1:13-20	237
1:13	237
3:5	216
7:2-4	196
7:2	196
9:4	196
9:10–17:2	225
10:10	210
13:17	196
13:18	19
14:1	196
20:15	216
21:6	195
22:4	196
22:13	195

APOCRYPHA
1 Esdras
1:33	206
1:42	206
5:49	206
6:7	22
7:6	206
7:9	206

Tobit
1:1	206

Judith
8:15	144
9:11	139

Additions to Esther
8:12	142
16:24	142

Wisdom of Solomon
5:16	144
12:5	156
14:23	156

Ecclesiasticus
1:30	206
2	139
2:8	139
2:13-14	139
5:15–6:1	135
6:14-17	137
6:15-17	137
6:29	134
8:12-13	136
14:26	134
19:8-9	135
22:20-26	121, 134, 135
22:20-22	121
22:22–23:11	121
22:23-26	120, 121
22:23	121, 122, 138
22:25	121, 122
22:26	121
24:23	206
29	136
29:1-7	136
29:6	135
29:8-13	136
29:14-20	136
29:14	136
29:22	134
34:16	134
48:12	134
51:2	139
51:30	139

Baruch
1:3	206
4:1	206

1 Maccabees
1:56	55
3:3	132
11:16	132

2 Maccabees
2:13-15	55, 56
2:13	56
2:14	56
5:9	132
6:12	206
8:23	206
8:31	36
13:17	132

PSEUDEPIGRAPHA
3 Maccabees
1:8-29	140
2:7	141
2:28-30	140
2:28	140, 142
3	141
3:10	141
3:16-19	140
3:20	141
3:21	141
3:27-29	141
4:19	141
5:6	142
5:25	143
5:35	143
5:44	141
6:6	140
6:9	139, 143

4 Ezra		*De specialibus legibus*		APOSTOLIC FATHERS	
8:3	80	1.83	144	*1 Clement*	
9:15	80	3.110	156	2:4	80
		3.111-119	156		
Letter of Aristeas				*2 Clement*	
9	51	*De vita Mosis*		6:8	80
10	51	2.114	197		
21	22			*Barnabas*	
28	22	JOSEPHUS		4:7	80
34	22	*Jewish Antiquities*		4:11	80
140	132	3.178	197	4:14	80
				5:9	80
Odes of Solomon		*Against Apion*		9:7-9	193
1:2	139	1.28-36	56	9:8-9	193
39:1-9	196	1.29	56	19:5	157
		1.34-36	56		
Sibylline Oracles		1.35-36	56	*Didache*	
2:280-282	157	2.5	140	2:2	157
3:765-766	157	2.202	157	5:2	157
8:244-250	198			13:1	79
		War			
Testament of Benjamin		2.229	55	Polycarp	
3:4	144	2.427	91	*To the Philippians*	
4:3	144	6.201-213	159	12:1	81
Testament of Reuben		MISHNAH		Shepherd of Hermas	
1:1	22	*Kelim*		*Similitude*	
		24:7	222	8.1.1-2	144
DEAD SEA SCROLLS				8.104.2-3	144
CD		BABYLONIAN TALMUD		8.3.2	144
19:10-14	195	*Horayot*		9.16.2-3	197
		12a	198		
PHILO				*Martyrdom of Polycarp*	
De cherubim		*Niddah*		12.2	61
126	144	13b	158		
				NEW TESTAMENT	
Legum allegoriae		*Shabbat*		APOCRYPHA AND	
2.53	144	55a	195	PSEUDEPIGRAPHA	
3.252	144			*Acts of Peter*	
		MIDRASH		5	197
De sacrificiis Abelis		*Genesis Rabbah*		27	197
et Caini		81:2	195		
843	144			*Apocalypse of Peter*	
				8	158

CLASSICAL AND ANCIENT
CHRISTIAN WRITINGS
Acts Eupli
1.1   66
1.4   66
2.1-2   66
3.3   66

Aeschylus
Agamemnon
1590-1599   159

Tetralogy
29, B, fr. 292b   139

Ammianus
Historiae
22.16.3   52
23.3.3   51

Ammon
*De sanctis Pachomio
et Theodoro epistula
Ammoni episcopi*
34.18   289

Apophthegmata Patrum
420.25   286

Appian
3.12.14   98
5.3.29   98
5.9.77   98
6   220

Aristotle
*De generatione
anamalium*
719b.17   139

Politica
1334b-1335b   154

Aristophanes
Wasps
300-302   46

Athanasius
*Apologia ad
Constantium*
4.2   68

Athenaeus
Deipnosophistae
1.4   43
5.214d-e   37
5.36-37, 203e   51

Augustine
*Breviculus collationis
cum Donatistis*
3.13.25   65

Contra Cresconium
3.27.30   65

Contra Faustum
11.2   33

Callimachus
Hymni
III, 6   286

Censorinus
De die natali
14.2   153

Cicero
De finibus
3.7   42
3.10   42

Epistulae ad Atticum
1.10.4   46

Epistulae ad familiares
13.77.3   53

Codes and Regulations
41   155, 156
92   156

Dio Cassius
Historia romana
42.38.2   51
49.43.5   59
50.31   98
52.36.1-2   59
56.23   59
66.24.1-2   50
73.24.1-2   51
73.24.3   51

Diocletian
*Edictum de pretiis rerum
venalium*
7.41-43   49

Diodorus Siculus
The Library of History
2   218
I   217
11   218
15   219
19   219
20   219

Diogenes Laertius
*Vitae
philosophorum*
5.42-50   35
5.52   36
5.62   38

Duodesim Tabulae
8   58

Epiphanius
*De mensuris et
ponderibus*
18   57
269-270   51

Epictetus
Diatribai
1.4.6   44
1.4.7   44

1.4.9	44	*Vita Constantini*		*Odyssey*	
1.4.14	44	4.36.2	67	2	90
1.4.16	44				
		Gaius		Irenaeus	
Euripides		Frag. 3	30	*Adversus haereses*	
Bacchae				5.30.1	19
ll. 1122-1147	159	Galen			
		De indolentia		Isidorus Hispalensis	
Eusebius		8–10	54	*Etymologiae*	
Historia ecclesiastica		19	39, 76	V 12, 2-13	296
1.4.5	30			6.3.3-5	34
4.37.1	68	*In Hippocratis*		6.5.1	41
5.1.22	64	18.2	39	6.5.2	42
5.1.47	63	3.17a.605-606	51		
5.1.53	64			Jerome	
5.8.5	19	Gellius		*De viris illustribus*	
5.19.4	22	*Noctes Atticae*		75	32
5.28.13-18	30	3.17	41		
5.38	64	7.17	52	Joannes Moschus	
5.52	64	7.17.2	34	*Fragmenta e Prato*	
5.62	64	18.5.1-12	34	*Spirituale*	
5.131	64	18.5.11	34	VII 3	289
6.12.3	28				
6.16.1-3	28	Dio Halicarnassus		Julian	
6.17.1	38	*Antiquitates romanae*		*Epistulae*	
6.39.1-4	64	4.49.2-3	159	23	54
6.39.5	64				
6.41.4	64	Herodotus		Justin	
6.41.5-6	64	*Historiae*		*1 Apologia*	
6.41.7-8	64	2.156.5	282	26.7	158
6.41.15-18	64			27.1	161
6.41.21	64	Herodas		29.1	161
8.2.1	65	*Mimiamboi*			
8.2.5	65	1, 7	282	*2 Apologia*	
8.8	65			12.1	158
8.10.10	65, 66	Hippocrates		12.5	158
8.11.1	65	*Aquis*		12.6	158
8.12.1-2	65	8.14	139		
8.12.6-7	65			*Dialogue with Trypho*	
8.12.10	65	*Historia Augusta*		79.3	133
8.13.1-8	65	15.7	51		
8.13.7	65	18.2-3	44	Justinian	
9.9.4	30			*Digesta*	
10.4.53	30	Homer		10.2.4.3	24
10.5.1-14	67	*Iliad*		22.4.2	24
		30	90	48.8.13	60

Juvenal
Satirae
15.78-83   159

Lactantius
De mortibus
persecutorum
12.2   66
15.7–16.1   67

Letter to Diognetus
5.6   158

Libanius
Orationes
1   220
1.148-150   53

Livy
Ab urbe condita
4.30.9-11   58
6.1.2   50
25.1.6-12   58
39.8-14   58
39.16.9   58
40.29   58

Lucian
Pseudologista
30   45

Lucian
De morte Peregrini
11   62

Macarius Magnes
Apocriticus
3.15   159, 160

Macrobius
Saturnalia
1.16.36   153

Manetho
Sacred Book
Fr. 76   217

Martial
Epigrammata
1.117.13-17 45
13.3.2   45

Muratorian Fragment
lines 73-80   31

Musonius Rufus
Reliquiae
15B   155

Origen
Commentarii in
evangelium Joannis
13.28.168   139

Commentarius in
Canticum
III.5   145

Selecta in Ezechielem
9   198

Orosius
Historiae adversum
Paganos
6.15.32   51

Palladius
Historia Lausiaca
LIX 1.2   285
XXXIV 6.8   285

Passio Sanctorum
Scillitanorum
10   62
14b   63
17   63

Peter of Alexandria
Paschal Homily
frag. 5.2   25

Plato
Phaedrus
267A   45

Pliny the Elder
Naturalis historia
Praef. 17   43
13.70   18
13.74-78   49
13.83   38
13.85-88   39
13.86   39
16.66   48
16.231   48
16.232   48
35.10   42

Pliny the Younger
Epistulae
3.5.17   46
7.19.6   60
10.96   62
10.96.1-10 160
10.96.7   160

Plutarch
Aemilius Paulus
28.11   41

Antonius
58.5   52

Caesar
49.3   51
62.5   98

Lucullus
4.4   37
42.1   42

Lycurgus
16.1-2   154

Moralia
497E   155
794.10   98

Sulla
26.1-2   35
26.2   37

Polybius
Historiae
12.27.4   42

Porphyry
De abstinentia
3.17.3   159
4.21.4   159

Ps.-Paulus
Sententiae
5.23.17-18 60
5.23.17   63
5.23.18   63

Ps.-Phocylides
Sentences
184-185   157

Res Gestae
22.11.8   53

Seneca
De Ira
1.15.2   154

De tranquillitate animi
9.4   47
9.5   51
9.6.7   47

Strabo
Geographica
13.1.54   35
13.4.2   52
17.2.5   157

Suetonius
Augustus
29.3   50
31.1   59
31.4   59

Domitianus
20   52

Iulius
44   42

Nero
6.2   153
38.2   50

Tiberius
63.1   59

Vitellius
14   60

Tacitus
Annales
2.30   63
2.32   59
4.35   60
12.52   60
14.50   60
15.41   50
15.44   61

Historiae
5.5   157

Tatian
Oratio ad Graecos
29.1   159

Tertullian
Adversus Marcionem
3.22.5-6   198
4.4.1-2   27
4.5.1   24, 26
4.5.2   27
4.5.3   26

Apologeticus
8.1   161
9.1   159
9.6-9   161
9.9   159
9.17   161
18.8   52

De praescriptione haereticorum
36.1-2   19, 24, 27
36.1   19

Theophilus
Ad Autolycum
2.30   26
3.1   26
3.20   26
3.23   26

Theodore the Studite
Epistulae
458.9-10   286

Thucydides
5.71.1   139

Timotheus I
Letter 47   29

Valerius Maximus
Facta et dicta memorabilia
1.1.12   58
1.3.3   59

Xenophon
Memorabilia
4.2   40

OSTRACA AND PAPYRI
BGU
1.23   123
1.73   104
2.1210.210   156
2.449.11-12   284
2.451   128
2.511   96
2.511, inv. 7118 98
2.601.27   287
2.601.27.13   287
3.714.15-16   287
3.714.16   287
3.823   104
3.948.15-16   284

BGU (cont.)			P.Bad.		14–15	188, 191,
3.969.8	98		4.46	117		234
4.1120.44	130		4.56	112		
4.1145.18	143				P.Cair.Zen.	
4.1147	131		P.Barc.		1.59034	127
4.1147.33	143		inv. 1	190	3.59342	127
4.1149	131		inv. 83	200	3.59384	127
4.1149.37	143				4.59620	128
4.1150	131		P.Bas.			
4.1151 verso		91	6	190	P.Col.	
4.1161	131				4.64.4	125
4.1161.25	142		P.Batav.		40 3.3.1.1	96
4.1166	131		20	201	40 3.3.1.1	
5.1210	104				col. I 2	98
5.1210.115-16		156	P.Beatty		40 3.3.1.1	
8.1810	129		1	188, 231	col. I 6	98
8.1811	130		2	114, 117,	40 3.3.1.1	
8.1829	128			188, 191,	col. II 11	98
9.162	94			194	40 3.3.1.1	
15.2471	113		3	117, 188,	col. II 14	98
16.2609	130			191, 232	40 3.3.1.1	
20.2863	107, 111,		6	190	col. II 21	98
	116		7	190	40 3.3.2	95
1104	154		7.9-10	113, 117	40 3.4	96
1126.20	130				40 3.5	96
1156.25	130		P.Berl.		40 4.1.1	95
			inv. 5513	292	40 4.2.2	93
C.Pap.Jud.			inv. 6982	98		
2.143	91		inv. 8877,		P.Dion	
2.156c	95		verso	95	11	130
			inv. 9780	297		
Codex Parisinus Latinus			inv. 10677.		P.Dura	
2179	63		323-326	295	10	188, 191
			inv. 11765	188, 189		
O.Narm.			inv. 13049	91	P.Egerton	
1.49	214				2	108, 190
			P.Bodl.			
O.Wilck.			1.6	292	P.Eirene	
1010	23		2	117	1.2	296
P.Alex.			P.Bodm.		P.Fay.	
30	130		1	191	331	216
			2	115, 188,		
P.Ant.				189, 191,	P.Gen.	
I 7	190			192, 233	3.92, frs A.1.9	133
			7–8	194	3.92, frs B.2.19	133

P.Hamb.
1.18 col. ii 622
1.28.11   143

P.Harr.
2.240   96

P.Herv.
1012   30

P.Hib.
1.35   125
1.35.10   133
1.93   143
1.93.1   142
1.93.4-5   128
1.95   125

P.IFAO
2.31   294, 297
inv. 237b   237

P.Iand.
I 4   190

P.Ital.
1.1.10   21

P.Jena
inv. 18 r.   292, 296
inv. 18r.   294
inv. 21 r.   292, 296
inv. 21r.   294

P.Köln
2.111   285
2.111, ll. 4-5   285
4.170   113
6.255   108
VI 255   190
8.351   104

P.Laur.
inv. PL II 31236

P.Leid.
2.W, Pag. 6.19   212, 221
2.W, Pag. 8.32   212, 221

P.Lips.
1.110   150

P.Lond.
3.897   125
3.897.5-6   144
3.985   22
3.985, line 18   23
6.1926   288
6.1926.1-3   288
7.2110   49
42   150

P.Lond.Lit.
11   96
27   96

P.Magd.Gr.
17   190

P.Mert.
1.28.14   287
1.28.8-9   287
1.28.9   287
2.130   293

P.Mich.
3.137   103, 231
3.158   64
3.208.8-9   284
8.488.18-20   284
8.488.19   283
222   188, 191, 194
inv. 25   94
inv. 4157a + 4170a   298
inv. 4157a + 4170a, l. 2   299
inv. 4157a + 4170a, l. 3   298

inv. 4157a + 4170a, l. 4   298, 299
inv. 4157a + 4170a, l. 5   299
inv. 4157a + 4170a, l. 7   298
inv. 4157a v. + 4170 v.   294
inv. 4800   93

P.Mil.
1.6   215, 221

P.Mil.Vogl.
2.66   216
6.264   97

P.Monts.Roca
IV 41   190
4.47   113
4.48   233
IV 48   190
4.51   200

P.Oslo
3.153.16-17   284
inv. 1046   113
inv. 1096   105

P.Oxy.
I 1   190
1.2   230
1.119.4-5   151
2.208   191, 230
2.260   22
2.260, 19-21   22
3.405   292
3.412   292
3.454   294
3.470   212, 221
3.508.11   127
4.654   110, 116
4.656   110, 116
4.657   191
4.658   64
4.668   191
4.719   22

P.Oxy. (cont.)		51.3606.		83	117
4.719, 26-34	21	230-35	104	412	78
4.744	146, 147, 150, 153	51.3614	116	483	53
		54.3758, 154-155	23	657	191
4.744 r. 14	148			1296, ll. 5-8	153
4.744 r. 15	148	54.3758, 207-209	23	2192	75
4.744 r. 2-3	149			5345	242
4.744 r. 8-12	148	56.3862	202, 284		
4.744 r. 8	151	58.3930	296	P.Paramone	
4.744 r. 9	149, 151	59.4006.3	288	14	285
6.289-90	196	60.4009	109, 111, 116	14, l. 14	285
6.847	188			14, l. 8	285
6.886	212, 221	60.4059 col. II 13	113	19.1	212
6.924	196				
7.1008	194	60.4059 col. II 3	113	P.Paris	
7.1022, 27-31	21			19.1	221
		60.4059 col. II 9	113		
8.1598	191			P.Petaus	
9.1171	109, 116, 191	62.4336	97	30	45
		63.3117	98	30, 3-7	45
10.1228	231	64.4401	237		
10.1242	96	64.4402	238	P.Princ.	
10.1335	191	64.4403	238	2.26	127
12.1473, 38-41	22	64.4404	243		
12.1475, 43-45	23	64.4404 l. 7	243	P.Ross.Georg.	
12.1562	23	64.4404, l. 36	243	1.23	201
13.1596	231	64.4405	235		
13.1603	292	64.4705	293	P.Ryl.	
14.1679	150	65.4445	238	3.457	111
15.1780	231	65.4446	239	3.457 v. 2	232, 233
15.1781	191, 230	65.4447	239	3.457	117, 232
15.1808	98	65.4448	240	3.457 r. 1	232
16.1874	285	66.4494	240	3.469	292, 294, 295
20.2264	95	66.4495	241		
24.2417	296	69.4706	292	4.627	216
34.2683	235	71.4803	241	4.628	216
38.2836, 17-19	21	71.4805	188, 191, 241	4.638	216
41.2955.3	98				
41.2955.5	98	71.4806	188	P.Schoyen	
41.2955.7	98	72.4934	187	1.20	188
41.2987	104	72.4964	188	1.23	112, 117
41.2990	64	76.5074	292	I 23	190
42.3016	104	82.76-91	196	2.26	112, 117
42.3021	96	82.5306	196	II 26	190
50.3523	190, 235	82.5306 ll. 20-22	196		
50.3528	190			P.Stras.	
51.3606.19	104	82.5607	196	7.680	202

P.Tar.
5, fr. G.2,
　1. 5-6　　　133

P.Tebt.
1.11　　　　125
1.34　　　　126, 144
1.40　　　　125
1.41.1-27　　125
1.112.41　　130
2.286　　　 105
2.291.43　　213, 221
2.308.7　　 210, 221
2.318　　　 105
2.328　　　 105
2.483　　　 104
3.758　　　 125
3/1.741　　 126
3/2.895.117　130
3/2.895.124　130
3/2.895.38　 130
Wall 5　　　104

P.Theon.
27.2　　　　97
29.37　　　 97

P.Turner
45, 23-25　　23

P.Willoughby
line 3　　　242

P.Yadin
1　　　　　209
2　　　　　209

P.Yale
299　　　　60

PSI
1.2　　　　190
1.85, verso　94
2.119　　　294
5.502　　　129

5.515　　　　129
5.515.15-16　143
6.666　　　　127
7.961　　　　105
10.1160　　　98
11.1200　　　190, 294
12.1285 v　　102
12.1291　　　191
12.1292　　　191
16　　　　　 294
16.1576　　　295

Pap.Castr.
7.2　　　　　91

Princ.Stud.Pap.
3　　　　　　113

SB
3.6277　　　143
3.6301　　　128
8.982, ll. 5-6　286
8.9882　　　 283
8.9882.11,5　284
8.9882.11.
　5-6　　　 287
8.9882.5　　283
8.9923　　　105, 113
12.10845.3　133
14.11858　　214, 221
14.12042.
　7-8　　　 284
16.12520.
　19　　　　97
16.12520.25　97
16.12816　　89
18.13786.7　104
20.14106.17　133
26.16373　　214, 221
26.16373,
　l. 6　　　 214
6301.11-13　143

T.Vindol.
1–4　　　　 39

INSCRIPTIONS
Rhodes Inscription
line 7　　　53

OTHER SOURCES
BKT
6　　　　　 295
6.2.1　　　 292
9.175　　　 292

ILS
1485　　　　156
18　　　　　58

LDAB
13　　　　　98
19　　　　　93
25　　　　　95
30　　　　　96, 98
33　　　　　95
36　　　　　96
45　　　　　96
194　　　　 295
295　　　　 92
341　　　　 94
470　　　　 91
477　　　　 92
542　　　　 92
607　　　　 90
627　　　　 90
637　　　　 91
653　　　　 92
655　　　　 92
656　　　　 91
769　　　　 297
1162　　　　90
1169　　　　92
1178　　　　92
1220　　　　90
1273　　　　89
1286　　　　297
1380　　　　96
1382　　　　96
1427　　　　89
1467　　　　89

LDAB (cont.)		6872	109	60106	90
1957	96	8119	112	60260	96
2283	96	8120	112	60262	96
2315	89	8632	96	60829	96
2423	96	10028	92	61281	96
2446	89	10733	92	61362	92
2448	89	14439	92	61496	92, 93
2460	292, 294, 296	145321	294	61497	91
				61508	91
2472	90	*MM*		61618	109
2627	91	91	23	61624	111
2643	92, 93			61627	115
2644	91	*NT*		61628	114
2655	91	P37	103	61857	113
2774	111			61929	112
2776	294	*PTA*		61933	113
2777	115	5	113	61937	110
2778	114	10	113	62595	98
3013	113	21	113	62996	91
3086	112			63000	91
3090	113	*SEG*		63274	91
3094	110	21.500	52	63527	108
3756	89			63552	92
3780	98	*TM*		63555	93
4016	294	58918	98	63663	109
4030	110	58920	93	63851	91
4188	91	58935	96, 98	66870	112
4192	91	58938	95	67315	96
4397	89	58941	96	68753	92
4401	89	58950	96	68869	112
4674	93	59200	92	69553	92
4736	108	59245	94	95830	95
4761	92	59371	91	98079	92
4774	91	59378	92	107779	91
4929	89	59443	92	704964	110
4930	89	59535	91		
4953	89	59551	92	*UPZ*	
5144	89	59554	91	1.4	128
5346	89	60048	90	1.64	128
5522	296	60054	92	1.119	125, 128
6596	92	60055	92	I 121	141

Index of Authors

Affleck, M. 41
Aland, K. 193
Allen, G. 9
Allen, W. C. 207
Allison, D. C. Jr. 208
Alonso, J. L. 130
Alston, R. 91
Anderson, H. 140
Andrews, E. A. 20
Arzt-Grabner, P. 131

Baarda, T. 273, 276
Bacchi, A. 143
Bagnall, R. S. 52, 155, 190, 227, 276, 285, 287, 288, 291
Bakke, O. M. 161
Banning, J. 205
Barker, D. 190
Barker, M. 198
Barnes, T. D. 68
Barrera, J. T. 165
Barrett, D. P. 188, 230, 277
Barth, G. 136
Barthes, R. 9
Basore, J. W. 47
Batovici, D. 291
Bauckham, R. J. 79
Bausi, A. 190
Bazzana, G. 88
Beduhn, J. 279
Beentjes, P. C. 122, 138
Bellinzoni, A. J. 276
Berti, M. 52, 53
Bigg, C. 79
Bingen, J. 128
Black, D. A. 277
Black, M. 199
Blomberg, C. L. 73
Bloom, H. 10
Blumell, I. H. 295

Blumell, L. H. 190, 200, 202
Bokedal, T. 189
Bonnard, P. 208
Bowie, E. 50
Bowman, A. K. 39, 69, 70, 90, 91
Braund, D. 146, 147
Braunert, H. 123
Breccia, E. 70
Brinkmann, A. 233, 277
Bromiley, G. W. 206
Brooks, C. 4
Brown, B. 177, 182
Brown, S. 190, 192
Brownlee, W. 164, 165, 175, 181, 182
Bruun, C. 101
Bruyn, T. de 201, 202
Burnet, R. 147
Burnett, N. 169

Cabrol, F. 281
Cadbury, H. J. 120
Caldwell, R. 298
Camp, C. 136
Camplani, A. 190, 296
Capasso, M. 90
Capponi, L. 209
Carlig, N. 291
Carlini, A. 294
Cary, E. 50, 51
Cavallo, G. 98, 103
Chantraine, P. 281, 282
Chapa, J. 285, 290, 291
Chapman, J. 20
Charlesworth, J. H. 29
Charlesworth, S. D. 193, 295
Chiesi, I. 89
Choat, M. 200, 284, 291
Clarysse, W. 89, 98, 103, 190, 191, 200, 226, 227, 229, 231, 232, 280, 298
Claytor, W. G. 92

Cole, P. 168
Collins, J. J. 120, 138, 140, 168
Colwell, E. C. 228, 234, 277
Comfort, P. W. 188, 230, 236, 238, 240, 277
Conti, E. A. 282
Cook, J. G. 160
Corley, J. 137
Cousland, J. R. C. 140
Crawford, D. 123–5
Creole, J. 277
Cribiore, R. 285, 287, 288
Crosman, I. 10
Cross, F. L. 33
Cross, F. M. 57, 181, 182
Crossan, J. D. 89
Croy, N. C. 140–2
Cugusi, P. 21
Cuvigny, H. 128, 129

Daniélou, J. 195
Daniel, R. W. 233, 277
Davenport, W. H. 65
Davies, W. D. 208
Davis, K. 177
Davis, W. D. 146, 149–51
Davoli, P. 89
Dehaene, S. 100
Deissmann, A. 141, 142, 148, 150, 153
Del Fabbro, M. 298
Derda, T. 281, 282, 288, 289
Derrida, J. 8
Di Lella, A. A. 120, 121
Dickey, E. 287
Dijkstra, J. H. F. 201
Dinkler, E. 194
Dinkler-von Schubert, E. 194
Donato, E. 6
Drexhage, H.-J. 147
Driscoll, M. J. 9, 10

Edgar, C. C. 146
Ehrman, B. D. 68, 277
Eidinow, E. 53
Eissa, M. A. 281
Elliott, J. K. 226, 230–2, 248, 277
Elm, S. 281, 283
Engels, D. 155
Epp, E. J. 85, 209, 210, 224, 225, 227–9, 232, 276–8

Eshkol, L. 180
Etaix, R. 205
Evans, C. A. 17, 70, 74, 75, 160

Fee, G. D. 246, 248, 278
Ferguson, E. 194
Finegan, J. 146, 194, 195, 233, 278
Fitzgerald, J. T. 48
Fleming, E. E. 170
Foucault, M. 9
ffrench, P. 8
Freund, R. A. 209
Friedrich, G. 206
Frow, J. 178, 179, 182
Funghi, M. S. 297

Gager, J. G. 58
Gamble, H. Y. 53, 66, 68, 169, 190
García Martínez, F. 165
Georges, K. E. 20
Giannerelli, E. 297
Gieschen, C. A. 195, 198
Gigante, M. 30
Gilbert, G. 73
Gilbert, M. 136
Golden, M. 154
Goldstein, J. 59
Gonis, N. 288
Gorman, M. J. 161
Gracia, J. J. E. 1–3, 5, 11, 12
Gray, P. 158
Gregory, B. 121, 135–7
Grenfell, B. P. 146, 149, 150, 212
Greshko, M. 177
Grossman, M. L. 168
Gulick, C. B. 43
Gundry, R. H. 206

Hacham, N. 140, 141
Hadas, M. 140
Hagedorn, D. 297
Hagner, D. A. 205, 206
Handis, M. W. 52
Harmer, J. R. 80
Harnett, B. 290
Harris, W. V. 45, 49, 154, 169
Hatzimichali, M. 52
Hawkins, J. B. H. 25
Head, P. M. 191, 228, 231, 234, 278, 279
Heger, P. 165

Heid, S. 194
Heikel, E. 149
Helbing, R. 150
Hempel, C. 165–7, 171, 172
Hick, R. F. 94
Hill, C. E. 279
Hoffman, A. 168
Holland, G. S. 48
Holmes, M. W. 80, 277, 279
Holmes, P. 19, 20, 27, 28
Holquist, M. 7
Holub, R. C. 10
Horbury, W. 128
Horn, C. B. 153–5
Hornblower, S. 53
Horsley, G. H. R. 24
Horsley, R. 169, 170
Horst, P. W. van der 159
Hoskier, H. 279
Houston, G. W. 34, 38, 45, 48, 50, 53, 54, 69, 70, 76
Hulley, K. K. 225, 279
Hunt, A. S. 146, 149, 150, 212
Hurtado, L. W. 82, 85, 187, 190, 192, 193, 199, 228, 247, 279, 291
Hurwit, J. M. 52
Huys, M. 152, 161
Hvalvik, R. 193

Jackson, J. 50, 60
Jacob, C. 36, 40, 43
Jaffee, M. 170–3, 182
Johnson, A. C. 146, 216
Johnson, L. T. 80
Johnson, S. R. 140
Johnson, W. 96
Johnson, W. A. 38, 45
Jones, H. L. 35

Kasher, A. 130
Kearns, C. 121
Kearsley, R. A. 130
Kelber, W. 170
Kellerman, J. A. 205
Kenyon, F. G. 83, 86
Ker, W. C. A. 45
Keyes, C. W. 127
Khalil, M. S. 164
Khalila, G. 156
Kiessling, E. 283

Kingsbury, J. D. 207
Kip, W. I. 65
Kittel, G. 206
Klinghardt, M. 225, 279
Kloft, H. 147
Kloppenborg, J. S. 88, 94
Klostermann, E. 208
Knipfing, J. 64
Koester, H. 83, 224, 247, 248, 275, 279
Kollek, T. 179
Konen, H. 147
König, J. 52
Kooij, A. van der Kooij 56
Köster, H. 80, 81
Kotansky, R. D. 233, 279
Kraeling, C. H. 279
Kraft, R. 166
Krentz, E. 207
Kress, G. 199, 200, 202
Kristeva, J. 8
Kruger, M. J. 279
Kwakkel, E. 106

La'da, C. A. 209
Lacey, W. K. 153
Lack, R.-F. 8
Lagrange, M. J. 206
Lake, K. 30
Lampe, G. W. H. 195
Lange, A. 56
Lanier, G. R. 243, 279
Larsen, M. D. C. 74
Lattke, M. 196
Laudien, A. 146
Leclerque, H. 281
Leeuwen, T. van 199, 200, 202
Leibovitz, L. 181
Leitch, V. B. 10
Lenaerts, J. 147
Levi, I. 121
Lewis, N. 146
Liddell, H. G. 221
Lieu, J. 279
Lightfoot, J. B. 80, 144
Lim, T. 173, 178
Lindemann, A. 157
Lindsay, D. R. 137
Litinas, N. 298
Livingstone, E. A. 33
Llewelyn, S. R. 130

Lohmeyer, E. 206
Longenecker, B. W. 194
Love, H. 100
Lu, M. 154
Lührmann, D. 136
Luijendijk, A. 190, 191
Luz, U. 206, 207

Macksey, R. 6
Magie, D. 44
Malik, P. 108, 191, 297
Maltomini, F. 297
Marböck, J. 121
Martens, J. W. 153–5
Marx, K. 182
McDonald, L. M. 31
McGowan, A. 159
McHoul, A. 183
McKechnie, P. 149–51
McNamee, K. 97, 98
McNeile, A. H. 206
Mecella, L. 292
Meier, J. P. 222
Merleau-Ponty, M. 163
Messeri, G. 147
Metzger, B. M. 68, 146, 225, 226, 230, 231, 233–5, 237, 243, 247, 254, 255, 259, 270, 272, 279
Millard, A. 169
Miller, O. 1
Miller, S. S. 91
Milligan, G. 146, 206, 213
Mills, S. 10
Minissale, A. 120
Minnen, P. van 89, 93
Mitchell, T. N. 73, 76–8
Modrzejewski, J. 141
Moi, T. 8
Morgan, T. 139
Moulton, J. H. 206
Mowitt, J. 3–8
Mroczek, E. 166
Mugridge, A. 84
Muhs, B. 89
Munteanu, D. 161
Musurillo, H. 62, 66, 98

Nägeli, T. 212
Navarette, N. V. 94

Netanyahu, B. 180
Nicholls, M. 43
Niditch, S. 172
Nolland, J. 221
Nongbri, B. 190, 226, 234, 279, 280
Noy, D. 128

O'Neil, E. N. 94
Obbink, D. D. 48
Occhi, S. 89
Oden, T. C. 205
Ogden, D. 58, 63, 161
Oikonomopoulou, K. 52
Oldfather, W. A. 44
Oliver, K. 9
Orsini, P. 98, 103, 190, 191, 200, 226, 227, 229–32, 280, 292, 298
Oulton, J. E. L. 28, 65, 66

Paap, A. H. R. E. 189, 201
Palme, B. 147
Papathomas, A. 292
Párassoglou, G. M. 214
Parker, D. C. 68, 224, 276, 280
Parker, H. D. D. 170
Parsons, P. J. 97, 107, 115, 234, 280
Parsons, P. J. 96, 97, 99
Perrin, B. 41, 42
Petersen, W. L. 81, 280
Piatowska, M. 123, 127
Pietz, W. 166
Plummer, A. 207
Pomeroy, S. 151, 155
Porter, S. E. 7, 10, 105
Pott, A. 280
Preisigke, F. 283
Price, L. 178, 180, 181
Puglia, E. 30

Rabinowitz, J. J. 209
Rackham, H. 38
Radice, B. 60
Raimondi, N. 89
Rathbone, D. W. 101
Reden, S. von 124, 127, 130, 138
Reed, J. L. 89
Reinhartz, A. 156
Rhea, J. 60
Richardson, E. C. 32

Rigsby, K. J. 127, 128, 130, 131
Rives, J. B. 159
Roberts, C. H. 98, 187, 190, 194
Robinson, J. C. 7
Robinson, J. M. 82
Roca-Puig, R. 200
Rodriguez, C. 93
Rohmann, D. 57, 59
Rolfe, J. C. 43, 50, 59
Rollston, C. 168
Rostovtzeff, M. I. 123, 124, 128, 130
Roth, D. T. 225, 280
Rothschild, C. 31
Rowlandson, J. 147
Royse, J. R. 194, 226, 228, 231, 233, 234, 244, 280
Ruffing, K. 147

Saad, I. abu 164
Sanders, E. P. 174
Sanders, J. T. 140
Sarefield, D. 57, 62, 64–6
Schaps, D. 46
Schiffman, L. 174
Schironi, F. 96
Schliesser, B. 136, 139
Schmid, J. 206
Schmid, U. 280
Schnabel, E. J. 31
Schneelmelcher, W. 31
Schofield, A. 168
Schorch, S. 56
Schrader, E. 233, 274, 276, 280
Schubart, W. 146
Schwartz, D. R. 56, 157
Schwartz, S. 138
Scott, E. 154, 155
Sedgewick, W. B. 149
Selden, R. 10
Senior, D. 222
Shackleton Bailey, D. R. 45
Sherk, R. K. 147
Skeat, T. C. 36, 46
Smarius, A. 63
Smith, P. 8, 156
Spawforth, A. 53
Specht, E. 148, 149
Stager, L. E. 156
Stegemann, H. 176

Stevens, A. H. 1
Stevenson, G. 197
Stevenson, J. 66
Stone, M. 166
Straus, J. A. 147
Strobel, K. 149
Stroppa, M. 293, 298
Suleiman, S. R. 10
Swanson, R. J. 235, 238, 239, 242, 250, 256, 260, 272, 280

Tabachovitz, D. 149, 150
Talmon, S. 165, 173
Theophilos, M. P. 208
Theron, D. J. 31
Thomsen, M. R. 10
Tompkins, J. 10
Tov, E. 166, 173
Trever, J. 164, 165, 175, 176
Trilling, W. 206
Tucci, P. L. 44, 50
Tune, E. W. 277
Turner, E. G. 97, 99, 107, 115, 294
Tutrone, F. 35, 42
Tyson, J. B. 280
Tyson, L. 10, 225

Ulrich, E. 173

Vaganay, L. 280
Valdés, M. J. 1
Vaux, R. de 175
Vogels, H. J. 246, 280
Vögtle, A. 206

Waetjen, H. C. 208
Walker, R. 222
Wallraff, M. 292
Warren, M. 191
Wasserman, T. 242
Wayment, T. A. 295
Werrett, I. 174
West, S. 149, 152
White, J. L. 129, 148
Wilcken, U. 123
Williams, D. S. 141
Williams, J. 8
Winter, J. G. 146
Wipszycka, E. 281, 282, 288, 289

Wise, M. 170, 171
Wisse, F. 82, 85
Witkowski, S. 146
Wittgenstein, L. 12
Woess, F. von 123
Wolfreys, J. 7
Woolf, G. 52
Wright, B. G. 120, 136
Wright, W. C. 54

Yadin, Y. 209
Yonge, C. D. 37
Young, I. 170
Yuen-Collingridge, R. 291

Zahn, T. 208
Zelyck, L. R. 108, 158
Zuntz, G. 149